The Narrow Gauge
in Britain
& Ireland

Cliff Thomas

Atlantic Publishers
Trevithick House, West End, Penryn,
Cornwall, TR10 8HE

ISBN: 1 902827 05 8

British Cataloguing in Publication Data
A catalogue for this book is available from the British Library

Printed by The Amadeus Press Ltd, Bradford

Contents

Photographs by the author unless otherwise credited.

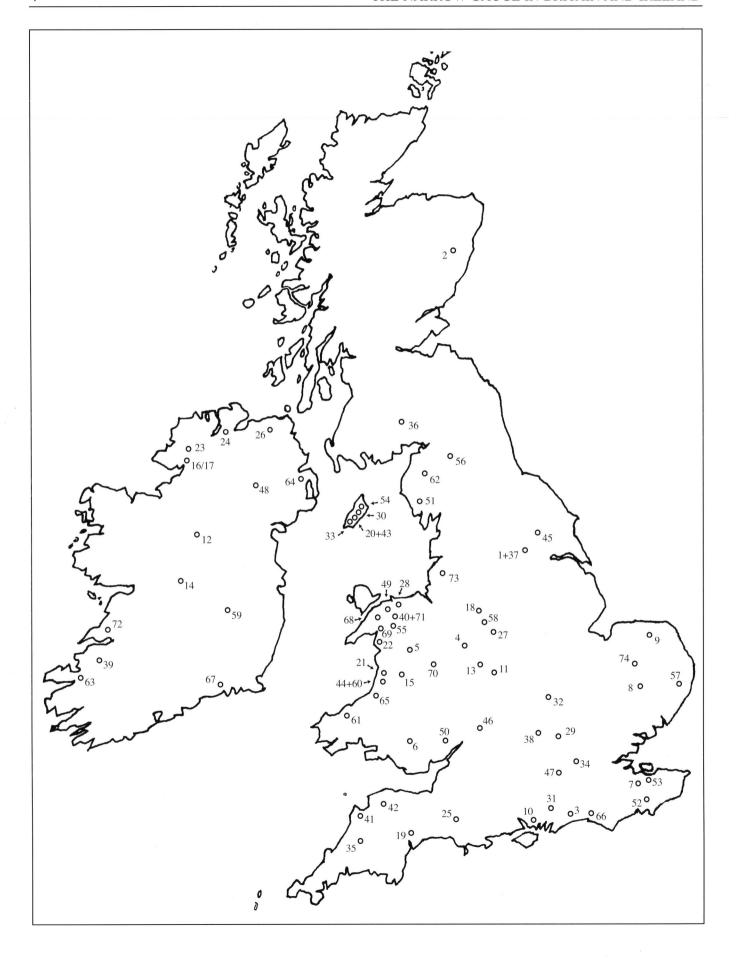

Narrow Gauge railways in Britain and Ireland

The Map opposite shows the location of all railways, museums & etc described in this book (other than closed lines). In the alphabetical list below, the first number is that shown on the map and the second is the page reference.

Celebrating the 50th anniversary of railway preservation - and a new era in the fortunes of the narrow gauge. Talyllyn Railway No.1 *Talyllyn* **pulls out of Wharf station during the July 2001 Jubilee Festival Week.**

CHAPTER ONE

Setting the Scene

The year 2001 marked the 50th anniversary of railway preservation - and it was a narrow gauge line that led the way. In 1950, the formation of the Talyllyn Railway Preservation Society started something never previously envisaged - the idea that a group of amateurs would give up their free time to work on and operate a railway, simply for the pleasure and satisfaction of doing it. At that time, it is unlikely that anyone conceived they were the pioneers of what would become a major preservation movement, but where they led, many have followed. From those early days of decrepit track and worn out equipment, the Talyllyn Railway has been transformed and, having proved it could be done, seeds were sown across Britain and Ireland, with an entire new leisure industry blossoming around the preservation and revival of locomotives and railways which would otherwise have been lost. People have found pleasure and fulfilment in making it all possible, and quite a few have found employment as well. At the opposite end of the spectrum, many others are happy to save, restore and operate equipment on a small scale - probably in a way that is only possible with the manageable size of narrow gauge equipment. As will be seen in the following pages, in all practical respects, narrow gauge lines have continued to lead the field, not simply in reopening closed lines and building new railways, but constructing passenger carriages, ordering new boilers and building replica locomotives.

In basic terms, narrow gauge is anything less than the standard 4ft 8½ins gauge between the rails, but it is not quite that simple! The 'battle of the gauges' between Brunel's broad gauge (7ft 0¼ins) and standard gauge (4ft 8½ins) for main lines was settled by Parliament in 1846. Prior to this, the choice of gauge for any 'local' railway was essentially an arbitrary decision, perhaps influenced by local tradition - many railways only became described as 'narrow gauge' retrospectively. For instance, mine owner, Charles Brandling, received Parliamentary approval to construct a railway to link his mines with the developing town of Leeds in 1758. When steam locomotives, designed by John Blenkinsop and built by Matthew Murray, were introduced in 1812 and proved successful, a justifiable claim to providing the first regular revenue earning use of steam traction, as opposed to experimental operation, may be made. The locomotives used a rack and pinion drive on one side and the gauge was 4ft 1in - so

although the Middleton Railway was changed to a conventional standard gauge industrial railway in 1881, there are some original 'firsts' which can be claimed for narrow gauge. Interestingly, the Middleton Railway would become the first standard gauge preservation project in 1959, just eight years after the pioneer TRPS had shown that a railway could be taken over and operated by volunteer labour!

No narrow gauge enthusiast will have any doubt concerning the 4ft gauge Padarn Railway, but the Glasgow Underground - of the same gauge - is a rather different matter, while the Lee Moor Tramway, of 4ft 6ins gauge ('Dartmoor Gauge') was narrow gauge by definition, but only just! At the other end of the scale is the question of minimum gauge and miniature, where definitions can become very blurred - consider the Ravenglass & Eskdale Railway which has progressed from its original conventional narrow (3ft) gauge, to miniature on conversion to 15ins, and has subsequently evolved into minimum gauge.

There are some measurements which offer a degree of broad uniformity within the wide range of narrow gauges. Ireland was the stronghold of the 3ft gauge with a large number of lines and lengthy route mileages built to this measurement. An extensive steam system and the Manx Electric Railway also made 3ft something of a 'standard' on the Isle of Man, although not all Manx lines were or are 3ft - the Snaefell Mountain Railway being 3ft 6ins and Groudle Glen 2ft. In England 3ft gauge was less common for public lines, the Southwold Railway being one, along with the Ravenglass & Eskdale Railway (until 1915) and the Rye & Camber Tramway, although it was widely adopted in industry - and virtually 'standard' for public works prior to 1914. The use of 2ft 6ins gauge is probably more widespread than many realise, including the Welshpool & Llanfair in Wales, the Lloyds/Bowater's industrial system in Kent - part of which survives as the Sittingbourne & Kemsley Light Railway - while several ex-Bowater's locos still work at Whipsnade Zoo, Bedfordshire. The Leek & Manifold was also of this gauge, but did not survive into preservation. Although out of the public eye, MoD lines built to this gauge and operated at a number of military depots added considerable mileage in this gauge. The Royal Engineers selected 2ft 6ins gauge when they built the (now-closed) Chattenden & Upnor Railway and this remained

the choice of British military authorities until they were obliged to change to 60cm gauge during WWI to match the French and German systems. The Admiralty, however, never did change - hence the survival of much equipment which has come onto the market via tender sales in recent years.

Much less common was 2ft 3ins gauge, although it was the choice of some important lines, notably the Talyllyn Railway and the nearby Corris Railway, also, Scotland's Cambeltown & Machrihanish Railway (closed in 1931). For many, the classic narrow gauge is just under two feet. The actual measurement varies slightly, hence the term 'nominal 2ft gauge' is often used as a generic description. The Ffestiniog, Vale of Rheidol and Leighton Buzzard lines are major 'nominal 2ft gauge' survivors, with the Welsh Highland part-way through reconstruction and the Lynton & Barnstaple Railway in the course of revival. The

Ashover Railway is probably the most notable line of this gauge to have been lost. Many other lines opened in recent decades have opted for 2ft gauge, often utilising equipment from closed industrial systems, and it is worth noting that stock from, say, the Dinorwic and Penrhyn systems has to be regauged to run on other lines, and the back-to-back wheel measurements have to be taken into account when locos make visits away from the 'home' railway. The adoption of 60cm (nominal 2ft) by the military, and the development of reliable internal combustion locomotives around WWI was also hugely influential in post-war development of the British narrow gauge.

Leaving aside debates concerning the very earliest plateways, tramroads, and tape measures, the narrow gauge has always enjoyed a special, almost indefinable, atmosphere. Originally, these railways almost always shared an intimate link with their

RIGHT: **Nearly half a century has passed since this scene of decay and dereliction at Harbour station (Ffestiniog Railway) was photographed. To realise how far we have come, it is well to have a reminder of where things were before determined preservationists arrived!** (*Peter Banner*)

LOWER: **Early days of Talyllyn Railway preservation. Precise details are not known, but** *Dolgoch* **is apparently pictured at Abergwynolwyn - the tracks visible in the foreground being rather intriguing since there was only a single siding at the station in the early 1950s. It is assumed that the 'extra' track is actually a stock of spare rails, perhaps lifted from the village incline in 1951. The date of the photograph has been narrowed down to between summer 1951 and summer 1953. David Mitchell, Managing Director of the TR, believes the lad coupling up may be Gareth Jones, who joined the Talyllyn's staff in mid-1951 and worked through the summer school holidays, and thus offers a best guess that the photograph shows the afternoon train in August 1951 - the first year of operation under Society auspices.** (*Don Doxey*)

OPPOSITE PAGE -
TOP: **What a contrast 50 years later!** *Dolgoch* **approaches Quarry in July 2001, the carriage immediately behind the locomotive is the restored Corris Railway carriage No 17.**

LOWER: **Simplex** *Mary Ann* **and George England 0-4-0ST** *Prince* **bring a train of vintage carriages across the Cob towards Porthmadog station. It is a timeless Ffestiniog Railway scene, but was actually shot in the early evening sun on 8 October 2000 towards the end of an FR Vintage Weekend – scenes of yesterday, today!**

The Ffestiniog Railway is also a scene of transformation, perhaps only the immaculate condition of Hunslet 0-4-0ST *Lilla* and the restored freight wagons gives a clue that this scene, captured outside Boston Lodge, dates from May 1998 and not decades earlier.

local communities. Many were initially built to serve industry, linking the quarry, mine, etc., with a port, canal or standard gauge outlet. Others linked rural communities, sometimes over considerable distances, especially in Ireland - where the equipment may have been bigger and the lines longer than in England, Wales and Scotland, but that special atmosphere was still there in abundance. Perhaps a major factor was the bewildering array of equipment employed, maybe compounded by the preparedness to make do and mend, for many were certainly impecunious. It was also the case that they tended to be in comparatively (and sometimes very definitely!) remote locations well away from the gaze of officialdom.

A common factor was economy. To build the railway, less land was required, sharper curves meant the route could hug the contours of the country and, if a cutting had to be made or a tunnel bored, less material had to be removed. With lower costs, in facilities, infrastructure and equipment, a railway could serve a small community or industry where a standard gauge line would be uneconomic. Of course, there are exceptions - Chelfham viaduct on the Lynton & Barnstaple comes to mind - and, where there was no alternative, the Ffestiniog bored tunnels to maintain its continuous downward gradient, but generally it is this ability to follow the landscape which accounts for the meandering (sometimes tortuous) course and tight clearances of most lines. Informality coupled with idiosyncrasy was very much a hallmark of the narrow gauge. While the scene in Britain and Ireland has changed to a huge degree, the tradition of individuality, which forms such a key element in its attraction, coupled with friendliness, remains just as strong on today's narrow gauge.

Although locomotives and equipment were often small, especially in comparison with the standard gauge, this was not necessarily the rule. While the diminutive 0-4-0T or 4wDM Simplex may seem typical, there was much variation and size. The Ffestiniog is famous for its 0-4-4-0 double-Fairlie locos, while motive power in Ireland (the Burtonport extension of the Londonderry & Lough Swilly Railway springs to mind) was both large and highly impressive. This variety remains today, especially with the importation of locomotives from abroad, including around a dozen big South African locos which are now in Britain, including 'NGG16's at work on the revived

Welsh Highland Railway (Caernarfon). If one wants really huge, visit the Buckinghamshire Railway Centre and see the 3ft 6in gauge ex-South African Railways '25NC' Class 4-8-4 on static display. The narrow gauge scene in these islands certainly offers something for all tastes!

Original railways have been saved and given new leases of life, old standard gauge trackbeds have been brought back into use by narrow gauge lines utilising combinations of preserved and newly-built equipment, small bands of enthusiasts have created entirely new narrow gauge lines for the pleasure of doing so and museum collections have been set up to provide a safe home for artefacts covering everything from tickets to locomotives. It is a wonderful and wide-ranging world, the 'problem' is less what should be included, more what has to be left out! This is illustrated by fact that there have been at least 43 railways and tramways of differing gauges and lengths on the Isle of Man alone - in addition to the obvious lines, this total includes temporary contractors' lines, mines tramways (including the wooden rails of the Bradda Mines Tramway), a craneway and the very obscure Peel Mortuary Tramway. This 'problem' multiplies exponentially in England, Wales and Scotland, and there were many industrial operations in Ireland as well. Narrow gauge tracks served industry in every conceivable form: mining, agriculture, construction contracts, internal factory and works systems - one may even include fishing - in 2001 tracks which served the fishing fleet remain across the shingle at Dungeness! Although many have now gone, others remain in specialist applications, solving problems such as restricted access (mines and tunnels) or where the ground cannot support the concentrated weight of road vehicle wheels, such as on peat bogs.

Accepting that offering a definitive history of every narrow gauge line in Britain and Ireland is a hopeless task, certainly within a book of this size, the emphasis has been given to passenger-carrying railways and the more significant museum collections to present a celebration of what has survived, with a flavour of what has been lost. Only the broadest of brushes has been applied to give a sample of industrial lines, and neither conventional town-type tram systems nor pier railways have been included, neither really fulfilling the traditional concept of narrow gauge.

Geographically, the starting point for inclusion in this volume was the narrow gauge railways of Britain. Plainly, Northern Ireland had to be included as part of the UK, but being limited by a political boundary in Ireland was ridiculous - especially so when the border came into being after the 3ft gauge systems had been built, and duly ran across the routes of two railways. The island of Ireland is therefore included as a whole, regardless of politics and government. The Isle of Man is an internally self-governing dependent territory of the Crown. It is not part of the United Kingdom, although the UK is responsible for the Isle of Man's external relations - the island's railways are jewels and their inclusion was obvious! Jersey, also, is not part of the United Kingdom and has its own Parliament, The States of Jersey, but being one of the Channel Islands, is one of the British Isles - sadly, this only enables the inclusion of a line which has been lost, other narrow gauge railways in the Channel Islands being either industrial or military in nature.

Place names

The spelling of many locations in Wales has changed in recent years. The most difficult decision within these pages relates to the Festiniog Railway, as defined by its Act of Parliament, or Ffestiniog as in Blaenau Ffestiniog. Latterly, the railway has been marketed as the Ffestiniog Railway and this spelling is now generally accepted in the style guides of leading publications, hence its adoption here - even for references prior to the preservation era. Some Irish place names also appear to have alternative spellings. The author has tried to adopt the more widely accepted spelling, but it seems to depend on which source one uses in some cases!

A background in industry

The employment of narrow gauge railway lines first arose in industrial applications. Initially they took the form of simple tramways, later the narrow gauge was adopted for the construction of 'proper' railways - the need for an economic method of transport was the simple explanation in almost every instance. The advantages of cheapness in construction have already been described, and such operations could be worked at comparatively low cost, allowing the advantages of rail transport to be exploited by industry where a larger operation made little or no sense. When that industry was situated in a remote location, perhaps amid mountainous topography, a narrow gauge line was often the only realistic option. But, narrowness of gauge need not equate to restricted capacity. The Ffestiniog Railway led the way, introducing steam haulage in 1863, a move which also meant that just three years later, it became the first narrow gauge line to receive approval from the Board of Trade to carry passengers. The FR was to demonstrate that further innovation could offer a viable alternative to doubling its line, or converting to standard gauge to handle the traffic. In so many respects, the

narrow gauge lines which developed in the mountains of North Wales to serve the slate industry provided a blueprint for others to follow - and the message passed around the world.

Slate extraction around Blaenau Ffestiniog resulted in the construction of the Ffestiniog Railway, and the other two great quarries in North Wales, the rival Dinorwic and Penrhyn operations which lay about four miles apart, each carving massive galleries into opposite sides of the same mountain range, had faced the same need for transport. The first tramroad to connect the Penrhyn quarries at Bethesda with Port Penrhyn on the Menai Straits opened in 1801. This was superseded when a new line was built between 1876-77 specifically with locomotive haulage in mind. While gauge is conventionally measured between the inner faces of the rails, Penrhyn originally adopted a gauge of 24⅛ins between the centres of the rail heads. As the size of rail sections increased, this naturally brought complications and the actual gauge becomes a matter of detailed debate. Quoting 1ft 10¾ins seems to be generally accepted, although other authorities say 1ft 10⅝ins - for what it's worth, Hunslet set the back-to-back of the tyres of most locomotives they supplied to Penrhyn at 20¼ins - hence proving the value of referring to 'nominal' 2ft gauge! The total system encompassed around 50 miles of track within the quarries at Bethesda, plus a main line of slightly over 6½ miles between the workshops and wagon marshalling yard at Coed-y-Parc down to Port Penrhyn, where there were further sidings. As the slate industry declined, so did

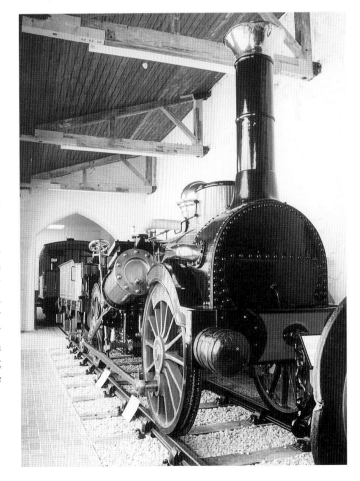

The magnificent 4ft gauge 1848-vintage Padarn Railway locomotive *Fire Queen* preserved at Penrhyn Castle. In the background, behind the loco's tender, is the Padarn Railway Directors Saloon Carriage.

LEFT: **War Department Light Railways Protected Simplex No 3098 is owned by the National Railway Museum and on loan to the Leighton Buzzard Railway where it is pictured leaving Page's Park with a run of skips on 20 November 1999. These locomotives were built for service on the western front, and examples subsequently worked sand trains on the 1919-built Leighton Buzzard line, while this locomotive found post-war employment at Knostrop Sewage Works in Leeds.**

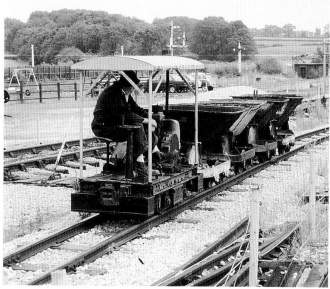

the fortunes of the Penrhyn Railway. Lord Penrhyn died in 1949 and in 1951 Penrhyn Castle - a huge castellated house and not a fortification - was transferred to the National Trust to cover death duties, the quarries being taken over by a new company. The passenger service (for quarrymen) on the Penrhyn 'main line' ceased in 1951 and the line was closed to all traffic on 24 July 1962, its work transferred to road transport. The track was removed in 1965 and the rails sold to the Ffestiniog Railway, also to become the destination for two of the Penrhyn main line locomotives, *Linda* and *Blanche*. Thankfully, *Charles* was also to enter preservation, at Penrhyn Castle. By about 1959, around half of the Penrhyn locomotive fleet was laid up, although the internal system in the quarries remained in use after the main line had closed. Steam finally ceased at the quarries in January 1965 (by which time internal combustion power was already in use) but fortunately, the surviving locomotives had all been acquired for preservation by about 1968.

The quarries at Dinorwic, opposite Llanberis, developed a little later than those at Penrhyn, but the method of transporting slate to the sea followed a similar pattern of narrow gauge railway development, although by a slightly different method. The first

CENTRE: **The extended Golden Valley Light Railway is a passenger carrying line, but with a collection of internal combustion locomotives, also forms a centre of industrial narrow gauge preservation. This August 1997 picture reproduces a typical industrial scene as the Lister Blackstone (53726/63) locomotive hauls a run of skips through the Swanwick Junction section of the railway.**

LOWER: **An example of battery-electric motive power, this is NG24, a Baguley Drewry loco originally built for use at RAF Chilmark, a munitions site near Salisbury. The loco is preserved at the Golden Valley Light Railway and is shown hauling two ex-MoD vans, on the Country Park section of the line.**

RIGHT: **The Ffestiniog Railway was originally operated by gravity in the downward direction and today's FR demonstrates this method of working during special events. In this picture, the train is approaching Penrhyn crossing.**

tramways in the quarry dated back to 1816 and, by 1824, the Dinorwic tramroad was constructed to connect the quarry workings with Port Dinorwic on the Menai Straits. Work on a completely new line commenced in 1841 and the 4ft gauge Padarn Railway opened two years later. Initially worked by horses, steam was introduced in 1848. This 'main line' element of the Dinorwic rail system was nearly seven miles long and provided the link between the 1ft 10¾ins gauge tracks within the quarries and the track of the same gauge at Port Dinorwic. At Gilfach Ddu, slate trucks were loaded onto transporter wagons, each of which carried four of the narrower gauge trucks, and they were offloaded some 250ft above Port Dinorwic and sent down an incline to reach the Port complex. The original steam motive power was provided by a pair of remarkable Horlock 0-4-0 tender locomotives named *Fire Queen* and *Jenny Lind*. These were replaced by three Hunslet 0-6-0STs, *Dinorwic* (1882), *Pandora* (1886 - renamed *Amalthaea* in 1909) and *Velinheli* (1895). A workmen's train service was operated over the Padarn Railway until 1947, the line closed in 1961 and was completely lifted by 1963. *Amalthaea* and *Dinorwic* were scrapped in August 1963. *Velinheli* had been dismantled for repairs in November 1953 but never reassembled, and most of the components were scrapped in June 1963, although the side tanks and chimney survived and are now in the Gilfach Ddu museum. Fortunately, *Fire Queen* was not scrapped, apparently being kept for sentimental reasons (an early example of preservation?) and, after many years' storage in a shed at Gilfach Ddu, is now cosmetically restored and displayed in the Penrhyn Castle museum. The Dinorwic Quarries closed on 10 July 1969 and, a month later, Dinorwic Slate Quarries Co Ltd went into liquidation. By this time a number of locomotives, no longer needed as the slate industry declined, had already been sold. An auction of the remaining equipment was held on 12/13 December 1969, when the last four steam engines were sold. The trackbed of the Padarn Railway on the northern shore of the lake now forms the

route of the Llanberis Lake Railway, opened in 1971. Many of the locomotives from the Penrhyn and Dinorwic quarry systems now haul trains on heritage lines, along with others which spent their working lives in the North Wales slate industry at such operations as Pen-yr-Orsedd, Dorothea and Cilgwyn.

Although fundamentally industrial systems, the Penrhyn and Dinorwic main lines also operated passenger trains to carry workmen. A number of other narrow gauge railways built to serve industry also carried people: the Bowater's line at Sittingbourne had carriages for its workers, the Glyn Valley Tramway quickly developed a passenger service, the Ashover was a public carrier in addition to its core business of transporting minerals, the Ffestiniog evolved into a passenger line, while the Leighton Buzzard Railway became a passenger line as the preservationists took over. All of these, and others, where passenger-carrying featured as an addition to the core business are covered in detail later in these pages, but a huge number of other lines served industry with no pretensions towards proper passenger traffic.

It is not known when the very first narrow gauge lines were laid, certainly the lineage can be traced back to the 1600s. These would have been hand-pushed by workers. The next development would be the use of horses and then locomotives: steam, internal combustion, electricity and, occasionally, compressed air. Some, normally where a steep gradient was involved although not always, made use of a cable and/or chain hauled by a stationary engine. The industries served covered just about anything where there was a load to be moved. Coal, ironstone, clay, sand, cement, brick, water and sewage works, quarried stone of all kinds, timber, agriculture, gas works systems, heavy engineering, construction and many more have, and in some cases still do, employ narrow gauge rail systems. Even the construction of the Channel Tunnel was aided by a narrow gauge railway - a far cry from the slate quarries of North Wales.

In Ireland, lines related to the peat industry did, and still do, account for the predominant mileage, but there were many

The Leighton Buzzard Railway holds regular Industry Train Displays to demonstrate how narrow gauge locomotives and stock used to serve industry. Running through the yard at Stonehenge Works in this 1998 picture is *RAF Stanbridge* with a munitions train, while a train of peat wagons waits in front of the building. The display arrangements have subsequently been improved to enable better public viewing and operate on sidings towards the top of the frame.

other lines serving industry, ranging from the steam-worked 1ft 10ins gauge Guinness Brewery at St. James's Gate, Dublin, through to the 3ft gauge British Aluminium Company system at Larne Harbour, and from the 3ft 6ins gauge Admiralty Railway at Haulbowline, to the Upperlands Horse Tramway which transported linen over the quarter of a mile which separated two parts of a factory.

Reference has already been made to gauge, and it is within industry that the range of measurements becomes bewildering - it has been estimated that there have been at least 30 different gauges employed between 1ft 3ins and 4ft 6ins in industrial applications. Many are long-gone, others are remembered because they had some form of link with more well known lines. There were far too many to offer comprehensive coverage in a work such as this, but the following provides a sample of the variety to be found.

Kerry Tramway - A 1ft 11½ins forestry line in Mid-Wales. After closure, its Bagnall 0-4-2T *Excelsior* was employed on the construction of the Lynton & Barnstaple Railway. The site had a later phase of use, and one of these locos, a Kerr Stuart 0-4-0T

(1158/17) went on to work at the Oakeley slate quarries at Blaenau Ffestiniog where it was named *Diana*, and later to the Pen-yr-Orsedd quarry. The loco entered preservation and spent periods (in non-working condition) at Llanberis and the Brecon Mountain Railway. Now privately-owned, restoration is in progress.

The Plynlimon and Hafan Tramway - chose 2ft 3ins gauge in common with the Talyllyn and Corris Railways. Opened in 1897 principally to transport road setts, it also had a handsome bogie saloon coach for passenger traffic - but the line lasted just two years before closure. One of the locomotives, Bagnall 2-4-0T *Talybont*, was regauged and used during construction of the Vale of Rheidol Railway and remained on that line following opening. The coach inspired the design of a new carriage built for the Launceston Steam Railway.

The Snailbeach District Railways - a line serving lead mines and a smelting works in Shropshire with a gauge of 2ft 4ins. Opened in the 1870s and taken over by the well-known figure of Col Holman F Stephens, the line finally closed in 1959, although most of it had been out of use for many years. The remaining steam locomotives all failed in 1946 and, towards the end, the line was operated by an agricultural tractor straddling the rails. The figure of Henry Dennis provided a link with the Glyn Valley Tramway, and Snailbeach locos 0-4-2ST *Belmont* and 0-6-0ST *Fernhill* were loaned to the GVT between 1885-1888 during its conversion to a steam line. In turn, the GVT loco *Sir Theodore* spent a period around 1905 at the Snailbeach system in connection with a new quarry, although not very successfully, the difference in gauge being too much. *Fernhill* was replaced by a new loco named *Dennis*, and three second-hand locos - one had been used during construction of the Leek & Manifold line - and two others were Baldwin 4-6-0Ts built for use in WW1.

The Pentewan Railway - this Cornish line of 2ft 6ins gauge opened in 1829 and was worked by steam from 1874. Although closed in 1918, a part of the track was relaid, to the original gauge, in 1926 by the Pentewan Dock & Concrete Co - some of which still survives. The line was notable for its locomotives, *Pentewan*, *Trewithen* and *Canopus*, each being built by Manning Wardle to replace the previous one. They all had an extraordinarily long wheelbase - a relic of an early plan by the engineer J B Fell to utilise lightweight timber viaducts. These were never implemented, although the replacement locos were built following the original principle!

Kettering Furnaces - An example of the 3ft gauge systems which served the Midlands ironstone industry. An ironworks was established in the 1870s beside the Midland main line near Kettering and 3ft gauge horse-worked tramways were operated before the first locomotive was acquired in 1879. Two 0-4-0STs supplied by Black Hawthorne followed, then three 0-6-0STs from Manning Wardle. An extensive network of lines served the ironstone pits. Many of these lines were of a temporary nature, while others took on a more permanent character with several bridges over public roads, and a viaduct constructed to cross a stream. The ironworks, and the last section of line, closed in 1963. Fortunately, one example of each type of locomotive has survived into preservation.

Lochaber Railway - This 3ft gauge line was built by the British Aluminium Co at Fort William, in the shadow of Ben Nevis in the Scottish Highlands. Aluminium smelting requires huge amounts of electricity, hence operations tend to be in areas where there is plenty of water, and at sufficient height to enable the use of hydro-electric generation. Construction of this works commenced in 1925 and a railway was needed to build the

pipeline and provide a service route for maintenance until superseded by roads in 1977. Several steam locomotives were employed by the contractors, Balfour Beatty but, when complete, the maintenance function was performed by diesels - including small Railcars called 'speeders'. Bauxite ore arrived at Fort William by sea, and was taken over the narrow gauge line to the works in trains hauled by two Kerr Stuart 0-4-2STs, both of which survive, albeit much altered.

The Betchworth Quarries - This quarry in Surrey, operated by the Dorking Greystone Lime Company, was unusual (although not unique) in having five separate railway systems employing four different gauges! These encompassed standard gauge (two of these locos survive, *Baxter* at the Bluebell Railway and 'Coffeepot' at Beamish), a hand-worked 19ins gauge system in the hearthstone mines, and a more recent 2ft gauge hand-worked system around the lime kilns. The main interest lays in the 3ft 2¼ins gauge system linking the quarry faces with the lime kilns. Two steam locomotives were introduced in 1880 and received the names *Townsend Hook* and *William Finlay* in 1930. An unusual feature was the working of waste material up an incline, with the locomotives running on a shallower incline hauling a cable connected to the wagons. From 1945, part of the system was worked by an O&K diesel *Monty* (OK7269/36) and the steam locos were out of use in the early 1950s. At this point, a new quarry face was opened and served by the fifth railway, of 2ft gauge, worked by a diesel. All of the narrow gauge locomotives have been preserved: Fletcher Jennings 0-4-0T's *William Finlay* privately and *Townsend Hook* by the Narrow Gauge Railway Society, based with the diesels plus some wagons at Amberley Museum, where a length of suitable gauge track has been laid.

Callenders Cables Construction Co of Belvedere, Kent - An internal industrial system utilising 3ft 6½ins gauge. The site later

The peat operations of Bord na Mona in Ireland continue to employ large numbers of narrow gauge locomotives on huge railway systems. Some of the machines are decidedly unconventional, such as this converted agricultural tractor which is mounted on a 4-wheel frame with the road wheels removed. The drive is conveyed from the rear axle of the tractor, by chain to the rear wheelset. This example was photographed on the Blackwater system, County Offaly, in 2001.

became British Insulated Callenders Cables Ltd (BICC) and employed several steam locomotives. Two, Bagnall 0-4-0STs *Woto* and *Sir Tom*, ceased work in 1968 and, after some 20 years in a dealer's yard, were sold for preservation, both being regauged to 2ft. *Woto* is owned by Patrick Keef of Alan Keef Ltd and regularly visits narrow gauge lines, while *Sir Tom* arrived at Threlkeld Quarry and Mining Museum in 2000 and, following reassembly, is due to return to steam in 2002.

Goathorn or Fayles Tramway - Built to 3ft 9ins gauge, the first line in this system, which transported clay, opened between Norden (near Corfe Castle) to Middlemere Creek, Poole Harbour, prior to 1860. It was abandoned around 1900, but in 1868 another line was opened between Newton Pits and Goathorn Pier, Poole Harbour. This line was extended to Eldon Sidings in 1905, with a further branch from Eldon Sidings to new pits to the west of Norden. The section to Goathorn Pier ceased to be used in about 1937. This left about four miles of track around Corfe, and when both existing steam locomotives failed this was relaid to 1ft 11½ins gauge in 1948, enabling the use of available diesel locomotives and stock. The former WHR 2-6-2T *Russell* had also been purchased by B Fayle & Co Ltd, but this historic locomotive suffered frequent derailments, even after being tried as an 0-6-2T. A broken axle finally forced *Russell* out of service by 1953. The tramway continued until the early 1970s, while *Russell* was sold for preservation and now runs on the Gelert's Farm-based WHR(P).

Saundersfoot - A 4ft gauge line dating back to 1832 which linked a coal mine with Saundersfoot harbour on Carmarthen Bay. A branch from Saundersfoot to Stepaside village was added in 1842, involving three tunnels through headlands, with only 6ft 6ins vertical clearance. Steam was introduced in 1874 on the section between Stepaside and Saundersfoot incline. In 1915, the original line to Thomas Chapel was extended to Reynalton, relaid and steam introduced. Closure was progressive between 1921 and 1930, then largely reopened in 1934 until final closure and dismantling in 1939. In more recent times, a miniature railway was operated for a time on part of the trackbed near Saundersfoot.

'Dartmoor Gauge'

The 4ft 6ins gauge Plymouth and Dartmoor Railway was a horse-worked line opened in 1823 between Plymouth and Princetown. Various branches were added later. The branch to Plympton was taken over and became part of the South Devon main line, the Princetown line was reconstructed to standard gauge after 1877 and became a branch of the GWR and part of the line at the Plymouth end also became a standard gauge branch. The central section from Laira Wharf to Marsh Mills and the Cann Quarry branch remained and were incorporated into the Lee Moor Tramway.

The Lee Moor Tramway, opened in 1858, formed an extension of the Plymouth & Dartmoor's 4ft 6ins gauge Cann Quarry branch to china clay workings at Lee Moor via a rope-worked incline. The section above the inclines was worked by two Peckett 0-4-0STs from 1899, while the lower (originally P&DR) part remained

horse-worked until closure of the much-reduced system in 1960. This section had several level crossings over later standard gauge lines, including a crossing of the main line at Laira over which horse-drawn trains had precedence! Both of the locomotives have survived. *Lee Moor No 1* is displayed at the Wheal Martyn Museum, St. Austell, while from the 1970s, *Lee Moor No 2* was housed, with the sole surviving Lee Moor china clay wagon, at Saltram House near Plymouth in a museum set up by the Lee Moor Tramway Preservation Society. In 2001, the Society had to move its collection away from this National Trust property and their new home is at Buckfastleigh, HQ of the standard gauge South Devon Railway.

Other significant industrial systems

The 3ft gauge tracks of the Kettering Iron & Coal Co have been mentioned, and other systems of this gauge were located at Islip, Eastwell, Scaldwell and Eaton with several other ironstone locomotives having survived into preservation. Metre gauge was also employed in the ironstone industry, the French-built 0-6-0T *Cambrai* (now owned by the Narrow Gauge Railway Museum Trust and kept at the Irchester Narrow Gauge Railway Museum) being an example which worked at the Loddington Ironstone Company quarries between 1936 and 1956. Lest anyone should assume that metre gauge in Britain is a comparatively recent phenomenon, note that the first such line of this gauge appears to date from 1841. Related to business ventures which included the development of a colliery at Clay Cross (see Ashover Railway section) George Stephenson was involved in setting up a limeworks at Ambergate in the 1830s. Limestone was quarried at the cliff quarry at Crich (which houses today's National Tramway Museum) and was transported some two miles over a horse-worked tramway, before being lowered down a self-acting incline to the limeworks. Although measured as metre gauge, its specific selection, as opposed to a measurement which happens to correlate to a metric equivalent, must be debatable.

Even today, narrow gauge railways offer the most effective means of transport over the soft ground of peat bogs. The 3ft gauge systems operated by Bord na Mona (Irish Turf Board) are covered in more detail in Chapter 7, but there have been bog railways in Britain in such places as the Somerset Levels. Environmental concerns have reduced the British locations where peat is extracted, aided by railways, to Hatfield Moor near Doncaster, and a number of bogs in the Scottish lowlands between Carlisle and Glasgow.

This selection merely scratches the surface: the horse-worked 4ft 2½ins gauge Peak Forest Tramway could have been mentioned, the 3ft 3ins gauge Cockenzie Tramroad, the 4ft 4ins gauge Fordell Railway, or the 2ft 11 ins gauge systems of the London Brick Company (4wVTB Sentinel *Nutty* from Stewartby, and a Motor Rail diesel and wagon from Arlesey being preserved) could have been described, as could countless others, many of which have been little recorded, if at all. Many were steam worked, others not. Regardless of location, as industries contracted and labour costs grew, many lines either fell out of use or were replaced by road transport.

CHAPTER TWO

Sadly departed

The survival and revival of the narrow gauge in Britain after the saving of the Talyllyn Railway, closely followed by the Ffestiniog Railway, has moved from miraculous to glittering - a wonderful story told in the later chapters of this volume. Railways which, just a few years ago appeared lost, are now under active restoration - and although the narrow gauge in industry has drastically declined much equipment has been rescued and is now in the care of new projects.

Half a century of preservation is a huge achievement. To put things in proportion, several railways did not last 50 years between opening and closure, and others did not exceed this by very much - indeed, just one of the lines described in this chapter comfortably exceeded the Golden Jubilee mark, and this was not a public carrier.

Although now just memories, a selection of these lines are described - a part of the great heritage of the British narrow gauge!

Campbeltown & Machrihanish Light Railway

This 2ft 3ins gauge line started as a colliery railway to transport coal from pits on the western side of the Kintyre peninsular to the port of Campbeltown on the eastern coast. It was built by the coal company on land effectively owned by the Duke of Argyle and was completed on 21 April 1877, running some 4¼ miles from Kilkivan pit to Campbeltown. As this pit was worked out, a new colliery - Drumlemble pit - was opened and the railway extended westwards in 1881, increasing its length to 4.7 miles.

The Campbeltown Coal Company took over in 1897, but the crucial change came in 1901 when a new turbine steamer started to call at Campbeltown. The advent of the Clyde tourist trade brought day trippers to Campbeltown who sought to travel on to Machrihanish by horse-drawn charabancs, which struggled over the poor roads. The opportunity of upgrading the railway to better handle the colliery traffic, and increase income by extending both ends of the line, was realised. A new Argyle Railway Company Ltd - later incorporated as the Campbeltown and Machrihanish Light Railway Company - applied for an Order to construct a Light Railway in May 1904, which was granted on 8 May 1905. The new company took over and upgraded the colliery railway, extended the line to the harbour

at Campbeltown (the new passenger terminus), added a passing loop at Lintmill and, at the western end, built a line into Machrihanish, the line to the colliery now becoming a spur off the new main line. The 6⅜ mile railway was inspected on 17 August 1906, the first fare paying passengers being carried the following day.

The reconstructed railway killed the horse charabanc traffic between Campbeltown and Machrihanish when it opened, but in 1913 it was itself threatened by the appearance of motor buses. By the late 1920s, two bus operators were in fierce competition - and both directly competing with the railway. The 1920s also saw strikes at the colliery. Moreover, the capital of the Campbeltown Coal Company had been eroded and coal production ended in September 1929. The railway struggled on without the coal traffic and in the face of competition for passengers, but locomotive problems early in 1932 spelt the end. The railway did not operate summer trains in 1932 and had effectively closed. Assets were liquidated in 1933, and *Atlantic* worked demolition trains the following year. By the end of 1934 everything had been sold or scrapped. The NCB did restart coal production and worked the colliery between 1946-1967, but it was far too late for the long-gone railway, the coal being carried by road.

All stock for the line was purchased new, and nothing survived closure to work on another railway. The first colliery locomotive was *Pioneer*, an 0-4-0WT built by Andrew Barclay & Co of Kilmarnock. A trailing truck was added, making the loco an 0-4-2WT, but it was out of use by 1906 and never incorporated into C&MLR stock. In 1883, another Andrew Barclay (269/83) loco arrived, an 0-4-0ST, *Chevalier* - also to receive a trailing truck and become an 0-4-2ST. *Chevalier* did enter the stock of the C&MLR and was overhauled during WW1, when its appearance was revised by adding a full cab. The loco was principally used to handle coal traffic and survived to the end. The coal company also purchased *Princess* in 1900, a Kerr Stuart 'Skylark' Class 0-4-2T (717/00) used to work light passenger traffic over the rebuilt line. Two larger locomotives were purchased specifically for the Light Railway, both Andrew Barclay 0-6-2Ts: *Argyle* (1049/06) and *Atlantic* (1098/07). For the opening of the Light Railway, four well-appointed bogie carriages were constructed by R Y Pickering & Co of Wishaw. Saloon vehicles with end balconies, a virtually identical fifth carriage was delivered in 1907 from the same maker. Pickering's also built carriage No 6, to the same basic style, but with a central luggage compartment.

Coal appears to have originally been carried over the railway in 'hutches' (colliery tubs) but, by 1884, at least 18 transporter wagons carrying four 'hutches' crossways on each had arrived. From 1910, new conventional 3¼ ton and 4½ ton wooden coal trucks entered service. Other stock consisted of a Pickering-built brake van (acquired on the insistence of the BoT to accompany coal trains down a 1 in 35 gradient, but really a box van with brakes which saw little use) and a goods wagon used for milk traffic.

Leek & Manifold Valley Light Railway

A child of the 1896 Light Railways Act, but with a highly unusual aspect - the application for a Light Railway Order was a joint application for lines to be built to different gauges. The first section was a standard gauge link from the North Staffordshire Railway's Churnet Valley line to Waterhouses (promoted by the NSR) then from Waterhouses a 2ft 6ins gauge railway to Hulme End, promoted by the Leek & Manifold Valley Light Railway Company. The L&MVLR would build the narrow gauge line, but it would be worked by the NSR. This helps to explain another distinctive aspect of the L&M line - its employment of transporter wagons to convey standard gauge wagons

over the narrow gauge line - the first such operation in Britain.

The LRO was made on 6 March 1899, and although the first sod of the 2ft 6ins gauge line was cut at Waterhouses on 3 October 1899, construction commenced in March 1902. The ceremonial opening of the narrow gauge line took place on 27 June 1904, opening to the public on 29 June. Waterhouses - Hulme End was 8¾ miles and engineered to the loading gauge of a standard gauge branch to accommodate standard gauge stock carried on the transporter wagons. There were also isolated lengths of 4ft 8½ins track in sidings for standard gauge wagons arriving on the transporters. There was an interchange station at Waterhouses, while Hulme End was the operating base of the railway, with locomotive and carriage sheds. Initially there were seven stopping places along the route, although an eighth was soon added.

Although busy during summer months with excursion traffic (largely from the Potteries) other traffic never really developed and the L&MVLR Company was not a financial success. Hopes of reviving the old lead and copper workings at Ecton never materialised and no appreciable goods traffic developed, although the transportation of milk provided a degree of trade, which developed further during WWI. The early 1920s brought mixed fortunes. A Creamery opened at Ecton, with standard gauge tanker wagons arriving and departing on the transporter wagons, and excursion traffic revived to some extent. However, several early stalwart supporters of the narrow gauge company

died and local passenger traffic fell away. Under the grouping of railways the NSR, and thus the Leek & Manifold, became part of the London Midland & Scottish Railway. But competition from buses was hitting traffic and the track needed renewal. The Creamery at Ecton closed in 1932, local farmers sending milk by road to a new dairy at Rowsley. With the last remaining source of regular traffic gone, the end was approaching and the railway closed on 10 March 1934. The standard gauge line from Leek to Waterhouses ceased carrying passenger in 1935, with freight services withdrawn in 1943. Meanwhile, with the track lifted, the narrow gauge line became a footpath on 23 July 1937 and, in 1953, the Redhurst to Butterton section was rebuilt into a road.

Although the railway was not an economic success, the appointment of Everard R Calthrop as Engineer ensured it was technically sound. Prior to his appointment, he had built the Barsi Light Railway in India and many features from this line's equipment influenced the Leek & Manifold. Two attractive 2-6-4Ts were built by Kitson & Co, No 1 *E.R.Calthrop* and No 2 *J.B.Earle* arriving in April 1904. The railway had four carriages, two all-3rd Class and two brake composites. Designed by Calthrop, and built by Electric Railway & Tramway Carriage Works Ltd of Preston, these bogie vehicles had a colonial appearance with end verandas and pitched roofs. Their primrose yellow colour set them apart from most passenger stock on the British narrow gauge, although they were later repainted into NSR red, then LMS maroon.

The railway only ever had eight freight vehicles, five of which were transporter wagons. The first four were built by Cravens Carriage & Wagon Co (two in 1904, two in 1907/8) with the fifth being built at Stoke Works, to a different design, after 1923 grouping. The other stock consisted of a bogie goods van and two low-sided bogie goods wagons. The bogie open's and transporter wagons, also saw service as auxiliary passenger vehicles up to WW1!

Both locomotives were scrapped after the railway closed, No 1 following use working demolition trains. The carriages were all broken up in 1936, and just one transporter wagon survived, being sold to the Ashover Railway. The signalbox from Waterhouses also survived and, in August 2001, was moved to the Amerton Railway to be restored - and once again used to control movements on a narrow gauge railway in Staffordshire!

Glyn Valley Tramway

This line dated back to the formation of the Cambrian Slate Company in 1857. Located high up the Ceiriog Valley, a means of transporting the slate out was needed, but constructing a suitable railway proved to be protracted and complex. The situation was resolved in 1870 when the Glyn Valley Tramway was incorpo-

rated by an Act of Parliament and, quite separately, Parliament passed the Tramways Act opening the way for tramways to be built in roads. A 2ft 4¼ins gauge (half standard gauge) line was constructed, the main line of just over 8 miles running from the Shropshire Union Canal near Chirk to Glyn Ceiriog. An incline from Glyn Ceiriog ran up to the Cambrian slate quarries (which had an internal narrow gauge system) and with other branches, the tramway totalled just over 11 miles. The line, worked by horse and gravity, opened for freight traffic in April 1873, and passenger services commenced in April 1874. At Chirk, there was an exchange siding with the GWR, but opposition from the Chirk Castle estate forced the line to adopt a stiffly graded route to the east of Pontfaen, which prevented it approaching Chirk standard gauge station. In 1878, powers were obtained to build a two-mile extension from Glyn Ceiriog to the granite quarries at Pandy and a deviation at Dolywern, but approval for the use of steam locomotives was refused. At Glyn Ceiriog, an incline to the Wynne slate quarries was added around 1884.

The breakthrough finally came in 1885 when the Glyn Valley Tramway Act was passed. This allowed conversion to steam, and with opposition from Chirk Castle now withdrawn, a revised alignment could be built from Pontfaen to the GWR's Chirk station, and a new wharf at Black Park Basin replaced Gledrid wharf as the interchange with the Shropshire Union Canal. The conversion work encompassed the laying of new rails, during which the gauge was slightly altered to 2ft 4½ins, a new station at Glyn Ceiriog (plus locomotive shed and turntable) and an extension to Hendre granite quarry. The rebuilding of the line was aided by the use of two locomotives from the Snailbeach District Railways, *Belmont* and *Fernhill*. Work progressed through 1887, and was largely completed the following year. Freight services were maintained throughout, but horse-worked passenger services having ceased on 31 March 1886, steam-hauled passenger trains did not commence between Chirk and Glyn Ceiriog until 15 March 1891.

Although built to transport slate, from about 1881 granite became the predominant traffic and the line's fortunes hinged on the status of the stone trade. Slate traffic fell during the early 1900s, while passenger figures steadily rose, but was more additional income than staple diet. Overall, the railway - for that is really what it was despite its roadside nature and tramway origins - did well enough up to WWI. Post-war, however, the granite traffic fell, costs rose, and losses were recorded. Decline set in during the early 1920s, and although a profit was recorded in the latter years of the decade, there was now motor competition to contend with (the material transported by the GVT helping to build the roads on which the motor vehicles ran!) and the line lost money from 1932 until the end. The last passenger service ran on 6 April 1933, the final mineral train was worked on 6 July 1935 and, in October of that year, an extraordinary general meeting put the company into voluntary liquidation.

As noted, the two borrowed Snailbeach locomotives were used during the conversion period 1885-1888. The GVT's own locomotives were built in 1888 by Beyer Peacock, *Sir Theodore* (2969/88) arriving in October that year, *Dennis* (2970/88) in the following April. Both were 0-4-2Ts (with the pony wheels

No equipment from the Leek & Manifold Light Railway has survived, but this Leek & Manifold /North Staffordshire Railway signalbox from Waterhouses has been saved. It arrived at the Amerton Railway in August 2001 and will be restored. To the left, Bagnall 0-4-0ST *Isabel* is taking water. *Carrie Thomas*

designed to lead since the locos were intended to always be driven cab first) with a casing around the boiler and the wheels and motion covered as part of the requirements for roadside use. A third similar, but slightly modified, loco was also built by Beyer, Peacock, 0-4-2T *Glyn* (3500/92) arriving in 1892. Tramway provisions were apparently forgotten when it came the fourth locomotive, an ex-WDLR Baldwin 4-6-0T (45221/17) which was rebuilt (including regauging from 60cm gauge) by Beyer Peacock for the GVT in 1921. All four were scrapped late in 1936. Independent of the GVT, two locomotives were employed within quarries served by the system: the Glyn Slate Co (later Glyn Ceiriog Quarries Co Ltd) which worked the Cambrian slate quarry had a 2ft gauge Bagnall 0-4-0ST on its internal system between about 1905 and 1921, when it was replaced by a Simplex 20hp petrol loco, and the Hendre quarry employed a 1880-vintage 0-4-0T (built by Lilleshall) between 1900 and around 1920, although it was not scrapped until 1944.

Trains were generally run as mixed (passengers and freight) with passenger stock being four-wheeled vehicles. Initially, a rather diverse selection of vehicles were acquired, covering the horse-worked period through to the introduction of steam-hauled services. From 1892, carriages were supplied by the Midland Railway Carriage & Wagon Co following a standardised form of two-compartment design, some being open's (which subsequently acquired roofs) the rest being enclosed coaches. After closure, most of the bodies were sold for use as sheds, hen houses, etc. Two of the closed bodies were eventually rescued and, following rebuilding, now run on the Talyllyn Railway. There were also two 3-ton covered vans, and two brake vans. Of the freight stock, the largest number of wagons were 4-ton, three plank vehicles with bottom side doors. These were for granite and coal traffic, and of particular interest was the presence of private owner wagons, some 20 of these vehicles being owned by the Ceiriog Granite Company. The stock also included tar wagons, bolster wagons and low-side open's (both based on granite wagon design), slate wagons, 2-ton open's (with the same underframes as the slate wagons) and side tipping wagons, although these were probably not used on the main line.

The Glyn Valley Tramway Group maintains a small museum in the old waiting room at Pontfadog.

Ashover Light Railway

Original proposals for a line to Ashover envisaged it being a standard gauge mineral railway. While surveying the route for the North Midland Railway between Derby and Leeds, George Stephenson saw the potential for developing a colliery in the Clay Cross area - the NMR providing a ready market and the means of transporting the output. George Stephenson & Company was formed and in 1837, while the Clay Cross tunnel was being driven, purchased land near the north portal where a colliery and coke ovens were developed and in production by the time the NMR was opened on 11 May 1840. On George Stephenson's death in 1848, his son Robert became Company chairman, although he resigned from the post in 1852 and sold his shares, the business becoming The Clay Cross Company.

This Company purchased the Overton Estate (including part of the Parish of Ashover) in 1918 with the aim of exploiting the minerals to be found, including limestone, fluorspar, barites and gritstone, which would be transported from Fallgate and Ashover by light railway.

Powers were applied for in November 1918 under the Light Railways Act to construct a four-mile standard gauge line between the (by then) Midland Railway station at Stretton to Ashover, plus a 2ft gauge rope-worked line to serve the Alton Colliery. The Light Railway Order was confirmed on 4 December 1919 but, in the event, the branch was never built and the colliery never reopened. The Consulting Engineer for the proposed railway, Lt Col H F Stephens, was asked to revisit the estimated costs. Following a meeting in March 1920, it was realised that a 60cm gauge line could be built not only over the Stretton - Ashover section, but extended to Clay Cross for about the same total cost as the planned standard gauge line. An application covering the revised proposals was made and, following a public enquiry held on 1 February 1922, the Minister of Transport confirmed the LRO on 13 November 1922.

Work had started in September 1922 and goods traffic was being conveyed between Fallgate and Clay Cross by January 1924. Meanwhile, an application for an additional LRO to extend the line to a better terminus at Ashover, and to serve two additional quarries, was approved in August 1924. After official inspection on 31 March 1925, the Grand Opening took place on 6 April 1925, with public passenger services starting the following day. The line ran from Clay Cross Works and, after skirting the town, ran south, then turned up the Amber Valley to Ashover, a total of 7¼ miles by rail, although just 3½ miles separated Clay Cross and Ashover as the crow flies! Wooden station buildings were provided at Clay Cross, Ashover Butts and Stretton with small shelters at other sites. The carriage and loco sheds were at Clay Cross, and an unusual feature was a triangle at both ends of the railway, allowing locomotives to be turned.

Ashover was a traditional destination for summer visitors and passengers flocked to the new railway. Although primarily conceived to carry minerals, providing a passenger service was always intended, with such income regarded as a bonus - probably just as well since passenger receipts for 1925 would be the high-point for the railway. The ALR carried good Bank Holiday and summer weekend traffic through the late 1920s, but competition from buses arrived and numbers declined. Winter services ceased after October 1934, but following poor patronage during 1936 - almost non-existent on weekdays - passenger services were suspended from 14 September 1936. The wooden shelters were removed and the railway, which never carried much in the way of general goods other than coal, concentrated on transporting limestone and fluorspar from Ashover and Fallgate to Clay Cross. There was some additional traffic between May and October 1942 when an opencast coal extraction site was operated at Woodthorpe Hall, between Hilltop Loop and Holmgate. A fan of sidings was operated by three diesels and an 0-4-0ST Kerr Stuart 'Wren' (KS3114/18). This loco subsequently entered preservation and, although part of the collection at Gloddfa Ganol, was loaned to the Bala Lake Railway between September

1980 and August 1985. Because of the Ashover connection, it was called *Ashover* for a time, but subsequently named *Dryw Bach* (Little Wren in Welsh). The Gloddfa Ganol collection was sold in 1998, the loco going to a private collector and was returned to steam in 2002. After the opencast operation ceased, one train a day sufficed for the remainder of the war.

The carriages were used for the final time on an 11 August 1937 excursion, the last public excursion operated on 8 June 1940 (using open wagons) and some special local outings were run between 1943-1946. On 24 August 1947 a train of four wagons was run for a Birmingham Locomotive Club trip - the last time passengers travelled over the whole line. The railway was running down and Clay Cross triangle was taken out of use in 1946, locomotives working bunker first from then on, and the Clay Cross Company informed Chesterfield RDC that it intended to close the railway and use road transport. At the end of 1949, the last remaining contract supplied from Butts quarry was terminated and the quarry closed on 28 January 1950, closure of the railway following on 31 March 1950. The track in Butts quarry was removed, but the main line left in place, albeit severed in places. These lengths of rail were replaced and obstructions removed so the Planet could work through to Fallgate from Clay Cross on 23 October 1950, enabling Clay Cross Company officials and a solicitor to inspect the line prior to selling the land - this did not apply between Fallgate and Ashover. Track lifting commenced on the day of this last trip. Although

Baldwin 4-6-0PTs were built for service during World War One, following which examples went to five narrow gauge systems in Britain, although none of these locos survived. This example is WDLR No 778 which is to be restored to operation by the Greensand Railway Museum Trust.

Milltown quarry had closed in 1946, the Clay Cross Company worked fluorspar deposits around Fallgate and the trackwork within the yard stayed in use, worked by small diesels. The use of locomotives ceased in 1968 and the last remnants of the railway system were abandoned in 1969. The trackbed from Ford to beyond Woolley was flooded by the Ogston reservoir in the late 1950s. The Ashover Light Railway Company, a wholly owned subsidiary of the Clay Cross Company, was wound up in 1950, a liquidator being appointed on 26 July 1950.

The principal motive power was ex-WDLR Baldwin 4-6-0Ts, four arriving in 1922: *Guy*, *Hummy*, *Joan* and *Peggy*. Following the ALR's construction, *Guy* was unserviceable, and two more of the type arrived in 1925, one being named *Bridget* and the other given the old plates from *Guy*. The fleet steadily reduced with locos cannibalised to keep others running. By about August 1948, *Joan* had worked for the last time, leaving only *Peggy* serviceable. Although the Baldwins were central to operations, there were experiments with other forms of motive power, including a petrol shunter (probably built by Muir-Hill), a 4-wheel Dick, Kerr petrol-electric locomotive (which eventually 'acquired' the unofficial name *Amos*), another petrol-electric loco (several had been purchased around 1927 for their electric motors) fitted with a McLaren diesel engine, and a Muir-Hill petrol loco. Finally, with the Baldwins now on their last legs, a new 48hp Planet diesel was purchased from F C Hibberd (3307/48) in 1948 to handle the remaining stone traffic from Butts quarry. This locomotive is now at the Ffestiniog Railway, named *Ashover*.

The railway had four carriages upon opening, the underframes and bodies being newly built by the Gloucester Railway Carriage & Wagon Co Ltd in 1924 and mounted on ex-WD bogies. Following closure, they saw use as store sheds at Clay Cross works, and later at a sports field at Clay Cross. Two, used as stands beside a football pitch, were moved to the Lincolnshire Coast Light Railway in 1961. The 1925 crowds following opening of the ALR resulted in two makeshift conversions of wagons into carriages, these reverted to wagons in 1926. This was possible following the purchase in 1926 of eight passenger vehicles from the 'Neverstop Railway' which ran at Wembley during the British Empire Exhibition in 1924/25. Clay Cross works removed the E E Baguley Ltd bodies from the steel frames and bogies, substituting new wooden frames and ex-WD bogies. These bodies were broken up in about 1944, the bogies being recovered. The wagon stock was also ex-WDLR, 70 wagons of types 'D' (entire side dropped in two parts) and 'E' (so-called well wagons, centre section only dropped) being purchased, although the bogies from some were used under the passenger coaches. The railway also bought a transporter wagon from the Leek & Manifold Railway in 1934. Following regauging, the wheels fouled the bogie frames on sharp curves and it never saw use, being cut up in 1951.

Rye & Camber Tramway

A proper railway, the promoters of the Rye & Camber Tramways Company Ltd apparently hoped to avoid the onerous requirements placed on 'railways' by calling their line a tramway. First discussed in January 1895, the 3ft gauge line was constructed (entirely on privately owned land) remarkably rapidly and the first trains ran on 13 July 1895! Other claims to fame include the involvement of Holman F Stephens who, at the age of 26 was awarded the contract to build the line, and remained its Consulting Engineer. Although this was only his second railway project, he was later associated with many enterprises, mostly distinguished by their impecuniosity, including a period with the Ffestiniog and Welsh Highland Railways. His assistant, William H Austin, who achieved some fame from his involvement with Stephens, drove the trains on the Rye & Camber line's opening day.

The railway was intended to transport golfers to Rye Golf Club and its original line ran for just over a mile to what was then called Camber station. An extension of a little over a mile opened on 13 July 1908 (to the public from the next day) to a new station named Camber Sands, the original terminus then becoming known as Golf Links station. All the original buildings were of corrugated iron, a style later recognised as typical Stephens. When Camber Sands opened, there was no building at all, although later a wooden structure (with corrugated iron roof) was added. The railway worked a certain amount of sand traffic from the original station (up to about 1909) and subsequently from Camber Sands (until about 1931) with sidings at both locations. A deviation of the line at Camber Sands was built for the 1939 season.

The line continued to operate during WWI, although passenger receipts were falling by 1916 and there was little sand traffic. By the 1920s, holiday-makers and day trippers were the most important source of traffic - many of the comparatively affluent golfers now arriving at the clubhouse by car! The railway had only operated during the winter up to this point with the help of a subsidy from the Golf Club, and only to Golf Links, and the subsidy ceased from the mid-1920s. The period 1930/31 brought more problems when several key figures involved from the beginning died, including (by this time) Lt Col Stephens, and operations were maintained by just two men.

The railway stopped operating on 4 September 1939, the day after war was declared. In July 1940, Camber was evacuated, the area being identified as of strategic importance, and early in 1943 the section between Rye and Golf Links was used by the Admiralty to transport men and materials in connection with the construction of a jetty into the River Rother. For a period, Rye booking office became a Guardroom, and the Rother Ironworks-built carriage body was removed from its frame and used as a bogie flat. The following year the line was used again, this time to bring shingle from Northpoint Beach to Rye, but now the track was in appalling condition. The railway was returned to its owners following the war, with a section leading to Golf Links station now in the form of a concrete road - ironically, now looking like a tramway!

The line never reopened for passengers and the lease from the Golf Club was terminated in 1946. The railway was practically dismantled by March 1947, and the Rye & Camber Tramways Co was dissolved on 7 February 1949.

Prior to opening, there had been thoughts of using a petrol locomotive, and electricity was also considered (the Volks Railway at Brighton had opened in 1883) but in the end, a steam locomotive was ordered. This was 2-4-0T *Camber* built by W G Bagnall of Stafford (1461/95). Other stock at the opening consisted of a Bagnall bogie carriage with 1st and 2nd Class compartments and two small, very flimsy looking 4-wheel wagons. A second bogie carriage was added in 1896, being shorter and taller than the Bagnall vehicle, and built by Rother Ironworks of Rye. By 1897, another locomotive was needed. After looking for a second-hand machine an order was placed with Bagnall's to build a new locomotive. Also a 2-4-0T, *Victoria* (1511/97) was slightly larger and more powerful than *Camber*, although of similar appearance. Three wagons were added to the stock in 1897 and, in 1918, two small 4-wheel wagons were acquired, rebuilt with seats and entered service as, well, passenger wagons! As road competition began to bite, and running costs were rising, in 1924, a locomotive (based on the Motor Rail Simplex type) was purchased from the Kent Construction Company. The only other item of stock was a ganger's trolley, propelled by moving

a pair of handles backwards and forwards. The Bagnall coach was preserved following closure, going to the Brockham Museum, and is now at Amberley awaiting restoration.

There have been several proposals for a Rye & Camber revival. At the time of writing, the Rye Bay Railway Company, having dropped a proposal for a 2ft gauge line on the original trackbed, is looking to build a 15ins gauge line on an entirely new trackbed to connect Rye and Camber without utilising Golf Club land.

Sand Hutton Light Railway

Similar to the Heywood lines, the Sand Hutton Railway was also an estate line, but came about in a rather different manner. Sir Robert Walker, Baronet of Sand Hutton Hall in the Derwent Valley east of York, established a 15in gauge private miniature line in the grounds of the Hall in 1910. Having decided to extend and upgrade the existing ¾ mile line, a Light Railway Order was obtained in 1920, but the availability of surplus 18ins gauge stock brought about a revised plan and work to rebuild the track commenced.

Three locomotives built between 1915-1917 for use at the Government meat depot at Deptford (London) were purchased in 1920, together with 75 2-ton open wagons, with a fourth locomotive added in 1927. All the locos were 18in gauge

This attractive scene was captured on 31 July 2000 during construction of the Dinas - Waunfawr section of the Welsh Highland Railway. Hibberd 4wDM *Upnor Castle*, from the closed Chattenden & Upnor Railway, is pictured with a works train shortly before reaching Waunfawr at the point where the river lays beside, and below, the track.

Hunslet 0-4-0WTs (HE1207, 1289, 1290 and 1291) with outside frames and Walschaerts valve gear. At Sand Hutton, HE1207 was named *Esme*, after Sir Robert's wife, although the others remained unnamed, retaining Deptford number plates.

The old miniature line was converted to 18ins gauge in 1921-22 and an extension built, connecting the system with Warthill station on the North Eastern Railway main line between York and Hull. By April 1922, a 1½ mile line had been added from the Sand Hutton main line to Claxton brickworks, the junction being roughly mid-way between Sand Hutton Central and Warthill. At the other end of the system, the line was extended to Kissthorns, and in 1923 further extended to Bossall and Barnby House. This brought the length of the main line (Bossall - Warthill) up to about 5¼ miles. A further ½ mile from a point near Bossall to Scrayingham was also authorised, but never built due to the cost of bridging the River Derwent. The hub of the system was at Sand Hutton Central, near the

LEFT: Bagnall's constructed the articulated 0-4-4-0T *Monarch* for the Bowater's industrial system in 1953. Following closure of the paper railway, the locomotive went to the Welshpool & Llanfair Light Railway in 1966, where it was photographed in action early in 1976. *Monarch* subsequently left the WLLR and is currently dismantled at the Ffestiniog Railway. It is believed that it could be regauged comparatively easily and forms something of a 'strategic reserve' for possible future use on the FR or WHR(C).

LEFT: **Built for use on the Lodge Hill & Upnor Railway (previously Chattenden & Upnor Railway) Manning Wardle 0-6-2T *Chevallier* (1677/15) was sold to Bowater's in 1950. When that industrial system closed, the loco found a new home at Whipsnade Wild Animal Park where it is pictured leaving Whipsnade Central station with a passenger train in 1995.**

Hall, where the locomotive shed was situated - the station being a gravel platform and hut.

The main traffic over the railway was agricultural products, coal and bricks from Claxton. When the brickworks was at its peak, three locos were in steam to handle the traffic. At Warthill, narrow gauge tracks ran on each side of a standard gauge siding. That at ground level was used to offload goods into Sand Hutton wagons, while a raised 18ins gauge line facilitated the transfer of products into standard gauge wagons.

A bogie passenger carriage was built by Robert Hudson & Co in 1924. It had a channel steel well-type frame, and the body, built with three internal sections, could accommodate 36 people. In the centre were longitudinal slatted wood seats for 20 arranged along the sides, one end was a semi-open section without windows which seated 10, and the other end was a saloon with six moveable seats, which could be used as a buffet. Access to the carriage was via an open veranda at one end. This was the only passenger vehicle on the line, but there was also a 4-wheel brake and parcels van. There were a number of Halts between Warthill and Bossall, and passenger trains ran on Saturdays only (another source says Sundays only) between October 1924 and July 1930, and for a brief period in 1925 on Wednesdays.

Claxton brickworks closed in 1929 and the railway was recording losses when Sir Robert Walker died in 1930. This was a period of agricultural depression and unemployment and although a passenger service may have been operated in 1931, all of the lines were closed at the end of June 1932. The railway was dismantled over the following 12 months and the locomotives were cut up on site, but the carriage survived. Following use as a pavilion for a ladies' cricket team at Harton, it was rescued in June 1967 and taken to the Lincolnshire Coast Light Railway where it received a new lease of life. Of the Sand Hutton line, little remains. Warthill main line station closed in 1959, and Sand Hutton Hall has also been demolished.

Chattenden & Upnor Light Railway

The Royal Engineers commenced construction of the 2ft 6ins gauge Chattenden & Upnor Railway, later to be renamed the Lodge Hill & Upnor Railway, in 1873. The initial work appears to have been largely a training exercise - the Royal School of Military Engineering then being based at Chattenden, near the River Medway, opposite Chatham Dockyard. The line commenced at Pontoon Hard, beside the river, and headed northwards (climbing steeply) towards Chattenden. Between Pontoon Hard and Chattenden was Church Crossing, where a spur led back to the Royal Engineers' Upnor Depot, north of Upnor Castle. The main base of the line, including locomotive sheds, was at

Chattenden adjacent to the barracks, and until around 1895 a line from Hoo (to the east) joined the main system here.

From Chattenden, the line continued northwards to, and around, Chattenden enclosure where stores and ammunition were kept. Up to 1891, the Navy's guns and ammunition were supplied by the Army. When the Admiralty took over this function, it acquired Upnor Depot, and in 1905 the Navy also took over Chattenden enclosure. Meanwhile, the Navy had constructed its own armaments depot at Lodge Hill, north of Chattenden, which was served by the railway. Up to now, the railway had been operated by the 8th Railway Company, Royal Engineers. In 1906, it was taken over by the Navy and the line became the Lodge Hill & Upnor Railway - the Royal Engineers relocating to Hampshire. The Navy added a further extension, connecting the Lodge Hill depot with an earlier single-track standard gauge branch that ran to Sharnel Street on the SECR system. This standard gauge link provided access to the ammunition dump from Woolwich and other centres over the main line system.

The system saw intensive use during WW2 and new stock was added. The last three steam locomotives ceased to be used in the 1950s. Manning Wardle 0-6-2T *Chevallier* (1677/15) was sold to Bowater's in 1950 and is now at Whipsnade Wild Animal Park. Unfortunately, other late survivors: Dick Kerr 0-6-2T *Fisher*, Peckett 0-4-2T *Norbury* and Avonside 0-4-2T *Burnett Hall* were scrapped in October 1954, November 1955 and May 1956 respectivly. Three diesel locomotives took their places: an 0-6-0 Hunslet (3301/46), a Drewry 0-6-0 (2263/49) and 4wDM Hibberd Planet (3687/54).

The railway was closed completely by the end of 1961. The diesels found new homes, along with several items of rolling stock. The Hibberd (Yard No 44) and four 1947-built bogie toastrack carriages (originally for workmen and 'other ranks') and the 1957-built 'combination car' (a passenger/guard vehicle for Officers and officials) went initially to the Welshpool & Llanfair Light Railway, the loco being given the name *Upnor Castle*. In 1968, the Drewry (Yard No 107, subsequently Yard No 58) also found its way to the WLLR, the loco's past being recognised by the WLLR which named it *Chattenden*. Later, *Upnor Castle* was sold to the Ffestiniog Railway and now operates on the WHR(Caernarfon) where it has been joined by the 'combination car', while the bogie coaches (two of which had been rebuilt into closed coaches in Wales, the other two remaining in original toastrack form) were sold to the Sittingbourne & Kemsley Light Railway in 1979.

The Jersey Railway

The first narrow gauge passenger train to run in Jersey operated on 15 March 1884 between St. Aubin and La Moye. The background to the 3ft 6ins gauge railway which ran from the island's capital, St. Helier, to Corbiere via St. Aubin, however, encompasses an earlier standard gauge railway.

First thoughts for a railway on Jersey have been dated back to 1845, but it was 1869 before a Bill in the name of the Jersey Railway Company was passed by the States of Jersey, the island's Parliament. A standard gauge railway was built between St. Helier and St. Aubin, the first train over this 3¾ mile line running on 28 September 1870, with opening to the public on 25 October. This company was bankrupt by the end of 1874, but in March 1871 a petition was made to the States by the owner of the granite quarry near La Moye to build a tramway to St. Aubin, granite and other goods then to be transferred to the Jersey Railway for carriage to St. Helier. The Bill for the St Aubin's & La Moye Railway & Granite Quarries Co Ltd was passed on 7 June 1871. It seems that this railway was intended to be standard gauge, but the requirement for some sharp curves led to the adoption of narrow gauge. By July 1877, 3ft 6ins gauge track had been laid between St. Aubin and Pont Marquet, the remainder of the line being unfinished since this company had hit financial problems. Although a trial was made by the island's first narrow gauge locomotive on 10 September 1877, all work stopped on 22 December, by July 1878 the company was bankrupt, and progress remained in abeyance until 1883.

In 1883, the standard gauge St. Helier - St. Aubin line of Jersey Railway Co, and the narrow gauge Aubin's & La Moye Company, were transferred to a new Jersey Railways Co Ltd - note the plural. Work to relay the St. Helier - St. Aubin line to 3ft 6ins gauge took place between February and September 1884, while the railway between St. Aubin and La Moye quarries (Corbiere) was authorised to open from 30 August 1884. Then, there was no physical connection between the two lines at St. Aubin, a junction being made the following year, with the first train over the full 7¾ miles of the connected lines operating on 5 August 1885. A now familiar tale continued, with the company entering voluntary liquidation in late 1895.

The Jersey Railways & Tramways Co Ltd was registered on 18 January 1896 and took over the assets of the Jersey Railways Co on 1 February 1896. An unprecedented event followed in February 1897 - the first dividend was paid to shareholders! Improvements were put in hand, including cutting a tunnel at St. Aubin in 1898 to eliminate a series of reverse curves, an extension from the terminus near La Moye quarries to the grounds of Corbiere Pavilion was opened on 1 July 1899, and new station buildings at St Helier were opened in 1901. A traverser was installed at this station in the following year. The first narrow gauge locomotives are believed to have been a pair of 0-4-2STs built by Black Hawthorne & Co in 1877 and it is thought that they were brought over by the contractor who narrowed their gauge. One carried a local name (*General Don*) but both left Jersey around 1899/1900. The Jersey Railways Company had operated initially with a pair of 2-4-0T Manning Wardle & Co locomotives, No 1 *St. Heliers* (916/84) and No 2 *St. Aubyns* (917/84) - there must have been a miscommunication over the spelling of the names! - with another 2-4-0T No 3 *Corbiere* (1418/93) built by W G Bagnall, added in 1893. A further Bagnall 2-4-0T was ordered, although No 4 *St. Brelades* (1466/96) arrived a fortnight after the Jersey Railways & Tramways Co took over. The final locomotive was Andrew Barclay & Co 2-4-0T No 5 *La Moye* (1105/07).

Financially, things now seemed to be on an even keel and 1913 brought record takings and a record profit. The outbreak of WWI dashed hopes of further record traffic, although special trains run in connection with German PoWs in 1915 enabled the company to pay a dividend, but traffic decreased markedly in 1916/17. In 1922 the company looked at introducing Railcars. After considering electricity and petrol, it opted for a Sentinel-Cammell steam Railcar, *The Pioneer No 1* making its first run on 18 June 1923. This was followed by *The Pioneer No 2* (later named *Portelet*) an improved, and more powerful version of the original, which arrived in January 1924, and a third in March 1925, this subsequently being named *La Moye* after locomotive No 5 was sold in 1928. These steam Railcars arrived just in time to help the railway compete for traffic, for in April 1923 a fleet of motor buses started to operate on the island. The railway company also inaugurated its own buses between St Aubin and St Brelades Bay, which acted as feeders by connecting with the trains, in August 1923. The tactics appeared to be working, since 1925 was the company's most successful year ever, but by 1928 private cars were having an adverse effect. Moreover, competition with the buses of Jersey Motor Transport Co Ltd was causing concern - a situation resolved by taking over that firm on 5 August 1928. The warning signs were clear, however. An approach by the standard gauge Jersey Eastern Railway in 1928 concerning the possibility of amalgamation had been rejected, and the standard gauge line closed on 21 June 1929. The JER was also operating Sentinel rail cars (although their introduction was too late to save it) and the narrow gauge line purchased Normandy in July 1930 and regauged it.

Winter services were suspended between St. Aubin and Corbiere from October 1931, and winter trains between St. Helier and St. Aubin ceased from the end of 1932. The early 1930s were marked by fierce bus competition, with profits from the Jersey Railways bus operations being swallowed up by railway losses. The train service closed for the winter on 30 September 1936 as planned, but never restarted. A fire at St Aubin station on 18 October 1936 destroyed the roof, along with 16 carriages. With the railway not paying its way, no money to deal with ageing locomotives and the insurance not covering the cost of replacing the destroyed coaches, the company abandoned railway operations. The Main Roads Committee of the States purchased the concessions and real estate in 1937 and the rails, rolling stock, and other movable equipment was offered for sale by tender in July of that year. The first steam Railcar had been withdrawn in 1935, and all remaining locomotives and Railcars were scrapped in 1937. The company was wound up in October 1937, with a new company, Jersey Road Transport, taking over all the shares in Jersey Motor Transport.

The St. Helier - St. Aubin section of the line ran largely around the coast and following the German occupation in July 1940, the invaders rebuilt the railway to metre gauge as part of their fortifications, adding a branch from Pont Marquet to the Ronez quarries. The Germans built a new 60cm (1ft 11½ins) gauge line at St. Ouen's Bay, and the old standard gauge Jersey Eastern Railway line between St. Helier and Gorey was also relaid to this gauge. These lines were worked by steam locomotives, but did not carry passengers, and were removed at the end of the war.

CHAPTER THREE

Decline and revival

The narrow gauge had declined steeply by the end of the 1940s. Many of the well known railways had closed, while road transport was biting into the passenger and freight traffic of those which were left. Attitudes had changed following WW2 and, it seemed, nothing would be quite the same again. Prior to the 1950s, nobody would have considered working on the railways without payment for the pleasure of doing so and the reward of what could be achieved. But now they did, and this was to be the salvation for many lines.

England

The once-strong presence of public passenger carrying narrow gauge lines in England had faded away totally when the narrow gauge reached its lowest ebb. Two of the most significant industrial systems hung on just long enough to keep the flag flying. The railway preservation movement was still in its infancy when moves to save a part of the Leighton Buzzard Railway took place in 1967. Those pioneers took on a railway which had never carried passengers and had no coaches or stations, and built up an entire new infrastructure by voluntary effort. The railway is now one of the leading narrow gauge preservation centres in Britain and, as a line born from WWI, has a reputation and expertise in caring for equipment of that vintage. It also specialises in the restoration of locomotives which spent their working lives abroad. The Greensand Railway Museum Trust, a separate body with its base at the LBR, is bringing these two specialities together in a project to restore to steam 4-6-0T Baldwin No 778. Constructed for service on the Western Front during WWI, the loco went to India before being brought to Britain. Its restoration is a huge task but, when completed, will represent a type of locomotive which worked on the Ashover Railway, Welsh Highland Railway, Snailbeach District Railways and Glyn Valley Tramway - plus another which served industry at the British Portland Cement Manufacturers' site at Rainham, Kent - truly an icon of British narrow gauge history.

At Sittingbourne, the line built to serve industry also carried its workers. Indeed, the 24-hour trains were probably unique on the British narrow gauge in carrying passengers throughout the night - something which has only more recently been revived on special 'gala' occasions at other railways. When no longer needed to serve industry, the concept of preservation was sufficiently established for part of the system to survive in a revised form. Times have not been easy for the Sittingbourne & Kemsley Light Railway, particularly so as the 1990s became the 2000s - but the determination of a comparatively small band kept the line alive and the new century should see an upturn in the railway's fortunes. Meanwhile, three of the redundant locomotives from the paper system found new lives hauling passenger trains through the animal paddocks of Whipsnade in Bedfordshire. These historic locomotives, along with carriages constructed onto the frames of ex-Bowater's pulp wagons, set Whipsnade apart from other small railways which run in zoos and parks, such as Marwell Zoo, Cotswold Wildlife Park and Child Beale. Also different is the North Ings Farm Museum in Lincolnshire. Although specialising in agricultural equipment, its 2ft gauge line even features steam. This railway dates back to 1971 when it was installed to serve the chicken farm - an agricultural railway handling feed, eggs and waste from the sheds until the poultry business ceased in 1981. The original locomotive and wagons were retained, and still see use around the farm, and have been joined by a collection of industrial diesels and a steam tram locomotive. These locomotives include the 4wDM Motor Rail *Penelope*, on loan from The Narrow Gauge Railway Museum, Tywyn. The line has been extended and now forms a circuit of just over a quarter of a mile, and a passenger train is operated for visitors.

The Leighton Buzzard Railway

The 2ft gauge line preserved by the Leighton Buzzard Narrow Gauge Railway Society provides a return trip of nearly six miles, covering a substantial part of an industrial railway dating back to 1919.

What was originally the Leighton Buzzard Light Railway was constructed as a direct result of WWI when cheap sand imports from Belgium ceased. Sand available from the Leighton Buzzard area was suddenly in great demand, but transporting it caused expensive damage to local roads. During the war, the Government met the repair bill, but when hostilities

LEFT: **The Leighton Buzzard Railway has one of the largest collection of locomotives (steam and internal combustion) in Britain. O&K 0-4-0WT *P C Allen*, Baguley 0-4-0T *Rishra* and Hunslet 0-4-0ST *Alice* are on the shed road, Kerr Stuart 0-4-0ST *Peter Pan* in the foreground, while Kerr Stuart 0-4-0ST *Pixie* arrives at Page's Park in the background with a train from Stonehenge Works.**

LOWER: **Orenstein & Koppel 0-6-0WT *Elf* at Leedon Loop on the Leighton Buzzard Railway. Originally built to serve the sand industry, the preservation society had to construct the carriages, this train showing examples of closed, semi-open and brake coaches.**

ended, the sand quarry owners had to find an alternative if they were to stay competitive. A private company was formed in July 1919 to build and operate a narrow gauge railway and by November of that year some four and a half miles of (very light) track had been laid, the line opening for regular traffic from 1 December 1919. The railway transported sand from the quarries southwards, principally to the screening and washing plants on the other side of the road from the present Page's Park station, and then into the LNWR sidings on the Leighton Buzzard to Dunstable branch line although there were also deliveries to operations to the north of Page's Park.

Originally, motive power was steam, being two Hudswell-Clark 0-6-0WT locomotives built in 1918 for war use but never delivered. They were unsuccessful and quickly replaced by ex-War

Department petrol and TVO powered locomotives which included both Protected and Armoured types. The 'Simplex' Motor Rail machines built in Bedford became the typical Leighton Buzzard motive power and it has been calculated that around 100 such locomotives worked within a two-mile radius of Leighton Buzzard town centre during the boom years of the sand industry! In fact, the Leighton Buzzard line was probably the first permanent railway in the world to be exclusively worked by internal combustion motive power. After WW2, traffic started returning to the roads. This trend continued, until in 1969 through working ceased entirely, sand trains then only running on the north section of the line between the Double Arches Quarry and Stonehenge Brickworks.

In January 1967, a group of enthusiasts planned to build a railway at Watford. They visited Leighton Buzzard with the idea of purchasing track materials, but although the disused parts of the Leighton Buzzard line were not for sale, an arrangement to use the existing railway at weekends was agreed. With the use of a temporary workshop, four Simplex diesels and some wagons were purchased, and by October a Society was formed. The idea then was to operate according to American practice, hence it became The Iron Horse Railroad. At Page's Park, work commenced on a station and locomotive shed, and the first public trains ran on 3rd March 1968 - with the passengers standing in borrowed freight wagons! By October 1969, the American idea was abandoned and the name changed to Leighton Buzzard Narrow Gauge Railway. The last commercial delivery of sand took place on 27 March 1977 and the Society took over responsibility for the whole track. Over the following years, the loco fleet has expanded and is now one of the largest collections of narrow gauge locomotives in Britain.

The site of what is now Page's Park station was originally a set of loops, forming a 'holding area' for trains waiting to cross the road. When the Society started to operate passenger trains, a station was needed, but in the early years this was simply a wooden platform near the shed. After the sand traffic ceased, a station building was erected across the old trackbed, behind what became the buffer stops. Subsequent developments have seen the construction of two platforms, several extensions to the locomotive shed/workshop (the base of the steam department) and the introduction of 'Dobbers Buffet' adjacent to the station building. 'Dobber' was the name given to the men who worked in the sand quarries and inside the building is a collection of enlarged historic photographs illustrating their work. The Society has completely relaid the line with heavier rail, a project finished in 2000.

The surroundings of the Leighton Buzzard line have changed substantially over the years. In the early 1970s, the line was threatened by the construction of new housing estates, but with support from the Local Authority, the original alignment was retained - it should be remembered that the railway was here many years before these estates. The railway continues where once there were green fields, until Vandyke Road is left behind. A short branch from the main line used to serve Chamberlain's Barn quarry (another now-disused sand quarry) and the setting is agricultural, although parallel to a road. The cheapness of the original construction resulted in some sharp curves and the absence of earthworks leads to surprising gradients where the track simply followed the contours of the land - the 1 in 25 of Marley's Bank is one of the steepest gradients tackled by steam locomotives in Britain. The line also features a number of level crossings over roads.

Passenger trains terminate at Stonehenge Works, named after the old Stonehenge Brickworks which was demolished in the 1980s and replaced by a modern tileworks on the adjacent Redlands site - and nothing to do with the ancient monument in Wiltshire! In its industrial days, the line continued on northwards up the hill to serve a number of sand quarries, those which remain in production now send the product out by road. The stretch of track, actually double for some way, which remains now serves as a storage siding, but it is a (very) long-term ambition for the line to be extended back towards the quarries, although this is unlikely to happen until the quarries have been finally worked out. The Stonehenge site is the base for the internal combustion locomotive collection. On selected dates during the year, many of these locomotives, together with appropriate stock, provide Industry Train Displays shortly after the arrival of a passenger service from Page's Park. A series of small trains are run, accompanied by a commentary, to show the way in which narrow gauge railways served many industries in the past. These include peat extraction, munitions, forestry, tile manufacture and, naturally, sand. They also provide the ideal opportunity to run the locos and stock in the collection. An occasional variation is provided by Quarry Machinery Displays, when a vintage Ruston Bucyrus face shovel loads runs of skips with sand which are then hauled away by a locomotive.

The collection includes some 11 steam and 43 internal com-bustion locos, although not all are in working order. The majority form the museum collection and are not 'traffic' locos, and many are privately owned, but the ITDs provide the opportunity to see members of the heritage fleet in action. Plainly, a full list of locomotives would be very space consuming!

Although the original Hudswell-Clark 0-6-0WTs were scrapped long ago, steam returned to Leighton Buzzard in the late 1960s with the arrival of the preservationists. The fleet which has subsequently been built up is a diverse collection assembled from all over the world. The oldest loco at the rail-way is De Winton 0-4-0VTB *Chaloner*, dating from 1877. The Society-owned steam locos are: O&K 0-6-0WT *Elf* (12740/36), O&K 0-4-0WT *P C Allen* (5834/13), Andrew Barclay 0-6-0T *Doll* (1641/19), Kerr Stuart 0-4-0ST *Pixie* (4260/22) and Baguley 0-4-0T *Rishra* (2007/21). Other locomotives are present on the railway by agreement with their owners, including ex-Matheran Hill Railway O&K 0-6-0T No 740 (2343/07) which has a flexible axle arrangement enabling it to work round sharp curves and which entered service in 2002 following restoration at Page's Park.

The collection of internal combustion locomotives includes *Festoon* (MR 4570/29) - the oldest of the sand quarry locos remaining on the railway - and the Protected-type Simplex which used to work on the line is represented by the National Railway Museum-owned No 3098 (MR 1377/18). The railway also owns a modern diesel, No 80, *Beaudesert*. Purchased in 1999 to provide reliable, modern motive power capable of dealing with any emergency as well as working passenger trains if necessary, the fleet number was selected since the loco was ordered and delivered in the 80th anniversary year of the railway. Although some wagons were fitted with seats for an inaugural run on the opening day in 1919, this was the only recorded occasion of passengers being carried on the line until the 1960s and the start of a rudimentary service by the preservation society. Over the ensuing years Society members have provided the present stock of coaches, either by building them especially for the railway, or restoring ex-military vehicles.

The Sittingbourne & Kemsley Light Railway

A significant 2ft 6ins narrow gauge industrial railway system, centred on the operations of Edward Lloyd Ltd, connected the paper manufacturing mill at Sittingbourne with the nearby wharves at Milton Creek. A pair of Kerr Stuart 0-4-2T steam locomotives - *Premier* and *Leader* - arrived in 1905 and the official start of operations was apparently in 1906, with a further loco-motive of the same 'Brazil' Class, *Excelsior*, following in 1908. The wharves at Sittingbourne silted easily and construction of a new dock at Ridham on the Swale commenced in 1913, the rail-way being extended to cover the three and a half miles between Sittingbourne and the new dock. In 1924, Lloyd's opened a new paper mill at Kemsley, beside the railway and roughly mid-way between Sittingbourne and Ridham Dock. The use of the rail-way increased and more locomotives were purchased. The traffic consisted of wood pulp, china clay and manufactured paper, and a passenger service for the Lloyd's employees ran right round the clock to a published timetable. Because of the loads of paper and the surroundings of the paper manufacturing plant, all the locomotives were equipped with spark arresting apparatus, hence the American 'balloon stack' appearance of the chimneys. In September 1948, the company was absorbed into the Bowater Group, becoming Bowater Lloyd Pulp and Paper Mills Ltd and in 1955 became Bowater's United Kingdom Pulp and Paper Mills Ltd

In 1965, a study of working practices reported that the railway should be replaced by road transport. The passenger trains were reduced in length and finally ceased to operate in September 1968, followed by the announcement that the railway would close completely in the autumn of 1969. Fortunately, the management of the paper company felt that at least a part of the line, which had become well known to enthusiasts and was treated with affection by the staff, should be preserved.

The railway was officially closed for industrial purposes in October 1969, but a section of the line was leased to The Locomotive Club of Great Britain at a nominal rent, along with some of the locomotives and rolling stock, to form the Sittingbourne & Kemsley Light Railway. Four of the Bowater's locomotives were sold - Manning Wardle 0-6-2T *Chevallier*, Kerr Stuart 0-4-2T *Excelsior*, Kerr Stuart 0-6-2T *Superior* and Bagnall 0-6-2T *Conqueror* (subsequently sold again) - and went to Whipsnade, while Bagnall 0-4-4-0T *Monarch* initially went to the Welshpool & Llanfair Light Railway and was later sold to a group of Ffestiniog Railway supporters.

The railway commenced operating as a preservation project on 4 October 1969, running from a site in Sittingbourne, where a station was built. The route traverses a viaduct of 118 spans and five bridges - the longest narrow gauge railway viaduct in Britain, possibly western Europe - then runs over the marshes to a terminus near Kemsley Mill known as Kemsley Down, preserving an industrial railway in an industrial setting. After the initial operation by The Locomotive Club of Great Britain, the SKLR became an independent entity from the LCGB in 1976 - although the two bodies retain a close relationship. The line, including the viaduct, is leased from Bowater's, as are the remaining locomotives, with the exception of Kerr Stuart 0-4-2T *Leader*, which is owned by a consortium of SKLR members. The passenger stock includes converted bogie pulp wagons, together with four coaches which originated from the Chattenden & Upnor Railway and were acquired by the SKLR in 1978 from the Welshpool & Llanfair Light Railway.

Unfortunately, problems with the concrete structure of the viaduct came to a head in 1992 when continued use was banned until expensive remedial work had been undertaken. While safe to carry the paper mills pipes, running passenger trains over it was not possible. Moreover, since the SKLR did not own the structure, it could not seek grants towards the cost of repairs. No public trains ran over it between Christmas 1992 and Easter 1996. Prevented from operating out of the station at Sittingbourne, the SKLR built a Halt at Milton Regis, immediately behind a supermarket. Although this allowed trains to keep running over the remainder of the line to Kemsley Down, passenger numbers plummeted, and the fall in income was not matched by a reduction

in operating costs - all at a time when funds had to be raised to cover the repairs.

These were dark days for the railway, but a programme was established whereby the work could be carried out in four phases, the first of which allowed for renewed running from Sittingbourne. Passenger numbers immediately climbed again and helped raise the funds for the remaining repairs, although it took three years to get back to 1992 pre-closure levels. The second and third stages of the work were carried out during the winter months of 1998/99 and 1999/2000, thus avoiding further closures. The carefully calculated business plan was nearly ruined shortly before the final stage (2000/2001) was due to commence when the railway endured an astonishing string of 23 break-ins at Sittingbourne and Kemsley Down in a six week period. The cost of repairing the damage and installing security systems soaked up the cash allocated for the repairs, but friends of the line rallied round, and with the help of a grant from the local Council, the SKLR survived.

Despite the problems surrounding the viaduct, the Kemsley Down site has been steadily developed. Vegetation has been cleared and rolling stock rearranged to provide an attraction for visitors. In addition to the working locomotive fleet, other motive power which has been preserved, such as the fireless locomotive *Unique*, is displayed and a 'Museum Walk' created for visitors to stroll past wagons (with explanatory notices) up to a picnic area. There is also a museum in a portable building, which sits on the chassis of an old pulp wagon in a siding underneath the structure - an arrangement probably unique in preservation! The locomotive shed at Kemsley Down is to be extended by the addition of an extra road on one side, and a new workshop. This will be followed by the addition of a carriage shed at the site.

Of the original Bowater's locomotives, Bagnall 0-6-2Ts, *Superb* and *Triumph* currently operate, while 'sister' loco *Alpha* has 'donated' parts to keep the others running, although could be restored in the future if the money can be found. Kerr Stuart 0-4-2ST *Melior* (dating from 1924 and similar to the earlier 'Brazil' Class locos, but fitted with Hackworth valve gear) returned to service in 1996, with work proceeding on *Leader*. *Premier*, however, needs major work and is not expected to see service for a long time. The SKLR also has two diesel locomotives, Ruston & Hornsby 0-4-0DM *Edward Lloyd* and Hudson-Hunslet 0-4-0DM *Victor*.

At Sittingbourne, the 21st century should see a major redevelopment of the station - at no cost to the SKLR. An agreement with the developer of a major retail complex on the site of former storage and warehousing units immediately below the railway, adjacent to its old car park, means the developer acquired the old car park and provided a new one, along with access to the station from the other side of the line. The developer is to construct a new station building for the railway, which the SKLR will fit out to replace the old ticket hut; the new building is to incorporate a booking office with two ticket windows, a small shop and toilets. A new platform is also being built on the opposite side of the tracks from the current platform. Although Milton Regis ceased to be a terminus in 1996, it retains the status of a Halt,

ABOVE: A mixed train on the Sittingbourne & Kemsley Light Railway, hauled by Kerr Stuart 0-4-2ST *Melior*, approaches the Halt at Milton Regis on its way back to Sittingbourne.

RIGHT: Bagnall 0-6-2T *Superb* runs into the Kemsley Down terminus of the Sittingbourne & Kemsley Light Railway.

but the platform which was used between 1993-1996 was removed and replaced with a small new platform built on the supermarket side of the tracks (the opposite side from the previous platform) at the beginning of 2000.

With the uncertainty of survival into the new century removed, thoughts turned to future developments - and the possible construction of a new station at Burley Crossing, funded by the local Councils to serve what will be known as the Church Meadows Country Park. With a passing loop and island platform, the station would not be precisely at the half way point of the running line, but the introduction of a passing place would be a significant step forwards for the SKLR.

Although not a current plan, it is not inconceivable that the line could be extended at some future date if either, or both, of the paper mills closed. At the Sittingbourne end, the SKLR would like to explore getting closer to the town centre. Although internal roads have been built over the tracks inside the current mill complex at Kemsley Down, if the mill closed, reinstating the line to Ridham Dock would be an ambition 'in principle'.

Wales

Many view Wales as the spiritual home for the narrow gauge in these isles. Certainly some of the oldest, and definitely the most influential - in the form of the Ffestiniog Railway - hail from this nation. Moreover, the Talyllyn was the first narrow gauge railway to be promoted as a public carrier of passengers and goods - and became the first public railway in the world to be taken over and run by volunteers.

When the Talyllyn Railway Preservation Society took over in 1951, it inherited a line which had all of its original locomotives and coaches and could run them over the entire length of a railway which never actually closed. For the first 85 years of its life very little changed on the TR but, over the following 50 years, much would alter, giving birth to an entire new movement of railway preservation and revival. The TR has a very special place in history, but many people had already looked at reviving the Ffestiniog Railway, closed in 1946 and remaining in a form of suspended animation. Early preservation ideas were thwarted by seemingly insurmountable problems and legal obstacles, but these were overcome. Even greater challenges had to be beaten to return to Blaenau Ffestiniog.

The trio of classic Welsh narrow gauge lines is completed by the Welshpool & Llanfair. Rather different from the other pair, it was a country railway and did not have its roots in industry, holding on just long enough to benefit from the proof of what could be done at the Talyllyn, although no trains ran for a period and part of its route was lost, it was able to come back from the brink.

The Talyllyn Railway

The slate quarry at Bryn Eglwys in the hills above Abergynolwyn was established around 1847. It was purchased in 1864 by Manchester-based cotton mill owners looking to diversify, since supplies of raw cotton had been cut off following the outbreak of the American Civil War in 1861. Although the war ended in

1865, the decision had already been taken to build a railway to transport slate from the quarry. Initially, the objective was Aberdovey, but the arrival of the standard gauge Aberystwyth and Welsh Coast Railway (the Cambrian Coast line) at Tywyn (or Towyn as it was then known) in 1863 brought an obvious change of plan. An Act of Parliament was obtained on 5 July 1865, although construction had actually started the previous year, and the first locomotive, No 1 *Talyllyn*, (delivered in the autumn of 1864) was employed on building the line.

Plainly, the use of locomotives had been intended from the start. Steam had been introduced on the Ffestiniog Railway in 1863 and the Engineer for the construction of the Talyllyn Railway was James Swinton Spooner, elder brother of Charles Eastern Spooner, so that decision is easily explained. Since the FR initially used steam in the uphill direction and continued to employ gravity for downward trains, the TR was probably the first narrow gauge railway to envisage steam working in both directions from the beginning. Interestingly, passenger traffic was envisaged from the start as well. The Board of Trade Inspector who visited the new line in September 1866 was not satisfied with various aspects. Among the changes made were the securing of carriage doors and barring of windows on the south side. The idea was that the track could then be slewed southwards under the bridges, producing acceptable clearances on the north side, although there is no evidence that the track was so moved. Securing the doors on the south side of carriages did not matter, since the station platforms are all on the north side of the tracks - and all carriages built since the Society took over have only been fitted with doors on the north side. A further inspection on 8 November 1866 approved the carriage of passengers (which had already commenced on 1 October!) and services officially started in December. Stations were added at Rhydyronen in February 1867, and at Brynglas and Dolgoch in 1873. The name of the railway did not reflect its destination - Talyllyn Lake being some three miles from the narrow gauge tracks!

The railway was really a line to carry slate over its full length, with a section in the middle used for passenger traffic. What is now the starting point for the majority of today's visitors was originally the end of the journey for the slate. Tywyn Wharf (formerly Towyn Kings) was simply a yard for slate storage with a wharf edge for transhipment onto the standard gauge - and what became the nucleus of Wharf station building was then simply an office. Tywyn Pendre, where the loco and carriage shed was built (now a much expanded base for the increased locomotives and stock under preservation) was the 'official' passenger terminus, although people were carried to Kings if sufficiently determined - the staff preferring to leave the carriages at Pendre since there was no run round loop in Wharf yard. Some 6½ miles from Tywyn, Abergynolwyn was the upper passenger terminus, then beyond it ceased to be a statutory railway and became a private mineral tramway. About half a mile from Abergynolwyn station, a winding house and incline, which dropped down to the village,

The Talyllyn Railway's No 1 *Talyllyn* crosses Dolgoch viaduct in July 2001.

were built shortly after the railway opened. The drum house straddled the tracks, with a loop around the rear (a turntable provided access to the incline itself) and the main line continued to the site of today's Nant Gwernol station, 7½ miles from Wharf. This was the limit of steam working, for the line now ascended the Allwyllt incline, at the top of which was ¾ mile of horse-worked tramway until reaching the Cantrybedd incline. At the top here was a further tramway serving the bottom levels of Bryn Eglwys quarry, and beyond were two further inclines to the higher levels.

William McConnel, one of the original partners in the Aberdovey (later Abergynolwyn) Slate Company which had acquired Bryn Eglwys quarry and built the TR, purchased the quarry and railway in 1881. A series of disputes between quarry workers and the owners of the two largest slate quarries in North Wales, Dinorwic and Penrhyn, between 1885/86 and 1896/97 respectively, boosted demand for slate from Bryn Eglwys and McConnel capitalised by adopting short term methods of working, knowing his lease expired in 1910. When this point came, no purchaser stepped forward and the quarry closed. Henry Haydn Jones, elected to Parliament as Liberal MP for Merioneth during 1910, initially tried to find a buyer for the quarry. These attempts were unsuccessful, and in January 1911 he purchased the quarry himself - an essentially philanthropic gesture which kept local people in employment - and the railway operating - but he had no capital available to invest in the quarry and continued the practice of thinning pillars in the underground workings - a means of gaining slate comparatively cheaply, but dangerous in the long run. His lease expired in 1942, but was renewed annually until 1946 when the inevitable roof collapse occurred (fortunately when no workers were present) which ended slate extraction.

Sir Henry Haydn Jones (he was Knighted in 1937) had been subsidising the railway and intended to keep it going during his lifetime. The last slate train over the mineral extension ran in 1948, but a passenger service on two days a week was sustained between Tywyn and Abergynolwyn. He died in July 1950, but his Executors continued to run trains through the season until October, the intention then being to obtain an Abandonment Order. There would probably have been some surprise in official circles that there was a railway to be abandoned if this had occurred! It had stopped appearing in Bradshaws Manual from 1893 and had (unlike its Corris neighbour) been overlooked both at Railway Grouping in 1923 and Nationalisation in 1947.

The railway had, however, attracted some attention from enthusiasts. A letter had been published in the Birmingham Post on 2 September 1949 but an October 1950 meeting held in Birmingham led to the formation of the Talyllyn Railway Preservation Society. Sir Henry's Executors agreed to allow the TRPS to take over the railway and the first trains under the auspices of the Society (five return trips) ran on 14 May 1951. Hauled by *Dolgoch*, these went as far as Rhydyronen, where the carriages were hand-shunted around the loco, the siding being used since there was no loop. This was followed by a Monday to Friday service starting on 4 June 1951.

While the railway and all of its original equipment had survived,

years of hand to mouth operations and no investment had left it in very poor condition. No 1 *Talyllyn* had been the favoured locomotive until the mid-1940s when serious wastage of the boiler and firebox had forced it into retirement in favour of No 2 *Dolgoch* which then made a 'come back'. The track was in a dreadful state, literally held in place by the surrounding turf, with rail ends jumping up as the weight of the loco met the other ends. Led by Tom Rolt, who took on the task of managing the railway for the first two seasons, volunteers kept trains running and the long process of recovery commenced. Rails from the closed Corris Railway were purchased, along with Corris locomotives Nos. 3 and 4 and some rolling stock, although an early disappointment was the discovery that No 3 could not be used since it regularly fell between the doubtfully gauged rails. Fortunately, following an overhaul by the Hunslet Engine Company, No 4 entered service in 1952 and took some of the pressure off Dolgoch. Rail was also recovered from the track beyond the Abergynolwyn Winding House in 1952 and, in the following year, a Territorial Army exercise relaid some of the worst sections of TR main line - and the first passenger carrying stock to be added to the railway since it's construction entered service.

By 1954, the project was looking secure, although it would be January 1967 before the last of the original wrought iron rails in the running line were finally replaced. During this period, other development work was being undertaken. A major remodelling of Wharf was put in hand during 1964/65 and the terminus became a proper station for the first time ever for the TR's Centenary year! A third passing loop was added at Quarry Siding in 1968/69 (the existing loops were at Pendre and Brynglas) allowing a three-train service to be operated. Accommodation for the increasing number of steam locomotives was provided during the 1960s when the loco shed was extended by knocking down the dividing wall into what had previously been a cottage. Passenger carriages were also being added to cope with visitor numbers and, in 1958, the steel frame for a new North Carriage Shed was erected at Pendre, replacing the barn which had occupied the site for decades. This building was followed in 1961 by replacement of the original wooden shed, which extended from the works building, by a new steel-framed structure, clad in wood, with brick dwarf walls and dubbed the South Carriage Shed. A third building, the West Carriage Shed was subsequently added.

There was a long-held ambition to extend the railway back onto the old mineral extension and carry passengers beyond Abergynolwyn to Nant Gwernol at the foot of the Alltwyllt incline. As noted, this section was not part of the statutory railway and tracing the landowners actually commenced in 1959, with surveys and plans prepared from the mid-1960s. The trackbed of the extension had to be widened to safely accommodate passenger trains and Abergynolwyn Winding House was demolished in 1968 to allow for the wider loading gauge required. Work officially started on building the extension when the first blasting of rock took place on 3 October 1970. A Light Railway Order was granted on 21 February 1972 and the ceremonial opening to Nant Gwernol took place on 22 May 1976, the first train being hauled by *Dolgoch*. Before this, work to

An unusual sight in Pendre yard captured in May 1998 - Barclay 0-4-0WT No 6 *Douglas* facing towards Wharf rather than up the valley as is normally the case for Talyllyn locomotives. *Douglas* is also working this train back-to-back with No 7 *Tom Rolt*.

reconstruct Abergynolwyn station had also taken place. The 1938-built slate building (which had replaced the original wooden shelter) was demolished and a new building erected in 1968/69. Subsequent development of the station included moving the loop westwards in 1975/76, along with extending the platform and building a blockpost. It is slightly ironic that the number of passengers on the revived Talyllyn actually peaked in 1973 in the midst of the effort to build the extension. This record year was almost matched in 1978, although numbers have since declined.

Although most of the major developments were complete by the 1980s, one issue from the early days remained. The 1889 Regulation of Railways Act required the fitting of continuous brakes to trains, but William McConnel had secured an exemption for the TR on the grounds of cost and low speed. The matter had been raised periodically by HMRI and, by the end of the 1990s, the TR had no option but to deal with it, hence a programme of fitting air pumps to locomotives and suitable equipment to carriages was put in hand and completed by 2001. Other progress in the 1990s includes enhanced access for passengers with a disability by the conversion of observation coach No 7 and two saloon coaches, while the opening of a new toilet building at Dolgoch in August 1997 concluded the provision of good quality, fully accessible, facilities at all three main stations.

As the Society celebrated its 50th anniversary, a major new project came to the forefront. The constraints of the Wharf and Pendre sites had been recognised for some time. Various options were investigated, but the solution unveiled early in 2000 was the construction of a new two-storey building to replace the existing museum and café at the western end of the original Wharf office building, with the later additions either rebuilt or demolished. The result would provide an enhanced cafe, an upgraded museum and improved shop, booking office and control office provision. The first floor would incorporate an education room, a museum/small exhibits gallery and a recreation of Rev Awdry's study as well as storage areas. A Golden Jubilee Appeal was launched, Planning Permission obtained and negotiations for grants commenced. The estimated £800,000 project was divided into two phases and work on the first element commenced in January 2002. In the same month, the Heritage Lottery Fund confirmed likely support for the remainder of the project.

The railway started with two locomotives, four passenger carriages, a brake van and around 115 wagons - and this sufficed until the TRPS took over in 1951. Both No 1 *Talyllyn* and No 2 *Dolgoch* were built as 0-4-0s by Fletcher Jennings & Co although they were very different in design, moreover, trailing wheels were added to *Talyllyn*, making her an 0-4-2ST. The coaches were 4-wheel vehicles, one being built by the Lancaster Wagon Co Ltd, the other three by Brown Marshalls, as was the 4-wheel guard's/luggage van No 5 which also served for many years as a travelling booking office.

The two Corris Railway locomotives purchased by the TRPS in 1951 were Hughes 0-4-2ST No 3 and Kerr Stuart 0-4-2ST No 4, subsequently named *Sir Haydn* and *Edward Thomas* respectively - although the latter has spent many years in the guise of the Rev Audry character *Peter Sam*. Barclay 0-4-0WT No 6 *Douglas* came to the line in 1954 (following regauging from 2ft) and 0-4-2T No 7 *Tom Rolt* (reconstructed from a 3ft gauge loco - see separate section for details) entered service in 1991. The railway has also acquired diesel locomotives: No 5 *Midlander* (Ruston & Hornsby 4wDM), No 8 *Merseysider* (Ruston & Hornsby 4wDH), *Alf* (Hunslet 0-4-0DM) and, most recently, No 10 *Bryn Eglwys* (Simplex 0-4-0DM) late in 1997.

The first passenger stock added by the Society in 1952 were ex-Penrhyn Railway workmen's carriages. These were joined

RIGHT: Something of a 'classic' scene, but soon to change as the Talyllyn Railway's Wharf terminus redevelopment proceeds. No 1 *Talyllyn* pulls away from the station on 26 July 2001.

OPPOSITE PAGE:
TOP: Talyllyn Railway No 1 *Talyllyn* in the woods on the approach to Quarry.

LOWER: The Talyllyn Railway's No 7 *Tom Rolt* pauses for passengers to board the train at Brynglas.

by other vehicles during the 1950s, the most notable of which are Nos 14 and 15 which are ex-Glyn Valley Tramway 4-wheelers and No 17, an ex-Corris Railway bogie carriage - all three being beautifully restored from the near-derelict condition in which they first arrived. The first new enclosed bogie coach to be constructed was No 18 which entered service in 1965. The design was based on an extended version of the GVT coaches and set a new standard of passenger accommodation. Bogie carriage No 10 received an enclosed hardwood body to the same basic design, although shorter, for the 1967 season but the TR could not build enough new bodies for further coaches itself, so further additions (to the same design as No 18) were built professionally.

The Ffestiniog Railway

The 1ft 11½ins gauge Ffestiniog Railway has many claims to fame, not least being the oldest unamalgamated railway company in the world (it avoided Grouping in 1923) and the first line in Britain of less than standard gauge to be authorised to carry passengers. Its preservation followed close on the heels of the saving of the Talyllyn Railway at the dawn of railway preservation - and returning trains over its full length to Blaenau Ffestiniog required massive effort and determination to overcome the severance of its trackbed.

In 1811 William Maddocks' mile-long embankment across the estuary of the River Glaslyn was completed. Known as The Cob, this allowed the land behind to be reclaimed, but the outlet of the river scoured out a channel at the western end. Powers were obtained in 1821 to capitalise on this by forming a harbour, which was completed three years later and known as Port Madoc. These developments led to talk during the 1820s of building a railway to connect the slate quarries at Blaenau Ffestiniog with

the new harbour. An Act of Parliament to incorporate the Festiniog Railway Company (incorrectly spelt with a single 'F') was passed on 23 May 1832 with construction commencing in the following year and it was opened on 20 April 1836.

At Blaenau, the line branched, the original terminus at Dinas serving the quarries at Rhiwbryfdir, with a branch to Duffws, although Duffws became the terminus from 1866. The slate was transported downwards by gravity over a line of nearly 14 miles which was engineered to an almost continuous gradient, save the use of two inclines, with horses pulling the empty wagons back up from the Harbour wharves. The inclines were eliminated when the Moelwyn tunnel was opened in 1842, and the route was further improved when the Garnedd tunnel came into use in 1851 - although the narrow bore of both accounts for the historical restriction of the FR's loading gauge.

The railway was so successful that before long there were complaints of delays caused by shortages of wagons, the problems including the time it took to return empties to the quarries. The 1840s were early days for steam power and locomotives were thought to be impractical on so narrow a gauge. The concept was still radical in 1860 when the FR Board asked for the use of steam locomotives to be investigated, but in July 1863 the first two locomotives were delivered from George England & Co - *The Princess* and *Mountaineer* - followed by *The Prince* and *Palmerston* in 1864. The arrival of steam revolutionised the railway, not least in bringing about the introduction of passenger services. Passengers were probably conveyed for the first time in October 1863, although the first carriages were delivered from Brown Marshalls early in 1864 with the first official passenger train running on 5 January 1865. Two improved and enlarged versions of the original locomotives, *Welsh Pony* and *Little Giant*, were added in 1867.

Despite the progress being made, the capacity of the FR remained under pressure and The Festiniog Railway Act of 1869 included powers to double the track. However, the arrival in that year of another revolutionary development rendered such work unnecessary. The double-ended loco *Little Wonder* was the first narrow gauge locomotive built to Robert Fairlie's 1864 patent. Constructed by George England & Co, it provided the power of a large locomotive, but mounted on a pair of short wheelbase bogies, could easily negotiate sharp curves. *Little Wonder* handled more than twice the load previously hauled by the 0-4-0s at higher speed while using less coal, and brought the FR national and international fame. The type went on to become synonymous with the Ffestiniog, and a grateful Robert Fairlie granted the FR free rights to build locos to his patent. The bogie concept was followed up in January 1873 when Brown Marshalls-built carriages Nos 15 and 16 arrived - the first iron-framed bogie passenger carriages to be built in Britain for any gauge - and the first bogie passenger carriages in the world to be built for a narrow gauge line. Slate traffic thus far had been to the harbour, with indirect transfer to the standard gauge railway network. Among the other provisions of the 1869 Act was the construction of Minffordd yard, which was opened in 1872, and provided direct transhipment to the Cambrian Railways.

The FR was at its peak in the late 19th century with the works at Boston Lodge building two new double-Fairlie loco-motives, *Merddin Emrys* (1879) and *Livingston Thompson* (1886) to join the double engine *James Spooner* which had been built by Avonside in 1872, the worn out *Little Wonder* being scrapped in 1882. However, the 20th century brought a period of decline and by 1908 traffic had fallen to such a degree that cuts were being instituted. The two-pronged tapping of the traffic at Blaenau was a factor: first by the LNWR in 1881 with its branch from Llandudno Junction, then in 1883 when the 1868-built 2ft gauge Ffestiniog & Blaenau Railway was regauged, creating a GWR link to Bala and beyond. Moreover, the demand for slate was also falling.

The FR came under government control during WW1, with part of Boston Lodge producing shells. This control ended in 1921 and attention turned to gaining tourist traffic, although the arrears of maintenance which had accrued during the war were never overcome. In 1923, the FR became one of the lines run by Col Holman F Stephens (an association which lasted until his death in 1931) and the Festiniog Railway (Light Railway) Order was obtained. In addition to allowing economies in working (e.g. reduced signalling requirements) this approved the building of the link with the Welsh Highland Railway in Porthmadog. As described later, the WHR's 22-mile line to Dinas closed in 1933, following which the FR leased it until 1936. This period also saw the introduction of internal combustion locomotives: the ex-WW1 machines now named *Moelwyn* and *Mary Ann*.

Tourism was already falling in the 1930s, then came WW2. Passenger services were withdrawn completely 12 days after war broke out, although some slate trains still operated. Indicating how far the railway had declined, in 1915 there were nine locomotives but, by 1939, just *Princess* and *Merddin Emrys* were usable. The railway ceased to operate on 1 August 1946, but could not be legally abandoned without an Act of Parliament. There was no cash for that, so everything was simply

Hunslet 2-4-0STT *Linda* and Alco 2-6-2T *Mountaineer* double-head a Ffestiniog Railway train off the Cob and past Boston Lodge in this May 1998 picture.

left where it was to gently rot. That said, a small diesel loco-motive continued to haul slate traffic at Blaenau between the Maenofferen quarry incline and the former standard gauge exchange sidings until 1962, so one might stretch a point and observe that wheels never totally stopped rolling over FR rails!

Following the lead shown in saving the Talyllyn Railway, attempts were made to revive the moribund Ffestiniog. A letter from the late Leonard Heath Humphries was published in the press and led to a meeting in Bristol on 8 September 1951. The Ffestiniog Railway Preservation Society was proposed in 1952, met for the first time in the following year and was incorporated as the Ffestiniog Railway Society Ltd on 24 December 1954. Meanwhile, a group led by Alan Peglar succeeded in gaining a majority shareholding in the FR company on 24 June 1954. This controlling interest was then passed to the Ffestiniog Railway Trust. The task facing the preservationists was huge with dereliction at Harbour and Boston Lodge, and nature reclaiming the track. The first train over the Cob in eight years ran in September 1954, with a 'special' for Directors and guests reaching Minffordd on 6 November. This was followed by the Simplex (now *Mary Ann*) hauling carriage No 17 and van No 1 through to Blaenau on 5 March 1955, but the year also brought the news that a Bill to approve a pumped storage scheme at Tanygrisau, which would flood part of the trackbed, had been submitted to Parliament.

Undeterred by the looming problems near the top end of the line, public services across the Cob commenced on 23 July 1955. Initially worked by the Simplex, steam arrived in the August after *Prince* had been fitted with a new boiler acquired back in 1945 by the old company. The line was progressively brought back into use, services running to Minffordd from 19 May 1956, Penrhyn from 20 April 1957 and Tan-y-Bwlch from 5 April 1958. Moreover, the double Fairlie *Taliesin* (named *Livingston Thompson* until 1932) returned to service in 1957.

The Central Electricity Authority (later Central Electricity Generating Board) scheme to flood the track north of the Moelwyn tunnel, brought years of legal wrangling. Eventually, compensation for loss of profits was awarded in 1971, although not the cost of reinstating the railway. The FR, however, was determined to return to Blaenau and started work on a deviation to by-pass the new reservoir as early as January 1965. Passenger trains returned to Dduallt on 6 April 1968, by which time work on a spiral to gain the necessary height from Dduallt was proceeding. Other progress included the return to service of *Merddin Emrys*, the entry into traffic of *Linda* and *Blanche* following their purchase from the closed Penrhyn system, the acquisition of ALCO 2-6-2T *Mountaineer* and 4wDM *Upnor Castle*, plus the construction of carriages to join restored examples of the original stock.

When work on the deviation commenced, the route by which the new reservoir would be by-passed had not been determined. Agreement was reached with the CEGB in early October 1971 that the course would be to the west of the lake. By this time the new Rhoslyn bridge to carry the extended line over the approach to Dduallt had been built, creating the only spiral track in Britain. Further up the line, drilling and rock

blasting took place at Tanygrisau in the winter of 1974 in prepa-ration for building a new station three feet higher than the old site. With the old Moelwyn tunnel now plugged, work to bore a new Moelwyn tunnel was undertaken between September 1975 and May 1976, although there was much finishing work still to be done after the basic bore had been completed. The first revenue earning train ran through to a temporary terminus at Llyn Ystradau, the newly formed lake, on 8 July 1977 and the new Tanygrisau station was opened on 24 June 1978. Blaenau was now just a mile and a half away.

A depot was established at Glan-y-Pwll and the track into Blaenau was finally made continuous on 24 May 1981. A new joint station with BR was built in the centre of Blaenau, beside the Queens Hotel, which involved swapping the old standard and narrow gauge trackbed arrangements, allowing the BR line to connect with the branch to Trawsfynydd nuclear power station. BR closed its old LNWR station and inaugurated its part of the new station on 22 March 1982, with the FR opening to its part of the new terminus on 25 May 1982, the official opening ceremony taking place on 30 April 1983.

The effort and expenditure in returning to Blaenau had taken its toll. A large overdraft had to be serviced, limiting further developments until a special share issue in October 1987 which raised over half a million pounds. Parts of the line had become run-down and the remainder of the 1980s were largely devoted to improving facilities. This effort encompassed station improvements, the construction of a carriage shed at Boston Lodge and the introduction of diesel powered push-pull trains. Although operations are centred on a professional staff, a huge input is required from volunteers, and during the 1990s a hostel building was constructed at Minffordd to add to the accommo-dation already available at Penrhyn.

The FR currently has three Fairlie locomotives in service, all built at Boston Lodge: double engines *Earl of Merioneth* (completed in 1979) and *David Lloyd George* (completed 1992) and single engine *Taliesin* (completed 1999) - for more details see Chapter 8. There are two other double Fairlie's. The boiler of 1879-built *Merddin Emrys* was dispatched to Israel Newton's in June 2001 for major repairs while the locomotive was rebuilt at Boston Lodge with the aim of returning to steam in 2002. *Livingston Thompson*, built 1886, is presently a static exhibit in the National Railway Museum. Of the other original steam locomotives, *Prince* and *Palmerston* survive in service, *Princess* is displayed in Spooner's Bar inside Porthmadog station and *Welsh Pony* is plinthed outside the building. The main line loco fleet was boosted in 1998 when the Bo-Bo Funkey diesel *Vale of Ffestiniog* acquired in 1993 from the Port Elizabeth Cement Company in South Africa entered service after the power unit and running gear were refurbished and extensive alterations had been made to its bodywork to fit the FR loading gauge.

A fleet of new carriages has been built up post-preservation to handle the available traffic, including stock with corridor connections. A programme of restorations has also ensured that the FR can operate heritage trains, including a rake of the 4-wheel 'bug boxes' which date from the beginnings of passenger services. In 1998, a Heritage Lottery Fund award of £375,000 (towards a

RIGHT: **Early morning steam
– a contre jour study of Hunslet
2-4-0STT** *Blanche* **hauling a
run of slate wagons across the
Cob on 8 October 2000.**

OPPOSITE PAGE:
TOP: David Lloyd George
**under floodlights at Boston
Lodge on 25 October 1997.**

LOWER: **The reconstructed
South African Funkey diesel**
Vale of Ffestiniog **(rebuilt to
meet the FR loading gauge)
departs with an evening train
from Porthmadog harbour on
1 August 2000.**

total project cost of £500,000) was announced, geared towards the restoration of historic stock. The project encompassed the construction of a new three-road shed at Boston Lodge, the restoration of Brown Marshalls-built 1872-vintage carriages Nos 15 and 16 and the renovation of a fleet of slate wagons. The coaches were totally stripped and rebuilt, returning to service in 2001, with the new building providing the infrastructure to facilitate future projects to a standard not previously possible.

The Welshpool & Llanfair Light Railway

The Oswestry and Newtown Railway brought standard gauge tracks to the town of Welshpool in 1860. Over the next 30 years a variety of schemes were put forward to connect the agricultural centre of Llanfair Caereinion with Welshpool. The breakthrough came with the passing of the Light Railways Act in 1896. This legislation was intended to make the promotion of rural railways cheaper, and included provisions for financial help from public funds. By accepting weight and speed restrictions on such lines, other requirements (e.g. level crossings and signalling) could be eased.

The various schemes eventually distilled into two proposals: the standard gauge Llanfair and Meiford Light Railway employing the Vyrnwy and Banwy valleys backed by the residents of Llanfair, and a narrow gauge line basically following the road between Welshpool and Llanfair which was supported by the people of Welshpool. A Public Enquiry was convened to determine which of the schemes should proceed and the announcement made on 4 September 1897 favoured the shorter, but steeply graded, narrow gauge line. Two years of discussions followed while The Welshpool & Llanfair Light Railway Co negotiated with the

Treasury and local authorities to secure the necessary finance, with the Cambrian Railways to make an agreement to work the line, and arranged the remaining issues of shares and debentures. The Light Railway Order was finally granted on 8 Sept 1899 and the ceremonial cutting of the first sod was on 30 May 1901.

The 2ft 6ins gauge line cost twice as much to build as had been estimated - and three-quarters of the total was met from local and state funds. The Board of Trade inspector was not satisfied following his 3 February 1903 visit, and asked for further work on a subsequent visit. The first freight train ran on 9 March 1903 and the line was finally passed as fit for passenger traffic on 3 April 1903, opening to the public on the following day.

The railway commenced in Welshpool where there were transhipment sidings with the standard gauge at Smithfield Road. The line then picked its way through the town for about a mile to Raven Square. The nature of the railway then changed as it progressed up the valley, including the 1 in 29 gradient with reverse curves on the ascent of Golfa Bank, down the other side through Sylfaen, to Castle Caereinion. Shortly after Cyfronydd, the railway passes over Brynelin Viaduct and runs parallel to the River Banwy until crossing it shortly before Heniarth. The river is then very close by for the remainder of the route into Llanfair Caereinion station, a total distance a shade over nine miles.

The Cambrian continued to work the line for the W&LLR Co until the end of 1922 when the Grouping of Railways Act came into effect. The W&LLR Co ceased to exist on 1 January 1923 and with the Cambrian Railways absorbed by the Great Western Railway, the W&L became a GWR country branch line, albeit narrow gauge. Freight traffic held up fairly well during the 1920s, but passenger traffic was not so good and the GWR started a review of the line in 1926. The report recommended closure, although it also looked at how the railway might be worked more economically. Services were cut back in 1930 and passenger trains finally ceased on 7 February 1931, although goods services - including coal, building materials, agricultural supplies and livestock - were retained. With the use of motor vehicles curtailed during WW2, the cattle and sheep traffic reached record levels. Freight, however, was declining by the time the railways were nationalised, the W&L becoming part of the Western Region of BR from 1 January 1948.

By 1950, closure of the unprofitable line was being considered, although no decision had been made when in 1952 BR confirmed it may be prepared to sell the railway. This arose from early preservation ideas, inspired by the formation of the Talyllyn Railway Preservation Society in the previous year. At this point, Welshpool Town Council were opposed to such a move - although there was some support for the possibility of creating a new terminus at Raven Square on the edge of the town. These, of course, were very early days for the preservation movement. Moreover, while the Talyllyn Railway was privately owned, nobody then had saved a line owned by BR.

The official last train ran on 3 November 1956, a special working for the Stephenson Locomotive Society with the enthusiasts conveyed in nine wagons and two brake vans. By this time, the preservation of the Talyllyn was clearly succeeding and the enthusiast revival of the Ffestiniog Railway was making progress. Encouraged by this, a Society aiming to save the W&L was founded on 15 September 1956. BR was not prepared to negotiate a sale of the town section and there were numerous problems to be overcome. A lease-purchase was agreed in the spring of 1959 and with it becoming clear that the centre of the revived railway would have to be at Llanfair, a selection of rolling stock was moved out of the yard in Welshpool - hauled by horses! A change in the organisation of the preservation effort came with the formation of the Welshpool & Llanfair Light Railway Preservation Co Ltd on 4 January 1960, the Society being finally wound up on 11 March 1961 when its funds were transferred to the Preservation Company.

Through the summer of 1961 work proceeded on clearing the track and acquiring rolling stock, and *The Earl* (having been overhauled at Oswestry) was returned to Welshpool on 27 July 1961. On the following day, the loco was steamed for the first time in four and a half years and hauled items of ex-Lodge Hill & Upnor stock (two coaches and some flat wagons) which had arrived via the standard gauge through the town to the sidings at Golfa and Castle Caereinion. This was followed by a Members Day in September when the first steam hauled train to work between Welshpool and Llanfair since closure was operated. A Light Railway (Leasing and Transfer) Order was applied for in November 1961 and issued on 3 October 1962, effective from 12 October. This specified that the south-west side of Raven Square would be the site of a new terminus - although there was a long way to go before this would become a reality, it confirmed that the town section would not form part of the preservation plans. Meanwhile, *Countess* had also been overhauled at Oswestry and having returned to Welshpool in October

1962, was also steamed for the journey to Llanfair. The pace was now accelerating. By the autumn of 1962 both *The Earl* and *Countess* were available, along with two 4-wheel diesel locos, two motorised trolleys, five bogie coaches plus some wagons and vans, and the first advertised passenger trains since 1931 were operated for Llanfair Fair prior to Christmas 1962.

The official re-opening train ran over the full length of the line from Welshpool to Llanfair on 6 April 1963, although just two days before, Welshpool Town Council completed the purchase of the section east of Raven Square. The last train to traverse the town section ran on 17 August 1963. Passenger services over the re-opened line ran between Llanfair and Castle Caereinion initially. Although the service was extended to Sylfaen in 1964, by August of that year the condition of the track meant that trains reverted to terminating at Castle Caereinion. Disaster, however, appeared to strike at the end of the year. During the night of 12/13 December the River Banwy rose, flooding the track at Dolrhyd Mill - but much worse was the damage done to the northern pier of the Banwy bridge. With trains unable to cross the bridge and no money to fund the repairs, services were now restricted to just the mile and a quarter between Llanfair and Heniarth and the whole preservation project was threatened. Fortunately, the 16th Railway Regiment, Royal Engineers, undertook rebuilding of the bridge as an exercise and, on 13 August 1965, *Upnor Castle* ran across the repaired structure, with passenger services recommencing over it the next day.

Llanfair was steadily developed as a base for the line, a locomotive shed being constructed between 1967-1971, while the Castle Caereinion section was reopened on 15 July 1972. Golfa Bank was cleared of undergrowth sufficiently to enable a members special train to run through to Raven Square in May 1963, but there was much to do before public services could be reinstated over the stiffly-graded route - including fitting continuous braking equipment to all of the coaches. The Welshpool Extension scheme was launched in May 1977 and work started on rebuilding the trackbed and constructing a new terminus. Public trains finally returned to Raven Square on 18 July 1981 - bringing the length of the line up to its present eight miles. Initially, the new terminus was provided with a signal box incorporating a booking office, but a proper building was required. The opportunity arose to acquire the redundant 1863-vintage building from Eardisley on the Hereford, Hay and Brecon Railway which had closed in 1964. The wooden building was dismantled, repaired and re-erected at Welshpool, adding a separate toilet block in the same style, the first WLLR ticket being sold from the booking office on 17 April 1992. There followed rebuilding of the old goods shed at Llanfair into a tea room, shop and booking office during 1993, progressive development also including a volunteers' hostel.

When the line opened, it was equipped with two 0-6-0T locomotives manufactured in 1902 by Beyer Peacock & Co Ltd named *The Earl* and *The Countess*, along with three end-veranda bogie carriages built by R Y Pickering & Co of Lanarkshire. This was a reduction from the initial plans (which had envisaged three locomotives and four coaches) due to financial problems which also deleted several cattle wagons from the initial order for freight stock. The GWR shortened the name of *The Countess* to simply *Countess* and both locomotives were rebuilt by the GWR at Swindon between 1929/1930 - *The Earl* receiving a new boiler. The goods stock was augmented by six new bolster wagons in 1905 to deal with the developing timber traffic.

The Earl and *Countess* (inclusion of 'The' has varied in preservation depending on the livery applied) have been joined by further locomotives from around the world. No 10 *Sir Drefaldwyn*, which arrived in Wales during 1969, is an 0-8-0T built by Franco-Belge in 1944 and rebuilt into its current form in 1957 by the Styrian Local Government Railways (Austria). Kerr Stuart 0-6-2T No 12 *Joan* came from Antigua (West Indies) and was in service between 1977 and 1991, Hunslet 2-6-2T No 14 was Sierra Leone Railway No 85 and repatriated in 1975, and tiny Andrew Barclay 0-4-0T No 8 *Dougal* was built in 1946 to work at Provan Gasworks, Glasgow. Tubize-built 2-6-2T No 15 *Orion* came to Britain in 1972 following service on the Jokioistan Railway in Finland, being moved to Llanfair in 1983 and entering service during 2000. There are also several diesel locomotives, the current line-up including ex-Lodge Hill & Upnor Railway 0-6-0DM Drewry No 7 *Chattenden*, Hunslet 0-4-0DMs *Ferret* and No 18 *Scooby* (now rebuilt with a cab and revised engine cover). Other locos have arrived and departed over the years, the most notable being the ex-Bowater's 0-4-0+0-4-0 *Monarch*.

Since the original carriages did not survive, passenger carrying stock from elsewhere had to be found for the reopening. Initially, five bogie carriages were acquired from the closed Lodge Hill & Upnor Railway, although these have all subsequently departed. In 1968, the Zillertalbahn Railway (Austria) donated five 4-wheel end-balcony coaches. Three were original ZB coaches with wooden bodies, the other two being ex-SKGLB steel bodied vehicles which had been sold to the ZB in 1957. This stock was supplemented by four ex-Sierra Leone Railway steel-bodied bogie coaches (built in 1961 by the Gloucester Carriage & Wagon Co Ltd) which were imported in 1975. The latest additions are a pair of 15-ton 54-seat bogie coaches of Hungarian State Railways origin, although they were acquired from a line in the Czech Republic. Arriving in July 1999, these vehicles will enter service following renovation. The freight stock includes original W&L wagons and vans, supplemented by vehicles from various sources.

As the WLLR moved into the 1990s and looked forward to the approaching centenary of its 1902-built locomotives, with the 100th anniversary of opening to be marked in the following year, an application was made to the Heritage Lottery Fund. The outcome, announced early in 1997, was an award of £495,000 spread over five years (1997-2001) representing a 60% grant towards projects - costed at a total of £786,000 - which amounted to a comprehensive overhaul of the entire railway. A sizeable part of the balance to be contributed by the railway was accounted for by volunteer labour, although £100,000 in cash had to be raised.

The Lottery award included provision for the refurbishment of the upper girders and decking of Banwy bridge. It was ironic, indeed alarming, that close on the heels of the 1997 Lottery

Keith Bide oils round *The Earl* at Raven Square, now the Welshpool terminus of the Welshpool & Llanfair Light Railway.

announcement, a routine inspection of the bridge revealed serious underwater erosion around one of the piers. Traffic over the bridge was suspended late in October 1997 amid echoes of the 1964 threat to the then fledgling preservation project. Temporary repairs kept things running and the following season was saved, until the next blow - a fire swept through the Llanfair tea room on the night of 26 April 1998 leaving the shop and refreshment room gutted and an original W&L van outside almost destroyed. The damaged building was repaired and returned to operation in September, but as attention turned to the bridge, October brought torrential rain and extensive flooding to the area, hampering progress on the bridge work. The 'underwater' repairs to the bridge structure had to be financed by the railway, but happily this work, along with the Lottery-funded attention to the upper parts, was completed in May 1999. Aside from a big improvement in the appearance of the bridge - it has

LEFT: Countess hauls her train over Banwy bridge on the return journey to Llanfair on 1 May 1998. At this time, the bridge pier was still the metal frame type which had been erected in 1964.

OPPOSITE PAGE:
TOP: The other original Welshpool & Llanfair Light Railway locomotive, *The Earl*, pauses at Cyfronedd in September 2000.

LOWER: The most recent steam locomotive to enter service on the Welshpool & Llanfair Light Railway is this Tubize-built 2-6-2T, pictured pulling away from Cyfronedd in September 2000.

almost reverted to its original look - it should now be sound for many years.

A substantial element of the Lottery award was to cover the full restoration of *The Earl* (last steamed in 1978, and then only for two weeks' emergency use) and *Countess* (then in service but with her 10-year ticket expiring at the end of 1999) in order that they could be in steam together for their centenary. The work included the provision of new boilers, cylinders and tanks for both. A surprising amount of the main line (as high as three-quarters) still contained original Dowlais rails and the Lottery package included provision for this to be replaced, the 1902 material then being relaid in less heavily used locations and what could be termed 'heritage sites' - basically, the stations. Much of the replacement material was near-new rail obtained from South Africa. Although not part of the Lottery award, a 2ft 6ins gauge Plasser tamping machine, built for use in gold mines around Johannesburg, was purchased in 1999 to reduce the amount of manual labour expended on track work.

Other projects included in the Lottery award covered the extension of the carriage shed at Tanllan (built in 1989) over two roads at the Welshpool end and the addition of a woodwork shop to the side. The latter was linked to a programme of restoration of W&L goods vehicles. Provision was also made for the rebuilding of two carriages, one ex-Zillertalbahn and an ex-Sierra Leone vehicle which had been used as a store and never entered traffic. Improvements to the passenger facilities at Llanfair encompassed the demolition of the old toilet block and the construction of a new toilet building, in a style compatible

with the other Llanfair buildings, beside the platform office in 2000. To round off the programme, a 90ft long single-road locomotive running shed was built at Llanfair during 2001 between the main line and adjacent industrial estate.

Isle of Man

As previously noted, the Isle of Man has hosted an astonishing number of lines. This section has to be restricted to those which carried passengers - and in huge numbers in their heyday. The majority of mileage was built to 3ft gauge, an additional 6ins was added when the electric line ascending Snaefell was built, while the Groudle Glen Railway - unconnected to the other systems - was constructed to 2ft gauge. While all these lines went into decline and, in parts, closure, the degree of survival and revival is remarkable. The Manx Electric and Snaefell lines remain intact and the Groudle Glen Railway has been resurrected. An original 1873-built locomotive has steamed into the 21st century between Douglas and Port Erin, two original 1893-vintage cars remain in use on the MER (and its newest tram was built in 1906), the Snaefell line still uses original cars (albeit with updated electrical equipment) and an original 1896-built loco still steams in Groudle Glen.

While a sizeable part of the route mileage of the steam line has been lost, ideas have been floated for a revival of the Douglas to Peel line. The Peel Heritage Trust proposed the relaying of some 600 yards of track as part of the 1998 'Steam 125' celebrations, envisaging a temporary line from the new

power station towards Douglas (to the Glenfabe road bridge) to be lifted again after the celebrations. Rail and sleepers - along with a loco and carriage - were to be borrowed from the IOMSR, but IoM Transport could not allocate resources to the project. Well over 90% of the Peel line trackbed remains as a heritage footpath, with ideas of reinstating a permanent line between Peel and St John's to provide a park and ride service to the Heritage Centre never quite fading away.

The first practical electric railway in the world was an exhibition line in Berlin in 1879. Its centenary was celebrated by the MER with a cavalcade of trams at Laxey on 31 May 1979 with MER cars 1, 9, 19 and 32 given historic liveries to mark the occasion. Little more occurred to promote the railways until 1983 when a Vintage Transport Weekend was held, with another the following year - neither being very successful.

This all changed in the 1990s, which were a golden period for enthusiasts of the Manx systems. A series of spectacular events, each linked to an anniversary, promoted the railways as never

before. *Sutherland* and *Caledonia* ceased to be exhibits in the Port Erin Museum and returned to steam, and the restored Upper Douglas Cable Tramway car No 72/73 ran on the Douglas Horse Tram tracks. While the scope for visiting locomotives was plainly limited in view of the gauge, the Manx Railways managed perfectly well between their own systems and some inventive thinking produced what amounted to a series of 'loco exchanges'. The anniversaries, with some of the highlights were:

1993 - 'Year of Railways' - MER Centenary, Douglas to Groudle. Beyer Peacock 2-4-0T *Loch* ran on the MER between Laxey and Dhoon Quarry. Original 1905-built *Polar Bear* visited from Amberley Museum in Sussex to be reunited with *Sea Lion*.

1995 - 'International Railway Festival' - Snaefell Centenary A third rail was laid between Bungalow and Summit, allowing 0-6-0T *Caledonia* to return to the mountain line which she had helped to construct 100 years before. All six Snaefell cars were taken to the summit, followed by a descent in company, three cars on each line. The only previous occasion when this occurred was on 14 September 1905 when the first car stalled, the third hit the second and the second car ran into first - no such mishap occurred on this occasion! *Caledonia* appeared on the MER between Laxey and

In August 1998, a short length of track was laid in the car park which now covers the old trackbed into Peel station. No 1 *Sutherland* was brought to the site by road and steamed, providing a reminder of how things used to be. Peel Castle can be seen in the background of this view.

Dhoon Quarry and the Groudle Glen line entertained visiting locos, Rishra and Chaloner from the Leighton Buzzard Railway.

1996 - Groudle Glen Centenary. *Polar Bear* visited again from Amberley to run with *Sea Lion*.

1996 - Upper Douglas Cable Tramway Anniversary.

1996 - Marine Drive Tramway Anniversary.

1997 - The 30th anniversary of Lord Ailsa taking a lease of the steam lines.

1998 - 'Steam 125' - Peel Line 125th Anniversary. MER tram No 33, towing a generator to provide its electrical power, ran on the Douglas - Port Erin line. No 1 *Sutherland* returned to steam for the first time in 34 years and ran on the MER between Laxey and Fairy Cottage. *Sutherland* also steamed in Peel on a temporary track in a car park, while the GGR entertained *Peter Pan* (from Leighton Buzzard) and *Jonathan* (West Lancashire Light Railway).

1999 - Port Erin Line 125th Anniversary and MER Ramsey Section Anniversary. MER No 33 again ran on the Port Erin line. MER Cars Nos 1 and 2 appeared together at Ramsey and *Sutherland* piloted a double-headed anniversary train to Port Erin.

2001 - The 125th anniversary of the Horse Tram system in Douglas.

Although the series of enthusiast spectaculars ceased after the 1990s, privately organised events have recreated many of the memorable times, and could be repeated

This period also heralded major investment in the infrastructure. New sheds were built for the Snaefell line (at Laxey) MER (Derby Castle) and steam line (Douglas and Port Erin) while the rebuilt Port Erin Museum opened in 1998. A massive investment in the track of both the Port Erin and MER lines has also been undertaken, along with refurbishment of the MER overhead equipment - the preparation of a five-year programme to allocate some £2million annually to priorities identified following a survey by Jarvis Rail being confirmed during the 1999 enthusiasts' events. Other changes have included the provision of platforms at Castletown, Santon and Ballasalla. Ideas for creating a high speed 'park and ride' service between Port Erin and Douglas have been mooted, with a similar plan considered for the MER - both proposals envisaging entirely new stock to run in addition to the existing services. Extending the MER along the promenade at Douglas has even been floated - a shade over 100 years after the idea first arose!

Whilst the systems nationalised by Tynwald inevitably grab most attention, the spirit of preservation centred on the Groudle Glen Railway is as strong as anywhere else. The railway played a full part in the special event weeks, and has contributed to a brand new project being undertaken by the Laxey & Lonan Heritage Trust to reconstruct the 19ins gauge tramway from the main adit of the Laxey Mine (near the *Lady Isabella* waterwheel) through an extant tunnel under the MER tram tracks and main road, to the Washing Floors at Laxey - an area once known as 'Little Egypt', apparently because of the pyramids of waste, but now laid out as gardens.

In 1999, this scheme was backed by several organisations and Planning Permission was granted. Civil engineering works were completed at each end of the formation early in 2001. On 16 March 2001, the first track was laid and ballasted, the work being done by 'volunteers' from the island's prison - with tools and knowledge contributed by GGR members.

Replicas of the diminutive 0-4-0T locos named *The Ant* and *The Bee* built by Stephen Lewin of Poole, Dorset which originally worked the line are to be built. *The Bee* will be in 'as built' condition, whereas *The Ant* will reflect the final condition of the locomotive with a larger water tank, extended rear frame and an injector on top of the boiler barrel. Both are being constructed by Great Northern Steam Services of Middlesborough, the company which built the reproduction Heywood loco *Effie*. Although initially planned as a passenger-carrying line to connect the MER and the *Lady Isabella*, it was realised that the gradients involved precluded this on a regular basis. However, a small coach is to be constructed to provide occasional rides. Otherwise, the line will fulfil a demonstration role and six replica tubs, which were used to transport ore from the mine, were delivered early in 2001.

The Isle of Man Steam Railway

The 15½ mile 3ft gauge line between Douglas and Port Erin is the last remaining section of a system which totalled some 50 miles.

The Isle of Man Railway Company was registered at Douglas on 19 December 1870. Tenders for construction were invited in the following year and orders placed for three locomotives, 29 four-wheel carriages and freight rolling stock. The 2-4-0T locomotives, *Sutherland*, *Derby* and *Pender* were built by Beyer Peacock and arrived in 1873. Over subsequent years, twelve more locomotives to the same basic design, but with increased dimensions, would be built for service on the Isle of Man, culminating in the final version, *Mannin* in 1926.

The 11½ mile line between Douglas and Peel was officially opened on 1 July 1873 (the first train had run on 1 May) and the first train over the Douglas to Port Erin section ran on 25 July 1874 followed by an official opening on 1 August. Two more locomotives and additional carriages arrived for service on the Port Erin line, followed by the first bogie coaches in the following year.

When the IOMR was first launched, its proposals included building a line to Ramsey, but this was dropped in December 1871. Pressure had continued to build such a line, and the Manx Northern Railway was registered on 17 March 1877. On 1 January 1878, Tynwald approved the construction of a 16 mile line between St John's and Ramsey - a route which included an impressive section parallel to the northwest coast of the island where viaducts crossed Glen Wyllin and Glen Mooar. The MNR ordered two 2-4-0T locomotives from Sharpe Stewart, along with six-wheel carriages, using the Cleminson flexible wheelbase system, from the Swansea Wagon Company. This line opened on 23 September 1879, initially being worked by the IOMR - an arrangement which continued until 6 November

LEFT: **The unusual opportunity to photograph steam and electric traction alongside each other arose at Douglas station in August 1998. IOMSR No 1** *Sutherland* **stands next to MER car No 33.**

OPPOSITE PAGE:
TOP: **A Beyer Peacock 2-4-0T double-header, No 11** *Maitland* **and No 10** *G H Wood* **pass Keristal on 30 July 1999.**

LOWER: **Dubs 0-6-0T** *Caledonia* **and Beyer Peacock 2-4-0T** *G H Wood* **pictured at Santon on 25 July 1997.**

1880 - although not without some friction between the two companies! In 1880 it was extended onto the quayside at Ramsey, and a third locomotive, *Thornhill*, was delivered - this being a Beyer Peacock of the same type as the IOMR fleet. The Foxdale Railway Company was registered on 16 November 1882, but was then leased to the MNR. Construction of a 2½ mile branch from St John's to Foxdale was started in April 1885 and 0-6-0T *Caledonia* (No 4 in the MNR loco fleet) was built by Dübs & Co, the line being opened in the following year.

The Manx Northern Railway had always been in a somewhat parlous financial state and was finally taken over by the IOMR in 1905, following which extensive work was undertaken on the northern section to bring it up to a proper standard. Unfortunately, in 1911 the Foxdale mines closed following financial collapse, thus eliminating a principal source of traffic on the Foxdale branch. The IOMR, however, was enjoying record passenger traffic. Recognising the problems presented by the original four-wheel coaches, a programme of close-coupling them into pairs had been completed by 1887, and bogie coaches had been added to the stock, the first seven in 1884, followed by seven more in 1895. Later, pairs of four-wheel bodies were mounted on new bogie underframes.

Tourism to the island stopped with the outbreak of WWI, although the construction of a PoW camp at Knockaloe (south of Peel) which was served by a steep branch line generated its own traffic. The camp closed in 1920, by which time (voluntary!) visitors were returning to the island, but the war had left a backlog of maintenance, and road competition started to be felt. The IOMR fought back, adding *Mannin* in 1926 and acquiring its own buses in 1928. Once again, tourism halted with WW2, although the initial financial problems were eased as military bases were developed on the island. By 1946, the railways were

again very run down and the quay line in Ramsey was used for the final time in 1948. Tourists did return, but it was not long before foreign holidays began to make their mark. To this was added increased bus competition and the rise in private car ownership. The first significant stock withdrawals started in 1958 and there were no winter services on the Ramsey line in 1961 or 1962, although trains did run during the summer. A pair of Railcars were purchased from the County Donegal Railway in 1960 and entered service on the Peel line in the following year in an effort to cut costs. But the railway was in trouble. So much so, that no train services operated at all in 1966.

The apparent closure initially resulted in the formation of the Manx Steam Railway Society, later to become the Isle of Man Steam Railway Supporters Association. However, salvation came in another form. The Marquis of Ailsa stepped forward and leased the entire railway system for 21 years, with the option of cancelling the agreement after five years. The first train ran under the new regime on 3 June 1967, although the Foxdale branch was not included in the reinstated services. Operating as the Isle of Man Steam Railway, locomotives were repainted, locos out of service were drawn out of the shed at St John's to be displayed and initiatives taken to develop traffic, including the operation of container trains and the transportation of fuel oil in tanks mounted on wagons. For all the effort, things were not working out and operations were cut short in the 1968 season, the final train running over the Ramsey line on 6 September and over the lines to Peel and Port Erin on 7 September. The lines to Ramsey and Peel would never reopen for passenger traffic.

Having previously announced that no trains would run in 1969 (although the option of cancelling the lease did not arise until 1972) discussions involving the Manx Government, the rail-

way company and the Marquis of Ailsa resulted in his agreement to run trains with Government assistance for a further three years, but only over the Douglas - Port Erin line. The Port Erin line duly reopened on 25 May 1969, St John's now being used only for storage, although some freight workings to Peel gasworks took place during 1970. The Ailsa period finished at the end of 1972, but it should be remembered that there would probably be no steam line at all today had he not attempted to keep the system going.

The railway company operated trains on the Port Erin line, with the support of the Manx Government, in 1973. But the end had plainly come for the Peel and Ramsey lines when the track, bridges and viaducts were sold for scrap towards the end of that year. Services continued in 1974, during which Tynwald decided to support operations between Port Erin and Castletown in the following year. This truncated operation was extended to Ballasalla for 1976, but this was also General Election year on the island. The railways were a major issue and the new Government purchased the steam line, which was placed under the control of the Manx Electric Railway Board - the two nationalised lines now being run as 'Isle of Man Railways', and services between Douglas and Port Erin were reinstated for 1977. Subsequently, the railway has been operated under the auspices of the Isle of Man Passenger Transport Board (1980) and the Department of Tourism and Transport (1986).

Without doubt, government control has kept the steam line alive. There has been some rationalisation - the removal of the canopies at Douglas in 1978, the sale of *Pender* (now sectioned and never to run again) in the following year and the sale of land at Ballasalla with consequent reconstruction of a new station in 1984. Other locomotives have been sold into preservation, at least one of which is due to run again in 2002. There have also been improvements, particularly during the 1990s. The Douglas terminus has been totally remodelled, with a modern carriage shed replacing the decrepit old structure and the signalbox moved closer to the tracks (having been marooned for many years on the other side of an access road). A new carriage shed has been built at Port Erin, where the museum has also been reconstructed. Perhaps more controversial has been the programme of adding raised platforms at Castletown, Santon and on the north side of the tracks at Ballasalla (the south side had a platform following the 1984 rearrangement) and the planned introduction of automatic barriers and lights at road crossings. A diesel locomotive, *Viking*, was purchased in 1992, track renewal programmes have been put in place and locomotives assumed to be destined to remain exhibits in Port Erin Museum have returned to traffic. The ex-County Donegal Railcars, which had fallen into a deplorable state, became the subjects of restoration. New bodywork has been constructed onto the renovated original running gear, but the work fell behind schedule (completion was due in 1999) and, with the project running substantially over-budget, work had come to a standstill by 2000.

A project to bury a sewage pipeline under the track of the southern section of the railway was approved by Tynwald on 16 October 2001. Work on the £13 million project commenced during the following winter and during 2002 the railway operated in two sections, Douglas - Santon and Castletown - Port Erin. An extension of the work was expected to mean that in 2003 the railway would operate between Douglas - Castletown and Port Erin - Port St. Mary, but when the track is reinstated over the pipe, it will have been totally relaid to a high standard.

Finally, various schemes for the introduction of high-speed commuter services have been explored. Although nothing definite had been decided as this volume was being prepared, it has been stated that steam would retain its place during the day, between the projected park and ride train services which would be worked by stock especially acquired for the work.

Manx Electric Railway

It is difficult to overstate the importance of the 3ft gauge MER, both in its pioneering use of electric traction, and its survival giving it the status of being the longest electric tramway in the British Isles and the oldest trams (Nos 1 and 2) to be operating regularly anywhere in the world.

The late 1880s were boom years for Manx tourism, particularly in Douglas. Although the Manx Northern Railway had opened its steam line to Ramsey in 1879, this followed a circuitous route via the north west coast, avoiding the steep gradients of the more direct passage along the east coast. The Douglas, Laxey and Ramsey Railway Company was formed in 1882, the idea being to build a branch from the Peel line at Quarterbridge (Douglas) to run via Onchan and Laxey, but did not progress.

In 1892, Tynwald approved plans to develop the Howstrake Estate above Groudle, provided a coast road and appropriate services were constructed out of Douglas. These plans were promoted by Alexander Bruce, of the Dumbell Banking Co Ltd and civil engineer, Frederick Sanderson. Moreover, R M Broadbent was planning to build a new hotel at Groudle and develop Groudle Glen as a tourist attraction. Douglas Bay Estate Ltd was formed by Bruce and his partners to build the road from Douglas to Groudle, which would incorporate a tramway.

Although very new, electric traction was seen as providing the answer to the steep climbs involved. Construction of the 2½ mile line started in early 1893, with a depot (including engine and boiler houses, dynamos, etc.) located on land reclaimed by filling in Port e Vada Creek. The first three motorised saloon cars and six trailers arrived in August 1893 and the first tram ran to Groudle on 26 August 1893 - regular services being inaugurated on 7 September, then over a single line.

Progress had been rapid, but thoughts were already directed towards Laxey. The Douglas and Laxey Coast Electric Tramway Co had been launched before the tracks reached Groudle (leaving the development of Howstrake to the Estate company) and Tynwald approved an extension of the line in November 1893. The second line to Groudle, to double the track, was opened in May 1894 and the extension to Laxey, terminating just short of Rencell Road, was officially opened on 28 July 1894. A car depot, along with a station and power station, was built at Laxey and an additional shed built at Derby Castle, along with upgrading of the electrical equipment to cope with what was now a 6½ mile line. At the cutting edge of technology

in its day - the line broke new ground in terms of distance, gradient profile and heavy electrical engineering - the railway was the subject of great interest in Britain and the USA.

The Douglas and Laxey Coast Electric Tramway Co changed its name to the Isle of Man Tramways and Electric Power Co Ltd in April 1894. This change followed its acquisition of the Horse Tramway along Douglas promenade, the intention being to electrify it and, as part of the package, the company built and opened the Upper Douglas Cable Tramway in 1896. Meanwhile, the line up Snaefell had been purchased at the end of 1895. The IOMT&EP company now owned two electric lines, a horse tramway and a cable-worked tramway - and was carrying huge numbers of passengers over its rail empire!

The next target was Ramsey. A petition was made to Tynwald in April 1896 by a London-based company, but was withdrawn when the IOMT&EP lodged a counter-petition in October. A revised petition was presented in March 1897 and, after various schemes in the vicinity of Laxey were put forward, Tynwald approved the extension in May of that year with construction starting officially on 1 November, although preliminary work commenced in August. At Laxey, a viaduct was built across Glen Roy to take the line into the present station site. The Snaefell line was also extended into the shared terminus which remains today, with the rustic Snaefell station building relocated to the new site to serve both lines - as it still does. Two gangs

worked on construction of the extension: one working south from Ballure and using the hired MNR locomotive *Ramsey*, the other working north from Laxey and employing the IOMR loco *Derby*. The company also purchased an Andrew Barclay 0-4-0ST loco and 45 ballast wagons. After construction was completed, the loco was sold in 1900, for the West Baldwin reservoir project. Also, the overhead current collection arrangements were altered, the original bow collectors being replaced by the trolley pole system, the extension being constructed to the revised pattern while the existing line was converted.

The extension was completed through to Ballure, just south of Ramsey and 17 miles from Douglas, in July 1898 with an official opening on 2 August. The remaining section into Ramsey included a section of grooved rail along Walpole Drive - a length officially classed as a street tramway, although the road surfacing over the tracks was never carried out. The line, with a final length of 17½ miles, was officially opened to the present terminus site in Ramsey (although its surroundings have

Steam on the Manx Electric Railway in 1995 during the 'International Railway Festival' was operated between Laxey and Dhoon Quarry. In this picture, *Caledonia* is passing Minorca station.

changed considerably since) on 24 July 1899.

Triumph, however, rapidly turned to disaster. The high cost of building the extension had been met by heavy borrowing, plus dividends were still being paid - but from capital rather than revenue. Warning signs in 1899 were followed by the collapse of Dumbells Bank in 1900 and catastrophe for Alexander Bruce and the IOMT&EP. Bruce faced arrest, but died in September 1900, and the IOMT&EP went into liquidation. The Horse Tramway and Upper Douglas Cable Tramway were sold to Douglas Corporation in 1901, and in the following year a bid for the electric lines was accepted. This was made by a syndicate, which sold the lines on 30 November 1902 to a new company - The Manx Electric Railway Company - as soon as it had been incorporated.

A period of investment followed. The track between Douglas and Laxey was already a concern, but even more so was the section above Bulgham Bay. This location, 2½ miles north of Laxey, is the summit of the line at 588ft above sea level. The rock face was cut back when the line was built, the road at this location being moved inland so that the trackbed could be built on the seaward side. The new company was apprehensive about the original construction and moved the

track further inland, onto solid rock, with the road being moved correspondingly, work being completed by 1903. Other enhancements included upgrading the electrical equipment and construction of a new car shed and goods shed at Laxey, new shelters at all the stopping places and new trailers. Control of the various hotels was regained and the final batch of new tram cars were received in 1906.

By 1907, the MER was on a sound footing to face the future, and there was a reserve fund available to see the line through the 1914-18 war when there was little work. The tourists returned in 1919 and although business fluctuated, 1922 produced a record. Another best ever year was recorded in 1925, but the following year saw the start of a recession which lasted into the early 1930s, moreover, buses were starting to arrive on the island. Other problems also overtook the MER. In April 1930 a fire at the Laxey car shed destroyed four trams, seven trailers, three tower wagons and other equipment. The depot was rebuilt and three new trailers were ordered. Next, in September 1930, severe flooding occurred at Laxey when the weir of the old hydro-electric plant was blocked. The new power station was damaged, and the company was held liable for the damage done to private property. A bad year also included the destruction by fire of the hotel and refreshment room at Dhoon Glen.

In 1934, the MER entered into agreement for the Manx Electricity Board to supply its power, consequent new equip-

The rare sight of Manx Electric Railway cars Nos 2 and 1 alongside each other at Ramsey on 24 July 1999, the day of the 100th anniversary of the MER reaching Ramsey.

ment including six sub-stations. Traffic remained good between 1935-1937, but then came WW2. A minimal service operated, although thousands of tons of mine 'deads' were moved from Laxey for use on the runways at RAF Jurby. A post-war boom came between 1946-1949, but decline set in from 1950. At the end of a loss-making year in 1955, the Manx Government was informed that operations would have to cease after the 1956 season (the same applied to the Snaefell line) and the company was prepared to sell the railway. Tynwald set up a sub-committee, surveys were commissioned and experts consulted. The upshot was the purchase of the MER, the Act being signed on 17 April 1957, with the formal handover following on 1 June.

Initially, there was a measure of investment with rails and sleepers ordered, the relaying of the Douglas to Laxey section being completed by 1965. However, the closure of the Ramsey line was also suggested. This was rejected, and when part of the embankment above Bulgham Bay collapsed in January 1967 reconstruction of the affected section was soon started rather than the opportunity taken to close the northern line. This work was completed by mid-July and normal services resumed. The location above Bulgham Bay was the scene of further problems in 1983 when a bulge appeared in the retaining wall, resulting in major work to stabilise and repair the trackbed.

In October 1975, the Ramsey line was closed, but the railways were a major feature in the November 1976 General Election for Members of the House of Keys and the Ramsey section was

reopened on 25 June 1977. Following the amalgamation of the Manx Electric Railway Board and Manx National Transport in 1983, the MER came under the auspices of the Isle of Man Passenger Transport Board and, at the end of 1986, a further reorganisation brought all of the nationalised railways under the control of the Department of Tourism and Transport.

The tram cars fall into eight basic batches of vehicles. G F Milnes supplied Nos 1-3 in 1893, these having enclosed bodies and open driving platforms. Nos 4-9 were supplied in the following year by the same manufacturer and are also closed cars, generally known as 'tunnel cars'. Nos 10-13, again from Milnes in 1895, were unglazed saloons which were withdrawn by 1902, No 12 being converted into a cattle van and No 10 (the only survivor of this batch) becoming a freight car, renumbered as No 26 and now preserved under the ownership of the Isle of Man Railway & Tramway Preservation Society Ltd (IOMRTPS). The other two were rebuilt as freight trailers in 1918. G F Milnes continued to supply new cars, Nos 14-18 (in 1898) being open with cross-bench seats and Nos 19-22 (1899) being the enclosed 'Winter Saloon' cars. Nos 24-27 were identical to Nos. 14-18, but entered service as un-motored trailers numbered 40-43. They were renumbered as 24-27 when motorised in 1903. The Brush type 'D' bogies employed resulted in the running boards acquiring steps, hence the nickname 'Paddleboxes'. The Electric Railway & Tramway Carriage Works Ltd supplied Nos 28-31 in 1904, these being open cross-bench cars, the removal of their air brakes in 1904 and consequent reliance on only hand brakes led to the term 'Ratchets' being applied to these cars. The final pair of cars were built by the United Electric Car Company (successors to ERTC) in 1906, Nos 32-33 being open cross-bench cars. A locomotive, No 23, was built in 1900 which 'borrowed' electrical equipment from No 17 every winter. This machine was damaged in 1914, but rebuilt in a totally different form in 1925 onto a new frame with a 6-ton wagon body at each end. The rebuilt vehicle has been preserved under the ownership of the IOMRTPS. Of the trailers (some of which have been renumbered several times), an especially interesting example is No 59. Built in 1895 as a special saloon on a four-wheel chassis for directors, it is the smallest item of MER passenger stock. By 1900 it had been mounted on a pair of bogies and became known as the 'Royal Trailer', having carried King Edward VII and Queen Alexandra in August 1902. It is normally housed in the museum (ex-goods shed) at Ramsey, but is used occasionally.

As noted above, four cars (Nos 3, 4, 8 and 24) were destroyed by the fire at Laxey in 1930, along with seven trailers. Another fire, during the night of 30 September 1990 at the bottom shed in Derby Castle, severely damaged Car No 22, but the vehicle was rebuilt and returned to service. A number of cars and trailers have not seen use in many years and are stored in Laxey shed. A check in 1998 confirmed that the trams included Nos 14, 15, 17, 18, 28, 29 and 30. Sadly, none of the three road/rail Bonner wagons obtained in September 1899 from Toledo, Ohio, survived.

Snaefell Mountain Railway

The first proposal for ascending the 2,036ft Snaefell mountain by railway arose in 1888. This was for a steam operated line from Douglas, via Laxey and was surveyed by Mr G Nobel Fell (the son of J B Fell who invented the Fell Incline Railway system) but did not progress. In 1894, the Isle of Man Tramways and Electric Power Company line (subsequently to become the MER) reached Laxey, followed by the formation of the Snaefell Mountain Railway Association. This body, including Mr G N Fell and members of the Isle of Man Tramways and Electric Power Company, met on 4 January 1895, although it was never registered under companies legislation - later leading to some controversy!

The route chosen was much as G N Fell had proposed, although electric traction was to be employed. The maximum gradient would be 1 in 12 and 3ft 6ins gauge selected, with a Fell system rail between the running lines. The reason for the

additional 6ins over the gauge of the Douglas - Ramsey coastal line has never been totally clarified, one theory being that it was to allow space for the braking system onto the Fell rail (the rail was never used for traction on the SMR) the alternative being to increase stability on the exposed parts of the mountain.

Construction started in January 1895, with 0-6-0T *Caledonia* hired from the Manx Northern Railway to work construction trains, a third running rail being temporarily laid for the 3ft gauge loco. A power station was built at Halfway (where the line crosses the mountain road between Douglas and Ramsey) equipped with four Galloway boilers, five Mather & Platt horizontal steam engines and dynamos to generate the current - the flue ran under the tracks to reach a 60ft iron chimney on the far side of the line. Mather & Platt supplied overhead equipment and six tram cars (with bow collectors rather than poles) were built by G F Milnes. A depot and station was constructed at Laxey on a ledge behind, and above, Dumbells Row (Ham and Eggs terrace) - this remains the site of the car shed, but is no longer a station.

The SMR opened on 20 August 1895 and the first paying passengers were carried the following day. In December that year, the Snaefell Mountain Railway Association sold the line to the Isle of Man Tramways and Electric Power Company - for nearly twice the sum that the line had cost to build! Notwithstanding the debatable nature of the transaction, the railway was popular and the Summit hotel was extended in 1896. That same year, a new hotel - called The Bungalow - was built at Halfway. In 1897, the Laxey terminus was moved further down the hill to just above the Laxey road crossing and the next year was relocated again to its present position on a site shared with the MER. The extension over the road at Laxey was (and remains) a single track, as opposed to the double track on the remainder of the railway, and brought the length of the SMR up to 4 miles 72 chains. The collapse of Dumbells Bank in February 1900 led to the Isle of Man Tramways and Electric Power Company going into Receivership, resulting in the sale of both the SMR and coastal lines to a Manchester based syndicate in 1902, followed by formation of the Manx Electric Railway Company which purchased both in November of that year.

There was a proposal to build a branch from Bungalow to Tholt-y-Will in Sulby Glen. This never progressed, instead, a charabanc service commenced in 1907, running (other than war years) until 1953. A mixed gauge siding was laid at Laxey in 1931/32 allowing SMR car bodies to be placed on MER bogies and run to Derby Castle for maintenance work.

All services ceased in 1939 when war broke out, although freight car No 7 transported peat from Bungalow to Laxey during fuel shortages. A post war boom followed reopening on 2 June 1946, but passenger numbers dwindled in the 1950s. In 1955, the Manx Government was advised that neither railway could be operated after the following season, resulting in nationalisation of the Snaefell line on 1 June 1957.

Manx Electric Railway car No 1 pictured running in Walpole Road, Ramsey, in July 1997.

The six passenger cars were originally unglazed, but windows had been fitted by 1896 and clerestories added during the winter of 1896/97. They had a dual braking system with a hand wheel operating the brakes on the bogie wheels, plus the Fell calliper brake acting on the Fell rail in the centre of the track. Car No 5 caught fire at the summit on 16 August 1970 and, apart from one end, was burnt out down to the chassis. A new body was built, without a clerestory and with bus-type windows and No 5 returned to service on 8 July 1971. No 7 was a freight vehicle without its own pair of bogies, the body being placed on a pair from another car when it was required to transport coal to the generating station during the winter. It seems that the bogies most often 'borrowed' were from No 5, leading to the theory that the regular changes had frayed the insulation of the wiring in No 5, resulting in the fire.

By the mid-1960s the line was ageing and the Fell rail becoming corroded. It was decided to replace it and new rail was specially rolled in 1967, the section between Bungalow and Summit being laid during 1968 and by 1973 about three-quarters of the Fell rail had been replaced. Meanwhile, studies into future policy for the SMR had been made and in 1976 London Transport was contracted to upgrade the electrical equipment of the cars. Seven redundant metre gauge tramcars came from Aachen in Germany, but the second-hand motors could not be fitted into the 1895-built bogies, so new bogies were constructed. The ex-Aachen control gear was fitted into the SMR car bodies and resistors (part of the rheostatic braking) were mounted on the roofs. The first newly-equipped car (No 1) entered service in 1977, Nos 2 and 3 being upgraded the following winter, and the final three in the winter of 1978/79. There were several problems. Increased resistor capacity was needed to overcome rapid overheating when using rheostatic braking. This had finally been resolved by 1982 when it became possible to use this braking throughout the descent (making the Fell braking on the new rail redundant!) while the bogies had to be rewheeled following several derailments. The passenger cars always had basically the same livery, other than a short period following nationalisation when Nos 2 and 4 controversially received corporate green and cream colours.

In 1904, one of the Mather & Platt steam engines was removed from the Halfway generating station to be replaced by a rotary converter fed from the coastal line power supply. In 1934, the SMR ceased generating its own power, agreement being reached for power to be supplied by the IoM Electricity Board. The generating station at Halfway was re-equipped with transformer rectifiers fed from Laxey, and in 1964 automatic switch gear was installed and the need to permanently staff the building ceased. Freight car No 7, known as *Maria*, was not needed to transport coal after 1934, although it did find some employment during construction work at the summit. Out of use by the mid-1950s, the body was totally reconstructed in 1994/95 and it finally acquired its own bogies, these being original 1895 bogies left over after the re-equipping of the passenger vehicles. The other original stock consisted of a Tower Wagon and a 4-wheel wagon. The latter was scrapped in 1982 and replaced by a wagon utilising another of the now-spare 1895 bogies. A second wagon

ABOVE: **A Snaefell car ascends the SMR with Sulby reservoir in the distance below.**

BELOW: **Special headboard carried by SMR cars during 1995 'International Railway Festival'.**

was also built for construction work at the summit, utilising another ex-passenger car bogie. At the beginning of the 1950s the Air Ministry built a radar station at the summit and introduced Wickham Railcars to the SMR, a separate shed being built to house them at Laxey. There have been four of these vehicles over the years to serve this installation, which is now operated by the Civil Aviation Authority.

The Bungalow Hotel was closed and demolished in 1958 and the only building at Halfway now is a hut, with toilets and a car park on the opposite side of the tracks. The old wooden station building at the summit was replaced in 1906 by a castellated hotel. This was destroyed by fire during the night of 5/6 August 1982 and rebuilt into the more modest structure opened in 1984 - the building now houses a cafe and bar. The car shed at Laxey was replaced in 1995 - the SMR's Centenary year.

The Douglas Horse Tramway

The 3ft gauge Douglas Horse Tramway along the promenade of the Manx capital celebrated its 125th anniversary in 2001. Thomas Lightfoot, a retired civil engineer, lodged a proposal at the Rolls Office in Douglas for a tramway along Douglas seafront in 1875 when the town was developing as a holiday

A rather intriguing combination is presented as the 3ft gauge IOMSR locomotive *Caledonia* and Manx Electric Railway trailer No 57 descend Snaefell with a 3ft 6in gauge Snaefell car! The Snaefell Centenary was marked in 1995 by the laying of a third rail up the mountain, the IOMSR loco and MER trailer then providing steam operated ascents of the mountain, with the Snaefell car added to provide additional braking during the descents.

resort, with the promenade under construction. In the spring of the following year an Act of Tynwald gave approval for a tramway to be worked by animal power from Victoria Pier (now part of the Sea Terminal) to Summer Hill. The first section, from Burnt Mill Hill to what is now the foot of Broadway, was opened on 7 August 1876. The line was extended to near Victoria Pier in early 1877, and later in the same year the stable building, which remains in use today, was purchased. This initial line was a single track with passing loops.

In 1882, Thomas Lightfoot sold the tramway to Isle of Man Tramways Ltd and, after the addition of several passing loops to allow increased services, the line was doubled during the 1880s. In 1890 the Tramway was extended to Derby Castle, and by the following year there were 26 cars in use on the line.

Another sale came in spring 1894 when the Tramway was purchased by the Isle of Man Tramways & Electric Power Co. The first section of the Douglas and Laxey Electric Tramway (later to become the MER) had opened the year before between Derby Castle and Groudle. The new owners planned to electrify it, either to run electric cars right through to Victoria Pier, or possibly intended to introduce smaller, more suitable, vehicles. Whichever, the important point was that the Tramway around the bay was viewed as an essential feeder to the electric line.

Negotiations with Douglas Corporation for permission to electrify it were lengthy, and apparently quite complex, since the Upper Douglas Cable Tramway was built as part of the overall 'package'. The plans for electrification effectively died in 1897, and with the IOMT&EP Co going into liquidation in 1900 following the collapse of Dumbell's Bank, plans to run powered vehicles along the promenade did not come to fruition.

The Horse Tramway (along with the Cable Tramway) was purchased by Douglas Corporation in 1901. At this time, the tram fleet stood at 36 cars - 13 double deckers, 3 single deck saloons, 14 open toastracks and 6 roofed toastracks. Subsequently 5 more cars were added. Accusations of cruelty over the work required of the horses resulted in all but one of the historic double deck trams being broken up. The one double decker which survived (No 14) is presently in the Manx Museum, Douglas, but in 1990

Upper Douglas Cable Tramway car No 72/73 pictured on the Douglas Horse Tram tracks running under its own power during the August 1995 'International Railway Festival'.

a single deck saloon, which had been a double decker at South Shields before conversion to a winter car at Douglas in 1908, was returned to its original double deck condition - although passengers are only carried on one deck. Douglas Corporation acquired its first motor buses in 1914 and the fleet rapidly expanded in the 1920s, but the horse trams survived, presenting a unique summer attraction. Winter services ceased in 1927 and were suspended during WW2, but commenced again in 1946. Over the years, the fleet has reduced and now stands at 16 toastracks, 4 winter saloons and 1 double decker, plus a further converted toastrack which is drawn out of Derby Castle terminus during operating days to serve as a shop.

The tracks of the 1.6 mile double line are set into the promenade road surface and shared with motorised traffic. The line out from the Derby Castle terminus is on the seaward side, with the return track from the Sea Terminal on the landward side. The depot at Derby Castle, which remains in use today, was started in 1895, the offices over the workshops being added in 1935. At about the same time, a magnificent cast iron awning was built over the terminal, but sadly this was condemned as unsafe and demolished in 1980. Shortly after leaving the Derby Castle terminus, the line having swung out into the road along the Queen's Promenade, are the stables. The horses are kept here during the operating season, but go out to pasture around

the island during the winter. When they are no longer able to haul trams, many go to the Isle of Man Home of Rest for Horses run by a charity at Bulrhenny, Richmond Hill, Braddan (just outside Douglas).

The aforementioned Upper Douglas Cable Tramway, which opened in August 1896 and closed in 1929, also terminated in Victoria Street, by the Jubilee Clock, near the Horse Tram terminus. The surviving parts of two Upper Douglas Cable Trams, which had been used as a dwelling, were restored between 1968-1976 to produce car No 72/73 - its mixed parentage reflected by the different numbers on each end. Normally stored at the horse tram depot, this vehicle is occasionally run along the promenade tracks. Initially, the tram was moved with the aid of a Land Rover, but in 1995 it was fitted with an electric motor and batteries and has subsequently run under its own power during enthusiast events.

Over a century after plans for electrifying the Tramway had apparently died, the concept reappeared in 2000/2001 when options for future transport strategy on the Isle of Man were examined in a consultative document prepared for Tynwald. Ideas included a high-speed commuter service between Port Erin and Douglas, the introduction of modern trams on the MER - and confirmation that it would be technically possible to extend the MER from Derby Castle, along the promenade to a new terminus near the Sefton Hotel! The document envisaged the relocation of the Horse Tramway onto the adjacent pedestrian walkway and raised the possibility of extending along the North Quay up to the steam railway station. Although examining the options does not mean that they will be implemented, it is fascinating to note the way in which old ideas can be revived - it will be interesting to see if the vision pursued unsuccessfully by Alexander Bruce and his Isle of Man Tramways & Electric Power Co eventually comes to pass!

The Groudle Glen Railway

The 2ft gauge Groudle Glen Railway ranks as one of the earliest narrow gauge lines to have been built specifically to cater for tourism, although not quite the first - Brighton's Volks Railway, for instance, was opened in 1893 and just predated it.

Towards the end of the 19th century, the tourist industry on the Isle of Man was booming. Powers to build a road, with a tramway alongside, from Douglas Promenade to Groudle were granted by Tynwald in 1892, the objective being to develop part of the Howstrake Estates. The first tramcar arrived at Groudle, where a new hotel had been built, in August 1893 with the official opening following on 7 September. The owner of the hotel, R M Broadbent, had also acquired the land on both sides of Groudle Glen and rapidly developed it as an attraction. Arriving on a tramcar, the Victorian visitors paid an admission fee to explore the paths and bridges down the Glen to the sea shore - or to the headland where they could view sea lions and polar bears in enclosures created by closing off an inlet at the base of the cliffs.

The success of the venture soon led to the idea of building a small railway as an attraction in its own right and to transport visitors to the zoo. Construction started in 1895 and the first passenger train ran on 23 May 1896. At first, there were three coaches and the Bagnall 2-4-0T *Sea Lion*. A further coach was soon added and, by the turn of the century, the Glen was being visited by over 100,000 people, with up to 40 return trips a day being run over the three-quarters of a mile railway at the peak of the season. In 1905, *Polar Bear*, a slightly larger and more powerful version of *Sea Lion* was delivered, along with four more coaches. Other enhancements included the addition of a passing loop and the construction of a loco shed.

The railway was closed during WWI and did not reopen until 1920 when new sea lions were placed in the zoo - the earlier animals were reported to have been 'released'! The Glen was now under new ownership and two four-wheel battery electric locomotives worked the trains until 1922. Steam returned for the 1924 season, although the electric locos operated again between 1925-26. The railway closed down on the outbreak of WW2 and by 1946 had suffered greatly from vandalism and theft - including the brass fittings from the locomotives. Operations recommenced in 1950 with *Polar Bear* and six coaches, although a landslip enforced the closure of the section between the headland and the zoo terminus at Sea Lion Rocks. Not good, but there were no animals in the zoo by this time anyway!

No trains ran in 1959, but in 1961 a new company took over the Glen and ran the railway. This was the 'fairground livery' period for *Polar Bear* and the six serviceable coaches. With *Sea Lion* still out of use, the line staggered on until the end of the 1962 season when the tubes in *Polar Bear* could last no more. In 1966 *Polar Bear* was sold to members of the Brockham Museum Association and was moved to Dorking, Surrey in the

following year. The loco was subsequently overhauled and steamed again in 1982 at Amberley Chalk Pits Museum, which remains her home, along with other items from the collection originally at Dorking. Also at Amberley are four Groudle Glen coaches, one being constructed using parts recovered from the Isle of Man in the 1960s, a second having components donated by the present GGR volunteers, while the other two are replicas, one incorporating removable seats to enable wheelchairs to be accommodated.

On the Isle of Man, *Sea Lion* and the remaining coach parts were rescued and moved away from the Glen. Meanwhile, the station building and loco shed at Lhen Coan were demolished and the rails up to the headland removed.

The period when William Jackson was General Manager of the Isle of Man Railway systems was, let's say, controversial. But, unintentional as it may have been, his actions led to the revival of the Groudle Glen Railway. The IOMSR Supporters Association was formed in 1966 with the intention of getting the 3ft gauge steam railway operating again. The group worked with Lord Ailsa on a number of projects after he leased the railway in 1967 and campaigned on behalf of the railway during the 1976 Manx General Election. Jackson acted as a consulting engineer for the MER, which came under Manx Government control in the mid-1950s, and was appointed Chief Executive of the MER on 29 October 1977, becoming responsible for the IOMR from 1 December 1977. At this point relations broke down and within two years there was no voluntary work at all on the IOMR. The members looked at possible sites on the island to build their own railway, but the appeal of Groudle and the restoration of something otherwise lost was overwhelming. Work started in January 1982 and what has been achieved is remarkable. Not only was the GGR trackbed overgrown, the drainage system had completely broken down with Lhen Coan having degenerated into a virtual bog. Moreover, the problems facing the volunteers were compounded by the absence of road access to the site.

While work on the trackbed was being progressed during 1982, the Association searched for suitable equipment. In October of that year eight 2ft gauge wagons were delivered to the island, two being used in the reconstruction work while the others were to provide the running gear for replica Groudle coaches. Next came the acquisition of a complete railway! The Dodington Railway had been built in 1959 at Dodington House, Chipping Sodbury, near Bristol. Although refurbished in 1976, it closed in 1982. The purchase included 1,080 yards of 20lb/yard rail, track fastenings, wooden sleepers, two points, two Hudson Hunslet 4wDM locomotives and three open bogie coaches. The icing on the cake was reaching agreement with the owners of *Sea Lion* for the loco to return to the island for as long as the Groudle Glen Railway runs.

Track laying commenced in spring 1983 and the section between Lime Kiln Halt and Headland was reopened to passenger traffic on 18 December. Having carried 700 Santa Special passengers, and another 200 on Boxing Day, the work continued on the Glen section down to Lhen Coan. Reopening a railway with Santa trains could be unique, but marking the opening of the first extension in the same way must reserve a special place

ABOVE: An evening study of Graham Morris' Kerr Stuart 0-4-0ST *Peter Pan* at Sea Lion Rocks during its August 1998 visit to the Groudle Glen Railway. Seated at the picnic table are the author's wife, Carrie, and the late Alastair Lamberton, one of the leading figures in the revival of the GGR.

OPPOSITE PAGE:
TOP: The two Groudle Glen Railway steam locomotives *Annie* (left) and *Sea Lion* are pictured together at Lhen Coan during a night photography session on 28 July 1999.

LOWER: Bagnall 2-4-0T *Sea Lion* passes Lime Kiln Halt on the Groudle Glen Railway in August 1999.

in history for the Groudle Glen line! Santa Trains between Lime Kiln Halt and Lhen Coan ran on 23 December 1984 and 850 passengers were carried.

The railway was officially reopened on 25 May 1986 and in October 1987, *Sea Lion* was handed over following work which had started on the island and subsequently continued at the BNFL Apprentice Training Centre at Sellafield, Cumbria, where a new boiler, cab and tanks had been constructed. The loco entered service at Christmas 1987. The railway was returned to its full length with the reopening to Sea Lion Rocks in May 1992 (on an alignment slightly further inland than previously) followed by the construction of a station building - with overall roof - in the style of the original at Lhen Coan. With a loco

shed/workshop already having been built, the restoration of the line's infrastructure was completed when a new shelter/museum/information building at Sea Lion Rocks was opened for the 2001 season - there are no plans to replicate the zoo!

When Leighton Buzzard Railway-based Kerr Stuart 0-4-0ST *Peter Pan* came to the Isle of Man in August 1991, it was not simply the first locomotive to visit the Groudle Glen Railway, but on 11 August 1991 became the first locomotive to run to Sea Lion Rocks since 1939. As part of the 1993 'Year of Railways' celebrations on the Isle of Man, *Polar Bear* returned to the Glen, along with the first three Amberley GGR coaches, for a three-week reunion with its old line and was in steam alongside *Sea Lion* for the first time in 50 years.

As the revived railway moves into the new century, the line is being progressively relaid with 30lb/yard rail, replacing the 20lb material. In addition to three bogie coaches which are based on the ex-Dodington vehicles, there are now three 4-wheel Groudle coaches (two examples of the 1896 type and one 1905 type) in service, all being considered to be 'original' since they incorporate all original metalwork except the axle boxes and springs which are new. A fourth is presently under construction on the island. Between 1993 and 1996 Andrew Barclay 0-4-0 wing tank *Jack* was resident at Groudle. Following its sale, Richard Booth set about constructing *Annie* which entered service in 1998. Other visitors to the GGR have included Baguley 0-4-0T *Rishra*, De Winton 0-4-0VTB *Chaloner*, Kerr Stuart 0-4-0ST *Peter Pan* (all from Leighton Buzzard) and Hunslet 0-4-0ST *Jonathan* (from the West Lancashire Light Railway).

CHAPTER FOUR

The leisure industry

Until the early 1800s, people rarely travelled far outside their communities, but railways brought travel within the reach of all. Main lines linked principal centres, with branches into smaller communities. Where standard gauge would be uneconomic, or an existing industrial railway could be upgraded, the narrow gauge offered a solution. But there was something else: a (comparatively) short train ride could be offered for purely tourist reasons - to the top of a hill or mountain perhaps, or to a beauty spot. People might even be inspired to take a ride for the sheer fun of doing so!

A purist could argue that the Vale of Rheidol does not belong in this section. It was promoted to serve the local community, but the tourist potential of Aberystwyth was understood. Freight traffic was not strong and from 1931 the line became a seasonal tourist railway. In fact, there is an argument it became a preserved railway from that time, under the care and protection of the GWR! The VoR became the last redoubt of British Railways' steam and the current management runs it as it always was - a railway which carries tourists and day trippers - preservation under a different guise.

The lines up Snowdon and the Great Orme and along the seafront at Brighton were plainly built to serve a specifically tourist market. But the wheel, so to speak, has come full circle. While railways lost out for a period in the face of bus transport, increased car ownership and air travel to holidays in the sun, taking a train ride 'just for the fun of it' became fashionable again by the 1990s. For all heritage lines, the majority of the business is not from railway enthusiasts but is 90% or greater 'Joe Public', so the attraction of steam is powerful in its own right. A fact duly exploited by the construction of new narrow gauge railways.

The Llanberis Lake Railway has been operating for over 30 years, successfully fulfilling the ambitions of those who promoted it and complementing the Snowdon Mountain Railway in developing Llanberis tourism. The railway at Whipsnade gave new life to historic narrow gauge equipment while enabling impressive numbers of zoo visitors to obtain good views of the animals.

Other railways described in this volume enjoy patronage for the same reasons, although they may be catering for a market quite different from that envisaged when they first opened. But the historic lines within this chapter are still doing today what they were originally intended to do.

Joining them are some later railways specifically built to serve only a tourist market, others are covered in the chapter dealing with railways constructed on old standard gauge trackbeds catering for the same leisure industry.

Notes covering three lines constructed in comparatively recent times to cater for the tourist business which have not survived (at least, in their original form as true narrow gauge railways) are also included.

Volks Electric Railway

Magnus Volk was born in Brighton, the son of a clockmaker who had emigrated from Germany. In June 1883, he approached his local Council with a scheme to build an electric-powered line on the seafront, which was ceremonially opened on 4 August 1883. Werner von Siemens had shown an electric railway system at the 1879 Berlin Exhibition, followed by the operation of a train at Crystal Palace in 1881. The potential for this form of traction had been spotted by William A Traill, and Siemens was involved in its use on the Portrush and Giant's Causeway Tramway (see Chapter 7) but although that line opened in January 1883, services worked by electricity did not start until November 1883. On this basis, the Volks line in Brighton can claim to have provided the first public electric rail service in the British Isles. In 1999, the line was named as the 'earliest public railway still in existence' by the Guinness Book of Records - a carefully phrased entry, with 'public' being crucial in relation to other (arguably more obvious) claims.

This first line was built to 2ft gauge and ran for a quarter of a mile, starting opposite the main entrance to the Aquarium near Palace Pier, eastwards along the sea front adjacent to Madeira Road (now Madeira Drive) to the western side of the Old Chain Pier. It was worked by a single 4-wheel car and employed a two-rail electricity supply. The line was successful and Magnus Volk received approval to extend it further east.

In fact, the railway was reconstructed rather than simply extended. A gauge of 2ft 8½ins was adopted and two new cars supplied. The new terminus was at Paston Place, at the site of

Not the average narrow gauge driver! Paula Jones, aged 18 and newly qualified, waits to depart from Peter Pan's station with car No 6 in May 2000. *(P G Barnes)*

the Banjo Groyne, and public services between Old Chain Pier and Paston Place commenced on 7 April 1884 (the official opening ceremony was on 4 April) - the original section still being rebuilt. The full line, named the Brighton Electric Railway, including the original length was 1,400 yards long with a passing loop part-way along. At first, the two-rail supply was retained, but an off-centre third rail was added in 1886. A further extension from Paston Place to Black Rock opened in May 1901, bringing the line up to a length of 1¼ miles. In June 1901, a private limited company, Magnus Volk Ltd, was formed to run the line. In May 1923 this company was reconstituted, although it was incorporated under the same name. The section of the extension immediately to the east of Banjo Groyne was built on a steel-braced timber viaduct over the sea. Over subsequent years, the shingle was washed around this structure until it was buried. In 1990/91, this now-hidden construction was replaced by a concrete raft to support the track.

By 1926, the line was carrying around a million passengers a year, being operated with 10 cars, and employing 50 staff during the high season. At the end of the 1920s, Madeira Drive was widened and the line slightly shortened at its western end. A new Aquarium terminus was opened in June 1930 - being

slightly away from the Palace Pier, patronage dropped quite markedly. The line celebrated its 50th anniversary on 4 August 1933, the year in which the Brighton main line was electrified. Rather underlining the innovation to be found on the narrow gauge, Col Gilbert S Szlumper, the Assistant General Manager of the Southern Railway, sent a telegram of congratulations which included the tribute, 'Your pioneer electric service set example which we have seized upon.'!

A new bathing pool was built at Black Rock in 1937. Although generating extra traffic, and meaning that a new station was constructed, it also caused another slight shortening of the line - the length now being 1.1 miles. Shortly after, in May 1937, Magnus Volk died and his eldest son, Herman, took over. The lease from Brighton Corporation was due to expire in 1939 and the Brighton Corporation (Transport) Act of 1938 gave the local authority powers to take over running the railway. The formal handover took place on 1 April 1940, but the outbreak of WW2 overtook events. In view of the threat of invasion, the

Changes down the years mean that the east end of the Volk's Electric Railway has had five different termini. The present Black Rock station was opened in 1998. *(P G Barnes)*

beach was closed from 2 July 1940 and the railway was surrounded by defences.

By the end of the war, the line was effectively wrecked. Years of neglect and salt corrosion had taken their toll, while the terminus buildings had been demolished. The Council decided to resurrect the railway and work commenced in 1947. Seven of the best remaining cars were renovated and public services re-started on 15 May 1948. Unfortunately, traffic went into decline in the 1970s, the impact of foreign holidays and the closure of Black Rock pool being contributory factors, and has fallen to around 200,000 per year. In 1990, although retaining the old initials, the railway was marketed as the Volks Excursion Railway - however, the name by which it is known to most has been retained for the title of this section. Although operated by full time staff employed by the Council, a supporters group - The Volks Electric Railway Association - was set up in September 1995 to assist the Council, and the railway's management, with the operation, maintenance, restoration and promotion of the historic line. Recent times have seen consideration given to extensions at both ends: a return to the Palace Pier at the western end, and to the new Marina from Black Rock when the future of a long-vacant Black Rock swimming pool has been determined.

All of the electric cars which have run on the line have been four-wheeled. The original pair were closed saloons, followed by two open cross-bench cars. A saloon was added in 1897, followed by two semi-open's for the 1901 extension to Black Rock. Further additions were made in 1910, 1926 and 1930 when a closed winter saloon was delivered. The reconstruction in 1947/48 resulted in the scrapping of three cars, leaving two open's and five semi-open's. In 1949, these were supplemented by two 1899-vintage Southend Pier cross-bench vehicles which entered service in 1950 and 1953. At the end of the 1990s, it was decided to return ex-Southend Car 8 'home' to be placed on display in the Southend Pier Museum, No 9 remaining at

Brighton. For most of its life, single-car services were run, but in 1963 suitable modifications were made to start operating two-car trains and paired running has latterly become the norm. After 115 years of operation solely with electric traction, a Simplex diesel was acquired in 1998 for use on works trains and to retrieve electric cars in the event of a breakdown. This loco was built in 1987, and was the last to be ordered from Simplex of Bedford before the firm closed down, although it was actually built by Alan Keef Ltd and bears an AK works plate with the number 40SD530. The machine was supplied to the Butterly Brick Company, initially for use at the Star Lane Works at Wickford, then moved to Cherry Orchard Works at Rochford, near Southend. In 1995/96 when the internal rail system ceased to be used, the loco was purchased by Alan Keef Ltd who regauged it and reprofiled the wheels to suit the VER track.

Although far from being a narrow gauge line, The Brighton & Rottingdean Seashore Electric Tramway has some relevance. At the end of the 19th century, Magnus Volk was thinking in terms of extending his railway to Rottingdean. This would have involved either a very steep climb to the cliff top, or an expensive embankment or viaduct, so he came up with the plan for the remarkable line which became known as the 'Daddy Longlegs'. Two lines of 2ft 8½ins gauge track were laid, 18ft apart between the outer rails, for a distance of just under three miles eastwards from the Banjo Groyne to Rottingdean - these tracks being covered by the sea when the tide came in. The 'vehicle' built to operate over this astonishing line has, understandably, been described as a combination of electric tram, pleasure yacht and a piece of mobile pier - all mounted on legs to raise the main body above the waves and deriving its electric power from trolley poles on the landward side of the route. As the line's own advertising put it, 'A sea voyage on wheels'! This line opened in November 1896, but suffered considerable damage during a gale in the December. This storm damaged the Volks Electric line as well and destroyed the Old Chain Pier. Services over the 'Daddy Longlegs' restarted on 20 July 1897, but it only survived until the end of 1900, after which sea defences were built across the route. Rebuilding the line further out to sea was not practical and it was abandoned. Volk then raised the possibility of extending his conventional line from Black Rock to Rottingdean as a replacement, but the finance could not be raised and that scheme was also dropped.

Vale of Rheidol Railway

The Vale of Rheidol (Light) Railway Act was passed on 6 August 1897, its objectives including the transportation of ore from the mines high up the valley to foundries in the town, timber, service to the local community and a recognition that Aberystwyth was developing as a tourist destination. The Act covered two railways, a main line of just over 11 miles between the terminus at Aberystwyth and Devil's Bridge, and a Harbour branch at Aberystwyth. Over subsequent years, there have been changes in the terminus and route within Aberystwyth which affect the length of the main line but, in broad terms, it is now about 11¾ miles.

After initial difficulties in raising money, construction of the 1ft 11½ins gauge line started early in 1901 and inspection followed on 12 August that year. It was not passed for public traffic, the

RIGHT: **No 8 *Llywelyn* approaching Devil's Bridge in July 2001.**

BELOW: **The Vale of Rheidol Railway at its lowest ebb - No 8 *Llywelyn* and train appear in BR rail blue in this September 1972 picture at Aberystwyth.**

track being much criticised, and the Inspector considered the railway to be unfinished. Goods trains did however start running, to generate some income and help settle the track. Further work was undertaken and the first 'official' (but private) passenger train ran on 5 November 1902. A further inspection on 25 November secured approval for public trains and passenger services started on 22 December.

The lead ore traffic did not meet expectation and fell away after peaking in 1906, although the conveyance of timber offered some compensation. In October 1910, the holdings in the independent VoR company were transferred to nominees of the Cambrian Railways, and the line was formally absorbed by the Cambrian in 1913. The Cambrian Railways were duly taken over by the Great Western Railway under grouping during 1922/23. The GWR immediately commenced a period of investment in the line. In addition to new locomotives and carriages, the permanent way - a serious problem from the start - received extensive attention.

The original locomotives supplied in 1902 were No 1 *Edward VII* and No 2 *Prince of Wales*. These were 2-6-2Ts built by Davies & Metcalf Ltd and the design was based on the Manning Wardle locomotives delivered to the Lynton & Barnstaple Railway in 1897/98. In addition, the company took over the 2-4-0T Bagnall employed by the contractor while building the line, which became No 3 *Rheidol*. This loco had been built to 2ft 5½ins gauge in 1896 for use in Brazil, but never delivered. It was then regauged to 2ft 3ins and sold for use on the Plynlimon & Hafan Tramway where it was named *Talybont*, bought back by Bagnall's when that line closed and regauged again for use by Pethick's. This motive power was supplemented by hiring 0-4-0STT *Palmerston* from the Ffestiniog Railway, the George England loco spending periods on the VoR annually between 1912-1915 and again in 1921/22. This connection was echoed when the FR's Alco 2-6-2T *Mountaineer* visited the VoR over 13/14 September 1986.

The GWR approved the construction of two new locomotives in January 1923 and Nos 7 and 8 were built at Swindon and ready for delivery by October 1923. The really interesting aspect is that although the construction of two locomotives had been approved, a third set of parts was made and completed by July 1924. No 2 *Prince of Wales* went to Swindon in 1924 and, supposedly, received a 'heavy repair'. In reality, the extra parts were used to construct a new locomotive, without official approval, and a brand new No 9 actually went to the VoR, the original No 2 *Prince of Wales* being no more. This fiction remained hidden until research in the 1980s revealed what had really happened - and would not be the only example of the VoR being 'looked after' by sympathetic GWR management! No 1 *Edward VII* went to Swindon by 1925 and was overhauled to serve as a spare engine, returned to Swindon in 1932 and officially withdrawn on 9 March 1935. No 3 *Rheidol* was withdrawn in July 1924, thus none of the original locomotives survive today. The three new Swindon-built locomotives were not named until 1956 when they became No 7 *Owain Glyndwr*, No 8 *Llywelyn* and No 9 *Prince of Wales*.

The Midland Carriage & Wagon Company of Shrewsbury

built 12 vertically planked bogie carriages for the opening of the line. Additional passenger accommodation for busy times was provided by carrying passengers in timber and open goods wagons - something the GWR was not prepared to live with, hence four bogie 'summer cars' were provided in 1923. In 1938, the GWR replaced the original carriages with new steel panelled bogie carriages, the three brake vans also being replaced at this time.

Although there was a boom in timber traffic during WWI, road competition was felt during the 1920s. Goods services officially ended on 1 January 1927, two GWR-built cattle vans being regauged and transferred to the Welshpool & Llanfair Light Railway. Year-round passenger services were withdrawn on 31 December 1930 - henceforth, the VoR became a tourist line operated during the summer only. When WW2 came, the line closed at the end of the 1939 season, reopening on 23 July 1945. Nationalisation of the railway system followed, with the VoR coming under the control of the Western Region of BR from 1 January 1948. Although there were closure rumours in 1954, the locomotives appeared in Western Region green and the carriages in chocolate and cream - without proper authority from 'on high'!

In July 1963 control of the VoR passed to the London Midland Region of BR. Also the year of the Beeching Report, the immediate impact was removal of the Capel Bangor and Aberffrwd loops, but 1967 was pivotal. The locomotives and coaches acquired a corporate BR Rail Blue livery, including the incongruous double-arrow logo. A scheme was drawn up to move the Aberystwyth terminus inside the standard gauge station, utilising the old Manchester & Milford bay platforms, and for the standard gauge loco shed (a 210ft long building built in 1940 to replace the demolished Cambrian shed closed in 1963) to become the new narrow gauge loco and carriage shed. On seeking approval, Euston responded that the railway should be closed. It was revealed that the line was losing £1,200 a year - something the Western Region had apparently disguised! Fortunately, the line still had friends, now in the form of the Divisional Manager at Stoke. Delaying tactics provided the opportunity for 'a word' with Barbara Castle,MP, Minister of Transport, when she visited Aberystwyth on 1 July 1967 - and the scheme was approved. The work was completed in time for the first train of the new season to depart from a new loop between bay platforms 4 and 5 inside the standard gauge terminus on 20 May 1968.

When first built, the Aberystwyth passenger station was in Smithfield Road (later renamed Park Avenue) and trains departed in a south-westerly direction to pass the loco sheds and yard beside the Afon Rheidol. The Harbour branch also started here (it fell out of use as goods traffic ended, the tracks being lifted around 1930) while the main line rounded a football field, passed under the Manchester & Milford line, until running parallel to the Cambrian tracks. In 1925, the line was extended from the station, across Park Avenue and round to the side of the standard gauge station, but the exit from Aberystwyth remained as before. Under the 1968 rearrangement, the line ran straight from the station past the loco shed (now its depot) eliminating the original sheds and yard, along with the circuitous route to the standard gauge via the riverside.

Talk of selling the line had attracted interest from various quarters. Although reprieved in 1967, private interest revived in 1969 with famous names such as Pat Whitehouse and John Snell involved. The Vale of Rheidol Railway Equipment Co Ltd was formed on 12 August 1969 and two 0-8-0 tender locomotives were imported from East Germany, ready to step in if BR changed its mind. Enthusiasts also took a close interest and the Vale of Rheidol Railway Supporters Association (VORRSA) was formed in 1970. The Equipment Company eventually sold the locomotives and was removed from the companies register in 1984. VORRSA continued as a supporters organisation until 1991 when it was effectively dissolved, becoming part of the Welshpool & Llanfair Light Railway organisation.

As noted, the permanent way had always been a problem. Second-hand rail had been used during construction, some as light as 32lb/yd (probably some was even lighter) and of poor quality. This problem was compounded by the use of sub-standard ballast and, in places, the formation itself was poorly built. On a line with tough gradients at the upper end, not unsurprisingly the track tended to slip downhill and curves did not hold their radius properly. The track gangs kept on top of things until the Cambrian took over, but neglect during WW1 took its toll. The GWR effected improvements almost amounting to reconstruction, but the track suffered again under London Midland Region control, coming to a head in 1986 when downhill rail creep and poor sleepers and track fixings resulted in a curve bursting near the 6½ mile post on 26 May. Little harm was done to passengers, but questions were asked in Parliament - crucially, why BR was running a tourist line and not concentrating on its core business.

BR finally decided to sell the line in 1988 and it was purchased in April 1989 by Tony Hills and Peter Rampton, the partnership which already owned the Brecon Mountain Railway. This arrangement continued until 1991, when their ownership interests were separated. Tony Hills kept the Brecon Mountain line (although he remained Manager of the VoR until 1996) while Peter Rampton became sole owner of the VoR until transferring ownership to the Phyllis Rampton Narrow Gauge Railway Trust. Although completely separated financially, the two railways retain a close friendship.

The top priority was getting the railway back on its feet. Some two-thirds of the sleepers and around half the rails needed replacement, the locomotives and stock needed attention and the facilities for visitors had to be improved. The recovery programme was threatened when a disastrous landslip occurred in April 1996. A mine, some 240ft deep, 40ft long and 5ft wide, which had last been worked in the 1800s, had collapsed, leaving a near vertical chasm, and took the hillside right back to the railway with it. Fortunately, the trackbed was not affected, being on solid rock, but the railway was effectively severed for seven weeks with trains operating only up to Aberffrwd while the hillside was reconstructed. The work was completed by mid-June, the railway then concentrating on summer operations.

The total renewal of the permanent way was completed by winter 2000/2001. All sleepers have been replaced with hardwood

No 7 *Owain Glyndwr* takes water at Nantyronen in September 1996.

and screws and clips have been employed to provide a stronger method of fastening than the original Dog Spikes. This programme also included replacement of the bridge over the River Rheidol (at a cost of some £130,000) and laying heavier rails in the main line. The following 12 months were set aside for general track fettling before moving on to the next stages of developing the VoR. These plans include improving visitor facilities and workshop at Aberystwyth. A car park is needed, and although the old standard gauge shed dwarfs the 2ft gauge locomotives, is not large enough to serve as a combined loco and carriage shed and workshop. The building will remain, but not necessarily as currently used. At Devil's Bridge, permanent buildings rather than temporary structures are planned, along with platforms and a proper car park. The original corrugated iron station building - which was Listed by CADW in 1988 - will, however, remain. Although the new owners reinstated the loop at Aberffrwd, unless a resolution to the water supply problems can be found, trains will continue to take water at Nantyronen.

ABOVE: **Progress on the Vale of Rheidol has been maintained, this view of No 8 (no longer carrying its** *Llywelyn* **nameplates) was taken at Capel Bangor on 28 July 2001, shortly after the station site had been cleared and relaid.**

OPPOSITE PAGE:
TOP: **Snowdon Mountain Railway trains terminate at Clogwyn when the weather precludes continuing to the summit. This 27 October 1997 view shows No 4** *Snowdon* **and a diesel locomotive at the station.**

LOWER: **This unusual view was photographed on 5 May 1998 in the SMR shed at Llanberis. A new dark blue livery had been applied to the right side tank (and cab) of No 2** *Enid,* **and masking tape is being placed in preparation for adding the light blue lining. One of the diesel locomotives stands in the background.**

Two of the locomotives have been rebuilt in the Brecon Mountain Railway workshops at Pant, No 9 *Prince of Wales* in 1990/91, and No 8 *Llywelyn* which returned to service in 1996, while No 7 *Owain Glyndwr* had a heavy overhaul in 1992. Currently, *Llywelyn* has an 'as built' GWR livery, complete with Great Western in full along the side tanks - since the locos were not named when built, it was felt that applying *Llywelyn* nameplates could not be justified with this 'original' appearance. *Owain Glyndwr* is also currently green, but carries nameplates. *Prince of Wales* has a red livery, along with a plate which not

only records the 1990 rebuild at Pant but the fact that the engine was wholly built at Swindon in 1924.

A start has also been made on the renovation of the carriages and all stock has been equipped with air braking equipment rather than the previous vacuum arrangements. The locos were converted to oil-firing by BR, No 7 for the 1978 season, No 8 in 1979 and No 9 in 1981, largely to eliminate the risk of fires in the forested surroundings of the line. Splendid views used to be a feature of the VoR, but became obscured by increased tree growth. Some cutting back has been done, but the future management of the woodlands remains an issue under discussion.

Early in 2000, the railway became unique, as the only narrow gauge line to have most of its locomotives and stock 'designated' by the Railway Heritage Committee. Although the powers of this committee normally only extend to main line public railways, any organisation which was once a subsidiary of the British Railways Board can come within its powers. Although now an independent company (as it was when first built) the VoR still operates under the same company registration number as established by BR prior to the sale. The designation covers all three 2-6-2T steam locomotives, 16 ex-GWR bogie coaches (four dating from 1923, the remainder from 1938), the four-wheel guard's van and 11 four-wheel wagons, some of which include ex-Plynlimon & Hafan Tramway examples from as early as 1897/98, pre-dating the VoR itself. Other equipment covered includes ex-GWR water cranes, an ex-Cambrian water tank, point levers and ex-Swindon Works patterns. The designation is

backed by the power of the law and no designated items can be sold or scrapped without the agreement of the Railway Heritage Committee - not that the VoR has any such intentions! The designation was supported by the railway and, having raised the heritage profile of the VoR, could assist grant applications. The designation, obviously, does not include modern equipment such as the 0-6-0DH locomotive or the Tamping machine, built by Plassers for working underground in a South African gold mine, which arrived at the VoR in 1991.

A very long term ambition is a museum at Aberystwyth. A collection of narrow gauge locomotives has been assembled over many years by Peter Rampton and the Trust. Most are in private storage, although others have arrived at Aberystwyth in recent years. As some are returned to steam, the availability of a loop at Capel Bangor opens the possibility of demonstration runs over part of the line. Once the future of the VoR itself has been secured, the aim is to turn attention to the museum project, although availability of money is a major issue.

Snowdon Mountain Railway

The 2ft 7½ins (800mm) gauge Snowdon Mountain Railway is the only public rack and pinion railway in Britain. Over a track length of 4⅘ miles, it climbs from 353ft above sea level at Llanberis to a station at 3,493ft above sea level, just 67ft below the summit of the highest mountain in England and Wales.

Snowdonia has long drawn tourists and by 1847 two 'refreshment' huts had been constructed by guides at the summit of Yr Wyddfa ('the burial place'), the highest of the peaks in the Snowdonia range. Visitor numbers accelerated when the standard gauge LNWR branch line from Caernarfon arrived at Llanberis in 1869 and the attractions of building a railway to the summit became increasingly obvious. A Bill was presented to Parliament for such a line in 1872 but was opposed by the landowner, Mr William Duff Assheton-Smith, who felt it would despoil the landscape. The North Wales Narrow Gauge Railway reached Rhyd Ddu, to the south of the mountain, in 1881 and the naming of its station as South Snowdon was plainly aimed at encouraging tourists to use it as the starting point for walking to the summit - to the detriment of Llanberis.

Renewed approaches to Mr Assheton-Smith brought a change of mind and in March 1893 the Snowdon Mountain Tramroad and Hotels Co Ltd was formed. The Royal Victoria Hotel was acquired and the ceremonial 'cutting the first sod' of the new railway was performed on 15 December 1894. The line was built in just 14 months by a workforce of 150 men, tracklaying being completed to the summit by January 1896. Built on private land, there was no requirement for an inspection, although an 'unofficial' inspection took place on 27 March 1896.

The public opening on Easter Monday, 6 April 1896 initially went well with two trains reaching the summit. Unfortunately, locomotive No 1 *LADAS* (the initials of Laura Alice Duff Assheton-Smith) left the rails just above Clogwyn while descending. The carriages stayed on the track, but the loco plunged into a ravine and was destroyed. The loco crew leapt to safety, but despite warnings to stay in their seats, two passengers jumped from the train, one subsequently dying from his injuries. Further minor injuries occurred when *Enid*, descending with the other train, collided with the halted carriages. The railway was immediately closed, not re-opening until 19 April 1897, by which time angled girders had been fitted to the rack and grippers to the locomotives, preventing the locos leaving the track.

Once re-opened, the line settled down to an uneventful, but successful pattern of operations. The Padarn Villa (now the Padarn Lake Hotel) was added to the portfolio and in 1904 the licences and goodwill of the two wooden huts at the summit were transferred to a new wooden building constructed just above Summit station. The railway operated through WWI,

SMR diesel No 10 *Yeti* is pictured on 5 August 2000 crossing the Upper Viaduct at Llanberis as it brings down the early morning 'works train' which conveys staff and water to the summit before the day's passenger operations commence.

A rare opportunity to see the smokebox of a Snowdon Mountain Railway locomotive as No 4 *Snowdon* (left) and No 3 *Wyddfa* (right) are prepared on 2 August 2000 in the yard at Llanberis for the coming day's work.

albeit on a reduced scale. Having sold the Padarn Villa during the 1920s, the company name was changed in 1928 to Snowdon Mountain Railway Ltd. The wooden building at the summit was replaced by the present structure in 1935 and a service continued to operate during WW2, this time as a cover for the military activities in the Summit building which included an experimental RAF radar station. Normal passenger services resumed in 1946 and in 1953 the Royal Victoria Hotel was sold.

Although it has been altered and refurbished since it was constructed, the Summit 'hotel' building has been the centre of a debate in recent times. While the railway remains the freeholder of the permanent way and the land on which the platforms at the summit are built, it ceased to own the freehold of the building in 1983 and now leases it from the Snowdonia National Park Authority (SNPA). In 1996, the SNPA (supported by the railway) considered applying for Millennium Lottery funding to rebuild the facilities. Environmental interests opposed the plan - and argued that all the buildings should be demolished, returning Summit to its natural state. This impasse effectively killed the project, but the National Park subsequently carried out a public consultation exercise to establish what people thought should be done. Late in 2001, a consultants' report recommending reconstruction of the existing building was accepted by the SNPA, with further consultation to follow before making a Planning Application.

The railway utilises the Abt rack and pinion system, the original rack rail being manufactured by Richard Cammell & Co with the running rails and rack laid on steel sleepers. The line is never flat, the gradient ranging between some 1 in 50 in Llanberis station to 1 in 5 at the steepest points. To prevent the track creeping down the mountain, there are upright steel joists periodically sunk into the trackbed for the sleepers to bear against. There are three passing places on the line: Hebron, Halfway and Clogwyn, of which only Clogwyn is staffed and

the movement of trains is controlled by radio communication with a Controller at Llanberis. When weather conditions prevent a safe ascent of the top section, trains may be terminated at Clogwyn, with the option of stopping at Rocky Valley if snow and ice prevent the train reaching Clogwyn.

The steam locomotives were all built by the Swiss Locomotive Works, Winterthur and there are two distinct types. The initial group: No 1 *LADAS* (1895 - destroyed 1896 and never replaced), No 2 *Enid* (1895), No 3 *Wyddfa* (1895), No 4 *Snowdon* (1896) and No 5 *Moel Siabod* (1896) had non-superheated boilers and are easily distinguished by the full-length side tanks up to the front of the smokebox. The later locomotives: No 6 *Padarn* (1922, formally *Sir Harmood*), No 7 *Ralph* (1923, formally *Aylwin*) and No 8 *Eryri* were provided with superheated boilers and have much shorter side tanks leaving much more of the boiler exposed. Sometimes termed 0-4-2T locomotives (the trailing wheels are mounted in a Bissel truck), this notation is not really applicable since the wheels only carry the weight of the locomotive and revolve freely. The drive from the horizontal cylinders is transmitted to two sets of pinions under the locomotive which engage in the rack. The counter-pressure brake, and automatic steam brake, is also applied to the pinions and not the wheels.

All of the early locomotives have been rebuilt by the Hunslet Engine Co, initially No 2 (1958), then No 5 (1959) and No 3 (1960) - but none so radically as was undertaken for No 4 *Snowdon*. Out of use since 1939, the cannibalised remains were taken to Leeds for reconstruction and little more than one frame plate and one cylinder from the original locomotive were reckoned to remain when it was completed in 1961 - the rest being entirely new! Hunslet also supplied new boilers for the later batch, although the rebuilds were undertaken at Llanberis. The railway has experimented with oil firing - in the 1970s using Laidlaw Drew burners and in the early 1990s using a 'Mexican

The three Llanberis Lake Railway Hunslet 0-4-0ST locomotives outside the shed at Gilfach Ddu, (left to right) *Thomas Bach* (nee *Wild Aster*), *Dolbadarn* and *Elidir*.

Trough' arrangement, both attempts being unsuccessful. Changing circumstances inspired experiments with No 4 *Snowdon*, the new conversion employing an improved burner design and the development of a suitable brick arch in the firebox. *Snowdon* was first tried in converted form just before Easter 1999. Various teething problems were identified and, following alterations, it worked its first trip in revenue earning service as an oil burner on 7 July 1999. The loco has worked successfully since, although no decision has yet been made on further conversions as this book was written.

This motive power sufficed until a 1985 share issue, by what had become Snowdon Mountain Railway plc, financed the purchase of two diesel locomotives and a new coach. No 9 *Ninian* and No 10 *Yeti* were built in 1986, followed in 1991 by No 11 *Peris* and in 1992, No 12 *George*. These 4-wheel diesel hydraulic locomotives were built by Hunslet, although only three were actually constructed at Jack Lane in Leeds, No 11 being built in Kilmarnock and having a Barclay serial number (775) as well as its Hunslet works number (HE9305).

To mark the line's centenary in 1996, No 3 *Wyddfa* received a deep maroon colour, an effort to reproduce the 'dark mahogany red' (or dark cherry red) believed to be the original locomotive livery. Further locomotives were repainted by their regular drivers

and other new liveries included: No 2 *Enid* (dark blue with light blue lining), No 5 *Moel Siabod* (black), No 6 *Padarn* (dark green), No 10 *Yeti* (maroon) and No 12 *George* (purple).

Six coaches were built for the opening of the line by the Lancaster Carriage & Wagon Company, five being open above waist level and fitted with roofs, the sixth having nothing above waist level. The frame of the latter was subsequently used for the caboose/water tank vehicle which still serves for works train use, along with an 1895-built 4-wheel flat wagon. Three more coaches, built by Schweizerische Industrie-Gesselschaft of Neuhausen, Switzerland, were added in 1922/23. Between 1951-1958, a programme to reconstruct the coaches was undertaken. Seven were rebuilt, one each year, with one being scrapped. The newer coaches can be distinguished from the older batch by the box which protrudes from the front to enclose the brake wheel. This stock was augmented in 1988 by an entirely new carriage, the East Lancashire Coach Builders Ltd body being mounted on a pair of bogies supplied by Hunslet. The coaches are not coupled to the locomotives but are pushed up the mountain, gravity keeping them in contact with the loco. They have a double rack pinion mounted on the bogie at the 'downhill' end and are equipped with a centrifugal governor. If the locomotive should begin to run away, this governor automatically applies the brakes when the speed exceeds 7½ mph.

In 1995, three diesel electric Railcars built by HPF Tredegar, arrived. These were to run either as a two-car or three-car set according to traffic requirements. Each of the units has a diesel

engine driving a fixed speed alternator, which then supplies electricity to an AC motor mounted onto a triple-reduction axle-hung gearbox. Power to the motor is controlled by an electronic inverter, with software designed so that each vehicle 'talks' to the others to ensure that speed and torque are correctly matched. There were problems from the start and, for a number of reasons, the units were not truly reliable, although some progress was made running a two-car set during 2001. Although the diesel locomotives have settled down to become solid workhorses, it is unlikely there will be further Railcars.

In 1998, Cadogan Properties decided to sell the SMR and Mr Kevin Leech acquired 100% of the shares in Snowdon Mountain Railway PLC. In June 1999, he re-formed it into a private company, Snowdon Mountain Railway Ltd and the SMR took its place, alongside Land's End, John O'Groats and The Needles Pleasure Park, in the Heritage GB Group, a holding company for operations under the ownership of Mr Leech.

Llanberis Lake Railway

Although 2001 marked it's 30th anniversary, the roots of this 1ft 11½ins gauge line are much older. It runs on the lakeside trackbed of the old 4ft gauge Padarn Railway (described in Chapter 1) which closed in 1961 and had been lifted by 1963. When the Dinorwic quarries closed, the end of this major industry was of understandable concern locally.

There was, of course, tourism, Snowdon (served by the

An historic train on the Llanberis Lake Railway. *Una* **(owned by the adjacent slate museum) is about to depart in company with** *Dolbadarn* **on 27 August 2001, this being the first time (so far as is known) that** *Una* **had ever worked on a passenger service in her entire life. The opportunity arose during a special event to celebrate the 30th anniversary of the railway when the author's book,** *Quarry Hunslets of North Wales***, was launched.**

Snowdon Mountain Railway) being the second string to Llanberis' bow. To provide local employment and develop the local tourist industry, Cymdeithas Rheilffordd Llyn Padarn was formed by a group of people to promote the construction of the Llanberis Lake Railway. At the 1969 auction of Dinorwic quarry assets, Mr Alan Porter (on behalf of the Trustees of the Cymdeithas) successfully bid for three of the Hunslets from the quarry. Mr Porter became Chairman of the Cymdeithas and the railway opened in July 1971. In 1976, the Cymdeithas was re-registered as Rheilffordd Llyn Padarn Cyf (Ltd), Mr Porter later being elected Honorary President of the Company.

The locomotives were *Red Damsel* (named *Enid* until at least 1908), *Wild Aster* and *Dolbadarn* - but what had been pur-chased - assembled or otherwise - was quite a mixture. In essence, the railway's then Engineer dismantled everything, laid the components out in three heaps and put them back as the three locomotives we see today. The nameplates for *Red Damsel* had disappeared by the time of the auction - and with doubts as to the 'proper' identity of the locomotive, she was named *Elidir* (after the mountain opposite Llanberis). *Wild Aster* was named *Thomas Bach* (Little Thomas) after the man who drove her in the quarries. Apparently, any similarity of the name, and blue livery, to other locomotives is coincidental! Later, *Dolbadarn* was painted yellow ochre, so all the locos had different colours for marketing reasons. There is a small fleet of diesels for shunting and works trains.

The locomotive shed is that used by 2ft gauge Dinorwic locomotives in quarry days, in one corner of the Gilfach Ddu works, which served the Dinorwic complex and has been developed into a museum of the Welsh slate industry. There is a link line between the railway and the tracks in the museum courtyard, enabling the museum's ex-Pen-yr-Orsedd Hunslet *Una* to appear occasionally on the lakeside line. The Llanberis Lake Railway's main station is close to the Vivian quarry entrance, the two-mile line passing the carriage sheds and under the 'Vivian Arch' onto a lakeside ledge through to Penllyn. There is a passing loop at Cei Llydan where passengers can alight on the return journey and visit a wildlife centre and picnic site beside the lake.

Meeting the aim of catering for tourism, the core market for the railway is coach parties, young families and senior citizens. Annual traffic steadily built up to around 60,000 passengers and the line carried its two millionth passenger in July 1997. Padarn Country Park, giving access to 700 acres of countryside, has developed around the railway, and the site at Gilfach Ddu has the slate museum, craft shops, and the nearby Dinorwic Quarry Hospital which has become a museum. Other Llanberis attractions are (obviously) the Snowdon Mountain Railway and Electric Mountain, a visitor centre offering guided tours into the man-made caverns created in Elidir to house an electricity generating complex. In the mid to late 1970s, the railway carried 'freight' traffic associated with the laying of underground cables beside the trackbed. A siding runs into a pumping station (which draws cold water from the lake to cool the buried cables) part-way between Cei Llydan and Penllyn, allowing heavy equipment to be transported to the site by rail.

A local Forum markets Llanberis as a destination for an entire day and promotes the village as a 'green gateway' to Snowdonia. The emergence of Victoria Dock in Caernarfon as a possible location for a new Maritime Museum led to speculation in the latter part of 1998 that this could take radical form by extending the Lake Railway from Penllyn into Caernarfon to link up with Rheilffordd Eryri - Welsh Highland Railway (Caernarfon). Although Swansea was selected, the concept did not completely die and a feasibility study was carried out during 2001, funded by The Welsh Development Agency. This confirmed that the Caernarfon to Llanberis plan could utilise parts of the trackbed of the old standard gauge Caernarfon to Llanberis branch which closed in the 1960s, and other parts of the old 4ft gauge Padarn Railway. Road and other developments preclude returning rails to the original Llanberis station site, but an end-on connection to the Llanberis Lake Railway could work. This would be a transport link rather than a heritage line, but funding such a link remains to be addressed.

Quite separately, the Llanberis Lake Railway pursued plans to build a half-mile extension from its Gilfach Ddu terminus towards the village. An application for Planning Permission was granted and it was hoped to build and open the extension in time for the 2000 season but, at the last moment, a problem arose with the funding package. Extending to a new station opposite the Snowdon Mountain Railway's terminus was supported by all the local tourist attractions - including the SMR - and late in 2001 a revised funding package was agreed. Work on the project commenced in 2002 and the extension was expected to be fully complete by the 2003 season.

At peak times, a two-train service runs while, at quieter times, just a single train operates. There are two rakes of carriages, one a set of fully enclosed vehicles including a coach adapted for use by passengers with a disability. A second set of summer carriages is used when the two-train service is operated. This set had semi-open sides, but a programme to add doors and adapt one vehicle allowing accommodation for disabled passengers on both trains, was implemented during 2001. As well as evening out use of the carriage sets, the line is more likely to need to run two trains with the new extension. With two passing loops (Gilfach Ddu and Cei Llydan) a three-train service will be theoretically possible.

The railway is run by professional staff without a volunteer supporting society, the core team of permanent staff being supplemented by seasonal staff in the café, shop and ice cream kiosk.

The Great Whipsnade Railway

Plans for an internal transport system at what was then known as Whipsnade Zoo in Bedfordshire were debated during the 1960s. Two events resulted in the construction of a 2ft 6ins gauge railway within the park; the announcement that the Bowater's Paper railway would close in the autumn of 1969, and the selection of Whipsnade as the first White Rhino conservation centre outside Africa.

Although Bowater's were keen that part of their industrial railway should be preserved - resulting in the present Sittingbourne and Kemsley Light Railway - a lot of equipment was surplus. At Whipsnade, an area of the park was landscaped to house the White Rhino herd, but the paddock could only be accessed by the public on one side. Constructing a railway would allow visitors to view the animals from the train. The availability of sturdy 2ft 6ins gauge Bowater's equipment provided the answer to the provision of locomotives and rolling stock, and plans were rapidly drawn up.

A company named Pleasurerail Ltd was formed by Mr (later Sir) William McAlpine, and others, to build and operate the railway under licence from the Zoological Society of London. Initially, the line was to be experimental, with the intention of extending it if successful. Although always intended to operate on a commercial basis, the people who set up Pleasurerail were also railway enthusiasts and, particularly in the early days, the line tended to 'feel' like a preservation project. Ex-Lodge Hill & Upnor Railway Manning Wardle 0-6-2T *Chevallier* (in dismantled condition) and Kerr Stuart 0-4-2T *Excelsior* were purchased privately, while Pleasurerail bought Kerr Stuart 0-6-2T *Superior* and W G Bagnall 0-6-2T *Conqueror* - all from Bowater's,

Following an early career working in industry on the Bowater's paper system in Kent, Kerr Stuart 0-6-2T *Superior* found a new lease of life hauling passenger trains in Whipsnade Wild Animal Park.

although not all were serviceable. The passenger coaches were conversions based on ex-Bowater's bogie frames and, although altered over the years, remain in use today.

The Whipsnade and Umfolozi Railway ran for 1,000 yards into the Rhino paddock from a small station. There were two platforms, but no run round loop, and a combined booking office/souvenir shop was created from a signal box relocated from the standard gauge Leighton Buzzard - Linslade line. A second box from that line was placed just outside the station, adjacent to a turnout accessing a yard complex. A special combined bridge/ditch/fence (known as a HaHa) was devised to allow the train to enter the paddock while preventing the animals escaping. The track ended in a sand drag just short of the far end of the paddock, the railway operating on a simple push-pull principle. At the end of the line was a signpost which pointed 'To Umfolozi 5,753 miles', being the original home of the Rhino herd sharing their new home with the fledgling railway and inspiring its name.

The first train, hauled by *Chevallier*, ran on 26 August 1970 and, by the summer of 1972, the railway was clearly popular with the public and had been accepted by the animals. Work began on an extension of about a mile through additional paddocks to make the railway a continuous circuit. A junction with the existing line was made at the throat of the station and the extra construction included four new HaHa's and what has become known as the 'tunnel', where a concrete walled cutting becomes a bridge under one of the zoo roads. A new station, with loop, was constructed behind the Sea Lion pool (then the Dolphinarium) and the signalbox from the old station relocated. The new station, Whipsnade Central, included a gated level crossing over Central Avenue.

The extended railway was officially inaugurated on 2nd August 1973 when *Conqueror* hauled a Royal Train for HRH The Princess Margaret. When the circuit was completed, exper-

iments established that running clockwise was the best method of operating, and this has remained. Between 1975 and 1990, a relaid siding in the disused original station accommodated 3ft 6ins gauge stock from Africa owned by artist and railway enthusiast David Shepherd. This consisted of a Sharpe Stewart Class 7 4-8-0 locomotive, an ex-Rhodesia Railways sleeping car and a converted 1938 Ford Prefect, reproducing a car used as an inspection trolley on the Zambezi Sawmills Railway.

By 1985, the zoo had decided to rearrange the animal displays and when the Rhinos were moved to a new location, the Whipsnade & Umfolozi title for the railway became redundant. The new name of Great Whipsnade Railway was adopted, a title which would not become dated again in the event of the animals, or indeed route of the line, being changed.

In 1990, the railway was sold to the Zoological Society of London, the last train under Pleasurerail ownership being hauled by *Superior* on 28 October 1990. Although ownership changed, management of the line initially did not, and the 1990s saw a period of enthusiast-oriented activity including a series of locomotive visits between Whipsnade and the Welshpool & Llanfair Light Railway; *Chevallier* and *Superior* visited Wales, while *Dougal* and No 14 (SLR 85) travelled to Bedfordshire. The development of an annual May Steam Up weekend at Whipsnade, featuring traction engines, etc., also resulted in special operation on the railway involving double headed working and demonstration goods trains.

A new manager in the mid-1990s implemented several changes. *Conqueror* (not used since about 1983) was sold, leaving the Park on 15 December 1994 initially going into private storage. The sale funded several improvements including re-cladding the loco shed and substantial work on *Superior* and *Excelsior*. A track improvement programme resulted in substantial relaying while the fitting of flange lubricators to locomotives and stock has also helped alleviate the historic legacy of sharp curves

Steam and snow! Kerr Stuart 0-6-2T *Superior* hauls a January 1995 train through a snow-covered Whipsnade Wild Animal Park.

not enter service when it arrived at the Park in October 1998. A full rebuild was completed during 2000. Meanwhile, time was found to resolve *Victor*'s problems and that loco returned to working order. *Chevallier*, which remains privately-owned by Sir William McAlpine although still at Whipsnade, was withdrawn from service in September 1995 and needs a thorough overhaul.

The two-mile line now runs through the Asia region and traverses three separate paddocks with a trip taking around 15 minutes. Over the years there have been numerous schemes to extend the line, none of which progressed. The railway is viewed as an essential element in the attractions of what is now called Whipsnade Wild Animal Park, providing a means of seeing animals in a way not otherwise possible and making a sizeable contribution to the Park's revenue. History has turned full circle in one respect - during 1998 a new enclosure was built beside the line to house Asiatic Greater One-Horned Rhino - a different species from that which inspired construction of the railway, and fenced off from the train, but steam and Rhinos are reunited!

The Great Orme Tramway

The tramway climbing from Llandudno up the Great Orme is effectively a 3ft 6ins gauge funicular, operated in two independent sections. At the lower end, it is a street Tramway, while it runs on the open slopes of the Great Orme at the upper end.

The Great Orme Tramways Act was passed on 23 May 1898 and construction of the lower section started in April 1901 with the first passengers carried on 31 July 1902. The upper section opened on 8 July 1903 and the line was largely complete by 1905. A serious accident on 23 August 1932 resulted in The Great Orme Tramways Company going into liquidation to avoid consequent claims - the insurance company denied liability when it was discovered that the (then) emergency braking system had been disconnected some years earlier! A new company, the Great Orme Railway Company Ltd, took over from the liquidator at the end of the 1934 season. Llandudno Urban District Council exercised its right to purchase the tramway and took over on 1 January 1949. It then passed to successor authorities under local government reorganisations: from April 1974 Aberconwy Borough Council, followed in 1996 by Conwy County Council.

Late in the 1980s, the Railway Inspectorate warned that action was needed if the tramway was to stay open. Aberconwy Borough Council placed operation of the tramway in the hands of its Trading Department, Grwp Aberconwy, and a five year business plan and £400,000 investment programme was agreed to commence in spring 1990. Summit station was rebuilt and Victoria station improved, but reconstruction at Halfway had not progressed when Conwy County Council assumed responsibility in 1996.

Inconceivably, as the tramway approached its 100th birthday, closure was a real threat. Although some £160,000 had been spent during the winter of 1996/97, when the Railway Inspectorate and the line's insurers visited prior to the 1997 season, the trams had

along the route. The yard has been remodelled, with revised sidings and a proper access road, and the passenger platforms at the main station have been reconstructed.

The railway has two 1951-vintage Fowler 100hp 0-6-0 diesel locomotives. The loco now named *Hector* arrived at Whipsnade having been purchased from the Welsh Highland Light Railway (1964) Company, while that given the name *Victor* was purchased from the Welshpool & Llanfair Railway where it was named *Wynnstay*. The railway also has a Ruston & Hornsby Ltd 48 DL Class diesel *Mr Bill* (after Sir William McAlpine!) which was acquired, plus some wagons and vans, in 1992 from the Broughton Moor Military depot in Cumbria. *Hector*, being equipped with vacuum braking can work passenger trains, but *Victor* has always been limited to non-passenger duties.

By about 1996 *Victor* was suffering various mechanical ills and looked likely to end up a source of spares for his companion. A search for a new large diesel resulted in the purchase of a 1981-built 340hp LyD2 from a sugar beet works near the Poland/Ukraine border. Although supposedly overhauled in 1992 when it received a new Romanian Mercedes/Maybach engine, followed by four years of service then storage, it could

Great Orme Tramway Cars Nos 5 and 4 pass at the loop on the lower section. Llandudno and the sea lies beyond in this view.

difficulty even getting down the track. In places, rail had been burnt out and, on some corners, cars parted company with the rails, running across concrete before finding the track again!

A new Transport Manager had recently been appointed, but only handed responsibility for the tramway in March 1997. He was given a week to have the line ready to open! A terrific effort saw 60 base plates changed, many new sleepers installed, sections of guide rail reinstated and 'top hats' and rollers replaced. Although the line reached a suitable condition to open for the new season, it had been a knife-edge decision as to whether it would run again. With that crisis resolved, a total refurbishment programme was planned, the first phase commencing during the 1997/98 winter when around £130,000 was spent on replacing over 50% of the rollers, pulleys and base plates. A further £220,000 programme was completed just before opening for the 1999 season.

With the tramway back to a reasonable standard, an application to the National Heritage Lottery fund was submitted in July 1998 and, in the following February, an award of £916,000 was announced as part of a £2.36 million work programme. This investment was soon increased to become a £4.5 million package, enhancements including the total reconstruction of Halfway. Work started in November 2000, the equipment inside the control room was removed and the buildings demolished. The new structure, operational for the 2001 season, is a single building incorporating a covered walkway for passengers to transfer between trams and a museum. The public can view the new

control room, which contains new electrical components, winding motors and gearboxes. Other work includes progressive relaying of the lower section over a four-year period, work on the lower section trams and a new radio system.

Four tramcars - Nos 4 and 5 arrived in 1902, Nos 6 and 7 in 1903 - were built by Hurst Nelson of Motherwell. Numbers 1-3 were 4-wheel vans (known as 'Jockey cars') built to transport coke to the Winding Station (the Winding House was steam powered until October 1957 when electric equipment entered service) and carry any goods traffic. They had gone by 1930, their fate being unrecorded. Two of the cars, Nos 4 and 5, are always on the lower section while cars 6 and 7 stay on the upper section. The 2000/01 improvement programme included complete reconstruction of the body of car No 5, plus major refurbishment of all four bogies of the lower section trams.

The 872-yard bottom section, from Victoria Station to the Winding House at Halfway, has two cables, one for each car, in underground conduits. A car is hauled up from Victoria Station by the winding engine, while the other is simultaneously lowered down. The cars are not directly counterbalanced, although there is some connection via the winding drums. This section has an average gradient of 1 in 6 and passes initially up Old Road, where traffic is banned during tram operation. Next comes a traffic light controlled junction, followed by a length of reserved track beside the road, with a passing loop just before the steepest section (about 1 in 3.9) on Killens Hill.

At Halfway, passengers transfer to an upper section tram. On this 827- yard section, there are three cables - one between each car and the Winding House with a third linking the cars via a pulley wheel at the summit. The tail rope between the cars provides a counterbalance between trams, the Winding House actually pulling the top car down, the tail rope in turn pulling the other car up. The upper section is less steep than the lower, the maximum gradient being 1 in 8, and cables and related equipment are above ground. On the top section, trams share the same track (other than the mid-way passing loop!) whereas on the lower, the tracks are interlaced.

Although the trams were originally fitted with poles, these did not collect electric current (as with conventional tramways) but provided a communication system via an overhead wire. This was replaced in spring 1990 by a dual use radio link, although the poles remained on the tram cars. The 2000/01 upgrade programme introduced a complex new radio system. Costing some £250,000, this included control panels on the driving platforms allowing the driver to control the tram by electronic communication with the winding house.

Alford Valley Railway

The operational base of this 2ft gauge line is at the old standard gauge Alford station, the terminus of a branch which linked Upper Donside with Kintore Junction until closure in 1960. The old standard gauge carriage shed now serves as a locomotive and carriage shed for the narrow gauge line, which does not utilise the standard gauge trackbed, other than within the yard area. The Alford Valley Railway Association was formed by enthusiasts in 1979 and a Light Railway Order for the 2ft gauge project was obtained in 1980. The initial track, internal combustion locomotives and some wagons were obtained from a line at New Pitsligo, used by a peat cutting operation.

Track was laid for some 1¾ miles to form a railway of two sections: from Alford station, through a golf course to Haughton Country Park, originally the grounds of Haughton House, and from Haughton Country Park station along one of the old entrance driveways to Haughton House to a caravan site at Murray Park. The Haughton Park to Murray Park section was officially opened in May 1980, with the second phase being in use from 1984. In recent years, the full track length has not been used, trains running over the first ¾ mile between Alford station and Haughton Country Park station. The line is operated by the Alford Valley Railway Company, a non-profit company, which ploughs income back into the railway.

The railway operates a steam locomotive, Fowler 0-4-2T (13355/14) *Saccharine*, which was brought back to Britain in 1979 and entered service around 1988 - the name alluding to its days on a sugar plantation near Durban, South Africa. There are also two Motor Rail Simplex 4wDMs (one with an original Dorman engine, the other with a Perkins engine) and a 1931-vintage Lister 4wDM. The locomotive fleet was enhanced in July 2001 when a new 3.5 ton steam outline (0-4-0T) diesel loco constructed by Alan Keef Ltd (AK63/2001) entered service. The railway has four carriages, two built by Severn Lamb for the Warwick Castle Railway and a third constructed with the help of Aberdeen Technical College. The other vehicle is the restored lower saloon of what was originally a 4-wheel double deck tram built for the Aberdeen Suburban Tramways Company. The vehicle could have originally been No 11 built in 1911, although the AVR believes it dates from 1895. Railway-style platforms have been fitted and the body mounted on a pair of 2ft gauge bogies.

The original standard gauge station building was reconstructed in 1982 and is part of the Grampian Transport Museum, a separate undertaking, although it works in concert with the railway on marketing, etc. This collection includes a 3ft 6ins gauge 1899-vintage Cruden Bay tramcar - reconstructed using the best parts of two trams from the line which used to connect the Cruden Bay Hotel with the Great North of Scotland Railway. Also noteworthy is the standard gauge Aberdeen horse tram No 1 from 1896.

Other pleasure lines which have come and gone

Rounding off this selection of lines constructed for the leisure industry are three 'modern' examples, all employing equipment available following the closure of industrial systems. As such, they were of much interest to enthusiasts, as well as serving the paying public.

The 18ins gauge Bicton Woodland Railway was constructed for commercial purposes, the availability of suitable narrow gauge equipment presenting the solution to a requirement. For the line's first 36 years, historic narrow gauge locomotives and equipment found a new lease of life and earned their keep - preservation being more a happy by-product than a specific objective. The railway remains, although post-2000 it adopted a different form, and one which does not fall within the parameters of this book. The stock, however, will before too long again provide the basis of a new narrow gauge railway.

The 2ft gauge line in the grounds of Knebworth House was built and run as a basically commercial operation, although the principals of Pleasurerail Ltd were enthusiasts. Over some 18 years, many interesting locomotives were housed at the site, all now at other lines where they are either operational or being overhauled. Although the narrow gauge has gone, a railway of a different form has subsequently been operated at the location.

The 60cm (2ft) gauge Lincolnshire Coast Light Railway was built by enthusiasts, but with the intention of commercial operation. The line ran for 25 years, seeing intense activity during its four-month summer seasons and, following closure, most of the equipment was put into store, but it could soon work again on a new site.

Bicton Woodland Railway

The gardens at Bicton, Devon (north of Budleigh Salterton) date from 1735. Bicton House and Home Farm were sold in 1957, the gardens becoming a separate attraction under independent

Fowler 0-4-2T (13355/14) *Saccharine* **outside the old standard gauge carriage shed at Alford. It now serves as a locomotive and carriage shed for the Alford Valley Railway.** *(James Gordon)*

ownership, opening to the public in 1961. Realising that an additional attraction was needed, in October 1961, the idea of laying a miniature railway arose. A survey was undertaken, but doubts concerned the suitability of 15ins gauge equipment for the gradients and sharp curves involved - and the cost of equipment looked prohibitive. A reappraisal led to the idea of adopting narrow gauge to provide the required power with shorter wheelbase stock.

The Royal Arsenal at Woolwich was founded in 1805 and a tramway was developed from the 1820s, becoming an 18in gauge system linking key buildings by the 1860s. The first steam locomotive arrived in 1871, and the railway was officially opened in 1873. The South Eastern Railway provided the main line connection to the complex, and the internal network connected the main buildings, a canal, and wharves on the River Thames. This system grew to over 30 miles of 18ins gauge track and 25 miles of mixed gauge (standard and 18ins) by the 1900s and peaked during WWI with over 100 miles of narrow gauge track, and more than 60 locomotives. The network was basically circular, minimising the need for trains to reverse, with branches and wagon turntables serving various locations, the 18in gauge coping with the sharp curves. The Royal Arsenal Railway was eventually run in six sections and included internal passenger services with 1st, 2nd and 3rd Class accommodation, the stock ranging from proper carriages through to open knifeboard vehicles. After WWI, production of armaments reduced, and the railway declined. By 1922, 10 steam locos remained and all passenger trains were 3rd Class. Stock started to be sold in 1933, but some revival came during WW2 when diesel locomotives arrived. The use of steam ceased in 1960 and the Arsenal closed in 1967.

The oil-fired 0-4-0T steam locomotive *Woolwich* was built in 1916 by Avonside Engine Co (1748/16) and had been in the yard of E L Pitt & Co Ltd at Brackley, Northamptonshire for 18

months after leaving The Royal Arsenal. Offered as a solution to the requirements of the proposed line in Bicton Gardens, the loco was inspected on 27 November 1961. Deciding that it would be suited to the planned new line, *Woolwich* was returned to working order by J & W Gower of Bedford, and with the spark arresting chimney replaced by a conventional chimney, a steam test - with the wheels jacked clear of the ground - was performed in their yard on 9 April 1962. Two days later, the locomotive was moved to Bicton, now sporting a blue livery, replacing the original Woolwich green. Six covered wagons and an open goods wagon were purchased from The Royal Arsenal during March. Since the covered wagons had carried explosives, regulations required that the wooden bodies be burnt prior to disposal, hence the Bicton line acquired only the bogies and frames.

The first track at Bicton Gardens was laid on 3 May 1962 in the area which would be the station, with the rest of the line proceeding in earnest from mid June and completed on 10 August 1962. The rail was flat-bottomed 30lb/yd material, laid on sleepers cut in the Estate sawmill from timber grown on the Estate, although ex-BR sleepers were laid under the points. Signals from the Exeter - Exmouth line were installed and the railway opened in 1963. The line commenced from a terminus at Bicton station, skirted the lake and entered the Pinetum. At Pine Junction a platform was built, the track then diverging around a balloon loop through the Lower Pinetum, before returning to Pine Junction and back to Bicton station - the loco now facing in the opposite direction from that on departure. The total length of track, including sidings, was 1,359 yards, although since the train traversed the Bicton Gardens station to Pine Junction section twice in a journey, passengers travelled over 1,617 yards (excluding sidings) during one complete trip. A siding was added at Pine Junction in June 1963 to accommodate

Peckett 0-6-0ST *Triassic*
shunts around in the yard at
Knebworth. The picture is
believed to have been taken
in 1983.

a buffet car, although this was lifted and re-laid at Bicton station in February 1966. Also in 1966, the 1962-built locomotive shed was extended, and an island platform built at the station.

An additional loco was needed to help with summer traffic and No 2 *Bicton* arrived May 1963. This was a Ruston & Hornsby (works number 213839) 16/20hp, built (apparently) in 1942 for the WD Storage Depot at Lion Brickworks, Scalford, Leicestershire. It later went to a 15ins gauge line in Sussex, but was never regauged. For use at Bicton, a body and cab were fitted. In February 1966, the opportunity to acquire another loco from The Royal Arsenal arose, an 0-4-4-0DM 88hp articulated diesel, built Hunslet Engine Co (HE4524/54) which entered service in April 1966 as No 3 *Carnegie*. This is one of just two diesels surviving from The Royal Arsenal railway, *Woolwich* being the only steam survivor.

The first carriages utilised the ex-Woolwich underframes with bodies constructed at Bicton Gardens to provide open and closed vehicles. These were supplemented by two ex-RAF Fauld coaches (one was later rebuilt onto an ex-Woolwich frame) a 4-wheel guard's van and the 1914-vintage ex-Woolwich goods wagon. The buffet coach was converted into a passenger coach in April 1966. Later, ex-LNWR Wolverton Works four-wheel wagons were acquired.

The railway did not operate during 1998, when Bicton Gardens were for sale. They were sold on 23 December 1998, the new owner announcing that the railway figured in his future plans. A franchise to run the line was agreed with a previous manager and the track brought up to passenger-carrying standard following a year without maintenance, so that trains could run during 1999. During the winter of 1999/2000, a major re-think resulted in the decision to sell the historic locomotives and

rolling stock and re-equip the railway with 'steam outline' locos and new passenger carriages supplied by Alan Keef Ltd. The track layout has remained the same.

No 1 *Woolwich*, No 3 *Carnegie*, seven coaches, three ex-LNWR Wolverton Works four-wheel wagons and a spare ex-Woolwich underframe were offered for sale. These were purchased by the Waltham Abbey Royal Gunpowder Mills Co Ltd and moved from Bicton Gardens on 17 October 2000. *Carnegie* was taken to the works of Alan Keef Ltd for an overhaul, *Woolwich* and the remaining equipment arriving at Waltham Abbey on 18 October.

Gunpowder production on the Waltham Abbey site dates back to the 15th century. Having become a research and development centre, The Royal Gunpowder Mills closed in 1991. The Waltham Abbey Royal Gunpowder Mills covers 170 acres, includes 21 Listed structures, and two thirds of the buildings are scheduled as ancient monuments. Supported by the Heritage Lottery Fund, the site opened as a visitor attraction in 2001 with the railway equipment initially placed on display. A running line is to be built on part of the route of the original narrow gauge railway which transported gunpowder from the Magazines to the Process Building prior to WWI. Although steam was never originally present on the site, the new home for the ex-Royal Arsenal locomotive seems very appropriate.

Knebworth West Park & Winter Green Railway

The 2ft gauge railway at Knebworth House was built by Pleasurerail Ltd, the company which also set up the 2ft 6ins gauge line at Whipsnade Zoo at about the same time. By July 1972, around a mile of track had been laid. The station and yard was to the west of Knebworth House and, from the station area, the line headed generally southwest into the grounds. On reaching a junction, the tracks divided at a sprung point and described a large (and irregularly shaped) balloon loop, to return to the junction and back to the station, trains now facing in the opposite direction from the start of the journey. There were sidings in the station area, and running sheds for locomotives and stock. The journey took about 15 minutes, with passenger trains running at an average speed of 7/8mph.

The railway appears to have been carrying passengers from the beginning of the 1972 season, with services advertised up to end of September 1972. A 'Stately Steam-Up' was held on 22nd July 1972 when Avonside 0-4-0T *Sezela No 4* disgraced herself by derailing - apparently the regulator initially refused to open, then did so unexpectedly with the loco in gear, whereupon she launched forth, and off the end of the track! The loco was then stripped down and overhauled, entering service in August 1973. Other locomotives on the railway at this time were Hunslet 0-4-0ST *No 1*, Hunslet 0-4-0ST *Lilla*, and three diesels.

Over the ensuing years, several other locomotives spent periods at Knebworth, although not necessarily in working order. These included Peckett 0-6-0ST *Triassic*, Bagnall 4-4-0T *Sezela No 23*, O&K 0-6-0WT *Sao Domingos* and O&K 0-6-0WT *Pedemoura*. There were also occasional visiting locomotives for special events, including Bagnall 0-4-0ST *Pixie* from Cadeby.

The steam locomotives have been at various other sites since leaving Knebworth, their current locations being: *No 1* Bredgar & Wormshill Railway now *Lady Joan*, *Lilla* Ffestiniog Railway, *Triassic* Bala Lake Railway, *Sezela No 4* Leighton Buzzard Railway, *Sezela No 23* North Gloucestershire Railway, *Sao Domingos* Bredgar and Wormshill, *Pedemoura* Welsh Highland Railway (Porthmadog).

Passenger vehicles for the opening consisted of five open-sided vehicles, each seating 30 people. Initially, at least, they did not have doors, brakes or safety chains.

The 2ft gauge line technically ceased operations on 14th September 1990, but it seems some track was relaid for a Bonfire Night Special that year. The track was then entirely lifted and removed, along with remaining equipment. A 7¼ins gauge miniature line was subsequently laid and operated at Knebworth.

Lincolnshire Coast Light Railway
The use of narrow gauge lines in the Lincolnshire potato industry was once extensive. A leading producer was W Dennis & Sons, their Littleworth estate having some 20 miles of 2ft gauge track by 1916. They started a new estate at Nocton in 1920/21 and developed a railway employing surplus War Department Light Railway equipment. This estate was sold to Smiths (potato crisps!) in 1936 and the narrow gauge system remained operational until the mid-1950s when improvements to farm roads aimed to replace the light railway lines. The Nocton system was largely out of use by autumn 1960, closing finally in 1969.

In 1958, a group of enthusiasts decided to create and operate a narrow gauge railway in Lincolnshire. The idea was to operate commercially in a promising location, utilising ex-WDLR equipment available from the contracting potato estates. A limited company was formed to finance the scheme and an approach to

Grimsby Rural District Council led to a suitable site being leased at Humberston, three miles north of Cleethorpes.

Construction of the 60cm gauge line commenced in April 1960 when a hired bulldozer levelled the trackbed and station sites. Commencing at a terminus called North Sea Lane station, where there were various holiday camps, the railway headed east, beside St Anthony's Bank and the road towards the sea for some 700 yards and used 20lb/yd steel-sleepered track, ballasted by boiler ash. At North Sea Lane there was a run round loop and siding, while the other terminus, named Beach (not far from 'The Fitties' and another holiday camp) had just a run round loop - both stations having a short platform. The railway was officially opened on 27 August 1960, trains consisting of a Simplex locomotive hauling a single open bogie coach. Despite the short season (trains stopped at the end of September) some 8,000 passengers were carried in the first year of operation.

For the following season, a passing loop was added mid-way along the line. Motor Rail locomotives arrived and additional coaches entered service. The big step forwards was the introduction of steam, ex-Southam Limeworks (1008/03) Peckett 0-6-0ST *Jurassic* hauling trains during the final week of the season. In 1962, a two-road running shed was built at North Sea Lane, an ex-Ashover Railway coach entered service and *Jurassic* regularly provided steam at weekends. Passenger figures were climbing - during the 1964 season some 60,000 passengers travelled over the line - in a year when all services were diesel hauled and steam did not figure!

The success of the railway attracted bus competition and the idea of extending the line to get the train closer to the Fitties Holiday Camp and caravan site had been conceived in 1963. During 1965, the railway was operated by paid staff while the volunteers concentrated on maintenance and preparations for building the extension. Negotiations with Grimsby RDC were concluded, but the railway was to be rebuilt on a new alignment. This was to the south of the St Anthony's Bank access road, about 30 yards from the original location, then parallel to the original alignment until swinging south east near the old Beach terminus, then parallel to the coast to a new terminus, near the Foreshore Inn, named South Sea Lane station - a distance of one mile, and more convenient for Fitties camp. Work on the new line was undertaken during 1966. By July, the track reached the site of the new Beach station (with passing loop) and, in August, a temporary platform was built 200 yards from South Sea Lane so that trains could run over the new route. The last passenger service over the old line ran on Sunday 14 August, and the inaugural train over new line operated the following day. The new main line was completed on 23 October 1966, using ex-Nocton and Penrhyn quarry rail, laid on ex-BR sleepers sawn in half.

A combined station/carriage shed was constructed at North Sea Lane, with half of the platform covered by an overall roof, the locomotive shed was relocated in 1968 and during 1969, the last materials were recovered from the original line. The 'new' railway was a success, in 1968 a traffic record was set when 70,000 passengers were carried - the trains being run 13 hours a day, seven days a week, during the four month season!

Lincolnshire Coast Light Railway Peckett 0-6-0ST *Jurassic* outside the shed in 1983, shortly before the line closed. *(David H Smith)*

Hunslet 0-4-0ST *Elin* (705/99 but now with a Marshall boiler) arrived in November 1969. Purchased by a director of the LCLR in 1962 from Penrhyn quarry, she had been overhauled and regauged to 60cm for use on the LCLR, but proved too heavy for the line and saw little use. Bagnall 0-4-0ST *Peter*, which had been purchased by the Narrow Gauge Railway Society, arrived in 1961 but never actually worked on the line and left in May 1963. The diesel locomotives were mainly Motor Rail Simplex's, although there was a Ruston & Hornsby 27/30 which was scrapped in 1968.

The rolling stock all came from Nocton, other than a skip frame and three coach bodies. The Nocton equipment included two bogie vans (WDLR ambulance vans), ex-WDLR 'D' drop-side open wagons, and 1-ton WDLR 4-wheel 'P' open wagons. The first coaches to enter service were based on 'D' wagons, with open bodies constructed by the LCLR. Two ex-Ashover Railway carriage bodies which had served as 'stands' at a football field following the withdrawal of Ashover passenger services were renovated and placed on ex-Nocton WDLR bogies. The other body was the saloon coach (and sole passenger vehicle) from the Sand Hutton Railway which was mounted on two reconstructed timber-framed 'D' wagons. The ex-Nocton vans were used mainly as mobile stores, although one was fitted out as a mobile booking office for South Sea Lane station during 1969.

In the early 1980s, the railway continued to thrive, but various problems then arose. Following an unfortunate incident, air braking was fitted to *Jurassic*, two Simplex locos and four of the coaches. The coal dispute and miners' strike in 1984 affected traffic but, more seriously, the local Council was insisting on various onerous conditions, including six foot high fencing on each side of the track. The combination of circumstances led to

closure of the railway in 1985 and the track was lifted shortly after. *Jurassic*, last steamed at the Leighton Buzzard Railway in 1987, has been in storage since. LCLR stock had been sold by the operating company to the Lincolnshire Coast Light Railway Historical Vehicles Trust, including one of the 'ambulance' vans (the other went to the South Tynedale Railway), two 'D' wagons and a 'P' wagon. These items were displayed at the Beverley Army Museum for a time, but are now stored in Lincolnshire. *Elin* was sold in 1986 and is now at the Yaxham Light Railway.

In 1993 *Jurassic*, five Simplex locomotives, the two ex-Ashover coaches, the Sand Hutton coach, two other passenger vehicles, two 'P' wagons and the rails were moved to Skegness Water Leisure Park in Winthorpe. Some of the stock deteriorated during a period of open storage, although restoration has taken place since the equipment was under cover at the Water Leisure Park site. Commencing at a sizeable shed, the new LCLR line has a fan of five sidings at this building merging into a single line to a run-round loop where a platform will be constructed. From the platform, the running line initially runs straight, then swings to the left as it approaches a wooded area. It continues, with a drainage dyke to the right, until reaching a run-round loop - a total run between loops of about 650 yards. Progress has been slow due to a limited number of volunteers and, at the time of writing, no public trains have run on this line. Meanwhile, Ashover coach No 2 has been restored to operational condition, the original longitudinal seating plan has been reinstated and the coach repainted - retaining the blue body with cream window surrounds which was adopted when first returned to operation on the Lincolnshire coast line. Unfortunately, the restoration to steam of *Jurassic* was delayed following the theft of various items early in 2001.

CHAPTER FIVE

On Standard Gauge trackbeds

For some decades, the Ashover Light Railway could be considered the last narrow gauge line of any significant length built in Britain. This claim has had to be modified more recently.

While the wholesale cutting back of the national system was not to be applauded, it left many attractive stretches of disused railway in its wake. In some cases, standard gauge restoration projects took shape, but, in others, the opportunity to construct a new narrow gauge line on the old standard gauge formation was presented.

The Bala Lake Railway was the first narrow gauge line to be built on an abandoned BR trackbed, its founder inspired by its scenic location. The South Tynedale and Teifi Valley lines were originally to be standard gauge restorations but changed circumstances resulted in revised plans, while the people behind the Brecon Mountain and Launceston Steam Railways were searching for suitable locations on which to achieve their respective narrow gauge ambitions. While the thinking behind the building of this group of lines varied, the advantages are obvious. Constructing a wholly new railway from scratch, certainly over any distance, is hideously expensive. An old trackbed provides a linear route which may not be ready-made, but presents far less problems (hence relatively less expense) in being brought up to suitable standard than attempting to construct over virgin ground - and securing planning approval is more straightforward. Carrying people for pleasure has not simply enabled the revival of closed lines, but made the construction of essentially new narrow gauge railways viable.

Rheilffordd Llyn Tegid (The Bala Lake Railway)

The Bala Lake Railway runs beside the southern shore of Llyn Tegid (Bala Lake) - the largest natural lake in Wales - on part of the trackbed of an old GWR secondary main line between Ruabon and Barmouth. After rationalisation in 1948, most of the line's traffic was diverted to the former Cambrian line between Welshpool and Machynlleth, the Llangollen to Barmouth section closing on 15th January 1965. The standard gauge Llangollen Railway has since reopened the Llangollen to Carrog section and plans to extend to Corwen.

George Barnes conceived the idea of building a narrow gauge railway beside the lake. By 1969, he had approached the influential figure of Tom Jones, resident in Llanuwchllyn and a Member of Meirioneth County Council. Alderman Jones was a railway enthusiast who saw the possibilities and backed the idea. He also revealed that the Council were in the process of purchasing the standard gauge trackbed, although with no firm plans for the land, simply envisaging the possibility of highway improvements and 'recreational use.' In 1971 Tom Jones, George Barnes and others formed a new company - the first to be registered in the Welsh language (Rheilffordd Llyn Tegid Ltd, later amended to Rheilffordd Llyn Tegid Cyf) - to build a 2ft gauge line.

A small diesel loco, rails and some wagons arrived in the winter of 1971 and tracklaying commenced in early 1972. The first 1¼ mile section from Llanuwchllyn was opened to the public on 13th August 1972. Further lengths were completed and opened in stages - Llangower being reached in September 1972, Pant-yr-hen-felin by the 1975 season and finally Pont Mwnwgl y Llyn (or Penybont) for 1976. The latter remains the terminus and is about half a mile from the centre of Bala. An extension into the town was envisaged, but has never been built.

The railway was conceived as a commercial operation. Initially worked by paid staff, there were volunteers from the beginning, a supporting Society becoming established in 1976. Following a financial crisis, volunteers took an increased role in operating the railway from the 1987 season and Society volunteers still support the nucleus of paid staff.

The HQ of the railway is at Llanuwchllyn. To build the narrow gauge line, the level was raised between the platforms and the station building reconstructed in 1979-80 by adding a new floor to make it two-storeys, along with a new entrance. The former waiting room is now a buffet, and the seating section was formally a waiting room at Barmouth Junction. The original toilet block and booking office were replaced by extensions based on the original style. A canopy, originally at the Cambrian station at Pwllheli, then moved to Aberdovey, arrived at Llanuwchllyn in 1979 and was added over the main passenger platform. The waiting room on the non-passenger platform serves as an office.

A loco shed, carriage sheds and workshops were constructed for the narrow gauge line with a resulting network of sidings.

The 1868 stone goods shed remains, now used for storage, although a grain store extension (built by the GWR in 1911) was demolished in 1998 having fallen into disrepair. The line drops down through fields towards the lake shore, which lays to the left of the train for the remainder of the route.

Midway along is Llangower station, serving a stony beach, with a passing loop. The terminus at Bala (Penybont) is on the site of an 1868 station which closed in 1886. The present station, opened in 1976, had a wooden platform which was replaced in 1988-89 with concrete block walling. The opportunity was also taken to lengthen it, and a bay platform and siding were added. Until the mid-1990s, a GWR corrugated iron shed, originally a lamp store, served as a platform shelter. It was replaced by a modern 'bus shelter' type construction - a modernised version of a GWR Pagoda waiting shelter! The old shed, restored to original appearance, is now at Carrog station on the Llangollen Railway.

George Barnes believed the ideal size for narrow gauge railway equipment lay somewhere between the 15ins gauge Ravenglass & Eskdale and the more conventional proportions of the historic Welsh 2ft gauge railways. This explains the appearance of the B-B diesel-hydraulic *Meirionnydd*, built by Severn Lamb in 1973, which looks like a main line diesel built to a smaller scale. Used extensively in the early years, it fell out of use, but was overhauled and equipped with a new engine in 2000. Henschel 0-4-0T *Helen Kathryn* was the first steam loco to run at Llanuwchllyn, although it was really too large and left in 1975. Regular steam-hauled services commenced in 1975 when Hunslet 0-4-0ST *Maid Marian* arrived. She was joined later that year by Hunslet 0-4-0ST *Holy War*, although the latter did not enter traffic until 1979. This pair has remained the core of the

steam motive power, and the transition of the railway to a more conventional narrow gauge line largely dates from the arrival of these locos.

Other steam locomotives have worked on the railway, including a Kerr Stuart 'Wren' and Hunslet 0-4-0ST *Jonathan*, although clearance problems restricted its use. In 1992, the Peckett 0-6-0ST *Triassic* arrived at the railway and ran in service until withdrawal in 1999 for overhaul. The railway has also entertained visiting locomotives, no less than four attending the biggest enthusiast event ever on the line over 14/15 August 1999. Designed to celebrate the Silver Jubilee of the Society (it is best not to calculate the dates too closely, the early years of the Society were somewhat shaky!) the visitors included De Winton 0-4-0VTB *Chaloner* and Hunslet 0-4-0STs *Cloister*, *Una* and *Alice*. For *Alice*, this represented a return, since her restoration was started at Llanuwchllyn, although she left before completion. Other visitors over the years have included Kerr Stuart 0-4-0ST *Peter Pan*, Hunslet 0-4-0ST *Britomart* and ex-Penrhyn Hunslet 0-4-0ST *Lilla*.

There are several diesel locos, many of which are privately-owned, although the company owns the useful 0-4-0 Baguley-Drewry/YEC *Bob Davies*, and *Chilmark*, a heavily rebuilt 40hp Ruston & Hornsby. In years past, there was an active Museum Association. Following the increased involvement of volunteers in running the railway, these activities declined and many of the locos and most of the slate-industry stock has moved away.

The coaches, all bogie vehicles, were also designed on the basis of a 'semi-miniature' outline. The first pair were originally completely open sided, and ran in this form for 25 years until sides were added up to waist level. The remainder, delivered in

The fireman cleans the grate of Bala Lake Railway Hunslet 0-4-0ST *Maid Marian* at Llanuwchllyn.

two batches of differing designs between 1972 and 1981 reflect the original concept of 'expanded minimum gauge', although they did progressively increase in size. The Society has a long-term project to construct a new coach for the railway, the design of which follows a more traditional narrow gauge outline. Although the line has been home to a considerable collection of goods stock, mainly ex-MoD vehicles, these were sold by their owner late in 2001 and started to leave the railway.

The Launceston Steam Railway

The GWR, in effect, reached Launceston when the broad (7ft 0¼ins) gauge Launceston and South Devon Railway opened in 1865. Some 21 years later, the London & South Western Railway opened its standard gauge line from Halwill Junction to the town. The LSWR terminus became a through station as that company's line was extended in stages to Padstow during the 1890s. The GWR line (regauged during the 1870s) closed in 1962, and the LSWR line (by then part of the Southern Region of BR) closed in October 1966. The sites of the two stations, along with locomotive sheds and turntables, have subsequently been obliterated under what became the Newport Industrial Estate to the east of the A388 road. The 1ft 11⅝ins gauge Launceston Steam Railway has been built on part of the LSWR trackbed westwards of the road bridge over the old LSWR line - the narrow gauge line's car park (immediately east of

Bala Lake Railway Hunslet 0-4-0ST *Holy War* pictured running beside the waters of Llyn Tegid in May 1997.

the bridge) being on the site of the old LSWR station.

In 1965, Nigel Bowman purchased Hunslet 0-4-0ST *Lillian* from the Penrhyn quarry in North Wales. It was taken to his parents' home in Guildford where a workshop and foundry was erected and the loco was rebuilt during 1966/67 - while Nigel was training to be a schoolteacher! By 1968, *Lillian* had returned to steam and was occasionally run on a short length of track at a friend's farm in Surrey. A career in teaching was now abandoned as Nigel had decided he wanted to build a railway to run *Lillian*. Various locations were looked at, including a section of the old Guildford - Horsham line, but permission was refused. Nigel and a friend even considered a section of the Lynton & Barnstaple trackbed. By 1971, he had identified Launceston as a possibility. An approach to the local Council by Nigel Bowman and Jim Stone (still one of the partners who own the railway, the others being George Pitt and Kay Bowman) brought a positive response and the task of purchasing the trackbed commenced, although it took considerable time to secure some parcels of land.

Much of the Launceston terminus was scheduled for housing, but the boom had quietened by the mid-1970s. Although it now has the charm of a small country station, it had been a rail-served gas works, the retaining wall for the coal delivery siding in standard gauge times now buried under the centre of the narrow gauge platform. Buildings used by the Launceston Gas Company now accommodate the workshops (the railway is practically self-sufficient, even undertaking boiler repairs) and museum (housing vintage cars, motor cycles and stationary steam engines, including a 1905-vintage Robey engine). The café and booking office arrived at Launceston in March 1985 to be erected on the site of the old gas works coal store. This structure was originally built by Boulton & Paul Ltd., sold at the first Ideal Home Exhibition in 1919 and erected as a three-bedroom bungalow at Cranleigh in Surrey, where it remained until being dismantled. The canopy, from Tavistock North station, was presented to the Launceston Steam Railway and erected during the winter of 1986/87. The ground level of the cutting where the station and run-round loop are located was raised during the spring of 1986.

The first ½ mile section of new line was opened on Boxing Day 1983, - an out-and-back trip, with no run round loop at the far end. A further ½ mile of track followed in 1985, with another ¼ mile added later in the year to reach Hunts Crossing, where a loop was laid enabling the loco to run round the train for the first time. The next extension, of ¾ mile, was opened to Deer Park (near Newchurches) in 1988. The railway achieved its current length of 2½ miles in the summer of 1995 when another ½ mile was added to reach New Mills, where there is a farm park (under separate ownership) that provides an attraction for railway passengers wishing to break their journey.

The route includes a two-arch bridge over the River Kensey, the parapets of which were destroyed by vandals after the standard gauge line closed, and had to be rebuilt. A bridge over a farm road also required attention. Although the masonry survived, the steelwork supporting the track had to be replaced - and the reconstructed handrails include boiler tubes from the Isle of Wight locomotive W20 *Shanklin*!

The rails were acquired from sources including: Penrhyn quarry (North Wales), Tan Dinas quarry (Anglesey), Horsham sewage works (Surrey), Fayles Tramway (Dorset) and the RNAD - the material includes rails originating from the Llandudno & Colwyn Bay electric tramway and the Lynton & Barnstaple Railway! The original sleepers were mainly either ex-BR or ex-RNAD, with some experimental concrete sleepers, cast by the LSR. Relaying in recent years, which includes ex-Vale of Rheidol rail, has largely employed Australian Jarrah sleepers.

In 1984, ex-Dinorwic Hunslet 0-4-0ST *Covertcoat* (HE679/98) was purchased to operate alongside *Lillian* (HE317/83) and, in 1986, James Evans brought his Hunslet *Velinheli* (409/86) to the railway, following the closure of the family-owned Inny Valley Railway. The dismantled components of Hunslet 0-4-0ST *Dorothea* were purchased in 1989 by Kay Bowman. *Dorothea* returned to steam (borrowing *Covertcoat's* boiler) at the end of 2001, although full completion and a return to service remain some time off. The line has two Motor Rail diesels, MR5646/33 is in working order, but the other, a WW1 vintage bow-framed machine, is currently engineless. There is also an electric powered inspection trolley.

The passenger vehicles, constructed by the railway, are designed to resemble historic narrow gauge stock. The body for the first carriage built at Launceston is based on an 1893 Manx

Not a typical Launceston Steam Railway working – home-based *Lilian* and visiting *Lilla* double-head a mixed train on 23 May 1998 when the line was not open to the public.

Ex-Penrhyn Hunslet 0-4-0ST *Lilian*, with Kay Bowman on the footplate, arrives at Launceston with a service train in July 1996.

Electric Railway trailer. The next is based on a vehicle that once ran on the Torrington & Marland line in Devon (and was originally a London Horse Tram) while the third carriage was again based on an MER trailer. The fourth vehicle, which entered service at the end of 1993, was modelled on the closed coach of the short-lived Plynlimon & Hafan Tramway. A fifth carriage which also saw occasional service was constructed for use on the Inny Valley Railway and incorporated material from a Methodist Chapel, including pews! By the late 1990s, its condition deteriorating, it was basically dismantled and became a flat wagon, although the interesting woodwork has been kept and it may be restored in the future. There is also a collection of slate wagons of Penrhyn, Ffestiniog and LNWR origin and some ex-RNAD box vans.

There have always been thoughts of extending the railway beyond New Mills, 2½ miles to Egloskerry, although this remains only a long-term possibility. More immediate plans envisage the reinstatement of the loop at Deer Park to provide a passing place. Nigel Bowman also intends to build a replica Brennan monorail, some components for which have been manufactured. Initially, the Brennan vehicle will be tried on one rail of the Launceston line, but eventually a dedicated track would be built. Nigel is also one of the driving forces behind the construction of a cliff funicular between the upper and lower parts of Launceston being promoted by the Launceston Civic Society. Components from the defunct North Bay Tramway at Scarborough have been purchased and are stored at the LSR.

The railway has been privately constructed, not supported by public funds. The only approach ever made for a grant - to the English Tourist Board - was refused and the railway has not sought outside finance since.

The Brecon Mountain Railway

The Brecon Mountain Railway runs on part of the trackbed of the standard gauge Brecon & Merthyr Tydfil Junction Railway, which opened in 1859 and closed in 1964. Tony Hills purchased Hunslet 0-4-0ST *Sybil* (HE827/1903) from the Pen-yr-Orsedd quarry in September 1963 and finished rebuilding her in 1968. In 1970, *Sybil* was moved to Llanberis while her owner, in partnership with Arthur Bailey, searched for a suitable site to build a tourist railway. Locations considered included Port Dinorwic, the old standard gauge trackbed between Bala and Dolgellau, and Caernarfon.

Analysis of every disused railway line in the country produced a shortlist including routes in the Lake District and Scotland but, around 1972/73, the Brecon & Merthyr Tydfil line emerged as the favoured option. BR had sold off everything except a bridge abutment, so the rest of the route had to be purchased from 12 different landowners. Scrap merchants had removed

TOP: **The Brecon Mountain Railway restored Baldwin 4-6-2 (61269/30) from (literally) being a wreck to this awesome sight during the 1990s. Running as BMR No.2, the loco is pictured in the excellent workshop at Pant.**

LOWER: **Arnold Jung 0-6-2WT *Graf Schwerin-Lowitz* makes a steamy departure from the Pant HQ of the Brecon Mountain Railway on 16 April 2001.**

everything: rails, bridge girders, even manhole covers. The ballast had gone (for road-making) and the buildings had been cleared, apart from the shell of the signalbox at Pontsticill and the station house, which had become a sheep shelter. By 1978 planning consents had been obtained and a start made on construction. The only section of the old trackbed which could not be secured was at Pant, resulting in a 600-yard deviation to bring the line into the present day station.

The station house at Pontsticill was rebuilt, the waiting room becoming a small workshop, and a shed erected to provide storage space. After repairing and replacing seven bridges on the 1¾ mile section between Pant and Pontsticill, tracklaying started in 1979. A landslide near Pant delayed work for two months, the 1ft 11¾ins gauge line finally opening to the public in June 1980.

Trains consisted of *Sybil* hauling a single coach up the stiff gradient, while 1908-built Arnold Jung 0-6-2WT *Graf Schwerin-Lowitz* was restored. This more powerful locomotive entered service in 1981 (along with a second coach) and has been the mainstay ever since. A new boiler was built for *Graf Schwerin-Lowitz* at Pant in 1993, oil-firing being adopted to obviate any fire risk in the National Park. *Sybil* is now stored in need of firebox repairs. At first, the ticket office at Pant was a garden shed - 19 break-ins in that first season meant that everything had to be moved away at night, including the shed, which was brought from Pontsticill on a trailer every morning - sometimes the train arrived at Pant before the station!

The railway is almost entirely within the Brecon Beacons National Park, but the terminus is just outside the boundary. The railway could attract grants on the basis of transporting people into the National Park in an environmentally friendly manner, hence a 40% grant helped fund a proper station at Pant. The first phase was opened in 1982, the inclusion of a flat combating the vandalism and theft problem. A shop, café, toilets and booking office, soon followed and further grants enabled the construction of a large workshop and running shed to start in about 1984. The HQ was fully completed by 1996. Although there are no plans for a southern extension, the building allows for such a possibility with no blockage of the running line.

Arthur Bailey ceased to be involved in the mid-1970s; Peter Rampton joined forces with Tony Hills and they developed the railway in partnership, buying the Vale of Rheidol Railway from BR in April 1989. They ran both narrow gauge lines until separating their interests in 1991, Tony Hills retaining the BMR, while Peter Rampton transferred ownership of the VoR into a Trust, although Tony continued to manage the VoR up to 1996.

Pontsticill station - beside the Taf Fechan reservoir (near the dam built in 1927 to create the lake) - was not intended to remain the line's terminus. In April 1994, work started on a 1¾ mile extension, alongside the water to a run-round loop known as Dolygaer at the northern end of the reservoir. Opened at Easter 1995 Dolygaer, as an interim terminus, has no platform, passengers remaining on the train while the locomotive runs round for the return to Pontsticill.

With the railway a proven success and the tracks reaching further into the National Park, additional motive power was required. This took the form of a 1930-built 4-6-2 Baldwin (works number 61269) from a cement works in Eastern Province, South Africa. Having been in an accident in 1974 and treated as a write-off by insurers, it was purchased as salvage and shipped to Britain. Restoration started in the early 1990s and it entered service in 1997, working in earnest from the following year.

The next extension added a further 1½ miles, running beside the banks of the Pentwyn reservoir, then climbing through plantations to reach Torpantau, 5 miles from Pant. Tracklaying was completed early in 2001, but still needed to be ballasted, lined and levelled. Opening is now likely in 2003. Just beyond Torpantau, at 1,313ft above sea level, is the highest railway tunnel in Britain. In time, a further ½ mile of track will be laid, taking the railway through this tunnel and bringing it up to a planned length of 5½ miles, although no completion date has been set.

The railway has an 0-6-0DH which is air-braked for use on passenger trains, but further steam locomotives will be added. With the line open to Torpantau, *Graf Schwerin-Lowitz* is expected to see less use, while the need for one loco of similar size to the Baldwin, and another not quite as powerful, is envisaged. Two new near-replica Baldwins based on Sandy River & Rangeley Lakes Railroad locomotives (2-4-4 No 10 built 1916 and 2-6-2 No 23 built 1913) will be constructed. Work during 2001 concentrated on machining the wheels and motion. When sufficient parts are ready, the frames will be cut and serious construction commenced,

although it will be some years before the pair - to be constructed at the same time - are complete. Further in the future, a 1928-vintage Hanomag-built 61-ton 2-6-2+2-6-2 Garratt (the most powerful locomotive ever built for the 2ft gauge) purchased from South African Railways in 1985 is in storage awaiting its turn, as is 2-8-2 'NG15' No.146 from Port Shepstone, South Africa.

The four coaches were designed by Tony Hills and built at Pontsticill, their appearance being influenced by American practice. The caboose, providing a brake vehicle with sliding doors capable of accommodating passengers in wheelchairs, is a near-replica of a 1903-vintage Sandy River & Rangeley Lakes vehicle, being built from original drawings. This stock runs on bogies from South African freight cars, and utilises couplings obtained from the Isle of Man. More recent construction has included pairs of flat cars and box vans, while a rail tamper came from South Africa during 2000. Two vertical-boilered locomotives which do not form part of the operating fleet are being restored when time permits. *Pendyffryn* is an original Pen-yr-Orsedd 1ft 11¾ins gauge De Winton 0-4-0VTB from 1894, while 1905-built 2ft gauge *Redstone* (named after its builder, the foreman fitter at the Penmaenmawr granite quarry) is basically a model of the 3ft gauge locos employed at Penmaenmawr.

The Teifi Valley Railway

The 1ft 11¾ins gauge Teifi Valley Railway has been built on the trackbed of a standard gauge branch line, although the origins of the line from which it branched were quite complex. Very briefly, a railway built by the Carmarthen and Cardigan Railway Company between Pencader and Llandysul was opened in 1864. This was 7ft 0 ¼ins broad gauge until conversion to standard gauge in May 1872. An extension to Newcastle Emlyn was added by the Great Western Railway and opened in 1895. The branch was closed to passengers on 15 September 1952, to freight on 28 September 1973, and the rails lifted.

A Teifi Valley Railway Preservation Society was formed in 1972 with the aim of operating passenger trains between Carmarthen and Newcastle Emlyn. This idea came to nothing, but two quite separate railways, of different gauges, have subsequently opened on parts of this trackbed. The Teifi Valley Railway, and the standard gauge Gwili Railway which is based at Bronwydd Arms and presently runs to Danycoed in one direction and is working on extending towards Carmarthen in the other.

The present Teifi Valley Railway Society was formed in August 1978. A Light Railway Order was obtained in December 1980 for the Newcastle Emlyn to Pencader Junction route (some 10/11 miles) and the purchase of the line from BR was completed in March 1981. Tracklaying started by 1984 westwards from Henllan, the new railway's base. The first terminus was at Pontprenshitw (roughly translated as 'shaky wooden bridge' and referring to the wooden scaffolding used when the adjacent viaduct was originally constructed) and the first train was operated on 24 August 1985 by the Hunslet 4wDM *Sholto* (HE2433/41), followed by an official opening on 9 April 1986. A further extension of about 1,000 yards was opened to Llandyfriog in 1990. A private limited company, originally named The Dyfed

Ex-Penrhyn Hunslet 0-4-0ST *Alan George*, **now fitted with a cab, draws a demonstration freight train into Henllan on 31 May 1997.**

Railway Company Ltd, now The Teifi Valley Railway Ltd, owns the trackbed and operates the railway. The Company is wholly owned by the Society (a registered charity) which provides volunteers to assist the nucleus of paid staff.

At Henllan, an office and stores building, along with two platforms, was all that remained from BR days when the TVR took over. The platforms were unsuitable for narrow gauge trains and everything now on the site has been built up by the Society, including a shed and workshops at the far end of the car park.

The route from Henllan is through woodland, and Forest Halt mainly serves the open-air Woodland Theatre. The end of the present two-mile running line is at Llandyfriog, where the locomotive runs round and proceeds back up the gradient which, in some places, is as steep as 1 in 30, to the site of an old quarry at Pontprenshitw where passengers can alight briefly and walk down steep steps to view the gorge and waterfall below.

The railway has two steam locomotives. Ex-Penrhyn quarry

Hunslet 0-4-0ST *Alan George* (HE606/1894) entered service on the TVR in 1987 and was the sole steam locomotive until early 1995 when 0-6-2 *Sgt Murphy* (KS3117/1918) arrived. Initially privately-owned, *Sgt Murphy* was subsequently purchased with the help of a Heritage Lottery Fund grant. A group of TVR members have also bought an 0-6-0T 'Joffre' Class loco, although this is a very long-term restoration project. In addition to the Hunslet diesel *Sholto*, the railway has Motor Rail diesels named *Sammy* and *Simon*. Progress on carriage projects included two vehicles entering TVR service for the first time in 2001. These were a new 14-seat 4-wheel coach based on the design of the centre-door (non-clerestory) Glyn Valley Tramway coach, and a coach with a fair bit of narrow gauge preservation history. Known as the 'Cote Coach' having been built in 1974/75 at Cote Farm, near Whitney, Oxfordshire, it became the WHR(Porthmadog) line's coach No 1 until being sold to a TVR Trustee - who was one of the original WHR members involved in building it. It is TVR policy to name each of its passenger vehicles, this pair being named *Emma* and *Nancy* respectively. The railway was hit by arson in November 2001 when the carriage

Teifi Valley Railway locomotive 0-6-2T *Sgt Murphy* (KS3117/1918) pauses at Pontprenshitw on 31 May 1997.

shed and all seven coaches were damaged. Coach No 4 was destroyed, the others being affected to differing degrees, but sufficient vehicles were repaired to maintain services.

The railway has plans for extending the running line in both directions, but has not been able to develop as rapidly as hoped. The borders of west and mid-Wales do not enjoy high tourism figures and the line has struggled. A substantial over-draft from the latter part of the 1990s has now been cleared and the railway hopes to secure European funding for developments which could secure the line's future. The initial objective is extending three miles into Newcastle Emlyn. The first stage, extending from Llandyfriog to the River Teifi, is comparatively straightforward and the TVR has the required rail in stock. The obstacle to be resolved is crossing the river. Once Newcastle Emlyn is reached, attention could turn to an eastward extension from Henllan to Pentrecwrt (Pentrecourt Halt in GWR anglicised days) with the long term ambition of reaching Pencader Junction. The railway still has the LRO for this entire length, although part of the trackbed was sold previously to raise money. If funding can be obtained and an eight mile railway developed, it could become the second biggest tourist attraction in the area.

The South Tynedale Railway

The South Tynedale Railway Preservation Society originally aimed to keep standard gauge trains running over the Haltwhistle - Alston branch of the Newcastle and Carlisle Railway - a line opened in 1851/52 to serve a lead mining area. Closure of the last colliery at Lambley in 1958 led to progressive contraction, with freight trains to Alston ceasing in 1965 and withdrawal of passenger services on 1 May 1976. The Society

had formed three years earlier, and negotiations to buy the line intact continued after closure. When BR lifted the track between Haltwhistle and Lambley, a more modest preservation scheme for the Alston - Gilderdale section was explored, but the required finance was not raised.

A re-think resulted in the Society's 2 July 1977 AGM opting for a narrow gauge line instead. With the support of local Councils, which had purchased the trackbed from BR, agreement to lease the Alston - Gilderdale section was reached in June 1980. A one-mile railway from Alston to a temporary Halt opened on 30 July 1983 and, following extensive repairs to a viaduct over the River South Tyne, services to Gilderdale Halt commenced in 1987.

The STR's Light Railway Order covered around six miles of trackbed through to Slaggyford, which was to be reached in two stages. Within three or so years, work started on the 1¼ mile extension from Gilderdale to Kirkhaugh, but proved far more difficult than anticipated. Essentially, the legislation changed between getting the LRO and building the track, compounded by complex paperwork issues - and construction proved costly. The biggest challenge was funding repairs to Whitley viaduct, just before Kirkhaugh. With no grant aid available, the 12-week project by contractors was financed by sizeable loans.

The HMRI inspection finally took place on 27 August 1999 with authority to operate between Gilderdale and Kirkhaugh granted on 3 September, the first public train running into the new station at Kirkhaugh on 4 September 1999. After all the frustrations, the extension had passed with flying colours and some very complimentary observations from the Inspector! The good news came in time for trips over the full line during the STR's 18/19 September annual Steam Gala weekend - a fine way to celebrate!

TOP: **The South Tynedale Railway enjoys a splendid scenic setting. Henschel 0-4-0T *Helen Kathryn* approaches Tyne Bridge, over the South Tyne river, on the way back to Alston.**

LOWER: **Henschel 0-4-0T *Helen Kathryn* arrives at the ex-standard gauge Alston station with a South Tynedale Railway train on 28 August 1999.**

With previous operations on the STR stopping just short of the County boundary, the first train to run over the new extension was also the first public service to work from Alston into Northumberland since 1976 when the old standard gauge branch closed. Presently, there is a single platform at Kirkhaugh although there is room to add a second. With no road access, a basic catering facility is provided from an adapted brake van during the lay-over before the train returns to Alston.

The next target is the 2½ miles of bare trackbed to Slaggyford, where the old station house is now in private hands, although the wooden waiting shelter and booking office at the site, along with the platform, survive and have received attention from STR volunteers. The railway has access to the trackbed and hopes to start work on the extension - with the inducement of seeing small locomotives working hard up a lengthy climb from the station on the return journey to Alston.

Extending beyond Slaggyford and reaching Haltwhistle remains a long-term ambition. A pre-feasibility study in conjunction with Tynedale Council established such an extension was possible, but there are no funds to commission a full report on the work involved. The 16-arch Lambley viaduct, a Grade II* structure in the care of the North Pennines Heritage Trust, was restored in the 1990s, but the Haltwhistle by-pass would have to be bridged, and Lambley station is in private ownership.

The railway is volunteer-run, except for a few months in the summer when some volunteers work every day on a paid basis to maintain services. The railway has enjoyed support from local authorities and funding organisations, helping to provide some impressive facilities. At Alston, the old station building is intact, although the railway only has the use of the booking hall, shop and a staff room, the toilets being provided by Eden District Council, and there is a privately run cafe within the building. The STR owns the freehold of an 'advance factory', originally built as a start-up unit to encourage local business. A new carriage shed has been built and there is also an excellent locomotive facility, with a workshop, separated by roller doors from an extension which forms the loco running shed. At Alston a signalbox, the upper part of which came from Ainderby (on the former NER branch to Redmire) is located on a new brick base beside the powered barriers controlling the level crossing into the car park.

Henschel 0-4-0T *Helen Kathryn* was to be joined in 2002 by heavily rebuilt Polish 0-6-0T *Naklo*, which operates as a tender loco. Awaiting attention is Hunslet 0-4-2T *UVE No 1*, purchased in January 1998 and needing a lot of work. Henschel 0-4-0T *Thomas Edmonson* is out of service, its future to be determined. There are several diesels, including the 100hp Hudswell-Clarke 0-6-0DM *Naworth* which handles passenger services at less busy times. The passenger stock consists of three 40-seat all-steel bogie saloon coaches, along with three wooden-bodied coaches (one equipped to carry wheelchairs) and two wood-bodied passenger brake vans. The ambition is to improve passenger stock when finance allows. There are a number of wagons for works and engineering use.

The Leadhills and Wanlockhead Railway

One of comparatively few narrow gauge lines in Scotland, the 2ft gauge Leadhills and Wanlockhead Railway can claim to be Britain's highest adhesion railway. Leadhills station stands at a height of 1,405ft above sea level and the line ascends to a height of 1,498ft - the maximum gradient is 1 in 40.

The trackbed was originally a Caledonian Railway branch from Elvanfoot on the main line, transporting refined lead from the mines at Leadhills and Wanlockhead to central Scotland. It was opened to Leadhills on 1 October 1901 and reached Wanlockhead a year later. To encourage tourism (and additional traffic!) a passenger service was run but, after the lead mines closed in the 1930s the end was in sight, with the final train running on 31 December 1938, the track being lifted early in 1939.

Construction of the narrow gauge line has been attributed to the capsize of a sailing boat on Bala Lake! Following this mishap, Alastair Ireland visited Llanuwchllyn to look at the Bala Lake Railway and got talking to George Barnes. The idea of building a short narrow gauge line on the old trackbed (Alastair, retired after a lifetime in banking, had a great interest in the locality) developed. The Lowthers Railway Society was formed in 1983, followed by lengthy negotiations before a lease was signed for part of the trackbed. Tracklaying finally commenced between the two villages in 1986.

A limited public service over a ¼ mile of track, operated by diesel motive power, commenced in 1988. The line has subsequently been extended and now runs for a mile up to the old County boundary between Lanarkshire and Dumfriesshire. The facilities at Leadhills have been built from scratch and include

A Scottish locomotive on a Scottish railway. Barclay 0-4-0WT *Jack*, owned by Nick Williams, pictured during a visit to the Leadhills and Wanlockhead Railway.
(Graham Morris)

a shop, small museum and signalbox. Initial ideas envisaged relocating the signalbox from Tulloch on the West Highland line, but this did not happen. What has emerged is probably better, for the newly-built structure incorporates original bricks from a viaduct built for the branch line on which the new line is built. This six-arch viaduct was built by the contractor for the famed Glenfinnan viaduct on the West Highland line, but the concrete structure was subsequently faced with attractive terracotta bricks. Many thousands of these bricks were recovered to build the signalbox, and represent the only 'preserved' item on the new line - everything else had been cleared long before the Society came on the scene. The lever frame was recovered from Arrochar (West Highland line) and controls the semaphore signals at Leadhills.

The line presently ends in a cutting, attractive when surrounded by summer heather, but not an ideal terminus. The aim is to extend to Wanlockhead (where there is a lead mining museum) and build a new station and run-round loop, but negotiations to secure access to the formation have been protracted.

The locomotive collection is presently all internal combustion and includes a 28hp Motor Rail Simplex *Elvan*, 32hp Ruston 4wDMs *Luce* and *Little Clyde*, Hunslet 4wDH *Clyde*, and 0-4-0DMF Hudswell Clarke *Nith*. Visiting steam locomotives have run on the line, the first being Graham Morris' 0-4-0T Kerr Stuart *Peter Pan* over 18/19 August 1990. Other are: *Montalban* and *Irish Mail* (West Lancashire Light Railway), *Chaloner* (Leighton Buzzard Railway) and the privately owned Barclay 0-4-0WT *Jack* - and *Peter Pan* has made further visits. The railway anticipates remaining an internal combustion-worked line with occasional visiting steam, although a Society member has purchased a 1913-built 0-4-0T O&K. Bought in Belgium, this loco is currently stored (in Scotland) with the hope of eventual restoration for running at Leadhills.

One of the passenger coaches and the guard's van were built by Society members, utilising the chassis from former peat line locomotives which worked at Kirkbride in Cumbria. An additional coach is based on a standard Talyllyn Railway chassis, dispatched from Tywyn in July 1990, the body being constructed by Society members.

The Gartell Light Railway

The 2ft gauge Gartell Light Railway is a private line, owned and operated by three generations of the Gartell family. Part of the present ¾ of a mile running line is built on a section of the old Somerset & Dorset Joint Railway trackbed south of Templecombe. The railway opened to the public in 1990 and Open Days are held on around nine Sundays a year. Being on private property, access is only possible on Open Days or for organised parties.

A loco shed and large carriage shed capable of housing all the passenger stock is at Common Lane, the main station. The track climbs fairly stiffly (initially 1 in 32, then 1 in 50) to Pinesway Junction where it joins the ex-S&D formation and continues for around half a mile on the old standard gauge trackbed to Park Lane. An extension line northwards from Pinesway Junction towards

Templecombe is planned, a flyover having been constructed to carry the extension over the existing line.

Initially, Lister internal combustion powered locomotives were employed. These left the railway in the early 1990s, being replaced by 4wDH Alan Keef No 5 *Alison* (in 1993) and 4wDH Ruston & Hornsby No 2 *Andrew* (in 1995). On 15 June 1998, a newly built steam locomotive was delivered. Named *Mr G*, the 0-4-2T was specially built for the railway by the North Dorset Locomotive Works at Shaftesbury, a firm which normally repairs traction engines and steam rollers. The design was based on the Groudle Glen Railway's Bagnall *Polar Bear* (now at Amberley) but with the wheel arrangement reversed. The loco made its public debut on 27 June 1998 following running-in trials and was named after Mr Alan Gartell, father of GLR owner John Gartell. Its debut train represented the return of steam-hauled passenger services on the S&DJR trackbed after 32 years! Public services hauled by *Mr G* commenced the following day, the draw of steam resulting in a 49% increase in passenger numbers over previous June Open Days. Operating dates have continued to see big increases in numbers, the advent of steam being credited as the biggest single reason.

The two builders of *Mr G* at the North Dorset Locomotive Works are regular volunteers at the railway and are to build their own steam locomotives, to be based on the railway. Both will utilise the same design of boiler, cylinders and other key components, but with variations in their appearance. The first is expected to be completed around 2004 and will be an 0-4-0ST tender loco The second will be an 0-4-2T, but with a bunker rather than a flat rear cab sheet. The railway itself is building a Bo-Bo diesel hydraulic locomotive, with a cab at each end, although progress slowed while work concentrated on developing the carriage stock. The original passenger vehicles were open-sided coaches from a Butlin's holiday camp railway. A programme to construct new all-steel bodies (mounted on the original bogies) was to be completed in time for Open Days in 2002, giving nine bogie carriages, six with the in-house steel bodies (painted S&D blue) and three with wooden bodies. The railway is worked by three locomotives, each hauling three carriages, producing an intensive service of 25 trains, with a departure every 15 minutes from Common Lane, on a normal Open Day!

It has been suggested that Gartell may be the most comprehensively signalled heritage railway, bar none! There are 20 - 30 working signals on the line, controlled by two fully operational signalboxes, with some of the sections just 100 yards long. An important factor concerning the extension is designing, and receiving HMRI approval of, the interlocking at Pinesway Junction where there is a 30-lever signalbox.

The Devon Railway Centre

The Devon Railway Centre is located at the old Cadeleigh Station, Bickleigh, near Tiverton, on what was the Exe Valley line. The station, built in 1885 and closed in 1963, was acquired by the Gicquel family in 1997. Work started on restoring the boarded-up station buildings - the goods shed and weighbridge hut had also survived. A 2ft gauge railway was constructed from

Mathew Gicquel driving Ruston & Hornsby LBT diesel (418770/57) at the Devon Railway Centre on 24 May 1998, very soon after opening to the public.

scratch and negotiates a circuitous route on the old standard gauge trackbed towards the river and back. This provides a half-mile ride and includes sharp curves, some as tight as 40ft radius, and two 1 in 30 gradients. There is a run-round loop near the goods shed, now housing the locomotive collection. Accessed via a 1 in 20 gradient, for a while this had the distinction of surely being the only locomotive shed in Britain to have a point inside the building, although this turnout was removed as it developed into a narrow gauge railway museum.

The Centre opened at Easter 1998 with passenger services worked by an LBT Ruston & Hornsby diesel (418770/57) and *Merlin*, a Hudson (LX1001/68) originally from Woodhead Tunnel and equipped with the 'steam outline' bodywork as fitted for work at Pembrey Country Park. Initially, the surroundings of the narrow gauge line were fairly open, emphasising the nature of the balloon loop and curves which appeared to wrap round on themselves. A programme of laying out gardens, walks, ponds and picnic areas, along with the planting of 200 trees, and a 'mine shaft', disguises the nature of the line, which might be extended in the future.

The number of locomotives at the site rapidly increased, mainly boosted by a collection owned by Peter Nicholson. These included ex-Kent Construction Hibberd 1747/31, two Hibberd Planets (2025/37 and 2201/39) and a Lister (6299/35), the latter being returned to action in June 2001 for the first time since the early 1970s. *Ivor* (MR8877/44) entered service during

2000, while *Merlin* was sold and departed in June 2001. During the 2000 season, another coach was added for the passenger-carrying line and one-time Pen-yr-Orsedd quarry 20DL Ruston (235711/45) was brought into operation following repairs to its brakes and gearbox.

The first steam-hauled trains ran over 29/30 July 2000 when Graham Morris visited with 0-4-0ST 'Wren' *Peter Pan* - a loco which worked in quarries belonging to Devon County Council before entering preservation - this was also the first time steam had worked on the old Exeter - Dulverton route since 1963. *Peter Pan* returned over 4/5 August 2001 and there are plans to bring a 2ft gauge steam locomotive to the line permanently in the foreseeable future.

Between the station platforms, 200 yards of standard gauge track accommodates the Baguley 0-4-0DM (3357/52), known as *Boris*, along with two Mk1 coaches which form the visitor reception area and house model railways, while 150 yards of 2ft gauge track and four points near the goods shed allow the running of demonstration freight trains. The rolling stock includes an example of 'Yr Tryclau Melyn' (the yellow truck), used to convey officials (and occasionally Royalty) within the Dinorwic quarry system, a 1ft 11½ins gauge GWR slate wagon from Blaenau Ffestiniog, a Ravenglass & Eskdale 15ins gauge granite wagon and a 2ft 10½ins gauge ex-Cattybrook Brickworks (Bristol) end-tipping wagon. A 200 yard length of 7¼ins gauge line was added for the 2001 season.

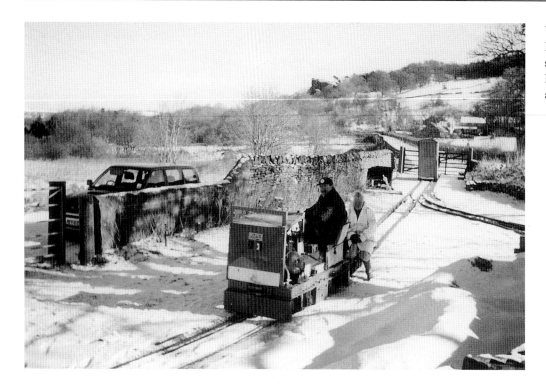

Winter on the Steeple Grange
Light Railway. Lister *Lizzie*
sets off through the snow in
December 2000 to prepare for
a Santa Special . *(P Sellers)*

The Steeple Grange Light Railway

The 18ins gauge Steeple Grange Light Railway runs on the trackbed of an 1884 branch of the old standard gauge Cromford and High Peak Railway. The branch closed in 1967. In the mid-1980s, a group interested in the Peak District National Park, the old standard gauge line and the trail on its trackbed, realised there was no possibility of reviving a part of the old High Peak line, but thought a short narrow gauge railway offered a way of conserving its memory. The Steeple Grange Light Railway Society was formed in 1988 and during 1988/89 track, some rolling stock and a derelict battery electric locomotive (still awaiting restoration) were recovered from the Ladywash Lead Mine at Eyam which was closing - hence the adoption of the unusual, but not unique, gauge. The initial passenger 'service' consisted of pushing an ex-Ladywash manrider up and down the first length, this low-key operation commencing in 1989. Around this time, a Greenwood & Batley Ltd battery electric locomotive was acquired from a Sheffield steelworks. By 1999, the railway had raised its profile as the running line was extended and additional locomotives and stock arrived. Services were mainly worked by the ex-Sheffield 'Greenbat' hauling a manrider salvaged from Bevercotes Colliery, Nottinghamshire.

The railway starts at Steeplehouse station, then climbs a 1 in 27 gradient to Dark Lane quarry. An extension to Killer's Dale station, where a passing loop has been laid, was completed early in 2000 and further track, using rail obtained from the Ravenglass & Eskdale Railway, was laid to Recreation Bridge, Middleton, early in 2001. Opening of this extension brought the track length up to half a mile. The next extension will add a further half-mile from Recreation Bridge to a station to be named Middleton Main Street. The owners of this section of trackbed intend to build a retail craft centre adjacent to the new terminus - requiring road access, they will construct a level crossing for the railway. The Society has obtained some 60ft lengths of Nottingham Corporation Tramway track from Crich, so the crossing will incorporate elements of a system which closed in the 1950s. The Society also made a start on another extension early in 2002, a quarter-mile branch into Steeplehouse quarry (towards the National Stone Centre) and will mean that Steeplehouse station will become Steeplehouse Junction, as it was in standard gauge days. During special events, incidentally, Steeplehouse station often acquires an overall roof, a gazebo-like tent being erected over the tracks!

A Society member has a petrol engined Lister named *Lizzie* which has worked on extension works trains and was intended to enter passenger service when fitted with air brakes. Unfortunately, the engine blew in 2001 - it is now intended to fit a replacement diesel engine. During 2000, the former BR narrow gauge diesel ZM32, was added to the railway's fleet. This Ruston 20hp loco (416214/57) originally operated on the 18ins gauge lines at Horwich Works - alongside the tiny 0-4-0ST *Wren*, now preserved at the NRM. ZM32 became part of the Gloddfa Ganol collection owned by Rich Morris and was regauged to 2ft. Following purchase by Steeple Grange Chairman, Michael Strange, it was regauged back to 18ins and air braking was installed. Still retaining its (faded) British Rail Blue livery, the loco was named *Horwich*, but a major gearbox failure frustrated plans for the loco to properly enter service. It was sent to Dorothea Restorations in 2001 for a complete rebuild and will be given a BR Green livery, and is due to return for the 2002 season.

Construction of a new dual gauge (18ins and 2ft) locomotive shed commenced in 1997, employing limestone blocks with sandstone quoins and lintels to provide a traditional appearance.

CHAPTER SIX

Enthusiast lines

The line in the garden of Cadeby rectory may be small, but was among the earliest of private preservation projects. Both the Cadeby Light Railway and the later Amerton Railway owed their construction to the acquisition of a locomotive - coincidentally both Bagnall 0-4-0STs.

The parents of the group of school friends who started what would become the West Lancashire Light Railway thought it would be a passing phase and, had early ideas gone differently, the Bredgar & Wormshill Railway could easily have been standard gauge - thank goodness both turned out as they did!

The railways in this chapter resulted from a group of people getting together to preserve some equipment and build a short railway to run it on. Rarely was it envisaged how things would turn out, but the result is a series of charming centres of preservation. They have mostly been built on private land, either bought for the purpose or by agreement with the owner, and provide short runs for the locomotives - a ride rather than a journey - to give pleasure to participants and visitors.

Really, only lines which open for the public, either regularly or by holding Open Days, are described. There are many more small private railways built and operated for entirely personal pleasure.

The Cadeby Light Railway

A new rectory was built in the village of Cadeby, Leicestershire in 1959 to replace the earlier Georgian house which had filled this function. Shortly after its construction, the Reverend E R 'Teddy' Boston was appointed Rector and noted the potential for turning a path between a screen of Beech trees and the A447 road in the, now reduced, garden into the trackbed for a miniature

Bagnall 0-4-0ST *Pixie* midway along the Cadeby Light Railway on Saturday 12 August 2000, with passengers enjoying the ride in an adapted wagon right behind the footplate of the locomotive.

railway. The cost of a suitable locomotive seemed prohibitive so, turning the usual situation (building a model because you cannot have the real thing) on its head, 'Teddy' Boston looked around for a full-size narrow gauge locomotive. Rejecting 3ft and metre gauge Midland ironstone locomotives as too large, he found Bagnall 0-4-0ST *Pixie* (2090/19) in a quarry at Cranford. The loco, owned by Staveley Minerals, had not been used since 1957, but when he made his first approach in 1961 the quarry owners wanted to keep the railway available in case it was required in the future. However, a visit to the Production Manager in 1962 proved opportune - the section of the quarry in which the railway was located was to be closed and the equipment sold. A cheque was written out on the spot to purchase *Pixie*.

The loco was collected in May 1962 and delivered to the Rectory garden in the first week of June. Meanwhile brambles, weeds and holly were being removed to clear the trackbed for a 2ft gauge line for *Pixie* to run on. Cranford quarry donated some track (including two points) which was lifted by enthusiasts in the July and moved to Cadeby, along with two wagons. Stone was obtained from Cliffe Hill Quarry and the trackbed consolidated by a steam roller. A short length of track was laid, more followed during the summer and by September the line had largely been built.

Pixie needed a complete overhaul and new slide bars, a new crosshead and new piston rings were fitted. She was steam-test-ed in April 1963, which was not simply successful, it turned into a trial run along the new railway! The summer was spent completing the track, including laying sidings, and monthly openings commenced. A further extension was added, bringing the track up to its present length, more sidings laid and several internal combustion locomotives added to the stock. Experience showed that the original 25lb rail was too light and most of the line was relaid during 1968 with 40lb material acquired from Baggeridge Brick Co. Although by no means certain, it is just possible that this rail was originally from the Leek & Manifold Light Railway.

'Teddy' Boston died in April 1986, however, his widow, Audrey Boston was able to purchase the house - thus the railway remained and the open days on selected dates have continued when passengers can ride up and down the line in adapted wagons. The OO gauge model railway, located in a 40ft x 20ft wooden shed also remained in place, but a brick-built museum building was constructed to house the considerable collection of other model railway equipment and railwayana which 'Teddy' had assembled and which used to be kept in the Rectory. The museum was opened by Wilbert Awdry in 1990.

The running line is just 97 yards long, commencing beside the model railway shed. A right hand curve takes it along that original path, parallel to the main road and past the 'workshop'

and museum building. A further curve to the right, the line now being on an embankment, brings the track to its terminus, further progress being barred by the driveway to the house.

The railway is operated by a small group of friends who own the locomotives and stock on the line, other than *Pixie* and other items owned by Audrey Boston. There are more than a dozen internal combustion powered locomotives, most being stored on sidings between the back of the house and the model railway shed. There are also several interesting wagons, including ex-Dinorwic stock, on a siding at the other end of the line, close to a 5ins gauge model railway in the Dell. A standard gauge 0-4-0ST Peckett (2012/41) is on static display beside the house.

The West Lancashire Light Railway

The West Lancashire Light Railway is, literally, the realisation of boyhood dreams - everything which has been built up at Hesketh Bank started with six school friends back in 1967. Aged between 13 and 19, those were days when lads rushed around the country 'spotting' during the final days (or so it appeared at the time!) of steam on British Railways. A couple of them were keen narrow gauge fans who realised the old brickworks in the area were closing down and there was equipment around of a size which they could handle, hence their own preservation project was born.

The location for their railway chose itself. Behind the back garden of 14 year old Jonathan Whitehead's home - with access through the back gate - was an old clay pit on a site owned by his relatives. At one time, the pit had been served by a 2ft 6ins gauge hand-worked line and a couple of lengths of 20lb Jubilee track were found in the undergrowth. After hack-sawing the metal sleepers off, 23 September 1967 is recorded as the date when work commenced on laying the first 150 yards of 2ft gauge track. A wagon was added and a railway was born. Things were initially hand-to-mouth as the line was developed. A scrap pile at the pit was raided to raise funds for sleepers and all sorts of other useful 'junk' was found.

The first locomotive, a Ruston & Hornsby 13HP diesel named *Clwyd*, bought for £25, arrived in April 1968. The group decided to build a shed, using rejected bricks from the adjacent Alty's Brickworks. Weekends were spent making countless trips up and down the Brickworks road with a wheelbarrow to shift the bricks onto the site, but before it was even completed, plans had expanded. In order to do some restoration work on the stock which was arriving, it was decided that a workshop should be built as well.

Clwyd had been pulling a home made 4-wheel passenger coach to provide rides since 1968 but, in the following year, the purchase of the first steam locomotive moved things to a more serious level. *Irish Mail* did not have a boiler when she arrived

after the Dinorwic quarry auction. This was solved during the summer of 1972 by the heroic recovery of *Alice* from near the top of the Dinorwic quarry workings. The boiler outer shell was sound, but a new inner firebox was needed, requiring significant sums of money. The group knew of a lot of locos and rails at local industrial concerns which were closing down and equipment was acquired, with some sold on, to raise the finance to plough back into the Hesketh Bank project.

By 1970, the track stretched to 370 yards, and two 'Silver Belle' bogie passenger cars from the Southport Pier Railway had arrived, followed by more locomotives and steady developments through the 1970s. The return to steam of *Irish Mail* in 1980 also produced problems - some of the neighbours being unhappy at the appearance of smoke and sounding of whistles - a pressure group was even formed to try and get the line closed. Other issues included the attention of HMRI, and the need for planning permission for what was now a 'proper' railway! The necessary consents were obtained, while traffic shot up as passengers discovered the line. With the operation having expanded hugely from its humble beginnings, a supporting Association was formed to supplement the original 'gang of six'. Things have moved on to a point far beyond anything envisaged by the school friends when they started and the formation of a Charitable Trust to safeguard the stock and formalise the future of the railway is being considered.

Care has been taken to ensure that the buildings at the line's Becconsall station capture the right narrow gauge 'atmosphere' with old materials used where possible to achieve the correct look and feel. The layout of the yard and buildings, however, was dictated when the first point was laid. The only material to hand was a couple of lengths of bent rail. The bends happened to be about 30 degrees, so the entire layout was formed around the resulting alignment! Developments in the late 1990s included a 33ft by 20ft extension to the running shed to house four additional locos. This was followed by replacement loco watering arrangements with a traditional cast iron tank placed on a base of 2,500 Accrington bricks recovered from an old sewage works, complemented by a water crane donated by BNFL from a site near Preston. Its precise origin is unknown, but being ex-standard gauge it was a bit big for its new home - solved by digging a 4ft deep pit to sink it into and reduce its height! A major project to develop the covered accommodation for locomotives and stock commenced in 2001, the first phase being construction of a 45ft long by 38ft wide three-road shed, two tracks being for diesel locomotives, the third a woodwork shop and paintshop. This will temporarily house the passenger coaches when the old carriage shed is demolished, the final element being the erection of a new four-road 70ft by 40ft museum building, following which the diesel/workshop building will be used for its intended purpose.

The running line is now some 430 yards long and follows a basically L shape at the top of a bank overlooking the site of the clay pit. Part way along is Willow Tree Halt, with a siding for stock storage (plus nameboard and willow tree!) followed by Delph station where there is a low platform and a run round loop. Beyond the station is a further 200 yards of overgrown line, used for storage. The question of an extension has been

West Lancashire Light Railway O&K 0-4-0WT *Montalban*, with a small diesel in front and a 'Greenbat' 4wBE behind, at Hesketh Bank on 26 August 2001. Behind the locomotives, the foundations for the new 45ft long by 38ft wide three-road shed are being prepared.

imported from Sena Sugar Estates Ltd sites in Mozambique. Henschel & Sohn 0-8-0T 'Feldbahn' (14676/17), which served during WWI as Deutsches Feldbahn No 913 and worked at Luabo Mill as SSE No 6 arrived in 2000, followed by Fowler 0-6-2T (15513/20) in the following year. The restoration of both is to be undertaken by contractors to speed their return to steam.

Also at the railway is *Jonathan* (HE678/98), named *Bernstein* in Dinorwic days and renamed after the owner's late son after being acquired for preservation, which arrived on long-term loan in 1986. In addition, the owner of ex-Penrhyn quarry 0-4-2ST *Stanhope* (KS2395/17) is basing his loco on the railway until such time as the Moseley Railway Trust finds a new site to operate its collection. The WLLR is also home to a significant collection of internal combustion and battery-electric locomotives.

The coaches have all been built in the railway's workshops. Original aluminium panels were stripped off the ex-Southport Pier vehicles, the underframes overhauled and new bodies fitted. The brake van is based on the chassis of an old diesel loco and a variety of other rolling stock has been acquired. The workshops also contain the components from the lower saloon of a Lytham St. Anne's tramcar, rescued from a local garden. Eventually, this will provide an all-weather passenger coach, complete with balcony ends.

The Bredgar & Wormshill Railway

This 2ft gauge railway owes its existence to Bill and David Best and a small group of friends. As the end of steam on the standard gauge Slough Estates industrial system approached, the brothers were on a shortlist to buy one of the two available locos. In retrospect, it is fortunate they were unsuccessful, for becoming committed to standard gauge would never have allowed the developments which have taken place at Warren Wood.

Shortly after the attempt to purchase the standard gauge loco had failed, the opportunity arose to buy a 2ft gauge diesel. Within weeks of this purchase, Alan Bloom put Schwartzkopf 0-4-0WT *Bronhilde* up for sale at Bressingham and by 1972 Warren Wood housed a steam loco, a diesel and 100 yards of track. The arrival of a steam locomotive attracted the attention of other railway enthusiasts, the first being Peter Howard who brought Arnold-Jung 0-6-0WT *Katie*. Sadly, Peter died in 1998, although his loco remains part of the collection. Within a year or so, a group of 10/12 people had gathered around the brothers. Although one or two have departed, two or three more have

considered but this hinges on future developments by the owners of the site. There is the potential to add around half a mile to reach the far end of the clay pit, but there would be problems. Obviously, it would depend on obtaining Planning Permission, funding the construction would be a significant factor, and the line would acquire a lot of new neighbours who would have to be considered. Moreover, there are no gradients to speak of on the current running line, but this extension would include a 1 in 40 bank, making the fitting of continuous brakes necessary. If the line did reach the end of the clay pit, there is always the possibility of breaking out onto the trackbed of a long-closed standard gauge branch - but that rather falls into the pipe dream category!

In addition to *Irish Mail* (HE823/03), the steam locomotive collection now includes 0-4-0WT *Montalban* (OK6641/13) and *Utrillas* (OK2378/08), the pair having been acquired in derelict condition in 1984 from a coal mine in Spain. In 1992 work commenced on Kerr Stuart 0-6-0T (KS2405/15) 'Joffre' Class loco which had been acquired in 1974. After 20 years laying disused the work required is substantial. Two further locomotives were purchased by Jonathan Whitehead from a large collection

joined, so basically the same group of a dozen or so friends have been working together for many years.

A series of extensions resulted in the basic half a mile of running line which exists today being completed by about 1980. The track, however, was not laid to a particularly high standard. The line, which is on privately owned property, was opened twice a year to benefit local charities, but a big event for a cancer charity attracted huge numbers of visitors - and gave the group a considerable fright! The railway, which included the main line running straight onto a small turntable, was fine for private pleasure, but totally unsuitable for public running.

The situation clearly needed to be re-appraised and they actually closed down while serious thought was given to what the group really wanted to do. Two of them made a scale model to show how the railway should be and this formed the pattern for future progress. It took around two years to revise the track layout, and another two years to fully sort everything out. The developments have continued, but following the basic plan which was established back in the 1980s.

A building to serve as a locomotive shed, restoration works and museum was constructed. By this time, more locomotives had arrived - Peckett 0-6-0ST *Harrogate* was acquired from the Ffestiniog Railway in 1987, followed in 1991 by 0-4-0ST Bagnall *Armistice* (from a private collector) and Baguley-Drewry 0-4-0 diesel *Bredgar*. The shed roads lead out onto a turntable which is served by a backshunt from the main running line. A few yards from the junction is Warren Wood station, complete with canopy and signalbox, where passengers join the trains. Next to the station is the carriage shed, while toilet facilities and a refreshment room have been built close by. Just after leaving the station, the tracks curve sharply downhill. This curve was subsequently eased somewhat, allowing *Harrogate* to return to action at the 13 May 2000 Enthusiasts' Day after an absence of five years. Skirting the woods, the train passes an old quarry working before entering the woods which surround Stony Shaw station. The entire track was relaid in 50lb rail during the mid-1990s - funded by the sale of some Baguley-Drewry diesels which had been purchased speculatively some years earlier. Towards the end of the 1990s a signalbox and two sidings were added to the run-round loop, platform and station building at this terminus. Stony Shaw marks the limit of the line for the foreseeable future, being on the edge of the land owned by the brothers.

The group, which has a wide range of skills, traditionally meets on Thursday nights to progress the various projects in the workshop, which also has an extension accommodating a well-equipped machine shop. Boiler work is contracted out (although the railway handles re-tubing), the wheel press is sometimes not quite big enough for some tasks, and they do not have a wheel lathe, but otherwise, the railway is pretty well self-sufficient. The result is very high-quality locomotive restorations which tend to be completed remarkably rapidly.

Generally, the team tried to only undertake one project at a time, but the increasing number of locos arriving at The Warren has slightly altered this plan in more recent years. In 1995 0-4-0T O&K *Eigiau* was purchased from Bressingham and while work on this loco was still proceeding, the Decauville 0-4-2T *Victory*

arrived from Australia in the following year. Next came an O&K 0-4-0WT (OK12722/36) purchased from the Brecon Mountain Railway in 1999, followed in January 2000 by two ex-Mozambique locos: 0-6-0 Fowler (18800/30) and 20ins gauge 0-4-2T Fowler (13573/12) which will be regauged. The collection grew again in March 2001 with the arrival of the dismantled components of O&K 0-6-0WT *Sao Domingos* (OK11784/28). In addition to the locomotives owned by Bill and David Best, Hunslet 0-4-0ST *Lady Joan* came to the line following its purchase by Rodney Tolhurst in 1997.

The museum shed is also home to a pair of restored 2ft 6ins gauge locos, No 105 *Siam*, an 0-6-0T built by Henschel (29582/56) and the La Meuse-built 0-4-0T (3355/29) as well as a collection of miniature locomotives. The railway has constructed five coaches for passenger use, the latest of which was a high-capacity open-sided vehicle which entered service in 2002. In the long-term, there are plans to build a 'super coach'. The line also has a small collection of freight vehicles which provide yet another attraction during special events.

Among more recent developments is a further, rail-connected, extension to the main shed to house the collection of vintage Bean Car Company vehicles which Bill Best has assembled into the largest collection in the country. Although the railway cannot be extended at the Stony Shaw end (unless the adjacent land becomes available) an extension to the running line which currently terminates beside the shed is possible. This would not add a great deal of track length, but would be a useful addition during special event days and allow Warren Wood to become a through station on occasions.

Being privately-owned rather than a commercial operation, the railway is not in competition with other heritage lines. The principal objective is the restoration and operation of locomotives which have been saved from becoming scrap. The railway is opened to the public on selected Sundays and has held additional special 'Enthusiast Days' when just about everything on the line can be viewed in steam.

The Amerton Railway

The Amerton Railway came into being as a result of the preservation of Bagnall 0-4-0ST *Isabel* - although the line was constructed many years after the locomotive was saved. Built in 1897 for the Cliffe Hill Granite Co of Markfield, Leicestershire, *Isabel* worked through until 1946, the quarry railway system being abandoned two years later. The locomotive remained in store until 1953 when she was purchased by Bagnall's for preservation to serve as a memorial to the locomotives built by the company and the men who built them.

Following restoration, *Isabel* was plinthed at the Bagnall works, remaining there until 1961, by which time the new management apparently found her something of an embarrassment! Under the care of the newly-formed Stafford Railway Circle, the local Council agreed that she could be displayed on a plinth in Victoria Park. Inevitably, her condition deteriorated and in 1977 *Isabel* was returned to what was now the GEC Castle Works for refurbishment before being returned to the Park. By late 1984, vandalism and the weather had taken their toll. Now under the ownership of Stafford Borough Council, *Isabel* once again returned to Castle Works. Various proposals were explored, but what finally emerged was the formation in 1986 of the Staffordshire Narrow Gauge Advisory Group, which approached the Council with a view to taking on the restoration of *Isabel*. By the following January, this had become the Staffordshire Narrow Gauge Railway Society. To meet the Council's requirements, the Society had to become a limited company, and work finally started in December 1987. *Isabel* was totally stripped down, the boiler refurbished and the locomotive rebuilt. She steamed again on 26 December 1989 (for the first time since entering preservation back in 1953) and was completed by October 1990, although her actual boiler test took place in January 1991.

While *Isabel* neared completion during 1990, consideration had turned to finding her a permanent home. As the owner of the locomotive, the Council stipulated that she must be kept within the Borough boundary. Various sites were considered, but the location which emerged was Amerton Farm at Stowe-by-Chartley - a 'greenfield site' on a working farm. A ceremonial cutting of the first sod was performed by the Mayor of Stafford on 26 May 1990 and the small band of volunteers started railway construction in the following month.

The railway was to be developed under a three-phase plan. Although subsequent events resulted in some changes, this largely reached fruition during 2001. Initial priorities were to build a secure shed for *Isabel* and other equipment, and construct about a quarter of a mile of running line. At that time, the field in which the first section of track was to be laid was occupied by cows, so fencing was a top priority! Over 2,000 tons of hardcore was placed (with the aid of a borrowed JCB) to form the trackbed and during Easter 1991, 246 yards of track was laid, followed by the construction of crossings over the line. The ballast came from Cliffe Hill quarry - a very fitting touch that this should be the source of the material for *Isabel*'s new home!

A 60ft by 30ft steel framed building was erected and *Isabel* was moved to Amerton on 26 October 1991. By Easter 1992, the railway was sufficiently completed to be inspected by HMRI and services over the initial 1/4 mile of track, worked by *Isabel* and one coach, commenced on 19 July 1992. With some income now being generated, further improvements could be made, including a ticket office and a shelter on the platform and the purchase of further rail and fastenings. The official opening by the Lady Mayor of Stafford took place on 27 March 1993.

At this stage, after leaving the station, the tracks ran through a field as far as a run-round loop. The original plan envisaged extending the line round across a marshy area, back towards the station (which it would re-enter just after crossing a bridge over a stream) completing a circuit of about half a mile. Work on this extension started in January 1994 and proceeded as far as the construction of the bridge. Unfortunately, this had to be put on

Bagnall 0-4-0ST *Isabel* running on the most recent extension of the Amerton Railway just prior to Christmas 2001, these workings being the first time that public trains had run over the extension, and indeed, right round the completed circuit.
Carrie Thomas

LEFT: Pearl 2 **hauls an Amerton Railway train back from Chartley Road on 6 May 2001.**

RIGHT: No 6 Druid, **a 20hp Simplex (8644/41) fitted with a Perkins engine and new body-work, and train at the Abbey Light Railway's Bridge Road station/HQ on 18 June 2000.**

hold while the future of the farm - and consequently the railway - were under negotiation.

The railway continued to operate and further locomotives and stock arrived. The turning point came in 1997. The position concerning the farm was resolved and the Society was promised a new 20-year lease and encouraged to proceed with its extension plans. The farm changed from a working farm to the attraction it has now become, allowing a reappraisal of the route for the extension. The year also saw *Isabel*'s centenary, celebrated with an Isabel 100 Gala over 17/18 May 1997, featuring five visiting Bagnalls: *Peter* (Amberley), *Pixie* (Cadeby), *Sea Lion* (Groudle Glen), *Armistice* (Bredgar & Wormshill) and Patrick Keef's *Woto*.

The new route for the extension expanded the size of the circuit to a one mile continuous round trip. In the process, this avoided the difficult marshy ground and created a more attractive run with twists and turns following the contours of the land in the traditional narrow gauge manner. Construction of a second bridge started in November 1997, a contractor prepared the formation of the new line, and the track was laid by volunteers. The original terminus has become a siding and the line to a new loop, named Chartley Road, was opened on 26 March 2000. Tracklaying was completed from Chartley Road back to the

starting point in April 2001. This was followed by ballasting and other fettling work during the summer, with the extension being used by public trains for the first time during the running of Santa Specials in December 2001. With the extension fully opened, a new platform with a picnic area will be built about 100 yards short of Chartley Road loop.

A second steam locomotive, *Pearl 2*, has joined *Isabel*. This is a newly-built 0-4-2IST, which entered service on 20 June 1999 - see Chapter 8. A third steam loco, an 0-8-0T Henschel & Sohn 'Feldbahn', is under restoration having arrived at Amerton in December 1999 following earlier importation from Mozambique. A collection of internal combustion locomotives has also steadily built up at the site with examples built by Motor Rail, Ruston & Hornsby and Hunslet. There are also two steam-outline locomotives built by E E Baguley Ltd of Burton, *Dreadnought* and *Golspie*. Three of the coaches were also originally built by Baguley, while the fourth was purchased from the Welsh Highland Railway (Porthmadog) - all of which are scheduled to be the subject of rebuilding to enhance passenger comfort. The four-wheel passenger brake van was constructed by Society members and wagons have been acquired from a number of sources. With long-term security and the track having

been extended to its planned limits, other developments are planned. These include the construction of a carriage shed near the existing loco shed/workshop, relocating the loop serving the main station and development of a museum in the ex-Great Northern Railway platform building recovered from Chartley station, which is being restored by members of the Staffordshire Industrial Archaeological Society. Also, in August 2001 the Leek & Manifold Railway/North Staffordshire Railway signalbox from Waterhouses was brought to the line. Following restoration, this will house the current open ground frame at the station.

Abbey Light Railway

The 2ft gauge Abbey Light Railway dates from 1974 when Peter Lowe submitted an application for Planning Permission to build a new railway. The idea was supported by the local Council and a start made on the Council-owned land in Kirkstall, just outside Leeds, two years later. Everything, including the trackbed, has been built from scratch.

The project, then and now, centres on the Lowe family and about half a dozen friends, the volunteer supporters being largely based on the White Rose Group of the Ffestiniog Railway

Society who gyrated towards a local railway project as well as forming FR working parties. The rails have a form of Ffestiniog origin too. The group recovered a lot of material and took it up to the FR where it was sorted into material the FR wanted to keep - the 'rejects' being brought back to Leeds for the planned new line!

With three tons of used rail and a couple of skips, a start was made on construction. The line crosses a Mill Race which is drawn off the River Aire; then enters a quite deep cutting and climbs up to the terminus near Kirkstall Abbey. A 1962 Priestman Cub Mk 5 excavator was available to do the digging, but while the bridge to carry the tracks over the stream was being built, there was a period when as fast as the holes for the piles were being dug out, local vandals were filling them back up again. The abutments of the bridge were formed with 'gabions' (cages filled with stone) - following a trial run of the construction technique in Peter Lowe's back garden!

While construction work and track laying continued, the group took a Lister diesel loco, a manrider and some V-skips up the Abbey end of the line to show local people what was going on and build up some interest in the venture. Although the odd running session had taken place, proper passenger carrying

Kerr Stuart 0-4-0ST 'Wren' *Peter Pan* at the head of a train of 'manrider' passenger vehicles in the Country Park section of the Golden Valley Light Railway on 22 October 2000. This visit by *Peter Pan* represented the first time that passenger trains had been worked by steam over the Brands Crossing to Newlands Inn section of the GVLR.

operations commenced after HMRI approval was given on 17 January 1986. The railway subsequently settled into a pattern of running on Sundays and Bank Holidays between about 13.00 and 17.00 with regular trains along the quarter mile of track, there being no need for a specific timetable.

At the 'town' end, the small shed erected early on has been supplemented by a sizeable building, the frame of which once served as the canteen of the local St. Ann's Mill. Inside, a machine shop has been developed, despite there being no mains electricity (and no water either) laid on to the site. The electricity is provided by a three-phase generator, while water is gathered from the roof of the building. Another slightly unconventional aspect of the railway is the ballast, which is almost entirely composed of crushed brick - the railway has its own crusher, obtained from Porthmadog where it was originally used for crushing fluorspar. The station at the Abbey end consists of a simple run-round loop beside a low 'platform' among the trees beside a weir.

The railway has entertained steam traction in the form of Graham Morris' 0-4-0ST Kerr Stuart 'Wren' *Peter Pan* and aims to have a resident steam loco of its own, a start having been made on building a 'Wren' from scratch. The frames and buffer beams have been cut out and erection started, along with the assembly of fabricated cylinders. Design work for the boiler has started, although construction is some way off and dependent on raising the cash.

The line was originally intended to continue a little beyond its current Kirkstall terminus, closer to the impressive ruins of the Cistercian Monastery of Kirkstall Abbey. Financing such an extension is a problem, and maintaining the existing level of service could present difficulties for the small group involved in the railway - plus, they would have to keep up with increased wear and tear on the track and equipment. Although passenger numbers would almost certainly rise, an extension does not look very likely for now.

The working fleet includes: No 1 *Loweco* a 6hp Lister (20449/42), No 3 *Odin* a 20hp Simplex (5859/34), No 5 a Ruston 20 (235654/46), No 6 *Vulcan* a 44/48 Ruston (198287/42), No 6 *Druid* a 20hp Simplex (8644/41) fitted with a Perkins engine and new bodywork and No 12 is a 'Greenbat' battery electric (2848/57). A number of other locomotives are at the railway, some undergoing work, others dismantled and awaiting their turn for restoration. The coaches are based on the ex-RAF Fauld ammunition wagon chassis', fitted with suitable bodies.

The Golden Valley Light Railway

This project started on 28 May 1986 when the Butterley Narrow Gauge Railway Association was formed, a self-contained (and self-funding) society which is one of a number of groups based on the Midland Railway Centre. The main running line for the MRC is standard gauge, centring on Butterley station, near Ripley. A short westward length runs across Butterley Reservoir to Hammersmith, but the main tracks head east to Swanwick Junction where the Swanwick Colliery Spur swings away, while the main line continues towards Golden Valley and terminates a little beyond Ironville. Swanwick Junction is the hub of the MRC's activities, among which is a large ex-main line diesel collection. The owner of one of these diesels had also acquired some narrow gauge equipment, and from this developed the 2ft gauge Golden Valley Light Railway.

The initial narrow gauge line ran between Butterley Park station, adjacent to the MRC's Matthew Kirtley Museum building, past some standard gauge sidings, to a platform at the eastern end of the site. This gave a length of about 400 yards over which the first official passenger train operated in June 1991. At Butterley Park, a two-road loco shed/workshop was built in 1993, while an additional stock storage area grew up around both sides of the other terminus, becoming known as Brands Sidings. On 4 March 1994, a new station platform was commissioned part-way along the line. Called Brands Crossing, this is beside the level crossing where the ex-Lindby signalbox is located and was aimed at capturing passengers who arrived on the standard gauge train.

The intention was always to leave the confines of the Swanwick site and run through the Centre's Country Park - with the added incentive of a pub at the terminus! The proposed route crossed a footpath east of Brands Sidings, so a Transport & Works Order was required. In fact, the Golden Valley's TWO was the first to be made for a narrow gauge line under revised procedures which replaced the previous Light Railway Order process. The TWO was made on 8 July 1997, coming into force on 29 July, by which time the track had been laid, but much work remained before the railway could be opened to the public. An event had already been organised for 16/17 August to mark the 50th anniversary of the last passenger train to run on the Ashover Light Railway with Kerr Stuart 0-4-0ST *Pixie* visiting from the Leighton Buzzard Railway. Although restricted to working passenger trains only as far as Brands Sidings, *Pixie*

became the first steam locomotive to work over the extension when an 'after hours' run was made with a works train.

On crossing the path at Brands Sidings, the scenic transformation is instant as the line enters woodland. The first 600 yards or so of the extension is built on the alignment of a much earlier line, the Butterley Company's old tramway to Codnor Park Forge. The remainder of the 900 yard extension was built on a deviation, constructed as a by-product of a Derelict Land Grant Scheme which funded restoration of the Cromford Canal at the mouth of Butterley Tunnel - the basin being immediately below the railway's Newlands Inn terminus.

The extension was inspected by HMRI on 19 May 1998, sooner than anticipated, resulting in rapid last-minute work. Approval obtained, the paperwork was faxed on Friday 22 May and the line opened on 23 May! The first train, drawn by *Campbell's Brickworks No 1* (Simplex 60S364), transported the new station nameboard to Newlands Inn - the paint was dry but there had been no time to fix it in place! The opening coincided with a Thomas event at the MRC and the Golden Valley line operated for nine continuous days, carrying some 2,250 passengers.

The track on the extension is surprisingly heavy 50lb/yard rail, obtained from British Coal - to meet the requirements of the Railway Inspectorate - and is fixed to the sleepers with Pandrol spring clips and baseplates. On 21/22 October 2000 privately owned 0-4-0ST Kerr Stuart *Peter Pan* (also based at Leighton Buzzard and a 'sister' of *Pixie*) visited and became the first locomotive to work a steam hauled passenger service over the full railway.

Normally, GVLR trains are hauled by internal combustion. Air brake-equipped Motor Rail 60S *Campbell's Brickworks No 1* is the mainstay, although a Huwood Hunslet (Hudswell-Clarke) 100hp double-ended mines loco has seen service and a back-up passenger loco, Simplex 'T' Class 102T20 entered service in 2001. There are other locomotives on the site, several in working order but without air-braking equipment, including: Motor Rail 8739/42 *Pioneer*, Simplex 40SD 529, an ex-Berry Hill Ruston 20DL (222068/43) and ex-MoD Baguley Drewry (3703/74) battery electric locomotive. In time, there will be resident steam in the form of O&K 0-4-0WT (OK7529/14) which arrived in January 1995. Work commenced late in 2001 following storage in the open, and will take several years. Passengers are carried in ex-colliery manriders. Eventually, traditional-type narrow gauge coaches may be built.

Having opened through to Newlands Inn, the station platform at Brands Sidings was no longer used. Work commenced in 2000/2001 to rationalise the layout on both sides of the tracks. Relaid sidings north of the running line now include interesting short-radius points and a diamond crossing to demonstrate the amazing track geometry of coal mining environments. On the south side, containers provide accommodation to work on maintenance and restoration projects which cannot be accommodated in the workshop at Butterley Park. A £60,000 project to build a 3-road running shed covering some 5,000 sq ft with a pit, wheel drop and gantry crane, was launched towards the end of 2001.

At Butterley Park, as well as the operational stock, items of four different gauges are displayed on isolated sections of track,

with interpretive panels showing the role narrow gauge railways performed in industry. This stock includes: 3ft gauge Hudswell Clarke 0-4-0ST *Handyman* (573/1900), a 100hp Hudswell Clarke single-ended mines loco, a manrider and a colliery tub; a 2ft gauge water works display provided by ex-Stoke Bardolph Ruston LBT (7002/0567/6) and two skips; and 2ft 1ins and 2ft 4ins gauge 100hp Hudswell Clarke double-ended mines locos.

The line serves as an internal transport system on the Swanwick site and, in future, this could be extended up to Brittain Pit Farm. Another possibility lays in the Country Park where it may be possible to run round a marshy area which formed a feeder reservoir for the Cromford Canal. No decision has yet been made on either option.

North Gloucestershire Railway

The North Gloucestershire Railway was formed in 1985 as the successor to the Dowty Railway Preservation Society (founded in 1962) which had operated standard and narrow gauge lines at Ashchurch. The Society moved to the present site at Toddington, alongside the standard gauge Gloucestershire Warwickshire Railway yard, in 1983. The North Gloucestershire Railway Company decided to concentrate on narrow gauge and sold off the standard gauge equipment. Its base includes a loco shed/workshop,

which also houses various exhibits for the public to view, along with a station platform and signalbox. The 2ft gauge line of some 400 yards runs to a Halt beside the standard gauge line's car park.

In 1999 work started on building an extension of the running line from beside the existing loco shed along the bottom of the standard gauge embankment, to Dilbrook. The rails (purchased from the Vale of Rheidol Railway) were laid on the cleared trackbed by 2001, and the trackwork largely finished early in 2002 - opening of the extension in 2002, possibly 2003, being the aim.

The collection includes four steam locomotives. Henschel & Sohn (15968/18) 0-8-0T Heeresfeldbahn (Army Field Railways) loco *Brigadelok* arrived at Toddington in October 1985 in derelict condition and was rebuilt, although its boiler ticket expired in mid-2001. Bagnall (2820/46) 4-4-0T *Isibutu* was supplied to the Tongaat Sugar Co in South Africa. On returning to Britain, *Isibutu* initially went to Knebworth in Hertfordshire and was acquired by a group of North Gloucestershire Railway members in 1983 and brought to Toddington. Now owned by the North Gloucestershire Railway Company, what turned out to be a very protracted overhaul, with the work including the replacement of the front half of the boiler, was finally completed during 2001. On returning to steam, the intention was that the locomotive would revert to its

LEFT: Henschel (15968/18) 0-8-0T pictured at the North Gloucestershire Railway on 28 May 2000.

RIGHT: O&K 0-6-0WT *Elouise* **steams into the yard of the Old Kiln Light Railway on 28 August 2000.**

original name of *Egolomi*. The other steam locomotives are Hunslet 0-4-2T (2075/40) *Chaka's Kraal No 6*, which returned to Toddington in 2000 following a period of operation on the South Tynedale Railway, and Arnold Jung (939/06) 0-4-0WT *Justine*. The collection also includes several Motor Rail and Ruston Hornsby diesel locomotives.

Old Kiln Light Railway

The Old Kiln Light Railway is owned, run and funded by about a dozen enthusiasts. Its origins lay in the Wey Valley Railway, which was founded in the early 1970s and ran around a disused pumping station in Farnham using equipment from local industrial lines. That site was acquired for redevelopment, and in January 1982 everything was moved to the current location at the Old Kiln Museum at Tilford, near Farnham, in West Surrey. About a quarter of a mile of 2ft gauge running line has been built round two sides of the Museum's Rural Life Centre, plus associated sidings and buildings.

The railway is independent from the Museum and visitors pay a separate fare to ride on the line, which operates on summer Sundays and occasional Saturdays and Bank Holidays, although not always with steam traction. There is no published timetable, trains running when there are potential passengers, but the volunteers make a point of talking to people and aim to provide an educational experience. Visitors who are especially interested in the railway will be shown around the shed and able to look at the equipment which is not otherwise on view.

Passengers join and leave the trains at roughly the mid-point of the running line where the shed, workshops and storage sidings are located. The shed has steadily been developed over a period of time. When it was built, an extension was incorporated by including an extra section of roof on the far side. This foresight allowed the subsequent addition of a machine shop.

Steam motive power is provided by 0-6-0T *Elouise* (OK9998/22) which arrived at the Old Kiln in 1986. There is also a collection of internal combustion powered locomotives, manufacturers represented covering Motor Rail, Ruston & Hornsby, Hibberd and Hunslet. The restoration of a second steam locomotive is progressing. Ex-Penrhyn Hunslet 0-4-0ST *Pamela*, has worked in preservation, but her boiler ticket had expired when Old Kiln member, Gerald Cannon, purchased her in 1984. The rolling chassis is complete, with the boiler, which definitely needs a new inner firebox, the next stage. This loco has a rather different appearance from the conventional cabless quarry Hunslets having been rebuilt at Penrhyn between 1951/52 using the cab, boiler and firebox from the Hudswell Clarke locomotive *Bronllwyd* on the Hunslet frames. When restored, *Pamela* will retain this form.

The chassis of the open passenger carriages were built by

Baguley in 1928 for use on the Lilleshall Railway. This line was closed during WW2 and the carriages stored until the early 1950s. They subsequently ran for a time at Alton Towers until eventually finding their way to Surrey, by then in a very poor state. New wheels and new decks have been fitted, and the seats had to be stripped down before being re-fitted across the frames - originally, they had longitudinal seats. The group has also built a replica Glyn Valley Tramway coach to provide enclosed passenger accommodation if required.

The internal combustion fleet is housed under an ex-mush-room shed, an open-ended corrugated iron structure curving in an arc from ground level on one side to the other. About half a dozen locomotives are therefore sheltered from directly falling rain. For the time being, some components have to be removed and stored in the main building, although it is hoped that the ends of this 'sub-shed' will be covered in to form fully secure accommodation in the future. There is also an oil store, which looks like a railway lamp hut. It is not, but is of historical interest since it housed the first petrol pump in Farnham.

The first section of track to be laid at the Old Kiln was from what is now the yard, down a gradient to Old Kiln Halt. Although located beside the Rural Life Centre's car park, the low platform cannot be used by passengers. On returning to the main station and yard, the track turns tightly to the right and continues to climb up to the other terminus. This also has a low

Ex-Penrhyn Hunslet 0-4-0ST *Elin* pictured at the Yaxham Light Railway in July 1996. The non-standard Marshall boiler fitted at Coed-y-Parc results in a more 'dumpy' appearance than her fellow ex-quarry Hunslets. At the time of this picture, she had a 14ins extension at the rear to provide additional room on the footplate, but the new firebox being fitted at the time of writing should allow this to be removed.

platform, although it is only used when running Santa trains. For Christmas operations, the volunteers which support the Rural Life Centre, known as the Rustics, 'man' the halt. Aimed at increasing their comfort, the previous very basic shelter was replaced by a new version which included the provision of a stove for the 2000 season. The 'building' is constructed on a metal base (apparently an old bed frame!) which means it can be lifted onto a wagon and moved down to the station as covered accommodation during the summer season!

Passenger fare income is ploughed back into the railway - otherwise funded by the group who run the line - and Santa trains have helped the railway break even financially and be less of a draw on the pockets of those who run it and have always 'chipped in' to fund improvements.

Yaxham Light Railway

This railway is dedicated to industrial preservation rather than passenger- carrying, with no public running dates as such. The owners will operate the line for organised groups of enthusiasts for a reasonable charge to cover expenses. Some special openings also take place in conjunction with the adjacent re-opened standard gauge line.

Yaxham station, built by the Norfolk Railway, opened for goods in 1846 and passengers the following year. It was reduced to an unstaffed Halt and BR finally closed the line in June 1989. However, standard gauge trains have returned to the station, following opening of the Mid-Norfolk Railway between Dereham and Wymondham Abbey.

The first narrow gauge line at Yaxham was laid by Mr D C Potter in the goods yard, on the south west side of the standard gauge trackbed, in 1967. In 1969, the Yaxham Park Railway was built on the north east side of the station, running for ⅝ mile in the meadows beyond and including a circular loop. This line was subsequently removed but in 1982 work on the present

Yaxham Light Railway commenced. This was a quite different railway, although a small part of the route lay on that of the earlier line. In 1988, a start was made on upgrading to 30lb rail, an incline of 1 in 38 was built down to the level of the standard gauge trackbed and additional land purchased for a 120 yard extension. The present track length is 360 yards, plus a service line to the loco shed.

Over the years, there have been nineteen locomotives on the Yaxham Light Railway. Although several have left, a new arrival is given the next number up in the series, the old number being left vacant. Steam is represented by 0-4-0ST *Elin*, purchased by the three partners who run the railway and arriving at the site on 25 October 1986. *Elin* was built by Hunslet (HE705/99) for the Penrhyn quarries, but was fitted with a Marshall boiler, originally supplied as a portable boiler, at Coed-y-Parc works between November 1938 and February 1939. A new saddle tank was provided to match the differently-shaped boiler. In 1997, the boiler was lifted for a new firebox to be made and she should have returned to service when this book is published.

At the time of writing, the collection of ex-industrial internal combustion locomotives at the railway included: Ruston & Hornsby No 7 16hp (170369/34), No 6 *Colonel* 16/20hp (202967/40) and No 14 20DL (222100/43), Motor Rail 20/28hp No 10 *Ousel* (7153/37) and No 13 (7474/40), Lister No 2 *Rusty* (32801/48) and No 3 *Pest* (40011/54), O&K 'RL1b' No 4 *Goofy*, No 18 F C Hibberd 'Planet' 39 Type, and a Hudson Hunslet (2666/42) fitted with a McLaren engine. Out of service since 1982 is *Coffee Pot*, a 4wVTB built at Yaxham in 1970 by Mr D C Potter with a Merryweather steam fire pump and lorry gearbox. The intention is to rebuild it into an 0-4-0 tram loco, although other projects have precluded much progress.

There are around 40 wagons of various types, allowing the operation of demonstration industrial trains, and two bogie passenger carriages - the larger example can transport enthusiasts around the line if required.

CHAPTER SEVEN

The Narrow Gauge in Ireland

The earliest rail track in Ireland was built in the 1740s during the construction of a pier. The first proper railway was the Dublin - Kingstown (Dun Laoghaire) line, built to British standard gauge (4ft 8½ins) and opened on 17 December 1834. This was followed in 1836 by a 6ft 2ins gauge line from Belfast, initially to Lisburn, later reaching Armagh. The potential for chaos was recognised and a Royal Commission on Railways was set up to determine the question of gauge in Ireland, Major General Pasley recommending 5ft 3ins - a proposal confirmed by an 1846 Act of Parliament.

The Ballymena, Cushendall & Red Bay line is generally recognised as being the first narrow gauge railway in Ireland. Built to transport minerals, its Act of Parliament was passed in July 1872 and allowed construction between 2ft and 3ft gauge - the latter being adopted. It opened in May 1875, but in the meantime, the Glenariff Iron Ore & Harbour Company had built a 4-mile private railway (being on privately owned land, it did not need an Act of Parliament) to transport ore from the mines to a pier at Carrivemurphy (Antrim) which opened in 1873. Two locomotives built by Robert Stephenson & Co were ordered. These were the first 3ft gauge locos in Ireland, but the mines ran out and within three years, the railway was abandoned. The locos remained at the site until 1885 when, at the sale to liquidate assets, they were bought by the Lough Swilly Railway, then re-gauging its line. It is not really known why 3ft was selected as the gauge for these lines, but was quite possibly influenced by the opening of the first sections of the Isle of Man railway system during 1873/74.

Plainly, broad gauge lines were comparatively expensive to construct and the narrow gauge offered a means of bringing railways to less populated areas. The Tramways of Ireland Act of 1883 stimulated the rise of the narrow gauge in Ireland by allowing steam to be used on tramways, and dispensing with the need for promoters to obtain an Act of Parliament, instead they could apply to the Lord Lieutenant for an Order in Council to build a line. Further legislation included the Railway Act passed on 14 August 1896, which made government funding available for railway extensions through 'congested districts' and the Light Railways (Ireland) Act of 1889 provided further encouragement to narrow gauge construction.

By the 1920s, over 530 miles of 3ft gauge track had been built in Ireland. This, sadly, was the high point for the Irish narrow gauge. Ireland was partitioned in 1922, Ulster remaining part of the UK with the Irish Free State becoming semi-independent (although not fully independent as the Republic of Ireland until 1949). For lines which crossed the border, this added delays for customs checks, and realigned the economic flows to their disadvantage. In the south, internal troubles affected several railways during the civil war, and in 1924, the Railway Act resulted in the amalgamation of 26 broad and narrow gauge railway companies into the Great Southern Railways in 1925. The GSR became Coras Iompair Eireann (CIE) in 1945.

In Northern Ireland, the Midland Railway (in England) had purchased the Belfast & Northern Counties Railway in 1903 with the aim of extending its interests across the Irish Sea. Since the BNCR had already taken over the Ballymena & Larne Railway, this had brought a narrow gauge line under the control of the Midland Railway (Northern Counties Committee), to which further lines in Antrim were added. The MR(NCC) also acquired joint ownership of the County Donegal Railway (with the Great Northern Railway) in 1906. When the railway companies in Britain were grouped in 1923, the Midland Railway became part of the London Midland and Scottish Railway, the MR(NCC) therefore becoming the LMS(NCC). On the nationalisation of railways in Britain, the LMS became the London Midland Region of British Railways, with the interests in Ireland under the former LMS(NCC) passing to the Ulster Transport Authority on 1 April 1949.

The narrow gauge lines in Ireland described here concentrate on passenger carrying railways. There were also extensive industrial systems, not necessarily built to 3ft gauge. Although several are mentioned, principally where equipment is preserved, no more attempt has been made to document such railways than has been applied to similar systems in the UK. Bord na Mona operated, and still operates, a huge mileage of narrow gauge for industrial purposes, with the Clonmacnoise and West Offaly Railway using one of these networks, as did the short-lived Bellacorick Bóg Railway at Oweninny, Co Mayo, and is included. The Annaghmore Turf Railway is mentioned in view of the Peatlands Park Railway now running over part of the previously production bog.

The extensive mileages of several of the Irish narrow gauge systems, in some cases massive when compared with narrow gauge railways in England, Wales and Scotland, has resulted in the development of a somewhat different preservation and revival situation compared with that which exists across the water with several operations limited to sections of an original railway. None of these projects took over an operational railway, or followed closely behind closure, in the same manner as the lines described in Chapter 3. And yet, they do not really fit well with the other chapter headings in this book - hence this chapter devoted to the entire island of Ireland. The arrangement generally mirrors that adopted for the railways described in the rest of this volume: the lines which are now but memories, then the era of preservation and revival where trains are once again running on old trackbeds, next those constructed on old (Irish) broad gauge 5ft 3ins gauge trackbeds, and finally - a glimpse of the industrial scene, 'new' projects and museums.

In the Republic, FAS - an Irish Government-funded employment training authority - has been crucial in reviving the narrow gauge. FAS has provided labour to assist schemes designed to attract tourists and develop long-term employment, while providing short-term employment and marketable skills for those involved.

Now Departed

The Schull & Skibbereen Tramway

Promoted and operated by the West Carbery Tramways and Light Railway Ltd, and operated as the WCT&LR, this 15½ mile 3ft gauge line ran from Skibbereen (where it connected with the Baltimore branch of the broad gauge Cork, Bandon & South Coast Railway) around Roaring Water Bay to the fishing port of Schull. A roadside line with steep gradients and sharp curves, unfortunately, it was also poorly built and although services finally commenced in September 1886, they were suspended in the following April. The problems were compounded by the poor performance of the Dick, Kerr 0-4-0T tram engines supplied for the opening. A new loco arrived in 1888, Nasmyth Wilson 4-4-0T *Erin*, but the line continued to lose money. In 1892, the Grand Jury appointed a Committee of Management and the original company lost control of the line. Henceforth, it operated as the Schull & Skibbereen Tramway

OPPOSITE PAGE:
TOP: Kitson-built 0-4-0T tram locomotive No 2 of the Portstewart Tramway, in the colours of the Belfast & Northern Counties Railway, is preserved in the Ulster Folk and Transport Museum.

LOWER: Peckett 0-4-0T 'Aluminium' class No 2 of the British Aluminium Co. Ltd. of Larne, County Antrim, worked on the company's four-mile system which transported ore within the plant and to the quays for shipment. It is now displayed in the Ulster Folk and Transport Museum.

and Light Railway. Two Peckett 4-4-0Ts were added (*Gabriel* in 1905 and *Kent* in 1914) and the last of the original tram engines went in 1926. Finally, a Cork & Muskerry 0-4-4T arrived in 1936 when that line closed. The railway was taken over by the GSR in 1925 under the reorganisation of Irish railways following independence. Fuel shortages caused temporary closure in April 1944, it reopened in November 1945. The last passenger train ran on 27 January 1947, and the line was formally abandoned by CIE in September 1952.

The Cork, Blackrock & Passage Railway

This 16-mile line ran along the western shore of Cork harbour and was basically a suburban commuter line which featured some appropriately rapid running schedules. The first 6½ mile section between Albert Street, Cork, and Passage opened as a broad gauge line in June 1850. This was converted to 3ft gauge in 1900 followed by an extension to Monkstown (opened 1902) and reaching Crosshaven in 1904. The Albert Street - Blackrock section was double tracked (unique on the Irish narrow gauge), the line then being single with passing loops. The railway suffered considerable damage during the Irish civil war in the early 1920s, and became part of the GSR at the beginning of 1925. The double track section was singled in 1927. Bus and lorry competition continued to cause the railway to lose money and the Monkstown to Crosshaven section was closed in June 1932, followed by the remainder in the following September. The four 2-4-2T Neilson Reid locomotives were transferred to the Cavan & Leitrim line where one was scrapped in 1936, the remainder surviving into the 1950s.

The Cork & Muskerry Light Railway

The 8-mile 3ft gauge line from Cork (Western Road) to Blarney opened on 8 August 1887, followed by an 11 mile branch from Coachford Junction (located between Healy's Bridge and Tower Bridge) to Coachford which was opened in March 1888. An 8½ mile branch from St. Anne's to Donoughmore was opened in May 1893 - although nominally independent, the Donoughmore Extension Light Railway was always worked by the Cork & Muskerry. The Great Southern took over under the railway company mergers following the 1924 Railway Act in Ireland. Having suffered damage during the Irish civil war, lost traffic never returned. This was compounded by bus competition, and the last train ran on 29 December 1934.

The C&M owned nine locomotives during its lifetime. Three Falcon 2-4-0Ts, *City of Cork*, *Coachford* and *St Anne's* were supplied for the opening (later converted to 4-4-0Ts) followed by a Kitson 0-4-2T No 4 *Blarney* in 1888 (sold 1910). Two 0-4-4T locos built by Thomas Green of Leeds, No 5 *Donoughmore* and No 6 *The Muskerry*, were delivered for the opening of the Donoughmore line, and 4-4-0T No 7 *Peake* was built by Brush Electrical Engineering Co (the successors to Falcon) in 1898. Also built by Brush was 4-4-0T No 8 *Dripsey* (similar to, but less powerful than, No 7) and the final locomotive was a Hunslet 4-4-0T, given the name *Blarney*, which arrived in 1919, but scrapped in 1927.

The body of Londonderry & Lough Swilly Railway 6-wheel carriage No 18 preserved in the Foyle Valley Railway museum. Although it retains its frame, there is no running gear, hence the body is stored on a CDR chassis.

The Clogher Valley Railway

This 37 mile long 3ft gauge roadside line linked the GNR stations at Tynan (Clones - Armagh line) and Maguiresbridge (Clones - Enniskillen line). It was opened in May 1887, and although its legal status was changed in 1894 from a tramway to a railway, its Sharp Stewart 0-4-2T locomotives with enclosed motion remained unaltered. In 1936, No 4, a Hudswell Clarke 2-6-0T was purchased from the Castlederg & Victoria Bridge line and rebuilt to become a 2-6-2T of conventional appearance. The railway was taken over by Tyrone and Fermanagh County Councils in 1928 and the improvements included the introduction of a diesel railcar, which took over (and dramatically speeded up) passenger services, and a rail lorry – both built by the Wigan-based firm of Walkers. Despite enhanced services, road competition took its toll and the losses continued, the final day of operation being on 31 December 1941. The steam locomotives were all scrapped, but the Railcar went to the County Donegal and became its No 10, and is now in the Ulster Folk & Transport Museum.

The Ballymena & Larne Railway

This 3ft gauge line opened for goods in July 1877, regular passenger services following in August 1878 - the first such on the Irish narrow gauge. At Ballymena, the line was extended to the broad gauge station in 1880, and ran for 32 miles to the port of Larne, where it shared a station with the 5ft 3ins gauge Belfast & Northern Counties Railway. The B&NCC took over the Ballymena & Larne in July 1899. In turn, the Midland Railway (of Britain) purchased the Belfast & Northern Counties Railway in 1903, the resulting Midland Railway (Northern Counties Committee) subsequently becoming the LMS(NCC). The Ballymena & Larne was noted for its boat trains, operated with newly constructed carriages, which were the fastest narrow gauge services in Ireland, as well as offering a standard of comfort never previously encountered in Ireland on the narrow gauge. The railway closed to passengers in 1933, although the section between Ballyclare Paper Mills and Larne harbour remained in use until July 1950.

The original locomotives on this line were built by Beyer Peacock, an 0-6-0T and two 2-4-0Ts which were very similar to those supplied to the Isle of Man. A 2-6-0ST was added in 1880, and another 0-6-0T in 1883.

A 4-mile line, operated by British Aluminium between 1900 and 1960 connecting the company's factory with the harbour at

Larne, connected with the Ballymena & Larne Railway. Peckett 0-4-0T No 2, which worked this line, was sold to George Cohen & Co in 1955 and was employed in the lifting of the Ballycastle Railway - it is now preserved in the Ulster Folk & Transport Museum. Peckett 0-4-0T No 1 was sold to a private owner, who steamed it in his garden, until being sold to Lord O'Neill in 1970 for the Shane's Castle Railway where it was named *Tyrone*. It is now at the Giant's Causway and Bushmills Railway.

The Ballymena, Cushendall & Red Bay Co

This 3ft gauge line was the first Irish narrow gauge line to be sanctioned by Parliament. It opened in May 1875 and ran over 17 miles between Ballymena and Retreat serving the iron mines in the area via sidings and branches. This mineral business collapsed and the line was taken over by the (broad gauge) Belfast & Northern Counties Railway in 1884, with a passenger service being introduced for the first time two years later. It thus also came under the wing of the LMS(NCC) in due course. A problem from the beginning, and never solved, was getting the line down from its 1,000ft summit to the coast in the space of four miles as envisaged by its title. Although passenger trains were introduced, they terminated at Parkmore, 3¾ miles short of Retreat - passengers having to use road transport to reach the tourist destinations of Cushendall and Glenariff. Passenger services ended in 1930, goods ceasing in 1940. The line made an end-on connection with the Ballymena & Larne Railway in Ballymena.

The original trio of Black Hawthorne 0-4-2ST locomotives were replaced by the B&NCR, a series of compound 2-4-2Ts being built for the company's narrow gauge lines in Antrim. The first pair were built by Beyer Peacock, the remainder being constructed at York Road works, Belfast.

The Ballycastle Railway

This 17 mile 3ft gauge line linked the coastal resort of Ballycastle with the B&NCR broad gauge Londonderry main line at Ballymoney. Opened in October 1880, it was not very successful and closed for a time in 1924, before being taken over and resuscitated by (what had now become) the LMS (NCC). There were originally three Black Hawthorne 0-6-0ST locomotives, with two Kitson 4-4-2Ts arriving in 1908 which were subsequently transferred to the Ballymena & Larne Railway in 1930 to work that line's boat train services. The original carriages were largely replaced by the carriages designed for the Ballymena & Larne boat train traffic, which were transferred to the Ballycastle line in 1933. The Ballycastle Railway closed in July 1950, its owners by then being the Ulster Transport Authority.

The Portstewart Tramway

Linking the seaside town of Portstewart with the Belfast & Northern Counties branch line between Coleraine and Portrush, this 1¼ mile 3ft gauge line was Ireland's first roadside steam

tramway. It opened in June 1882, but by 1892 the company was bankrupt, with a Receiver appointed. Operations continued until 1897 when the line was put up for sale, the only offer being made by the BNCR which then assumed control. Since the BNCR was acquired by the Midland Railway in 1903, which was in turn grouped along with other British railway companies in 1923, the Portstewart tramway became a part of the London, Midland & Scottish Railway! The tramway was in poor condition and the LMS(NCC) decided on closure - the last tram running on 30 January 1926. The first two locomotives were identical 0-4-0T tram engines built Kitson & Co of Leeds, while the third (also a Kitson) had slightly smaller wheels and therefore a higher tractive effort. No 2 (dating from 1883), is preserved in the Ulster Folk & Transport Museum, the other is in Hull Transport Museum.

The Londonderry and Lough Swilly Railway

The first section, between Londonderry and Farland Point (a section which lasted just three years) and Buncrana opened in November 1863 as a 5ft 3ins gauge line. A 3ft gauge line was opened from Tooban Junction to Letterkenny in June 1883, and in 1885, the original Londonderry - Buncrana section was re-gauged to 3ft. In July 1901, an extension from Buncrana to Carndonagh was opened, and in March 1903 the notionally separate Letterkenny & Burtonport Extension Railway was opened. This brought the total system up to 99 miles of track - although 50 miles of this was contributed by the Burtonport Extension - the second longest narrow gauge system in Ireland. At Letterkenny, it connected with the County Donegal Railway line from Strabane via a spur, the companies each having their own stations, there being little cooperation between the two. The partition of Ireland in 1922 brought great problems for the railway with customs delays at the border and changes in the pattern of trade in north Donegal. The railway was losing money by 1925 and approaches to the CDRJC concerning joint operating - and a unified 223 mile 3ft gauge system - were rejected. Closure came in stages: Buncrana - Carndonagh in October 1935, Londonderry - Buncrana (to passengers) in September 1948 and goods August 1953, Gweedore - Burtonport first in June 1940 although revived until final closure in 1947, Letterkenny - Gweedore June 1947, and Derry - Letterkenny in August 1953. In the 1920s, the company started to run buses, and remains in existence as a bus operator!

The first Lough Swilly narrow gauge locos were three Black Hawthorne 0-6-2Ts (the first in 1882, the other two in 1883), followed by an 0-6-0T from the same builder in 1885. In addition, two 2-4-0T locomotives built by Robert Stephenson & Co for the Glenariff Iron Ore & Harbour Company were purchased when that operation's assets were sold in 1885. In 1899, the first big engines arrived in the form of two 4-6-2Ts built by Hudswell Clarke, followed by two more in 1901 for opening of the Carndonagh line. Further pairs of 4-6-2Ts were delivered in 1904 (Kerr Stuart) and 1910 (Hawthorne Leslie). Andrew Barclay supplied four 4-6-0Ts for the opening of the Burtonport Extension. The locos became bigger still, the next pair, for use on the Burtonport line, being 4-8-0 tender locos built by Hudswell Clarke in 1905. The final motive power was also sizeable, a pair of Hudswell Clarke-built 4-8-4Ts in 1912.

The Bessbrook & Newry Tramway

This 3 mile 3ft gauge tramway connecting the flax mills at Bessbrook with the town of Newry opened in October 1895 and closed on 10 January 1948. It employed hydro-electric power (following just two years after the Giant's Causeway line) supplied through a third rail between the running rails, except at Millvale level crossing where there was an overhead supply. Two motor cars and a trailer (all being bogie vehicles supplied by Ashbury) formed the original stock. Two more motor cars and a trailer were supplied by Hurst Neilson in 1921, and two Dublin & Lucan trailers were acquired in 1925. There were 27 4-wheel freight wagons - with flangeless wheels! These ran on additional rails laid on each side of the main running rails at a slightly lower level - the flangeless wheels allowing the wagons to be hauled on the road, thus easing transhipment problems.

One of the original power cars, No 2, has survived. Originally equipped with an open driving platform at one end (the tramway had a turning loop at each end, obviating the need for reverse running) the bodywork was to be renewed in 1920, but a new power car was purchased instead. However, in 1942, the passenger compartment was replaced by the body of one of the ex-Dublin & Lucan trams - No 24, built in 1900. Following closure, in 1950 the rebuilt power car returned to its original builder, Mather & Platt, in Manchester where it became a cricket pavilion - complete with glass panel to display the electric motor! In 1955, Mather & Platt donated the tram to what is now the Ulster Folk & Transport Museum.

The Castlederg & Victoria Bridge Tramway

Seven miles long, this 3ft gauge line ran from Victoria Bridge, on the Londonderry & Enniskillen broad gauge line, to Castlederg. Opened in July 1883, there were three intermediate stations, which had sidings but no passing loops. The original locomotives were Kitson 0-4-0T tramway engines (two for the opening, another in 1891), but these had gone by 1912 having been progressively replaced by a Hudswell Clarke 2-6-0T which arrived in 1904 (to the Clogher Valley Railway on closure), a Hudswell Clarke 0-4-4T in 1912 and a Beyer Peacock 2-4-0T (similar to the Isle of Man type) obtained in 1928 from the Ballymena & Larne line when it closed. A Railcar seating 24 passengers was constructed at Castlederg in 1925. Powered by a 20hp Fordson paraffin engine, this machine had controls at each end. Already running at a loss and with accumulated debts, the line closed during the railway strike which took place in Ireland between 31 January and 7 April 1933. The last steam locomotive to traverse the line left Castlederg on 27 July 1934, to move the stock to Victoria Bridge for auction. A locomotive and some wagons were purchased by the Clogher Valley line, while what remained of the Railcar was acquired by the County Donegal and formed the basis of CDR Railcar No 2.

RIGHT: Ex-Bord na Mona Andrew Barclay 0-4-0WT No 2 (AB2264/49) and passenger coaches, which form the 'Stradbally Woodland Express', pictured in the station of the 3ft gauge line operated by the Irish Steam Preservation Society.

Preservation and reconstruction

The Stradbally Woodland Express

Located in the grounds of Stradbally Hall, Co Laois, the train runs with a 'Stradbally Woodland Express' nameboard and the volunteers who run it agreed that this should be the description of their railway. Operated by the Irish Steam Preservation Society (ISPS), formed in early 1966, the railway was the first steam operated narrow gauge railway with regular public access to be built, maintained and operated by volunteers in Ireland.

A Traction Engine Rally held behind the Market House in Stradbally on 26 December 1965 created huge interest. Some 8/9 engine owners viewed the town as a convenient centre and approached the owner of nearby Stradbally Hall. Agreement was reached with the late Major E A S Cosby that future events could be held in the grounds of the Hall, an arrangement continued by his family to the present day, with the August Bank Holiday Steam Rally now a major event - note that this Irish Bank Holiday does not correspond with that in Britain.

The first railway element was introduced for the 1966 event when Guinness Brewery locomotive No 15, which had been acquired by the ISPS, was placed on blocks and steamed at the Rally entrance. This is one of the unusual 1ft 10ins gauge 0-4-0T locomotives built to the design of Samuel Geoghegan for work at the St. James's Gate Brewery in Dublin, which could be mounted on a converter truck and shunt 5ft 3ins sidings as well. The compact design met the requirement of working a spiral tunnel linking two parts of the Brewery, which made 2½ turns on a 1 in 39 gradient. Similar locomotives are preserved at Amberley, Tywyn, the Guinness Museum in Dublin and the Ulster Folk and Transport Museum in Belfast. For the 1967 Rally, about 50 yards of 1ft 10ins gauge track had been laid which No 15 steamed along. This track was extended a little for the 1968 event, with No 15 again in steam.

Towards the end of 1968, Bord na Mona disposed of three 3ft gauge 0-4-0WT locos which had been built in 1949 by Andrew Barclay. No 2 (AB2264/49) and No 3 (AB2265/49) were acquired by the Society, No 3 then being sold to Lord O'Neil for use on the Shane's Castle Railway where it was named *Shane*, and is now at the Giant's Causeway & Bushmills Railway. No 1 was sold separately to the Talyllyn Railway Preservation Society and was to form the basis of TR No 7 *Tom Rolt*. For the ISPS, the acquisition of No 2 opened the way for a more comprehensive railway at Stradbally Hall and it was decided to cease operating the Guinness loco. A museum of steam and vintage farm machinery had been opened in 1968 in a building in Stradbally itself and No 15, along with three 4-wheel passenger wagons from the Guinness system, was moved in.

The passenger wagons were essentially a slatted knifeboard seat for four people, mounted on a chassis frame. Two of these wagons were later transferred to the Guinness Museum.

The 1ft 10ins gauge track was lifted and laying of a new 3ft gauge line commenced. Initial thoughts envisaged a three mile line around the Estate but, as work progressed, the small group involved realised this was too ambitious. A more modest scheme was prepared, and developed, today's ⅝ mile of running line being completed in 1982. The track commences in a locomotive shed, then runs into a platform where passengers join and leave the train. There is a passing loop, although the loop line is used for stock storage. The track climbs up through the woods to a junction where trains normally take the line to the right, to run round a sizeable balloon loop, still in a heavily wooded setting, before returning to the junction and dropping back down into the station. The loco pushes the carriages back round the circuit for the next trip, thus returning the train to being the right way round at the station.

There are also diesel locomotives on the railway. The wholly original *Nippy*, a Hibberd Planet 4wDM (2014/36) arrived in April 1986 from the Shane's Castle Railway and was soon put into running order. A Ruston & Hornsby 4wDM (326052/52), which had been fitted with a Lister HR6 air cooled engine in 1982, was donated to the Society by the Electricity Supply Board in 1991 and is also in working order. Hunslet 4wDM

(2281/41) however no longer has an engine and is somewhat derelict, with no plans for restoration. There are two semi-open passenger carriages with toastrack seating. The larger is based on the shortened underframe of Cavan & Leitrim Railway coach No 7, with new upperworks built by Joseph Bennett & Sons of Stradbally and entered service in 1973. The other is a shorter brake carriage based on a flat wagon from the British Aluminium Co at Fort William which came to Stradbally via the Shane's Castle Railway - the underframe and wheels arriving in April 1986, although conversion into a passenger-carrying brake vehicle was not completed until 1990. The locomotive shed was first built to accommodate the Guinness loco, then being around a quarter of its present size. It was doubled in length to accommodate the Barclay 0-4-0WT in late 1968, and doubled again when the Ruston arrived in 1991.

In more recent years, the museum in Stradbally has been closed and had effectively become a store, the Guinness locomotive and passenger truck remaining inside, but not available for public viewing. During 2000, funding became available in partnership with the Laois Leader Rural Development Co Ltd and a refurbishment programme for the building commenced. It is hoped that internal decoration will be completed in 2002 and funding secured to bring in new exhibits to supplement those in the building, and others stored off-site.

The Society is an entirely volunteer organisation and runs

Although the revived section of the Tralee & Dingle railway is normally operated by steam, its 1892-built Hunslet 2-6-2T No 5T (HE555/1892) underwent a heavy overhaul during 2001. Services during that season were worked by a 115hp Hunslet diesel (HE9256/86) hired from Bord na Mona, presenting a different photographic opportunity for this 19 September 2001 picture.

the railway for pleasure. Considerable help with sales of track material is provided by Iarnrod Eireann, and a retired Chief Permanent Way Supervisor has helped the group maintain the track to a high standard over many years. The railway operates on all Irish Bank Holiday Sundays and Mondays between Easter and October, and on other occasions when there is a special event in Stradbally and is entirely dependent on fare income. The Annual August Steam Rally can generate very large numbers of passengers - over 2,100 have been carried in a single day! The railway can also be opened for organised parties by prior arrangement and details of special short notice operations are posted on the ISPS website.

Tralee & Dingle Light Railway

Opened in March 1891, the main line ran from Tralee (the capital of Kerry) to Dingle, a distance of 32¾ miles. Some 10 miles from Tralee, a branch at Castlegregory Junction ran for 6 miles to Castlegregory itself. Much of the route across the Dingle peninsular traversed sparsely populated areas, and involved considerable climbs and descents. There was never much passenger traffic, but cattle fairs kept things going. Passenger trains

ceased in 1939 and regular goods services ended in March 1947, although periodic cattle train 'specials' ran until June 1953 when the line finally closed.

Three Hunslet 2-6-0T locomotives were supplied in 1889 for the opening. Hunslet also supplied a tram-like double-cab 0-4-2T with covered motion for the Castlegregory branch in 1890, although this was unsuccessful and scrapped in 1907. A Hunslet 2-6-2T was delivered in 1892, followed by the purchase of two Kerr Stuart 2-6-0Ts in 1902/03. Another Hunslet arrived in 1910, this being a 2-6-0T. The roadside nature of the route accounted for the fitting of cowcatchers and acetylene headlamps to the locomotives. The carriages were all bogie vehicles and the majority of 4-wheel wagons were for carrying cattle.

On the closure of the Tralee & Dingle line, four of the locomotives were transferred to the Cavan & Leitrim Railway, which was still operating by virtue of the Arigna coal traffic. When the C&L finally closed in 1959, 1892-built Hunslet 2-6-2T No 5T (HE555/1892) became the sole surviving Tralee & Dingle locomotive having been saved from scrapping by an American enthusiast, Edgar T Mead of Erna, New Hampshire. The loco was shipped across the Atlantic and displayed in the Steamtown Museum in Vermont. This Museum was moved to Pennsylvania in 1985 and No 5 no longer fitted into the Museum's plans. Back in Tralee, there was a revival of interest in local industrial history and a project to restore the windmill at Blennerville was being promoted. A local journalist, Peter Levy, traced Edgar Mead and the idea emerged of repatriating the locomotive. A committee was formed in Tralee to progress the return of No 5 and with sponsorship from Tralee Urban

District Council, local businesses and donations from individuals, the project gathered pace. Edgar Mead donated No 5 to the Tralee group, and with the aid of a special rate for shipping by Atlantic Containers, the locomotive returned to Tralee in August 1986.

The plan had been to display the locomotive at the main line station in Tralee, but its return generated so much interest locally that ideas for providing a railway for it to run on emerged. Consideration was given to laying a third rail along part of the 5ft 3ins gauge Tralee to Fenit section - a concept stimulated by the Great Southern Railway Preservation Society running steam hauled trains on the Fenit line - but this presented practical difficulties, and would not capture the atmosphere of the old narrow gauge line. Much of the T&D trackbed had been built over for housing in the Tralee area, but the section from the old basin station remained undeveloped. This fitted well with the restoration of the windmill at Blennerville and the canal which parallels the River Lee between Tralee and Blennerville. The idea of reinstating the railway between Tralee and Blennerville became part of the Lee Valley Development Scheme and was supported by Bord Failte (Irish Tourist Board), the objective being to provide a tourist attraction while preserving the memory of the old railway. With the scheme now written into the development plans for the area, the Tralee - Dingle Engine Restoration Committee promoted the scheme in early 1987 with the publication of a booklet which was partly a facsimile of an original Tralee & Dingle company publication, with additional material explaining the project.

The next step was the formation of the Tralee & Dingle Steam Railway Company. Some IR£100,000 was rapidly raised, while the local Council purchased the trackbed. The restoration of No 5 took some three years, the work being done by a team from the North Yorkshire Moors Railway. The restoration was also supported by FAS, Shannon Development and CIE. The first trains over the 3 kilometres (1½ miles) of revived 3ft gauge line ran in December 1992, with the official opening on 10 July 1993 - making it the first narrow gauge steam railway restoration to provide a regular passenger service in Ireland. The railway is operated by paid staff, employing men who worked on its reconstruction. The railway is open between May and September and traffic averages around 25,000 passengers a year, the highest total recorded being 30,000 in a year.

At the Tralee end, a new station was built at Ballyard (not on the original formation) on the southern edge of the town. The station, sharing a car park with the Aqua Dome, consists of just a platform and run-round loop. The line crosses a road over a gated level crossing, followed shortly by traversing the River Lee on a newly-built bridge. Regaining the original trackbed, the railway runs over the salt marshes (which can sometimes be under water) in the estuary of the River Lee. After crossing a tributary of the river by another bridge, the line parallels Kearney's Road into Blennerville. This station consists of a newly constructed platform on the site of the original station with a run-round loop. Across the road from the buffer stops is the restored windmill, with a craft shop and restaurant in the surrounding complex. Blennerville is also the operational base of

the railway. Just short of the platform, a turnout leads immediately into a gated level crossing over Kearney's Road and into the yard with a single-road shed and stock storage sidings.

In addition to 2-6-2T No 5, the railway has an ex-Bord na Mona Ruston & Hornsby 40DL (371967/54) for use on works trains and shunting. Four metre gauge passenger carriages were acquired for the revived line from Bilbao, Spain, although only two were refurbished and regauged. The other pair remain in open storage in the yard. Although there are suitable bogies, this pair have never been brought into use since the platform at Blennerville limits the length of trains which can be accommodated. During the 2001 season, the boiler from No 5 was lifted and sent to Israel Newton's works in Bradford (UK) basically for a 10-year overhaul. Trains during that season were hauled by a 115hp Hunslet diesel (HE9256/86) which was hired from Bord na Mona.

The above-mentioned booklet (reprinted without alteration in 1999 in view of its historic interest) to promote the revival of part of the Tralee & Dingle line included a small map of the proposed route. In the event, Ballyard station was not built in quite the same location as shown. This map also showed two possible extensions at the Tralee end of the line, one of which would not work in view of the revised station location. The initial section of the other represents what was constructed, although there are no current plans to continue in an easterly direction as the map indicates. The area around Ballyard station, however, is within the Lee Valley Park which is being progressively developed. For the railway, these plans envisage the construction of a building at Ballyard station in the style of the original T&D station (which still survives in private ownership) to serve as a visitor centre and small museum.

Although operated by the Tralee & Dingle Steam Railway Company, the line is sometimes marketed as the Tralee & Blennerville Railway to avoid giving a misleading impression to potential passengers as to the line's actual destination.

The County Donegal Railways

The County Donegal Railway Joint Committee network became the most extensive narrow gauge system in Ireland, and Britain, with nearly 125 miles of 3ft gauge track. Its origins lay in the 5ft 3ins gauge Finn Valley Railway opened between Strabane and Stranorlar on 7 September 1863. At Strabane, this line shared a station with the Londonderry and Enniskillen Railway, which was leased to the Irish North Western Railway. In turn, the INWR was amalgamated into the Great Northern Railway (Ireland) in 1876.

The Finn Valley company wished to extend westwards to the town of Donegal. A new company, the West Donegal Railway Co, was formed on 21 July 1879 to build the line. The West Donegal line was constructed to 3ft gauge and ran from Stranorlar, through the Barnesmore Gap in the Blue Stack Mountains, to a temporary terminus at Druminin (later named Lough Eske) some four miles short of Donegal - the cash having run out. The line opened on 25 April 1882, motive power being three Sharpe Stewart 2-4-0Ts. The railway was finally completed and opened to Donegal on 16 September 1889, the new station being built by the Donegal Railway Station Company and leased to the WDR!

In 1892, the Finn Valley and West Donegal companies amalgamated to form the Donegal Railway Company, and the system expanded. A 19-mile extension from Donegal to Killybegs opened in August 1893, the Stranorlar to Strabane section was regauged to 3ft in July 1894, utilising a new route into Strabane, and a 24-mile branch from Stranorlar to Glenties opened on 3 June 1895. A line from Strabane to Derry opened on 1 August 1900 - Victoria Road station being on the opposite bank of the River Foyle from the broad gauge Great Northern terminus, although Donegal wagons could be winched over the Craigavon bridge to the GNR yards for transhipment of loads. Donegal - Ballyshannon opened on 21 September 1905, making a total of 105 miles. The railway was purchased by the Midland(NCC) and the Great Northern Railway on 1 May 1906, and henceforth run by the County Donegal Railway Joint Committee for the two owning companies. A line from Strabane to Letterkenny was built and opened on 1 January 1909. Although the Strabane and Letterkenny Railway was nominally independent, it was always worked by the CDRJC and brought the total CDRJC system up to 124½ miles. The Letterkenny extension had been opposed by the Londonderry & Lough Swilly Railway, which provided a link between Letterkenny and Derry, and relations were cool. Each had its own station, although the lines were connected.

The 1920s were a difficult period with the 'troubles' followed by the partition of Ireland and associated difficulties of running a line which crossed the border. Road competition was rising, although the CDRJC bought its own vehicles in an effort to feed traffic onto the railway system, and experimented with Railcars as an economy measure. By the end of WW2, the system was run-down and there was little cash to rectify matters. Road competition was biting hard by the 1940s and losses grew, although the CDRJC maintained standards during these difficult times.

The first section to close was Stranorlar to Glenties, with regular passenger and freight services ending in December 1947, the final freight being run in September 1949, with closure becoming official in March 1952, followed by demolition between 1953/55. The cost of working the Strabane to Derry section was actually charged to The Ulster Transport Authority, so steam remained the rule over this route, there being little reason to use its more economic Railcars from the CDRJC's viewpoint! The UTA closed this line in December 1954, although a 'special' was run in June 1955. The end for the remainder of the system came on 31 December 1959 and from 1 January 1960, the CDRJC became solely a bus and lorry operator, a situation remaining until 1971 when the company was absorbed by CIE (the state transport body) and the bus routes taken over by Bus Eireann, the road passenger division.

The original locomotives were three Sharpe Stewart Class 1 2-4-0Ts built by Sharpe Stewart, the last of these being scrapped in 1926. Six Class 2 4-6-0Ts were supplied by Neilson Reid in 1893 (the last of these was scrapped in 1937) and two Class 3 4-4-4Ts built in 1902, also by Neilson Reid, survived until both were scraped in 1933. Later locomotives

were all supplied by Nasmyth Wilson between 1904-1912 and comprised four Class 4 4-6-4Ts, five Class 5 2-6-4Ts and three Class 5A 2-6-4Ts. The locomotive fleet was renumbered and renamed in 1928, with further changes in 1937.

The pioneering use of Railcars was introduced by Henry Forbes, who had joined the CDR in 1910 as Secretary, became Traffic Manager in 1916 and after 1928 was Secretary and Manager until he died in November 1943. In 1906, a small 4-wheel Inspection Car built by Allday & Onions of Birmingham had entered service. This was rebuilt in 1920 to carry seven passengers (and mail) and became Railcar No 1. A coal strike in 1926 encouraged its use, and two further machines were acquired that year from the Derwent Valley Railway and regauged from 4ft 8½ins to 3ft. This pair were replaced in 1934, the new No 2 being based on an ex-Castlederg & Victoria Bridge Tramway vehicle, while the chassis for No 3 came from the Dublin & Blessington Steam Tramway - the latter having eight wheels and the only double-ended Railcar to run on the CDR. Later converted into a trailer, this vehicle is preserved at Cultra.

The development of the type continued and in 1930/31 Nos 7 and 8 - the first diesel Railcars in the British Isles - were introduced. The chassis' were built by the GNR in Dundalk and employed Gardner engines, with bodies from O'Dohertys, coach builders in Strabane. Modern articulated Railcars started to arrive from 1934, the first Walker machine, No 12 (with the body built at Dundalk by the GNR) arriving that year. Also added to the fleet was the first articulated Railcar in Ireland, which had been supplied to the Clogher Valley Railway, becoming CDRJC No 10 on arrival in 1942 following closure of the CVR. The final development provided Nos 19 and 20 in 1950, although the Railcars subsequently built for the West Clare Railway were of the same type. This CDRJC pair were sold to the Isle of Man Railways and at the time of writing are part-way through a major reconstruction programme.

The Railcars were successful, reducing operating costs while offering the flexibility to stop virtually anywhere to pick up or set down passengers. As the older Railcars were withdrawn, they were converted into trailers, while the more modern machines were able to haul red painted vans carrying parcels and mail.

The entire system had been demolished by the end of 1960 and on 1 March 1961 a public auction took place at Stranorlar (Co Donegal) and Strabane (Co Tyrone). There were 124 lots, including steam locomotives, seven Railcars, 14 bridges (the longest was the 229ft span over the River Finn outside Clady), wagons, bogies, cranes, signalboxes, rails and sleepers. The majority was purchased by a Dublin-based foundry. Prices realised included working locos for £550, £250 and £160, and a Railcar for £95.

Much of the equipment was saved for preservation. A number of items were secured by the (then) Belfast Transport Museum and are now housed in the Ulster Folk & Transport Museum. The other source follows the intervention of Dr Ralph Cox, whose name will be encountered elsewhere in the text. He came from New Jersey and planned to build a narrow gauge railway in the United States. Viewing the CDR locomotives, Railcars and stock as being suitable for this scheme, he initially made private purchases of various items. He was subsequently successful in bidding for further equipment at the 1961 auction, but apparently could not raise the funds to ship the items back to the USA and his plan had collapsed by about 1968. Some of the coaches were vandalised and later scrapped and (surely incredibly) No 11 *Erne*, the last Baltic tank in Britain and Ireland, was cut up as late as 1967 at Letterkenny, but his involvement certainly saved much equipment from destruction.

There are presently two restoration projects based on sections of the old County Donegal trackbed which are described in the following sections, plus the Ulster Folk and Transport Museum and the Foyle Valley Railway, where ex-CDRJC equipment is preserved.

The Fintown Railway (An Mhuc Dhubh)

Before describing the railway and its origins, some explanation concerning its description is in order. A Gaeltacht is a designated area of Ireland where Gaelic remains the primary language and old traditions and culture are still a part of everyday life. Such areas receive special support to aid development, and with the Fintown district laying within such an area, the financial input of Udaras Na Gaeltachta has been crucial in rebuilding the railway. Publicity and written material on the project is dual language and the railway is promoted as An Mhuc Dhubh Historic Railway. The Gaelic translates as the Black Pig, the description which local people gave to the arrival of steam locomotives in the district - puffing, 'snorting' and billowing black smoke! Material concerning the line also features the description Cumann Traenach na Gaeltachta Lair (CTGL) which means Central Gaeltacht Train Society - the body which operates the line. The cover of the Society journal features the description An Mhuc Dhubh, with 'The Fintown Railway' beneath. Although it may be described as the Fintown - Glenties railway restoration project, the term Fintown -

Glenties Railway does not appear in any literature.

The County Donegal line from Stranorlar - Glenties was opened in 1895, incorporating a magnificently scenic section beside Lough Finn, but closed to passengers in 1947. The origins of the project to reinstate a 3ft gauge railway along the shore of Lough Finn date back to 1991. Joseph Brennan was involved with the County Donegal project at Donegal town station which aimed to rebuild a section of the CDR to the Barnesmore Gap. He approached the Development Committee for Fintown, which existed to find ways of regenerating the locality, with the idea of rebuilding the rail link between Fintown and Glenties. The Development Committee backed the idea and a committee was formed to promote the scheme. Many meetings were held, principally with local farmers to gain permission to cross their land and the 'first sod' was turned at Fintown station in 1992, although the first track was not laid until October 1994. Advice on tracklaying was provided by Foyle Valley Railway (North West of Ireland Railway Society) members, with a team of FAS workers undertaking construction, largely with picks and shovels.

The target was to open on 3 June 1995 - the exact centenary of the arrival of the original County Donegal line. This was achieved, the line then being ⁹⁄₁₀ of a mile. Opening day featured large crowds seeking a trip on the revived railway, and the 1995 season holds the record for passengers. Further money from Udaras Na Gaeltachta has enabled development, although the number of workers available since 1997 has reduced. The running line extended a section at a time during winter periods when the railway was not operated and reached its present length of 2¼ miles in 1999, this being a little short of the end of the lake shore. It is planned to lay a further 600 metres of track, and a siding, when finance and labour is available. The long-term objective of extending to Glenties remains, but is equally dependent on funding.

The railway commences from the platform of the original CDR Fintown station. The building is currently a Health Centre,

Simplex 102T and ex-Charleroi tram trailers at Fintown station. The water tower and station building are original CDRJC structures.

one room being available to the railway as a toilet facility, and the water tower is also extant. For the 1995/96 seasons, a grounded half-body of an LMS (NCC) 3ft gauge coach served as a ticket office/souvenir shop. From 1997, a portacabin filled this role. With no run-round loop at either end of the line, trains are worked push-pull. The line runs along the lake, with stops to open and close gates between fields, sheep being constant companions of the track, which is not fenced off - the author is assured that no animal has ever come to grief! The original CDR goods shed remains at Fintown, used for storage. A new industrial unit-type shed was constructed alongside the old structure in 2000 (the land having been purchased in 1997) although doors had yet to be fitted late in 2001. There are two roads inside this building, but in late 2001 only one was connected to the main line; however, it has already been realised that the building is too small and should be extended - as with other enhancements, this depends on finance.

The principal locomotive for passenger trains is a Simplex 102T. This machine worked on the Shane's Castle Railway and carries the No 6 which appears to date from that period and is essentially the same as No 2 *Rory*, now at the Giant's Causeway & Bushmills Railway. Passenger stock comprises three ex-Charleroi tram trailers from Belgium. These enclosed single-deck 4-wheel vehicles went from Belgium to a private light railway in the Cotswolds, then to the Shane's Castle Railway. Although the majority of Shane's Castle equipment was purchased for the Giant's Causeway line, Simplex No 6 and these coaches were not required for that scheme and were sold to the Fintown project. The coaches initially retained their old liveries but, by 2001, FAS funding had covered the repainting of two into a red and white County Donegal livery, with the third due to be similarly repainted during 2002. There is a second locomotive, Ruston & Hornsby 4wDM (329680/52) acquired from Bord na Mona where it was fleet number LM77. Intended for shunting and permanent way duties, this loco can work passenger trains on dry days although, being very light, suffers from slipping when the rails are wet. In addition to a pair of 3ft gauge bogies, the only other item of rolling stock is a four-wheel permanent way van. The body is from an ex-standard gauge British Rail vehicle which has been mounted on a 3ft gauge chassis. Aside from providing crew accommodation, it has a Ratcliff power tailgate - unusual, if not unique, for a narrow gauge vehicle in Britain and Ireland!

The half-body of the above mentioned coach is of considerable interest. The acquisition of the Ballymena & Larne Railway by the British LMS has been described earlier. With the B&LR narrow gauge stock being quite aged (dating back to the 1870s/1880s) the LMS(NCC) started building five new coaches at Belfast (York Road) in 1928 to work a fast boat train service between Ballymena and Larne. Four of these (Nos 350-353) were 50ft long, the fifth, No 318, was constructed on an old Ballymena & Larne underframe and somewhat shorter at 43ft. The boat trains ceased in early 1933 and the five coaches went to the Ballycastle Railway. That line closed in July 1950 and two of the new-build coaches, along with the shorter coach, were purchased by the CDRJC, the 'new' coaches becoming

CDR No 57 (ex-NCC No 352) and No 59 (ex-CDR No 351) and the shorter coach becoming CDR No 58 (NCC No 318) and all ran on the CDR until closure at the end of 1959. After the 1961 auction, one of the coaches was converted into a home by the purchaser and located at Gartan, Co Donegal. The Fintown project was offered this coach, by now only half of the original body and, with its CDR background, was accepted and moved to Fintown - but was it half of No 57, 58 or 59? The answer may have emerged during 2001 when another half coach body was discovered by CDRRS (Donegal Town) members. Detective work indicates that the two part-bodies are the two halves of CDR No 58. Perhaps it will be possible for the halves to be reunited and restored on one of these CDR restoration projects.

The railway project wishes to develop the 'visitor experience' and in 1998 a boat was leased for use on the Lough, and in 2000 a 45ft pleasure boat was purchased. At the time of writing, this is in the railway yard at Fintown awaiting renovation, safety equipment, and attention by a marine engineer, the plan being to offer passengers an outward ride on the train with a return cruise down the lake.

Although there is a Society (CTGL) with a committee, there are no volunteers on the project, the railway being operated by paid staff. The atmosphere is notably relaxed - perhaps best defined as a refusal to be slaves of the clock - although visitor numbers appear to be healthy. Until such time as the project at Donegal station progresses to the construction of a running line, the Fintown Railway is the only operational narrow gauge passenger railway in Co Donegal.

County Donegal Railway Restoration Heritage Centre

The South Donegal Railway Restoration Society was formed in 1991 with the aim of restoring a nine-mile section of the railway from Meenglass (near Ballybofey) to Keadue at the southern end of the Barnesmore Gap. Three years were spent on this plan before the project was abandoned, not the least of the problems being the construction of a road by-pass around Donegal town over part of the old line. Further possible locations for reviving part of the line were subsequently examined, but without success. As the vision of restoring an operating railway faded, so did the level of support. However, the advent of the FAS schemes in Ireland made the development of a Railway Museum and Heritage Centre at the old Station House in Donegal Town possible, plus progressing the restoration of various items of County Donegal stock which the Society has secured for preservation.

By the 1990s the station, still owned by CIE, had fallen into dereliction but with the assistance of FAS workers, has been completely renovated. The Heritage Centre was opened to the public at Easter 1995, the operating organisation now being named the County Donegal Railway Restoration Society. Two ground floor rooms form a museum for photographs, memorabilia and other exhibits (including model railway layouts featuring parts of the Donegal system), another is a video viewing area and the original toilet block has been transformed into a shop.

Outside the station building is CDRJC brake third coach No 28 from 1893. The body was recovered from a caravan park in

CDRJC class 5 2-6-4T No 5
Drumboe **is pictured in September 2001 following a fair degree of cosmetic restoration to improve its appearance, with a concrete pipe temporarily serving as a chimney! Having raised its profile, the County Donegal Railway Restoration Society aims to launch a long-term project to return the locomotive to steam.**

north Donegal and has been restored to original condition, except the guard's compartment has been altered to accommodate passengers in wheelchairs for when it returns to service. Meanwhile, it requires a pair of bogies and air brakes before it can run on rails again. Work has also commenced on trailer No 5, a lightweight vehicle built for use behind Railcars. The body of the trailer was thought to have been destroyed following use as a ticket office at a football ground, but was rediscovered at Doochary in November 1993. Although not on public view, other County Donegal vehicles at the site and elsewhere include: Railcar No 14, half of coach No 58 (see Fintown section concerning the other half), and the body of red wagon No 12. Cattle wagon No 295 could join the collection.

Also at the site is CDR No 5 *Drumboe*, a Class 5 2-6-4T built in 1907. The locomotive was among the equipment purchased by Dr Cox when the CDR closed, but was never shipped to the USA. After some 30 years in open storage at Strabane, the locomotive was placed on loan to the CDRRS by the North West of Ireland Railway Society. During 2001, three local volunteers set about a cosmetic restoration of Drumboe. The work is unconventional in some respects, but has improved the overall presentation of the locomotive. When finished and painted, the loco is to be displayed in front of the station to raise its profile prior to a major fundraising effort aimed at restoration to working condition. Drumboe has been surveyed by Bob Meanley of Tyseley Locomotive Works, Birmingham and the cost of work required is estimated at some £210,000, of which the Society hopes to raise a significant proportion from UK and USA funding sources.

Having established a fine Heritage Centre, a business plan (funded by grant aid) was prepared in 2001 to take the Society forward. Planned developments over three years include more

interactive displays with working models, providing refreshments, and rebuilding the station platform area together with a short length of track. The next step would be the construction of a three-quarter mile line out to Gorrells crossing, creating a working railway on part of the old trackbed from the station. This would take the form of a tramway to link a planned supermarket complex on the edge of the town with the station, which is very close to 'the diamond' (the town square) in the centre of the town. It would form a park and ride for residents of Donegal town and car-born shoppers arriving at the complex - an environmentally friendly proposition all round. The tramway would be operated with new equipment similar in outline to the original Donegal stock, and would form the starting point for a heritage line, without being dependent on a short tourism season. The Society has been advised that a gas-fired, environmentally suitable locomotive could easily be designed and built to look like *Phoenix*, as converted to a diesel tractor by the CDR. In the short term, while awaiting construction of new vehicles, a small diesel, owned by a member and located on the Cavan & Leitrim Railway, could be employed, along with Trailer No 5 once a suitable vacuum braked chassis has been found. The Society has also been gifted the old Donegal engine shed, and the water tower at Inver station, both of which will be dismantled stone-by-stone and reconstructed in new positions on the station site to support the planned working railway.

If these plans come to fruition, then more adventurous schemes may be explored, ranging from setting up a 7¼ins gauge line in the Barnesmore Gap, through to a very ambitious proposal which has been studied by the independent consultants Symonds Group, who were also consultants for the Welsh Highland Railway. This looked at nothing less than building a 42-mile 3ft gauge line to link Derry with Donegal!

The CDRRS is a voluntary Society, some 70% of whose members live in the UK, which has employed workers under the FAS scheme to assist its objectives.

Cavan & Leitrim Railway

The 3ft gauge Cavan & Leitrim Railway opened for goods traffic on 17 October, and to passengers on 24 October 1887. The railway had a 33¾ mile main line from Belturbet (Co Cavan), via Ballinamore to Dromod (Co Leitrim), with a branch from Ballinamore which reached a length of 14¾ miles when it was extended to serve the Arigna coalfields. The line ran through a sparsely populated area, with livestock providing the principal traffic. Subsequently, coal from Arigna provided the traffic which kept the railway going, but when a power station opened at Arigna in 1958, the writing for the railway was on the wall. The line was originally worked by eight 4-4-0T locomotives built by Robert Stephenson & Co. The coal traffic extended the life of the railway after many other narrow gauge lines had succumbed, hence equipment from lines such as the Cork, Blackrock & Passage and Tralee & Dingle Railways was transferred to the C&LR during the 1930s and 1940s - a situation which has resulted in the railway being referred to as a working museum by the 1950s!

Conversion to diesel operation was rejected on the grounds of cost against the available traffic and closure came on 31 March 1959, the railway being the last narrow gauge line in Ireland to be worked exclusively by steam. The line was steadily reclaimed by nature, although much of the infrastructure survived, including the station, locomotive shed and water tank at Dromod, which would form the base for reviving a part of the old line.

The driving force behind the restoration of Dromod station and part of the old line is Michael Kennedy. He steadily acquired a substantial collection of narrow gauge equipment, most of which was kept in his garden at Dungarvan, although some was at the GSR station in Mallow. Between 1989-92 a railway museum was set up at Cahir, County Tipperary, but looking for a suitable site for a railway project, Dromod was the ideal choice - the station building remained, and was alongside an operating broad gauge CIE station.

The station building had not been inhabited for 10 years and was owned by a New York resident, while the C&L trackbed was still owned by CIE. The station and a part of the trackbed were purchased, some 40 lorry loads of equipment were brought to the site and restoration of the buildings commenced. The first track was laid at Dromod station on 22 December 1992, The Cavan & Leitrim Railway Company was re-established on 2 June 1993 and by 1994 the first trains ran over a track which was just under a quarter of a mile long. The project received financial assistance from a European Union border counties initiative (INTERREG) and The International Fund for Ireland and full-time staff were employed. The station building at Dromod was refurbished, and new workshops and a carriage shed built, with Phase One of the project completed when the first passenger train on the 'new' line ran on 27 May 1995. The track was

extended to Clooncolry Halt, giving a running line of just over ½ mile of 3ft gauge track, in 1996 - this remains the present limit of operations.

Trains leave Dromod station and run to Clooncolry, pause, and are pushed back (there is no run-round loop) to a low platform opposite the main shed. The passengers then detrain for a guided tour of the shed. The equipment ranges from 2ft gauge Arigna mine coal wagons, through a 3ft gauge West Clare wagon to a china clay wagon from North Devon dating from the 1880s. The shed accommodates a number of locomotives, some restored (including a 2ft gauge 1941-vintage ex-War Department Hudson-Hunslet 4wDM (2659/42) recovered from a bog in Tipperary and 4wDM Fowler (3900011/47) *Dinmor* and a collection of ex-Bord na Mona diesels. Following this educational tour, the train returns its passengers to the station.

Steam haulage is provided by 0-4-2T No 1 *Dromad* (spelt in Gaelic form). The basis for this locomotive is a Kerr Stuart (3024/16) loco built for Balfour, Beatty & Co Ltd and used during construction of the Lochaber Water Power Scheme in Scotland. In 1918 it was sold to the British Aluminium Company at Lochaber and named *Sir Murray Morrison*. It was sold for its scrap value (£60) in 1970 to the Hampshire Narrow Gauge Railway Society which removed various useful parts, then passed the remains on to Alan Keef Ltd - basically a frame and wheels. These were purchased in 1988 by the Irish Narrow Gauge Trust, with Alan Keef Ltd being commissioned to undertake the restoration. The boiler employed was built by Robey, a firm often associated with traction engines but, in this instance, it had been used in the laundry of a Bristol hotel! Other parts with unlikely origins have been employed, including spectacle glasses from a Great Northern broad gauge locomotive and the whistle from a London Underground train. Cowcatchers were fitted, a feature of the original C&L locomotives, and *Dromad* was steamed for the first time on 3 June 1994, passing a boiler inspection at the end of that month. The loco arrived at Dun Laoghaire on 10 July 1994 and reached Dromod station in the early hours of 11 July. Its first steaming on its new line took place over 13/14 July.

The railway also has a second steam locomotive, Avonside (1547/08) 0-6-0T *Nancy*. After spending its working life at Harston and Eastwell iron ore quarries in Leicestershire, she was purchased by Lord O'Neil for the Shane's Castle Railway and dismantled. Following closure of this line, the components were purchased by the Cavan & Leitrim Railway and sent to Alan Keef Ltd. After being stored for some years, work commenced late in 1999. Restoration of the frames was complete, with the reprofiled wheels fitted to produce a rolling chassis, by the spring of 2001 with attention then turning to the cylinders and motion.

In addition to the equipment in the main shed, a sizeable collection of internal combustion locomotives and ex-Bord na Mona Railcars can be found in the yard. The passenger carriages comprise Tralee & Dingle Railway coaches Nos 7T and 10T (acquired by Michael Kennedy prior to the move to Dromod, one is presently in service, the other now just a chassis), West Clare Railway trailer 47c, and a veranda-ended coach built by Alan Keef Ltd in 1997. The collection used to include Isle of

The volunteer driver of 0-4-2T No 1 *Dromad* awaits the 'right away' from Dromod station on the Cavan & Leitrim Railway. The loco is based on the chassis of Kerr Stuart (3024/16) with a Robey boiler.

Man carriage F21, but this was sold back to Manx Transport in the 1990s. The site is also home to a fleet of buses, including examples owned by Irish narrow gauge railways. Adjacent to the station, but not yet restored, is the signal cabin from Gormanston (North Dublin) which was moved, along with its 24-lever frame, to Dromod on 15 August 1999.

The present running line stops a little short of the R202 road, but the long-term aim is to extend a further 5¼ miles to Mohill station. A local heritage committee owns this building and was restoring it, but interest apparently waned and the station has now been vandalised. A renewed effort, in concert with the local Council, was made during 2001 and with a FAS scheme due to start in January 2002, it is hoped that the extension of the railway will progress. A major issue, however, is gaining possession of the trackbed - the total of 27 acres is owned by no less than 47 landowners!

In addition to being run by an enthusiast, Cavan & Leitrim Railway Supporters Association members volunteer their help, including driving *Dromad* - justifying the C&LR's claim to be the only narrow gauge railway in the Republic of Ireland operated by enthusiasts which runs every day during the summer.

Each of the termini of the original Cavan & Leitrim Railway linked with broad gauge lines. At Dromod, the connection was with the Midland & Great Western Railway's main line between Dublin and Sligo and CIE trains still call at the broad gauge station. At Belturbet, the connection was with the Great

Northern Railway's branch to Ballyhaise on the Clones to Cavan line. In a project unrelated to the revived Cavan & Leitrim Railway, Belturbet station was opened to the public in the summer of 2001 following a major restoration programme. Also surviving from the old C&L and preserved in the Ulster Folk & Transport Museum is 4-4-0T No 2 *Kathleen*, built in 1887 by Robert Stephenson & Co. and carriage No 5, while loco No 3 *Lady Edith* is preserved in the USA.

West Clare Railway

The West Clare Railway ran from Ennis (adjacent to the broad gauge Limerick & Western Railway station) to Miltown Malby, a distance of 27 miles, and was opened in July 1887. An extension, actually the South Clare Railway although it was operated by the West Clare, was added southwards from Miltown Malby to Moyasta Junction (16 miles), where the line divided. The main line continued west to the coastal town of Kilkee (five miles), while a four mile branch from Moyasta Junction ran to Kilrush on the Shannon estuary. The South Clare section opened for goods traffic in August 1892 and for passengers some four months later. The railway achieved fame as a result of a trip made by concert hall performer, Mr Percy French, who was due to appear in Kilkee. His train failed at Miltown Malby, he sued the railway for lost earnings - and wrote the song *Are ye right there, Michael? Are ye right?*, thus immortalising the railway.

Originally steam-worked (the final pair of Hunslet 4-6-0T locomotives delivered in 1922 were the last steam locos to be built for the narrow gauge in Ireland, other than industrials built for Bord na Mona) the line received its first Railcars in 1928 when two petrol-engined Drewry Railcars were purchased for the network by the Great Southern Railway. Four Walker Railcars were bought by CIE for the West Clare in 1952, along with four ex-Tralee & Dingle coaches (rebuilt with new bogies) to work with them. The Railcars were almost identical to the County Donegal Railcars Nos 19 and 20 which subsequently went to the Isle of Man. In 1955, three centre-cab 230hp Bo-Bo locomotives built by Walker Bros (F501 and F502) arrived, following which the line was completely dieselised. The decline in traffic, however, was terminal and the last train ran over West Clare metals on 31 January 1961.

Moyasta was really no more than a suitable location for the Kilrush branch to diverge from the Kilkee line, with a link line added to form a triangle, suitable for turning locomotives and Railcars. Nearby is a bar (public house) which was there prior to the arrival of the railway, but little else. The bar, however, turned out to be the catalyst for today's West Clare Railway. Taken over by Joe Taylor (who also owned some adjacent land which included part of the old West Clare trackbed) he saw the potential for opening a tourist railway, promoted the idea locally and purchased the Moyasta station site in 1996.

Moyasta station was renovated and served as an interpretation centre for the old West Clare, then track was laid and, by 1998, a passenger service commenced over some 400 yards of the old WCR trackbed. This was operated using a diminutive Railcar, loaned to the fledgling line by the revived Cavan & Leitrim Railway. The machine, powered by a Ford Escort engine and weighing three tons, was Bord na Mona No C47 (works number 3) which had been built in 1958 and acquired and moved to the Cavan & Leitrim base at Dromod in January 1993. This machine sufficed until about 1999 when the West Clare line purchased its own locomotive, the Railcar returning to Dromod where it remains on display.

The running line has been progressively extended and by mid-2000 had reached 1¼ miles. The current track runs from the level crossing gates on the N67 Kilrush to Kilkee road, through the northern platform of Moyasta Junction and then in a basically north-easterly direction. Trains are worked push-pull, there being no run-round loops. Passengers are shown a short video of the old West Clare line in the station building before joining the train. The booking hall contains a small sales counter and there are toilet facilities. The water tower on the station platform has been restored and a signal box erected, with ex-CIE semaphore signals added for the start of the 2001 season. On the southern side of the triangular platform, grounded ex-CIE broad gauge saloon coach body came into use as a tea room during 2000.

The line's diesel locomotive is L101/89 built by RFS in Doncaster for use on the Channel Tunnel construction project and, following rebuilding, was supplied to the WCR in 1999 by Alan Keef Ltd. The chassis and bogies for the two steel-bodied coaches were supplied by Alan Keef Ltd, the frames being newly constructed, and mounted on ex-Bowater's bogies which Keef's regauged. The bodies were constructed by F Keating Engineering of Kilrush, the first coach entering service in 2000, followed by the second early in 2001. In the long-term, it is planned to introduce steam motive power. The last surviving WCR steam locomotive, 0-6-2T No 5 *Slieve Callan* (Callan Mountain - the highest in Co Clare), has been leased from CIE. Built in 1892 by Dübs, the loco stood for many years on a plinth outside Ennis station, but was moved (not without some local protest!) in the late 1990s and following a tour of the locality to generate publicity, was taken to the Ross-on-Wye works of Alan Keef Ltd for restoration. At the time of writing, the boiler has been removed, the progress is dependent on the revived WCR generating sufficient funds.

Although Joe Taylor sold the bar at Moyasta in 1997 and the railway project has been purchased by Jackie Whelan, Joe remains very much part of the running and development of the line. Immediate plans envisage laying track (the rail is in stock) over a one mile section, which has already been fenced, on the other side of the N67 road in the direction of Kilkee, with a shed for the loco and stock to be built near the road crossing on the Kilkee side. Further extensions are not ruled out, but depend entirely on generating funds and securing grants to aid the railway's development as a tourist attraction.

Giant's Causeway & Bushmills Railway

The original 3ft gauge Giant's Causeway Tramway was conceived by William A Traill (and his brother Dr Anthony Traill) of Ballylough. Their scheme was launched in 1879, the Bill allowing construction receiving Royal Assent in August 1880. The company was officially entitled the Giant's Causeway, Portrush, Bush Valley Railway & Tramway Co Ltd, reflecting wider (but never fulfilled) ambitions for a minor railway empire in Antrim. The potential for electric power was recognised from the beginning and the Siemens Company, which displayed the first electric railway system in the world at the 1879 Berlin Fair, was appointed as electrical engineers for the tramway, Dr William Siemens becoming a director. A generating station was built at Walkmill Falls with water turbines producing the electric power and the line became the first commercially operated hydro-electric powered tramway system. However, a third rail, laid 17ins above ground level, was employed and its use in the urban parts of Portrush (and a branch to the market place at Bushmills) was prohibited by the Board of Trade, hence two steam locomotives were purchased to work in those areas, although they also worked over the full length of the system at busy times.

Opening was approved in January 1883 and steam-worked operation commenced, although various electrical problems were not solved until the following September. The official opening between Portrush and Bushmills was on 28 September

The last surviving West Clare Railway steam locomotive, 0-6-2T No 5 *Slieve Callan* pictured at the Ross-on-Wye works of Alan Keef Ltd. The boiler has subsequently been lifted from the frames in preparation for the full overhaul which will take place as the funds are raised by the revived West Clare line.

1883, with services worked by electricity commencing in November. A further Act of Parliament covered the Bushmills to Giant's Causeway section, opened in July 1887. The raised live third rail caused a number of accidents and conversion to an overhead trolley system, was completed in July 1899. At this time, four new power cars were obtained, and an old saloon re-equipped, although steam continued in use.

The line carried considerable traffic during WW1, and again during the second world conflict when Portrush became an evacuation centre for Belfast during the 1941 blitz, and an army camp was built between Portballintrae and Giant's Causeway in 1942. Traffic declined at the end of the 1940s and the line badly needed re-equipping. The tramway closed for the winter on 30 September 1949 and never re-opened, an Abandonment Order being sought in September 1950, issued in the following September, and all equipment was sold at a public auction on 15 September 1951.

The tramway commenced beside the broad gauge (5ft 3ins) Belfast & Northern Counties Railway station in Portrush, where a dual gauge branch ran to the harbour. The tramway anticipated this carrying sizeable tonnages of iron ore for export, but the

trade never developed and the branch ceased to be used after June 1888. On leaving the town, the tramway ran on the northern edge of the main road to Bushmills, a clifftop location overlooking the sea, and the ruins of Dunluce Castle. At Bushmills, there was a sizeable station, tram sheds and a short branch into the centre of the town, this being the intended (but never built) start of a planned line to Dervock. The line then became a true railway on a reserved track. After crossing the River Bush over the Victoria Jubilee Bridge, it skirted Runkerry Strand before arriving at the Giant's Causeway terminus - a route of a little over eight miles. The two original locomotives were worn out early in the 20th century (the chassis of at least one had become a wagon by 1908) and a further pair were acquired, all being Wilkinson 0-4-0VTB tram engines. The later pair certainly carried names, No 3 *Dunluce Castle* (not the 4-4-0 now preserved at

Cultra!) and No 4 *Brian Boroimhe*, and were sold around 1926. They were used on a breakwater project on the River Bann in the 1930s, although their subsequent fate is unknown. Three items of stock have been preserved: saloon No 2 (which was rescued after serving as a garden shed at Whitrock, Co Antrim) and toastrack No 5 are in the Ulster Folk and Transport Museum, while Power Car No 9 - which served as a holiday home and tea shop in Youghal, Co Cork - is being restored at Howth Castle.

A totally different project would eventually lead to the return of trains between Giant's Causeway and Bushmills. The 3ft gauge Shane's Castle Railway was built by Lord O'Neill in the grounds of his ancestral home on the banks of Lough Neagh. Essentially a happy combination of enthusiasm for the preservation of steam and an additional visitor attraction, it opened in 1971. The railway was just over 1½ miles in length, with much of it basically a roadside tramway. A 1904-vintage 0-4-0T Peckett built for the British Aluminium Company which worked at Larne until being sold to a private owner, a Mr W P McCormack, was sold to Lord O'Neill in 1970 and became No 1 *Tyrone*. The other loco was an Andrew Barclay 0-4-0T which was one of a trio built in 1949 for Bord na Mona. Two were purchased by the Irish Steam Preservation Society (see The Stradbally Woodland Express section) with No 2 remaining at Stradbally, and No 3 being sold on to Lord O'Neill and becoming No 3 *Shane*. The third was eventually reincarnated as the Talyllyn Railway's No 7 *Tom Rolt*. There was originally a small Simplex named *Rory*, the name later being transferred to a larger Simplex acquired from Blue Circle Cement which became the surviving No 2 *Rory*, and a similar machine was the No 6, now at the Fintown Railway. An Avonside 0-6-0T (1547/08), which already had the name *Nancy*, was purchased and dismantled, but never ran at Shane's Castle and is now owned by the Cavan & Leitrim Railway. The passenger stock consisted mainly of 4-wheel carriages based on the chassis of wagons built by Allen's

of Tipton for Charles Tennant & Co Ltd for use on Glenconway turf bog, near Dungiven. The bodies were constructed at Shane's Castle and there were eight semi-open's (with roofs but no doors) and four fully open's, the design of these bodies being based on the style of Penrhyn quarry workmen's carriages. There were also three tram trailers from Charleroi, Belgium, which are now at Fintown. A sizeable collection of County Donegal stock which had been purchased by Dr Cox and was under the stewardship of the NWIRPS was stored at Shane's Castle for some 10 years while that Society sought a new base (see Foyle Valley Railway section).

For various reasons, the decision was made that the Shane's Castle Railway would have to close, and in August 1993 it was announced that the equipment was to be sold. In the event, the line ran in the following year, but operations ceased at the end of the 1994 season. During 1993, David Laing had been involved in setting up Robert Guinness' steam museum near Dublin. His various interests included driving on the Shane's Castle line for more than 20 years and, inevitably, he learned of the planned sale in advance of the public announcement. A discussion more than two decades earlier, while walking the path which was now on the old Giant's Causeway trackbed, with the Secretary of the National Trust in Belfast was recalled. The gist of it was that instead of surrounding the approach to the Giant's Causeway with car parks, a train or tram could provide a park and ride service from Bushmills. Wishing to avoid the break-up of the Shane's Castle collection, David Laing conceived the idea of building a new line on the Giant's Causeway trackbed which would utilise the locomotives and stock from Shane's Castle. Letters were sent to the two local Councils which were now the owners of the trackbed, the Tourist Board and possible funding sources.

Although it took a long time, and considerable personal commitment from David Laing, the project received support and a non-profit distributing company limited by guarantee

A specially posed Giant's Causeway & Bushmills Railway train prior to public opening. No 2 *Rory*, the brake van and three repainted ex-Shane's Castle coaches are pictured just to the north of the new bridge over the River Bush where the formation widens to accommodate the mid-point passing loop.

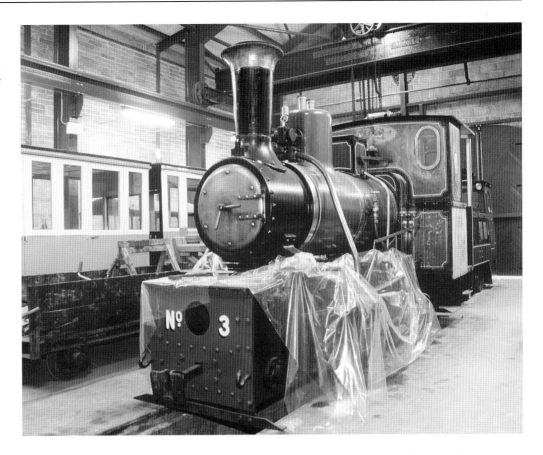

No 3 *Shane* pictured in September 2001 inside the new shed at Giant's Causeway. The plastic sheeting is to cover the motion while the loco is prepared for repainting. The heavy steelwork and overhead crane were originally part of the structure of the Shane's Castle workshop.

(which has charitable status) with volunteer directors was set up. The rail and equipment for the proposed project was purchased, with the help of substantial donations from private individuals, from Lord O'Neill. This encompassed No 1 *Tyrone*, No 2 *Rory*, No 3 *Shane*, 12 passenger carriages, wagons and 1.6 miles of 75lb rail.

It had been hoped that a start on building the new railway could be made on 29 September 1999 - the 50th anniversary of the last tram running on the old Giant's Causeway line - but discussions were still continuing with various bodies. By the end of the year - six years and four months after the idea was first raised - construction finally commenced when the two-mile length of the new Giant's Causeway & Bushmills Railway trackbed was cleared by Enterprise Ulster workers. The old pedestrian bridge over the River Bush was removed in January 2000 by a joint Army/RAF team using a Chinook helicopter. The stonework of the old tramway bridge piers was then reduced in height to accommodate a new bridge being built for the railway by the Mabey Group of Twyford. By early 2000, a mile of 3ft gauge track had been laid from the Giant's Causeway end of the line towards the bridge. The Simplex diesel No 2 *Rory* was brought to the line on 16 June 2000 to work ballast trains on the section of track which had been laid and the first passenger train, described as 'an exploratory trip', to run over the first section of new railway operated on Monday 19 June 2000.

After various difficulties had held up work on the new bridge, it was finally in place by August 2000, following which track was laid over it and across the golf course. By the summer of 2001, the rails had reached Bushmills. As noted, the 75lb rail obtained from the old Shane's Castle line only covered 1.6 miles of the 2

mile new line. The balance of the rail is 50lb material purchased from the Vale of Rheidol Railway. The rail is laid on new wood sleepers with the work being supervised by Cecil Wright, a former Section Inspector with Northern Ireland Railways.

The base of the railway is at Giant's Causeway, nor far from the National Trust visitor centre which leads to the Causeway itself. A new station building, locomotive shed/workshop and carriage shed has been constructed from breeze blocks with a rendered finish that blends into the local landscape. The design of the locomotive and carriage sheds is based on part of the Portrush tram depot of the original Giant's Causeway Tramway, while the station building draws inspiration from early County Antrim stations. Within the locomotive shed/workshop, the framework and overhead crane which used to form the structure of the workshop at Shane's Castle has been incorporated. At Bushmills, it had been hoped that the original station building, which is now in use as a private residence, could be secured. This did not prove to be possible and the new line terminates on the other side of the road, almost opposite the original building. For the time being, no new structure will be erected here, but eventually it is planned to construct a corrugated iron replica of the 1887 structure originally imported from Switzerland by Col. W A Traill which served as the Causeway station building. A platform was constructed early in 2002 with Army help, and a passing loop installed just to the north of the River Bush bridge.

It had been hoped that a full fare-paying passenger service over the railway would commence during June 2000. Unfortunately, work did not proceed as rapidly as had been anticipated. The station at Giant's Causeway was pretty well complete by the end of that year, but other tasks remained outstanding. No 1 *Tyrone* and No 3 *Shane* were moved to the railway on 25 April 2001 from secure storage, although their arrival was aimed largely at generating publicity, since *Tyrone* was immediately moved down to Ballymena for a 10-year examination. Subsequently, vacuum ejectors for the continuous brakes have been fitted to both *Tyrone* and *Shane* at Giant's Causeway, along with the installation of a vacuum pump on No 2 *Rory*. The preparations were set back again when Foot & Mouth disease broke out in Britain early in 2001, and the decision was made that opening would be delayed until Easter 2002.

The locomotives are to run in different liveries, each to represent the three major pre-nationalisation railway companies in Northern Ireland: No 1 *Tyrone* in crimson lake (Northern Counties Committee of the LMS), No 3 *Shane* sky blue (Great Northern) and No 2 *Rory* holly green (Belfast & Co Down). Of the 12 4-wheel ex-Shane's Castle coaches, the eight semi-open's (including the brake van) have been fitted with doors and safety glass (to protect passengers from golf balls!) and continuous brakes. They have been painted in honeysuckle, cream and mushroom, with black ends, and upholstered seats have been added. Of the other Shane's Castle coaches, one of the open's has been rebuilt with an enclosed body and higher seating capacity, while two others are to be converted - one will be a brake van/wheelchair coach, the other a 1st Class observation car. The railway also has a veranda-end bogie carriage which ran at Shane's Castle and this could become a dining carriage.

The railway has been designed so that it can be operated by a core of three paid staff: David Laing, a secretarial assistant and a Chief Engineer. For the time being, no supporting society has been set up, so the permanent staff will be supplemented by paid full and part-time seasonal workers.

Listowel & Ballybunion Railway

Charles Francois Marie-Therese Lartigue was born in Toulouse in 1834. His raised track monorail system seems to have been inspired by the sight of a camel caravan during an 1881 trip to Algeria. Before long, over 60 miles of track to transport Esparto grass and using mules for the haulage had been built following these ideas. He patented the system in 1882 and further lines followed. Realising that steam power was needed, Lartigue approached Anatole Mallet in 1884 and a vertical-boilered locomotive designed by Mallet was built by S A Metallurgique of Tubize, Belgium, which worked trains round three miles of demonstration track at Tothill Fields, Westminster in 1885/86.

Meanwhile, in Ireland, the broad gauge main line had arrived at Listowel in December 1880 and proposals were soon mooted for a line to link this town and Ballybunion. It is not clear why the Lartigue system was selected, but an Act of Parliament was passed on April 2 1886 for the line, and the Listowel & Ballybunion Railway Company was incorporated on April 16 1886. Construction started in September 1887, assisted by the loco used on the Westminster line, and the 9¼ mile line was ready for an official opening ceremony on 29 February 1888, with opening to the public on 3 April.

The Lartigue system has the main running rail mounted at the top of an 'A' frame, which places it about a metre above ground level. The locomotives and stock straddle the frame, and have guide wheels, which run on guide rails mounted part-way down each side of the 'A' frames.

Switch tables were the Lartigue equivalent of points or turnouts, with the centre of the track on the tables (which actually describes a gentle arc) not over the central pivot! There are many tales concerning balance, the number of people on each side of a carriage having to be equal, and the like. Folklore involving cows balanced by two calves, and even pianos and calves, has developed, but these stories are unlikely to have any substance and probably arose from a highly embroidered speech by Joseph Bigger, MP for Belfast, in the UK Parliament.

Three 0-3-0 locomotives, designed by Mallet, were built by the Hunslet Engine Company of Leeds (HE431, 432 and 433) in 1887. These had two horizontal boilers which hid the wheels, cylinders and motion. The passenger carriages were built by Falcon of Loughborough and ran on two two-wheel bogies (four in-line wheels) with outward facing seats in bodies suspended on each side of the track. The passenger vehicles appear to have comprised: one 1st Class, four composites, seven 3rd Class, two guard's vans (complete with attached stairs for crossing the track) and a mobile staircase, also to allow passengers to cross from one side to the other. There were also covered wagons, cattle wagons, open wagons and iron hopper wagons for transporting sand.

At Listowel, the Lartigue line's terminus was beside the broad gauge station and yard, the line then ran parallel with the broad gauge before swinging away towards Lisselton, the passing place on the line. Originally, the train simply continued to Ballybunion, but an intermediate Halt was established at Francis Road in 1912. At Ballybunion, there was a short extension to a sand siding. Overall, the line had quite lengthy straights and few curves, although little of the route was level - the steepest gradient being around 1 in 50.

All of the line's buildings were of corrugated iron construction, but the use of reinforced concrete for parts of the infrastructure was novel, being employed for the first time in Kerry, possibly Ireland. The road crossings were unique, farm roads being crossed by 17 examples of 'Flying Gates' which were double drawbridges mounted in vertical frames and operated by chains, the drawbridges dropping down to allow a crossing of the track at the level of the main running rail. In contrast, there were eight locations where wider roads were crossed by a variation of switch tables, a 12ft length of straight track being pivoted in the centre to turn at right angles to the running line to allow traffic to pass.

The line operated independently up to late 1916 when all Irish railways came under British Government control for the remainder of WW1. This control ended in August 1921, but the company was then trading at a loss, problems including reduced tourism in the area and the increasing impact of motor vehicles. The line was then badly damaged in 1922 during the Irish civil war. The Lartigue was not included in the railway company mergers which followed the 1924 Railway Act in Ireland and with its locomotives and equipment in a poor state, a High

The partially-completed replica (diesel powered) Listowel & Ballybunion monorail locomotive pictured in the works of Alan Keef Ltd on 8 September 2001.

Court Order to permit closure was granted on 7 October 1924, the last train running on 14 October.

The broad gauge North Kerry line ceased to carry passengers in 1963 and freight services were withdrawn in 1977, although the track remained in place. CIE finally sought an Abandonment Order in 1987, by which time interest in local industrial heritage was undergoing a revival. Less than 20 miles away, the scheme to restore a section of the Tralee and Dingle Railway was gathering pace following the repatriation of Hunslet 2-6-2T No 5T (HE555/1892) - see the Tralee & Dingle Railway section - and the tourist potential for a Lartigue project of some kind in Listowel was spotted, its leading advocate being Michael Guerin. When it became clear that opposition to the abandonment of the broad gauge line was not going to succeed, he pressed the Council to purchase part of the trackbed, including the disused broad gauge station. The Lartigue Monorail Committee was formed, Michael becoming its Secretary, and proposals for three projects were formulated: the display of a working Lartigue model inside the old GS&WR goods shed, a Lartigue Museum in the disused Listowel station and a passenger-carrying miniature Lartigue line running round a circuit which encompassed part of the old monorail route. Michael wrote a book, *The Lartigue Listowel & Ballybunion Railway* to mark the centenary of the line's opening which was published in 1988. By the end of that year, Listowel UDC had endorsed the Committee's proposals, and the restoration of a part of the Lartigue was included in a discussion document prepared by Shannon Development, with an 'Operational Viability Study' prepared by consultants appearing in July 1990.

The Council purchased the section of trackbed into Listowel by the end of the 1990s and the broad gauge station was incorporated into a housing scheme, leaving the old goods shed and remainder of the old 5ft 3ins gauge Great Southern & Western Railway's trackbed available for the Lartigue Project. Around this time,

Jimmy Deenihan, TD, member of the Dail (Irish Parliament) for North Kerry was looking at potential projects to promote tourism, and with some past family connections with the old Lartigue asked an American Intern at the Dail to prepare a survey of heritage lines in the UK. The result was the formation of a Lartigue Project Committee and an application to the National Millennium Committee in 1999 which awarded IR£175,000 to the project. Over IR£40,000 was added by the Ireland Funds (an international organisation which supports projects both north and south of the border) and financial help was also given by Kerry County Enterprise Board and Tuarha Chiarrai (the Leader Company for North and East Kerry), along with contributions from local businesses and individuals. The project was also supported by FAS which provided free labour, the fundraising only having to cover materials. The total project was originally costed at just over IR£853,000, of which some IR£500,000 covered phase one, a train operating on a 500 metre track complete with locomotive/carriage shed, although with a sizeable element of the cost having to be paid in Sterling, the relative strength of the Irish Punt meant that some estimates had to be revised upwards.

The first phase of the project commences at the old GS&WR goods shed and consists of a long rectangular area of the ex-broad gauge trackbed, which heads almost due west out of Listowel, as far as the junction with the road to Ballybunion. Outside the old goods shed is a platform, adjacent to a turntable. Working westwards, there are two switch tables with passenger platforms beside lines which form a run-round loop. From the western switch table, a line also runs into the locomotive and carriage shed. The running line continues westwards, with a drawbridge crossing shortly after the shed, until reaching a switch table and turntable, which form a run-round loop at the far end of the line, accompanied by passenger platforms. The motive power consists of a single, diesel powered, replica

Lartigue locomotive and two replica carriages, one 3rd Class and one 3rd Class/guard (incorporating cross-over steps) giving a total train capacity of 40 passengers. The key features which set the Lartigue system out as being so different are all included over the 500 metres of running line.

The contract to design and build a locomotive, two coaches and the track components was awarded to Alan Keef Ltd. The original 0-3-0 locomotives had a booster cylinder in the tender, although the tender drive was not successful and subsequently removed. With cost and ease of operation over the comparatively short runs required at Listowel to take into account, the decision was made that a diesel powered reproduction was the sensible solution. Some compromises over the wheel arrangements and drive have been necessary and the reproduction locomotive is actually an 0-2-0, with the drive transmitted to the tender (itself an 0-2-0) which pushes the locomotive. The engine is a Perkins diesel located on the right hand side of the tender, while the left side houses the equipment associated with the hydrostatic drive. The design of the newly built track has been modified slightly to allow the use of standard material to keep the cost at acceptable levels. The main running rail for the revival project is conventional 30lb/yd material, while the pair of guide rails are S7 section, a light continental rail material.

A formal order was placed in August 2000 and rapid progress was made, with the first section of assembled Lartigue track being shown at the 9 September 2000 Alan Keef Ltd Open Day. Six months of progress followed as the track components were built and work commenced on the locomotive and tender. Unfortunately, the project was delayed when Foot and Mouth disease hit Britain early in 2001. Kerry is predominantly an agricultural area, and with the export of material from Britain placed on hold, the completed track components could not be exported until May 2001. Work on the locomotive continued and the largely complete machine was unveiled at the 8 September 2001 Alan Keef Ltd Open Day.

Meanwhile, in Listowel, the GS&WR trackbed was surrounded by security fencing and the area cleared, followed by the delivery and levelling of 10,200 tonnes of ballast. A modern industrial-type building was erected to form the locomotive and carriage shed and the bases of the turntables and switch tables dug out and cast in concrete. Although the Foot and Mouth epidemic prevented the export of the track components from Keef's, restrictions on movement within Ireland also stopped the delivery of old CIE sleepers, thus preventing much progress on preparing the track components during the early/mid part of 2001. The combination of various delays set the project behind schedule, although all of the materials had arrived by the end of the year. During the winter of 2001/2002 the track sections were installed, while work continued on the loco, first carriage and switch tables at Keef's. The railway was expected to open in early summer 2002.

With the first phase complete, attention will turn to phase two - renovation and conversion of the old goods shed into a museum/interpretive centre/café which is due to commence in 2003 and is budgeted at IR£370,000/400,000. The long term plan envisages landscaping the field where the old Lartigue yard was situated to form a recreation and interpretation area.

The field has been donated to the Lartigue Project Committee and the plans visualise a path around this area with seating, and additional excavation around the remains of the surviving original turntables and switch tables.

Little remains of the original line. In addition to the switch bases at Listowel, the corrugated iron goods shed still stands just beyond the boundary of the field which has been donated to the project. The overbridge at Tempaillin Ban also survives and was renovated in 1997. For many years, the memory of the Lartigue was kept alive by Michael Barry. A Lisselton farmer, he collected support trestles, rails and even parts of a coach from surrounding land and assembled about 40ft of track on which the remains of the coach were located.

New Projects

Foyle Valley Railway

The North West of Ireland Railway Society was formed in 1970 by railway enthusiasts and former railwaymen with the aim of preserving the railway heritage of the North West of Ireland, with particular emphasis on the County Donegal Railway, Great Northern Railway(I), LMS(NCC) and the Londonderry and Lough Swilly Railway. Initially, this took physical form by caring for, preserving and restoring items of County Donegal equipment which had been purchased by Dr Cox, but never shipped to America. The first base for the Society was on the eastern bank of the River Foyle in Derry, on a part of the site of the old CDRJC Victoria Road station. A small museum was established, hard work and enthusiasm compensating for the lack of money. Unfortunately, the owners of the station site sold the premises and the NWIRS had to move out in the late 1970s. Lord O'Neill offered to provide storage space for the rolling stock until the Society found a new base and the equipment was moved to Shane's Castle, where it stayed for some 10 years.

In the mid-1980s, the Society approached Derry City Council, pointing out that the City, with its significant past railway connections (served by four different railway companies, each with its own terminus - and of two different gauges), was the ideal place for a railway museum to be developed. The Council agreed, and in the course of identifying suitable premises, realised that it owned the trackbed of the Great Northern Railway (the broad gauge line from Derry, through Strabane and Omagh to Portadown which had closed in 1965) as far as the border with the Republic of Ireland - and the GNR goods shed on the western bank of the Foyle near Craigavon bridge.

With the help of European funding, the goods shed was converted into a museum, opened in 1989. The exhibits were essentially the CDR equipment originally owned by Dr Cox, although for various reasons, some items were now owned by Derry City Council, with the rest in the ownership of the NWIRS. Construction of the 3ft gauge Foyle Valley Railway commenced in 1991. There is a fan of tracks out of the museum building at the northern end, from which a running line was

County Donegal railcar No 12 pictured inside the Foyle Valley Railway museum building. The bonnet of railcar No 18 is just visible to the left.

built on the river side. A passenger platform is located beside the wall of the museum, facing the river, and the track was progressively extended in a south-westerly direction along the river bank, reaching a length of three miles by 1997, about a mile short of the border. The first section from the museum is on the trackbed of the old GNR siding which ran off the docks, a short section was then built on land purchased from the adjacent houses, with the remainder back on the old GNR main line trackbed. The railway was developed and equipment restored with the aid of an 'Action for Community Employment' programme.

Initially, while the Council maintained and managed the museum building, the Society ran the railway as a volunteer-based operation. In 1997, the Society took over the management of the FVR project, and with the aid of grants from the City Council, employed a secretary and two drivers to provide the train rides in restored CDR Railcars Nos 12 and 18. The Railcars could run as a back-to-back pair, or if one Railcar was in use, with a 3ft gauge Simplex at the rear to 'pilot' the return journey. Rides were provided through the 1990s, the length of run progressively increasing, there being no need to have run-round loops. About a mile down the track from the museum is a workshop compound where the restoration of stock was progressed with the aid of grants from different sources, including the National Fund for Ireland and the Peace Fund.

Unfortunately, relations between the NWIRPS and City Council started to break down around 1999/2000, and following the construction of a cycle path adjacent to the railway, public trains over the Foyle Valley line ceased in July 2000, although the Council operated a 'special' for a party of enthusiasts with a Railcar during 2001. The reasons behind the dispute are outside the scope of this book, but progress on restoring coach No 30 had come to a halt and there was some doubt concerning the future of the collection at the time of writing (particularly the

items owned by the NWIRPS) and future operation on the FVR; the planned extension of the running line to Carrigans, then on towards St. Johnston (a distance of eight miles) was also on ice.

The restored equipment currently inside the museum consists of CDRJC Class 5 2-6-4T *Columbkille*, CDRJC diesel Railcars Nos 12 and 18, CDRJC carriage No 14, the body of Londonderry & Lough Swilly Railway Cleminson 6-wheel carriage No 18 (which has its own frame but no running gear and currently sits on a CDR chassis), ex-Clogher Valley Railway luggage van No 19 (which subsequently ran on the CDR) and an 0-4-0DH Motor Rail Simplex dating from 1974. Outside the shed is unrestored CDRJC Class 5 2-6-4T No 4 *Meenglass* (built 1907). Other items currently stored in the workshop compound and not on public display include an ex-CDRJC goods wagon and the major project to restore CDR carriage No 30 which has involved the construction of a replica body to replace that destroyed while stored at Stranorlar following the closure of the CDR, for fitting onto the original chassis.

Waterford & Suir Valley Railway

The start of this new 3ft gauge line dates back to 3 July 1997 when a meeting, convened by the Chief Executive of Waterford Chamber of Commerce, was held to further the idea of promoting a steam railway on the trackbed of the closed 5ft 3ins gauge line between Waterford and Tramore. A preliminary feasibility study carried out in October 1997 identified several problems concerning the likely cost, practicality and viability of the scheme, so a further study was made, looking at the Waterford to New Ross and Waterford to Dungarvan lines. The former did not find favour, but the trackbed of the 5ft 3ins gauge Great Southern & Western line to Dungarvan, which had ceased to

The present Waterford & Suir Valley Railway passenger train consisting of a rebuilt Simplex 60S and two carriages supplied by Alan Keef Ltd. is pictured on 17 September 2001 (prior to public opening) at the temporary terminus beside Mount Congreve Nurseries.

carry passengers in 1967 and closed completely in 1982, was identified as being in good condition, and complete to Kilmeaden, offering the prospect of a five-mile journey through outstanding scenery. Efforts now concentrated on this route. What had started in 1997 as a 'Steam Train Restoration Group', progressed in 1998 to become the Waterford Tourism Railway Development Group, then the Waterford & Suir Valley Railway Project in 1999, with the Waterford & Suir Valley Railway Company Ltd being formed in 2000. The project has received help from a range of business sponsors and, crucially, has been supported by organisations such as Bord na Mona, CIE Heritage and FAS, together with the Waterford local authorities. The railway project is administered by a voluntary committee, although paid staff have been employed to construct the line under the FAS scheme. The railway is intended to be a self-financing addition to local tourism.

The sale of the trackbed to Waterford County Council was approved by the CIE board in September 1999, with a stipulation that the W&SVR be granted access to the Kilmeaden - Bilberry section for the development of the narrow gauge railway. A month later, agreement was secured to accommodate the planned line in the design of the new £90million Waterford road

by-pass and the way was clear for work to start on preparing track. This work commenced in February 2000 at the Waterford Crystal site. Ex-CIE track panels were 're-sized' by leaving the rail and fastenings in place on one side of the broad gauge sleepers and moving the fastenings and rail at the other end inwards to 3ft gauge, the sleepers themselves being reduced in length. Re-sized panels started to be taken to the site of the new line in June 2000 and by September, the first ⅞ of a mile of track had been laid and packed. Re-sizing continued at Waterford Crystal and by June 2001 2¼ miles of track had been laid from Kilmeaden to the site of the old lime kilns beside Mount Congreve Nurseries. A sleeper-built platform was constructed at this river bank location as a temporary terminus, while further tracklaying continued in 2002.

Although the passenger line commences from the site of the old Kilmeaden station, where only the platform remained, track was laid in the opposite direction up to a 'shed' for the locomotives and carriages, the basis for which are two 60ft shipping containers, joined end to end and raised 3ft above ground level, the floors having been removed. The lower section, between the ground and the container sides has been sheeted in steel and the whole structure painted. The far end doors remain in place to allow for possible extension at a later date by adding a third container. In theory, this is a temporary building, although it will probably remain in use for some time. With secure storage on the site, the stock was moved to Kilmeaden in May 2001, following a period of storage in the Waterford Crystal car park, and the first train ran over the line - a Sponsors and Friends Day special - in the late summer of 2001.

At that stage, the line constituted a basic railway with a platform at each end, but no run-round loops. Work scheduled for 2002 included the installation of loops, refurbishing and erecting an ex-GS&W footbridge at Kilmeaden and the preparation of a car park. The railway expected to formally open to the public, initially at weekends only, in June 2002 over the section to the Mount Congreve Nurseries. A further extension of about 1.4 miles was expected to come into use later in the year, with the line due to reach Bilberry during 2003, bringing the railway up to five miles. A number of developments at this station are envisaged. The majority of this route lies immediately beside the River Suir, providing an attractive waterside location. Closer to Waterford, the new by-pass includes a new river bridge, with the railway set to run for a mile on one side of the new road, then passing underneath and covering a further mile on the other side before the road swings away from the river. In the long-term, it is hoped that the railway might be further extended to Gratton Quay in Waterford itself, bringing it up to about six miles in length.

The first stock for the line were two diesel locomotives gifted to the project by Bord na Mona in July 1998. In July 1999, a passenger train, consisting of a rebuilt Simplex 60S equipped with a new engine and two carriages, was ordered from Alan Keef Ltd. The loco, and one coach, were displayed at the 11 September 1999 Alan Keef Ltd Open Day in advance of delivery early in the following year. The steel-built coaches are unusual, with roughly two-thirds of the accommodation in the form of open crosswise seating, with the remainder being an enclosed saloon accessed from an end veranda. Of the ex-Bord na Mona diesels, a Deutz 4wDM had been refurbished and was working on the line in 2001, while the second loco was being renovated at a site away from the railway. The introduction of steam is envisaged in the long term.

Museums and Industry

Clonmacnoise & West Offaly Railway

A significantly different operation from any other railway described in this volume, the 3ft gauge Clonmacnoise & West Offaly Railway is operated by Bord na Mona as a means of providing visitors with a guided tour of part of its major peat extraction activities on Blackwater Bog. The passenger carrying railway operates on tracks which are shared with the industrial element of the operation - a unique experience in several ways!

Bord na Mona is a Statutory Corporation established in 1946 to acquire, develop and manage peatland areas and is a major railway operator, having an estimated 1,200 miles of permanent and temporary narrow gauge track (mainly 3ft, but some 2ft gauge) at its various operating locations. It has four Divisions: Peat Energy, Horticulture, Solid Fuels and Environmental, along with small enterprises, of which the Clonmacnoise & West Offaly Railway is a rail tourism/education

venture. The Blackwater production bog is one of many raised bogs in the Midlands of Ireland and has an area of around 8,000 hectares encompassing parts of four Counties: Offaly, Westmeath, Roscommon and Galway. The bogs in these Counties are interconnected by a 3ft gauge railway system with a total mileage in the region of 160 kilometres. The development of Blackwater Bog commenced in 1953, with milled peat production starting in 1961.

The tourist train project was developed by Bord na Mona with financial assistance from the European Regional Development Fund - administered by Shannon Development - between 1989 and 1993. The first trains worked on a trial basis for one month in 1991, with the full service being introduced in 1992 when a specially commissioned coach was delivered. The passenger line operates round a basically square route on a 5½ mile journey. Tickets are sold from the counter of a tea room adjacent to the yard of the peat railway, with the visitor complex including a craft shop and toilets. The passenger station consists of a low raised platform equipped with picnic tables under a roof. The train comprises a single diesel locomotive and a specially constructed coach and a commentary is given by a guide throughout the tour. After reversing out of the station, past a display of machinery employed in the peat extraction process, onto the main line, the train passes the throat of the operational yard. On one side are peat extraction areas, while on the other is the 'island farm' on a 'gravel uplift' which has fertile mineral soil, in contrast to the surrounding bog. The train passes a location where the peat extraction process has been completed and the area has been returned to a wetland state for wildlife, then conifer tree plantations which are also experiments to establish potential future uses for the cutaway bog when the extraction process has finished.

The train stops at roughly the half-way point where passengers can alight and be shown how peat used to be manually dug. The train then skirts a production bog and part-way along the final leg of the run passes a turnout which is the means by which trains of milled peat leave the bog system and run to the ESB (Electricity Supply Board) power station at Shannonbridge, and return having discharged the loads. Around one million tonnes of milled peat a year goes to the power station, emphasising the scale of industrial use over the narrow gauge system. In contrast to early power stations which burnt sod peat, the milled peat produced for Shannonbridge is a fine-grain material which is blown into the furnaces and can also be compressed to form briquettes, a solid fuel substitute for domestic coal.

Production commenced at different bogs from around 1939, each having a local numbering system for its locomotives. From about 1954, the system was rationalised, with all Bord na Mona locomotives being given numbers in a national scheme (by date order) with the prefix LM - apparently for Locomotive Machine. Since many locomotives lose their original works plates in their working environment, the presence of these numbers is crucial in working out the identity of individual machines.

The trial operations in 1991 carried passengers in a vehicle which had been rebuilt by CIE at Inchicore Works from a former Walker Bros Railcar, which had previously worked on the West

Clare Railway. The locomotive used at this time is understood to have been LM111, a 4wDM Ruston & Hornsby 40DL (379079/54). The coach was subsequently withdrawn and moved away from the site, to be stored at a Bord na Mona depot. The original locomotive also ceased to be used for the tourist train and was replaced by examples of the 0-4-0DM Hunslet 'Wagonmaster' type, fitted with Ford 2713E 6-cylinder engines, which were previously employed on the production operation on the bog. Two of these locomotives, both built in 1979, are now employed on tourist train duties and are Bord na Mona No LM323 (HE8924/79) and LM322 (HE8923/79), although at the end of 2001, LM322 was out of use, apparently in need of repairs. For their new role, they were repainted into a green and yellow livery, thus being easily distinguished from similar machines still employed in peat production at Clonmacnoise which are in brown and cream Bord na Mona livery - although some Bord na Mona locomotives around the working yard are painted yellow! For the start of the full operation of the tourist railway, a specially constructed 52-seat air-conditioned passenger carriage, numbered as TC1, was built by Metro Walker of Clara and delivered in 1992. With the train established, a second coach, TC2 52 was built by J Managan &

Sons, Edenderry, and commissioned in 1994. This pair are painted in the same green and yellow livery as the locomotives.

A barrier precludes public access to the works yard (unless permission is obtained to enter) but a range of internal combustion locomotives used on the production bogs can normally seen, ranging from the interesting to bizarre. Although the passenger carriages have the Clonmacnoise & West Offaly Railway name plainly emblazoned on their sides, and the line's literature is similarly identified, the local authority brown tourist signs directing visitors to the line actually give the name as being the Blackwater Railway!

Bord na Mona also used to operate the Bellacorick Bog Railway at Oweninny, Co Mayo, as a similar kind of tourist train to the C&WOR, but this line closed around the end of the 1990s, apparently because it did not generate sufficient passenger numbers.

Peatlands Park Railway

Peat lines are not limited to the Republic. The Annaghmore Turf Railway was an unusual operation south of Lough Neagh, Co Armagh. Around 1907, the Irish Peat Development Company built a 3ft gauge railway about eight miles long. Up to the 1950s, this line was worked by the only electric locomotives in Ireland. These were built in Belfast and resembled sheds on a railway underframe, with overhead trolley poles mounted to one side. These machines were replaced by two diesels (a Planet and a Schöma) in the 1950s, but the commercial operation

Bord na Mona Hunslet 'Wagonmaster' 0-4-0DM No LM323 (HE8924/79) and passenger carriage of the Clonmacnoise & West Offaly Railway pictured at the stopping point part-way round the tourist trip on the Blackwater Bog network.

The first internal combustion engined rail vehicle to operate in Ireland, and among the first in the world. Built in 1906 by Allday & Onions as an open-top inspection vehicle, in 1926 (now enclosed) it became CDRJC railcar No 1. Withdrawn in April 1956, it is now preserved in the Ulster Folk and Transport Museum.

ceased in the 1960s. Part of the line was revived as a tourist attraction in what was now the Peatlands Country Park, the Peatlands Park Railway opening in 1988. The pair of original diesels provided the motive power, carrying passengers in replica turf wagons. A diesel built by Alan Keef Ltd arrived in 1993 and a former GSR/CIE inspection car (regauged from 5ft 3ins) provides an enclosed coach. There is also a short section of 2ft gauge track and a Hudson-Hunslet diesel loco.

Near Peatlands Country Park, peat is extracted commercially from the bog. The Sunshine Peat Co runs this operation and reinstated another part of the railway using 2ft 6ins gauge to take advantage of ex-Admiralty equipment. There is no public passenger service over the system, and the line passes under the M1 - probably the only incidence of an NG railway crossing a British motorway.

Ulster Folk & Transport Museum

Today's Irish Railway Collection at the Ulster Folk and Transport Museum dates back to the 1950s when various railway vehicles were assembled in the old Belfast & County Down Railway running sheds (by then under the auspices of the Ulster Transport Authority) at Queens Quay, Belfast. The railway and road exhibits were subsequently displayed at Witham Street, Newtownards Road, in Belfast - now entitled the Belfast Transport Museum. In 1967, the Ulster Folk Museum (set up in 1958) and Belfast Transport Museum were merged and the combined collections developed on a large site at Cultra, Holywood, just outside Belfast. The site is bisected by the Belfast to Bangor railway line (served by Cultra Halt) and the A2 road, the Folk Museum being on the southern side, the Transport exhibits on the northern side. The rail transport galleries were opened in October 1993, with entry to the hall containing the railway collection at a high level, a walkway providing an overhead view of the collection until descending to floor level.

The centre of the hall is a turntable, with fixed flooring surrounds, a branch of the 5ft 3ins gauge main line allowing broad gauge exhibits to be brought in and out. The broad gauge locomotives all face the turntable, while the narrow gauge (mainly, but not exclusively, 3ft gauge) are arranged around the other exhibits.

The 3ft gauge exhibits include CDRJC Class 5A Nasmyth Wilson & Co 2-6-4T No 2 *Blanche* 'hauling' CDR carriage No 1 (originally a tri-composite, later converted into a directors saloon) and CDR Trailer No 3 (originally a 5ft 3ins gauge Drewry Railcar built for the Dublin & Blessington Steam Tramway), alongside a 'station platform' displaying the huge station name board from Strabane. Alongside is another 'train' - Cavan & Leitrim Railway 4-4-0T No 2 *Kathleen* at the head of Cavan, Leitrim & Roscommon Light Railway and Tramway Company carriage No 5 and Castlederg & Victoria Bridge Tramway carriage No 4. Other 3ft gauge items displayed include the first internal combustion engined rail vehicle to operate in Ireland (and one of the first in the world) CDR Railcar No 1, CDR Railcar No 10 (originally built for the Clogher Valley Railway) and 4wD No 11 *Phoenix* (originally built for the Clogher Valley Railway as an 0-4-0VTB steam locomotive) and 0-4-0T tram locomotive No 2 of the Portstewart Tramway.

Other equipment includes: 22ins gauge Guinness brewery system steam loco No 20 and later F C Hibberd diesel, 3ft gauge 0-4-0T Peckett No 2 from the British Aluminium Co at Larne, 2ft gauge Hunslet diesel from the Admiralty Railway at Lisahally, Lough Foyle and a pair of Motor Rail Simplex's, along with various wagons. The road transport hall adjacent to the railway collection gallery also houses saloon No 2 and toastrack No 5 from the Giant's Causeway and Motor Car No 2 from the Bessbrook & Newry Tramway Company, plus other tramway exhibits.

There is no 'reserve' collection of vehicles not displayed, although occasionally broad gauge items are exchanged with the Railway Preservation Society of Ireland.

CHAPTER EIGHT

Taking the Lead

The lines which survived into the era of preservation naturally retained their own carriage stock, sometimes including vehicles dating back to the construction of the railway. Only a rare few - including the Vale of Rheidol, Snowdon Mountain and Isle of Man Railways - had sufficient vehicles to

handle the passenger traffic which has subsequently arisen. Even the Talyllyn Railway had to rapidly acquire, rebuild, and construct from scratch, vehicles to convey the passengers who, by purchasing tickets, were providing the cash to pay the bills incurred in preserving and developing the railways.

For the new wave of narrow gauge lines, providing passenger stock was a high priority. Some early solutions were highly inventive, and other answers have included the conversion of ex-military stock. Surviving carriage bodies were rescued, restored and mounted onto suitable underframes and running gear, but lines soon turned to the construction of new carriages to resolve the problem.

Attention also had to be given to the locomotives. The standards of engineering have rapidly climbed as old skills were re-learned and modern techniques and machines applied to the care of vintage locomotives. Overhaul standards quickly rose, but the point was soon reached where components could not have further life squeezed out of them - especially the central element of all steam locomotives, the boiler. The narrow gauge led, in accepting

This Leighton Buzzard Railway train is being hauled by No 80 Beaudesert *which, in addition to being able to work passenger services when required, can perform any recovery operation envisaged on the railway. The loco is a radically rebuilt Simplex 'T' series machine, the conversion work having been undertaken by Alan Keef Ltd and it was delivered in time to appear during the line's 80th birthday celebration event on 26 June 1999 - hence its fleet number. Following painting and completion of various details, it officially entered service on 8 August 1999, becoming the newest narrow gauge diesel to enter service on a British heritage railway at that time. The carriages on the LBR have been built by volunteers over the years, the railway originally being an industrial line to transport sand.*

that the way forwards lay in building new boilers rather than continued efforts at patching up life-expired units. In this, narrow gauge railways remain well in advance of standard gauge colleagues, for no more than a handful of new standard gauge boilers have been constructed at the time of writing, and none bigger than ex-industrial locomotives and 0-6-0T 'Terrier's'. Admittedly, the cost of a new narrow gauge boiler is substantially less than for a much larger standard gauge unit, but there is comparatively less money available to narrow gauge railways, thus balancing the equation. Although practicality is an important motivation for building new boilers, there is a preservation issue as well. It has been realised that constantly repairing original boilers amounts to the progressive scrapping of historic material. By constructing new, the original boiler can be placed in a state of conservation and displayed, allowing the study of the original techniques employed by the old manufacturers. Moreover, if the time comes when the locomotive is to be displayed rather than operated, the modern boiler can be removed and the original replaced, allowing the exhibition of a genuinely original locomotive.

Some standard gauge locomotives entered preservation direct from service, mainly industrials, although a few were privately purchased from BR, and some locomotives saved for the national collection are allowed to be put into operational service, but the key to the many standard gauge heritage lines was the survival of so many locomotives sent to Barry scrapyard, but never cut up. Initially, motive power for new narrow gauge projects was available from industry, indeed several railways grew from projects aimed at the preservation of individual locomotives. As the number of railways grew, and operations on the older established and preserved railways expanded, the need for more motive power arose. Many locomotives have been imported from abroad and received new leases of life in Britain, but there was no Barry Island stockpile of native machines to draw on!

Inevitably, attention turned to new construction. In some cases this was to fulfil the need for additional motive power, in others to meet the desire to recreate a type which was scrapped

ABOVE: Modern equipment in evidence to aid the repair and maintenance of narrow gauge motive power. This May 1998 picture shows the tender of 2-4-0STT *Blanche* lifted clear of the floor while the locomotive receives attention in Boston Lodge, Ffestiniog Railway.

long ago. Described in this chapter are a selection of the newly constructed locomotives which are running, or will enter service before too long, on narrow gauge railways in Britain.

Earl of Merioneth

The construction of *Earl of Merioneth* was an early example of new locomotive building in the era of preservation - but it could be said to have simply followed a pattern established by the Ffestiniog Railway's works at Boston Lodge many decades before.

Articulated locomotives built to Robert Fairlie's 1864 patent have come to be a hallmark of the Ffestiniog Railway. The first to enter service was *Little Wonder* built by George England &

Although an oil-burner, *David Lloyd George* had 'bunkers' and coal to provide the illusion of being coal fired during the October 2000 Vintage Weekend on the Ffestiniog Railway.

Co in 1869 (withdrawn in 1882), followed in 1872 by *James Spooner* (built by Avonside and withdrawn in 1933) and the Vulcan Foundry-built single Fairlie *Taliesin* in 1876 (withdrawn 1932). The first Fairlie to be built at Boston Lodge was the double engine *Merddin Emrys* in 1879, followed by *Livingston Thompson* in 1886 (renamed *Taliesin* in 1932).

The fledgling preservation project which reopened the Ffestiniog Railway in 1954 worked initial trains with internal combustion motive power, the George England 0-4-0STT *Prince* returning to steam in 1955. The double engine *Taliesin* (previously *Livingston Thompson*) returned to traffic in September 1956, and in April 1961 was renamed again, becoming *Earl of Merioneth*. The other surviving double engine, *Merddin Emrys*, needed a great deal of work and, after boiler repairs and the rebuilding of its superstructure, returned to traffic for the 1961 season. Unfortunately, the boiler problems continued and the locomotive missed the 1962 season.

Earl of Merioneth (nee *Taliesin*, nee *Livingston Thompson*) was in need of an overhaul, but had to be kept in service. It became obvious that the boilers of both double engines had reached the end of their lives, hence two new superheated boilers were ordered from Hunslet Engine Co in 1968. Taking advantage

of a good price, these were not built to the original wagon-top design with a tapered section between the raised firebox casing and barrel, but were basically a double ended version of the boiler the company had recently built for 0-4-0ST *Linda*.

Merddin Emrys returned to traffic in November 1970, the new boiler solving her performance problems, but causing a considerably revised appearance. *Earl of Merioneth* was then withdrawn in 1971 for the fitting of its new boiler. In view of what had happened to *Merddin Emrys*, it was realised that the old outline of *Earl of Merioneth* would also be lost. A group called the Active Forty advocated that instead of effectively destroying the old superstructure, it should be retained for preservation and a completely new locomotive constructed. A Fund was launched to cover the difference in cost, and building of a new *Earl of Merioneth* started in 1972. At the time, it was believed that the loco would not only be required quickly, but that there was a need for the machine to be capable of making a return trip to Blaenau Ffestiniog without taking water, hence the design incorporated huge slab-sided water tanks. In the event, the return to Blaenau was not achieved until 1982 and other priorities arose which slowed down work on the new loco.

The new *Earl of Merioneth* was finally completed in 1979, being officially launched into traffic on 23 June. The locomotive was virtually all-new, incorporating little more than the frame plates and cylinder castings from earlier units. It is also oil fired, following a policy adopted by the FR from 1970.

Two newly-built Ffestiniog Railway double-Fairlie locomotives, *Earl of Merioneth*, with *David Lloyd George* behind, at Minffordd on 3 May 1998.

Aesthetically, the loco won few admirers - certainly criticism of *Merddin Emrys* paled when the new *Earl of Merioneth* appeared! Changes have been made over subsequent years to alleviate its visual impact: the brass dome covers and chimneys from *Merddin Emrys* (withdrawn with cracks in the areas where the firebox meets the boiler barrel) have been fitted, the plates moved more to the centre of the tanks, and a revised paint scheme implemented which includes a reasonably complex pattern of lining.

Considering the motivation behind its construction, it was probably appropriate that *Earl of Merioneth* should be the loco to work the first train back to Blaenau on 25 May 1982. To round things off, the original *Earl of Merioneth*, saved by the construction of the new loco, had the name *Livingston Thompson* reinstated and following cosmetic restoration is now displayed in the National Railway Museum at York. The third name which has been applied to this locomotive, *Taliesin*, was 'reserved' against the ambition of building a new single Fairlie to replicate the original holder of the name. This came to fruition in 1999 - see later.

David Lloyd George

The background to the Ffestiniog Railway's Fairlie locomotives is described above. Having returned to Blaenau Ffestiniog in 1982, the time had come by the late 1980s for the FR to turn its attention to improvements along the length of the railway and the experience offered to passengers. What emerged was the INCA Programme (INcreased CApacity) which took advantage of funds available under a series of tourism development initiatives promoted by local and national authorities. A major investment in the future, the INCA Programme was to provide a new six-coach train, a new double Fairlie locomotive and improved passenger facilities at the three main FR stations. Four of the coaches for the new train were totally new construction, while two were extensive rebuilds of carriages built some 10 years previously. The standard of accommodation was a major step forward and the set was equipped for push-pull operation in conjunction with a diesel locomotive as well as being capable of use in a 'conventional' train.

So far as the locomotive was concerned, the objective at the time was not to actually have three double Fairlie's in operation, but to build a new boiler, superstructure (tanks, cab, etc.) and cradle frame - the upper chassis on which the boiler is mounted and rides on the power bogies. The intention (then) was that the new loco would replace *Earl of Merioneth* and use the bogies from that locomotive which would be about due for its first major overhaul as the new machine was completed. However, a parallel

ABOVE: Single-Fairlie *Taliesin* leaves Porthmadog Harbour station on Saturday 1 May 1999, following its official naming ceremony, with a special train for the people who contributed the funds which made the project possible. At that time, the loco was temporarily painted black, the current deep red livery being applied subsequently.

LEFT: Talyllyn Railway No 7 *Tom Rolt* pictured at Tywyn Wharf station.

project to build two new power bogies, complete with new cylinders, motion and wheels was also put in hand at Boston Lodge. One was earmarked for the single Fairlie construction project to build *Taliesin*, the other being intended to become a spare - with all of the power bogies being interchangeable.

A key decision was that the new locomotive would have the appearance of a traditional double Fairlie - more so than the rebuilt *Merddin Emrys* and definitely not a repeat of *Earl of Merioneth!* As already recorded, the two 1968 Hunslet-built

boilers were not constructed to the traditional wagon-top design and by the late 1980s it was already apparent that there were problems with cracks developing around the throatplate of the firebox outer wrapper. These boilers also had wider fireboxes than the older design which meant that the cradle frames had to be built out sideways to go round the firebox. The lesson that G P Spooner had been right with his original design was taken on board and the new boiler, designed by Bob Meanley of Tyseley Locomotive Works, had fully tapered second rings, and the firebox was waisted so that it would fit between straight frames. It also had four superheater flues at each end, two more than the Hunslet boilers. The boiler, along with the rest of the locomotive, was slightly larger than the earlier Fairlie designs, but retained the correct proportions. The boiler was constructed by Bloomfield Steel Construction of Tipton in the West Midlands and was delivered to Boston Lodge on 1 August 1991.

The official naming ceremony was performed by Dr William R P George, grandson of David Lloyd George on 6 April 1993 and the new loco entered service. Perhaps inevitably, circumstances have modified the original plans. The aforementioned cracks identified on the Hunslet-built boilers resulted in the withdrawal of *Merddin Emrys* at the end of 1995, thus *David Lloyd George* and *Earl of Merioneth* provided the double engine motive power on the FR in recent years. An appeal was launched in 2000 to fund the modification and repairs to the boiler of *Merddin Emrys*, with the aim of returning the loco to service for 2002/3. The FR Society would also like to complete the construction of a new power bogie and, if possible, build another.

An interesting design feature of *David Lloyd George* is that only three of the tanks contain water, the fourth containing fuel oil, the locomotive being oil-fired. On at least one occasion, the loco has appeared during an FR Vintage Gala with coal in fake bunkers - but it cannot be converted to coal burning as can *Taliesin*, the lumps were present for effect only!

Taliesin

The original Ffestiniog Railway 0-4-4T single Fairlie *Taliesin* was the third Fairlie-type loco built for the FR. Constructed in 1876 by Vulcan Foundry, it was, in effect, half of its predecessor, double Fairlie *James Spooner*. By about 1932, *Taliesin* was withdrawn and dismantled at Boston Lodge.

The construction of a replica dates back to an evening in 1986 when two FR Society Directors, Andy Savage and Gordon Rushton, discussed the idea over a bottle of brandy. Deciding the scheme was feasible, a plan to raise the necessary cash by covenanted subscriptions was developed. This was publicly launched in early 1989 with the target of raising £250,000 to fund the construction of the new loco at Boston Lodge on a contract basis, with input by volunteers, and major parts such as the boiler to be constructed by outside contractors. The initial minimum of 200 covenanters was quickly passed, the total actually reaching 240.

With experience of building double Fairlie *Earl of Merioneth* in the 1970s and *David Lloyd George* under construction (completed 1992), Boston Lodge had the drawings available for a standard power bogie along with the casting patterns. Although few drawings of *Taliesin* existed, the decision had already been made to construct the loco to a slightly larger size than the original, the standard power bogie being adopted and all other dimensions being slightly increased to retain the correct proportions. The consequently larger boiler allowed a superheater to be fitted, along with an increase of boiler pressure from the original's 160psi to 200psi. The locomotive has also been designed to either burn coal or oil and it only takes a few hours to convert

Taliesin from one to the other, the oil tank (located in the bunker) being craned in or out.

The new power bogie was constructed immediately after the two for *David Lloyd George* were finished, meanwhile, detailed computer-aided drawings were produced. A search of Boston Lodge revealed a surprising number of original components. The driving wheels were discovered, but could not be used because cracks were found in them. Other parts unearthed included the reversing lever and links, hand brake column, chimney and nameplates. Incorporating these components into the new loco resulted in references to it actually being a 'major rebuild' of the original!

The main frame and bogies were complete by mid-1996 and the rolling chassis was displayed during the October FR Vintage Weekend. By the following May's FR gala, the smokebox and water tanks had been added and the boiler, built by Bloomfield Steel Construction, was delivered in July 1998. Originally launched as the 'Taliesin 2000' project, it was becoming apparent that the locomotive was going to be completed well ahead of schedule and *Taliesin* was officially named in a ceremony at Harbour station on the morning of Saturday 1 May 1999, although at that point, the loco was temporarily painted black. Present for the ceremony were FR Society Vice-President Andy Savage, Gordon Rushton (with a bottle of brandy - reputed to be the same one involved when the project was conceived!) and FR Vice-President, Bill Broadbent, who unveiled the nameplate. *Taliesin* then hauled a special train carrying contributors to the project and entered service working public trains on the following day. The loco was finished in its lined maroon livery in time for the following October's FR Vintage Weekend.

Tom Rolt

Purists might debate whether Talyllyn Railway No 7 is a newbuild locomotive or a major reconstruction of a pre-existing loco. John Bate, who led the project for the TR, describes the task in his own book as 'to a considerable extent simply a matter of rearranging existing components'. This author feels he is being a little modest and that the reconstruction was so radical that it is reasonable to include *Tom Rolt* in this section!

In the mid-1960s, the pioneer project to preserve the TR had established itself with rapidly growing traffic, but there was concern at the motive power situation. *Talyllyn* and *Dolgoch* were not considered to be sufficiently powerful or reliable and *Sir Haydn* had not been used since 1957. The mainstay was *Edward Thomas*, with *Douglas* just about providing a back-up. John Bate (by then working full-time for the TR) looked at what was required starting with a 'clean sheet' and by February 1966 had developed an outline scheme and drawing for an 0-6-2T which his study concluded would produce a suitable locomotive. Estimates for the construction of proposed new locomotives were obtained and the subject debated through into 1968, by which time various alternative schemes had been proposed. By the end of the year, discussions were in progress with Hunslet concerning the possible supply of an EVA type 0-4-2T.

ABOVE: **Alan Civil, who built the loco, on the footplate of** *Pearl 2* **at the Amerton Railway.**

LEFT: Annie, **with owner and builder, Richard Booth, on the footplate, at Sea Lion Rocks station on the Groudle Glen Railway.**

On 20 January 1969, an offer came of 3ft gauge 1949-built Andrew Barclay (AB2263/49) which could provide all the main components required at a scrap value price. This 0-4-0WT was one of three built in 1949 for Bord na Mona (Irish Turf Board). The trio carried both Bord na Mona numbers (in the usual Locomotive Machine system they applied to all motive power) and conventional numbers: No 1 LM43 (AB2263/49), No 2 LM44 (AB2264/49) and No 3 LM45 (AB2265/49) and had a

weight of 10½ tons, 8½ins x 12ins cylinders, 2ft diameter driving wheels and a tractive effort of 5,527 lbs. They were designed to burn peat, and went to Portarlington, but were not successful - it is said that apart from not steaming well, despite being equipped with spark arresting chimneys they tended to set fire to the product they were supposed to be assisting in harvesting!

No 2 entered preservation under the ownership of the Irish Steam Preservation Society and remains, in full operation, at the Society's line at Stradbally, Co Laois, while No 3 kept its number and acquired the name *Shane* when it entered service on the Shane's Castle Railway, and retains both number and name at the Giant's Causeway and Bushmills Railway. The opportunity to purchase No 1 was taken by the TRPS and the loco arrived at Liverpool on 12 March 1969 and the Talyllyn Railway on 26 March. Perhaps ironically, by this time Sir *Haydn* had returned to service.

Other projects had to be pursued, not least being the commencement of work on the extension to Nant Gwernol and no real work was done on the new loco until 1971 when it was dismantled. In October 1971 a start was made on the frames to prepare for regauging at Pendre and work progressed until spring 1975 when the boiler was placed (on blocks) on the chassis of what was now an 0-4-2T and all work halted. The Nant Gwernol extension had continued to take priority (it opened in 1976) but the situation had changed significantly from the time when a new locomotive had been considered essential. Principally, traffic on the TR had peaked in 1973 and started to decline, while the position concerning the other locomotives had steadily been improved.

The project remained in abeyance until about 1987/88 when the loco was moved back into the workshop, and work recommenced on the chassis. By 1990 the pace was accelerating and the locomotive was sufficiently ready for a naming ceremony on 6 May 1991. For most of the time that the locomotive had been at the TR it had been known as *Irish Pete* - a pun referring to its origin and fuel. Second thoughts prevailed and the name *Tom Rolt* was chosen, after the man who played a crucial role in the preservation of the railway. His widow, Sonia Rolt, performed the naming, but at that point, the loco was not fully complete, having only one injector and a number of other details outstanding. *Tom Rolt* was ready for service on 27 July 1991 when it hauled its first train and entered regular traffic on 15 August 1991.

The principal components derived from the Andrew Barclay loco are the boiler, wheels and cylinders. The loco has a very different appearance from the 'donor' machine, not least because of the new large side tanks. The 14 ton 5 cwt loco has 8½ins x 12ins cylinders, a boiler pressure of 180lbs/sq in and a tractive effort of 5,527lbs at 85% boiler pressure. A couple of interesting details are that the chimney was found in a store at Dinorwic and the cab window frames were supplied by the Ffestiniog Railway to a Fairlie design.

Annie

Built by Richard Booth for use on the Groudle Glen Railway, 0-4-2T *Annie* is a replica of a Bagnall which was built in November 1911 and delivered to the Gentle Annie Tramway of Gisbourne, New Zealand, on 23 March 1912.

Construction commenced in December 1995 when the frame plates, stretcher and buffer beams were cut and profiled by the IoM Steam Packet Co at its Fort Street, Douglas, works. Initial erecting took place in Richard's next door neighbour's garage and parts produced by sub-contractors were added as

they arrived. In mid-April 1996 the frames were moved into the IOMSR workshops at Douglas where the proximity of machines and tools increased the pace of construction. The potential problem of the cylinders was resolved when the owner of another replica of the loco in Perth, Western Australia, agreed to a set of castings being made from his patterns. These duly arrived and were being test-fitted by the following November, by which time the tanks, bunkers and cab had been progressed. The all-welded boiler - basically a copy of that on *Polar Bear* but with the dome combined with the manifold on the firebox wrapper and the clacks mounted on the backhead - was built by Valentine Engineering in Northamptonshire. In fact, many chassis components share the same dimensions as those of *Polar Bear* - in many respects, *Annie* is basically *Polar Bear* in reverse!

The boiler was delivered in late June 1997 and the locomotive was ready for its test steaming on 25 October 1997. Following tests, the boiler was lifted for the Bagnall Price valve gear to be fitted. On 26 April 1998, *Annie* was moved out of the Douglas works on a trailer and a fire lit. This formed a test for the 'big day' on the following Saturday - 2 May 1998 - when *Annie* (in pink undercoat) was to appear alongside *Sutherland* for the Beyer Peacock 2-4-0's return to steam. *Annie* was almost complete, although the absence of the main steam and blast pipes prevented much movement! The loco first moved properly under her own steam on 11 June on a short test track outside the works. The paint was then applied, the maroon is the same colour as had been applied to *Caledonia* when that loco returned to service. *Annie* left Douglas on 27 June and was taken to the Groudle Glen Railway where she was formally 'inaugurated' when Sharon Booth appropriately broke a bottle of Gisbourne Chardonnay over the buffer beam.

Pearl 2

Although inspired by an 1890s Bagnall inverted saddle tank design, an example of the type being *Excelsior* which worked on the Kerry Tramway and was later employed on the Lynton & Barnstaple construction contract, *Pearl 2* is not a specific replica of a 'lost' locomotive. After 40 years in engineering, including 11 years at Bagnall's, Allen Civil, who had led the restoration of 0-4-0ST Bagnall *Isabel* (1491/1897) for service at the Amerton Railway, as well as previously owning several standard gauge locomotives, decided to construct his own loco - based on Bagnall practice, but adapted to meet modern requirements.

Work on building *Pearl 2* started in 1995 and she was a rolling chassis in time to be displayed during the 1997 celebrations of *Isabel*'s 100th birthday at the Amerton Railway. The loco was 'officially' named at Allen's home on 8 August 1998 and arrived at Amerton on 5 September, making her debut hauling passenger trains on 20 June 1999. She remains based on the Amerton Railway, although she spent six weeks in August/September 2001 visiting the Launceston Steam Railway.

The chassis of the 0-4-2IST is very similar to Richard Booth's *Annie*, although the wheels are slightly larger, the size being determined when Allen was offered four Ruston tyres - he simply made the patterns for the wheels accordingly and had the castings machined to fit the tyres! Her 5½ x 7½ins cylinders are also larger than those of *Annie*. The frames and buffer beams were cut to profile by a contractor and the boiler was built by Valentine Engineering in Northamptonshire. All other machining and erecting work to construct the locomotive was undertaken by her owner. The boiler, with a circular marine-type firebox, is effectively identical to the boilers of locos such as *Pixie* (Cadeby Light Railway) and *Armistice* (Bredgar & Wormshill Light Railway) - one size bigger than the boiler made for *Annie*. Other differences from *Annie* include the dropped footplate and full cab.

Pearl 2 has an all-welded water tank, is equipped with taper roller bearings for all the wheels and is fitted with an air pump which enables her to work passenger trains on the Amerton line. Her name? Mrs Civil's name is Pearl and the locomotive was named after her - with the 2 added to differentiate between them!

Taffy

During the 1960s, Alan Keef had owned two De Winton vertical boilered locomotives, one being 2ft gauge, the other 3ft gauge. These were sold in the late 1960s as Alan Keef Ltd expanded its narrow gauge construction and restoration business, but Alan came to regret the decision to part with them. When the cylinders of an original 3ft gauge De Winton became available, the opportunity to construct a replica locomotive was taken.

The cylinders originated from the 1878-built *Penmaen*, which worked at the Penmaen East granite quarry at Penmaenmawr, North Wales, until falling out of use, certainly by 1943. Work on building the replica 0-4-0VTB started around 1987 and was carried out by Alan Keef with backing from the works facilities. Although the cylinders made the project possible, almost everything else was constructed from scratch and *Taffy* is basically a replica of the 1877-vintage *Chaloner* (based at Leighton Buzzard) from which all basic dimensions were measured. A new frame was built, along with new wheels, tank, bunker and boiler. A Ruston & Hornsby diesel loco contributed some components, while a few other parts came from the original *Penmaen*, including some valve gear components, the safety valve base and hand rails.

Taffy made its debut in steam at the 2 September 1995 Alan Keef Ltd Open Day. Although she successfully worked passenger trains on the works demonstration line, unfortunately a crank axle broke. Following repairs, the loco saw some use, although it was not truly completed until 2001 when most of the remaining details were finished.

Lyd

The original Lynton & Barnstaple Railway Manning Wardle 2-6-2Ts *Yeo*, *Exe* and *Taw* were scrapped in 1935 after the line closed, along with the Baldwin 2-4-2T *Lyn*, while 2-6-2T *Lew*, built in 1925 under Southern Railway ownership survived to be exported to Brazil - rumours occasionally circulate that it has been 'discovered', but holding one's breath is not recommended! Both the L&B and its Manning Wardles retain a deep affection among enthusiasts who, inevitably, wish to recreate them. There are two projects to build replicas, of which *Lyd* is further advanced.

James Evans founded The Lyd Project, having been fascinated by the L&B since his teens. After securing the original works drawings for *Lew*, he decided to produce a replica. Production of components started c. 1994 and, part-way into 1995, cylinders had been cast and machined, buffer beams and tyres made, and the frame plates paid for. By this time, he was supporting projects at the Ffestiniog Railway and an agreement emerged by which the project was relocated from Cornwall to Boston Lodge and ownership of the components was transferred to the Ffestiniog

0-4-0VTB *Taffy* pictured hauling an ex-Penrhyn workmen's carriage at the 8 September 2001 Open Day at the works of Alan Keef Ltd.

Lyd suddenly looked like a locomotive, albeit an 0-6-0, when pictured in May 1999 following the return of the rolling chassis from ESCA Engineering. Admittedly, this angle does disguise the fact that there was no boiler behind the smokebox!

Railway Trust. James remained deeply involved, not least in undertaking design work where modifications from the original drawings are necessary. The change also made it possible to broaden the appeal for funds - a covenant scheme was set up and substantial income generated from the FR guest driver programme. For the FR, it provided continued work for skilled staff at Boston Lodge - and a new locomotive for the FR and WHR(C).

The locomotive is to be visually very similar to *Lew* in 1925, but incorporating improvements over the original. Metric material dimensions enforce certain changes, the slightly increased thickness of plate for the boiler enabling a higher operating pressure. The loco will be oil-fired, although convertible to coal firing. Where performance can be improved without changing the external appearance, this will be done - assuming the original Manning Wardle trio were a Mk1 design and the 1925-built *Lew* represented Mk2, James Evans views The Lyd Project as producing a Mk3 version of the Manning Wardle 2-6-2T design.

Parts (including forgings for the rods and fly cranks along with the valve gear) arrived at Boston Lodge during 1995 followed in 1996 by components including the six driving wheels, main horn guides, front-end stay and slide bar brackets. Although FR staff had other priorities in early 1997, some 1600 hours of paid time were allocated to the project during the summer to progress the frames, which were displayed during the October 1997 FR Vintage Weekend. In March 1998, the water tanks were delivered, after construction by a Cornish marine engineering company. To prevent corrosion, green paint was applied - the temptation to add the prominent 'Southern' logo was irresistible!

During 1998, there was a shortage of skilled staff to work on the loco. In an effort to accelerate the project the frames, and a

collection of components, were moved out of Boston Lodge in January 1999 and taken to ESCA Engineering with the aim of producing a rolling chassis complete with springs, axleboxes, driving wheels, cylinders and motion brackets. The plan for the chassis to be returned to Porthmadog for the Ffestiniog Railway's May gala ('Railffest99') was achieved. *Lyd* suddenly looked like a locomotive - albeit an 0-6-0 since the pony trucks were not built. On the chassis were side tanks, smokebox wrapper - and original L&B chimney as fitted to *Yeo*. This was acquired from Pilton yard in 1935 by Murch Bros of Little Torrington and fitted to a Ruston Proctor steam roller named *Pride of Barum*. James Evans purchased the roller in 1997 to secure this historic item! For the record, although light-hearted references were made to the effect of this transforming *Lyd* into a rebuild project, the rivet patterns on the chimney prove that it came from *Yeo* and not the later *Lew*.

As the end of 2000 approached, the order of construction was changed. The cash available would have either covered finishing the locomotive, less the boiler, or funded the boiler, leaving the rest of the money to complete the loco to be raised. The decision was to go for the boiler and an order was placed with Israel Newton & Sons of Bradford in December 2000. The 200psi boiler - costing some £36,000 - is of welded construction, but employing flanged joints between plates.

At Boston Lodge, work continued during 2001 on machining the coupling rods, connecting rods and cylinder cover castings, the plan being to have most of the outside motion in place by the end of the year, although progress slowed following another round of staff shortages. If additional cash is raised to fund the pony trucks, progress should be made during 2002 with the aim of producing a working chassis, complete with boiler. When the project started, the cost was estimated at £200,000 and it was hoped to have the loco in service by 2002. Costings have since risen, and meeting the target date, while possible, depends on raising the funds.

Yeo

The Lynton & Barnstaple Railway Association project to rebuild the line took a considerable step forwards in March 1995 when Woody Bay station was purchased. With high hopes that the return of rails to the L&B trackbed was now within sight, thoughts among members turned to motive power. The Lynton & Barnstaple Locomotive Group emerged and Project Yeo was launched in June 1996. After some initial problems, a new team was in place to take the concept forwards by the following autumn and had agreed to commission a technical specification and seek charitable status. The Project is close to, but not part of, the L&B Association - although the objective is to build a locomotive to run on the revived L&B.

The charitable status of the Project was confirmed in May 1997 and a set of drawings for the original locomotives was secured free of charge. A full Technical Specification Document - amounting to 566 A4 pages - was prepared by BB Project Services in 1998 and forwarded to contractors with invitations to tender.

The quotation supplied by Winson Engineering, Daventry, was accepted in June 1998. The projected price was £199,837 (plus VAT) with construction, and payment, to be undertaken in stages over a period of time - anticipated as three to three and a half years. Winson's completed the initial manufacturing drawings and started construction by September 1998. The side pieces of the main frames were then cut out, stress relieved and surface ground to dimensions. By the end of 1999, the main frame bolt holes had been drilled and initial erection of basic frames carried out. This included the front and rear drag boxes, frame stretchers and brackets, and the basic frame structure was viewed at the works by members and supporters in June 2000. Unfortunately, business problems struck Winson's in April/May 2001 following which the work completed was removed from the factory and relocated to a site in Essex. Despite this setback, it was already apparent that the original target of steaming the new loco in 2001 was not going to be achieved.

The stated aim is to produce a replacement locomotive rather than a replica. With construction employing modern methods, the objective is to produce a locomotive which will look and perform as it would have done in 1935. It will also be given the Manning Wardle works number 2048. This arises since two L&B Association members set up Manning Wardle & Co Ltd as a private limited company in 1997, having purchased the trademarks of the old company which ceased trading in 1927.

Lady Madcap

The original *Lady Madcap* was the only Hunslet supplied second-hand to the Dinorwic quarries (or Port) operation. The 0-4-0ST (HE652/96) was built for the Groby Granite Co Ltd to work at their quarry in Leicestershire and named *Sextus*. In 1909, the locomotive was returned to Hunslet's for overhaul but, on completion, the Groby Co asked if Hunslet would supply a new 0-6-0 loco, and take the reconditioned *Sextus* in part exchange. Having agreed to this, when Dinorwic needed a loco in 1910, *Sextus* was offered. After modifications to meet Dinorwic requirements, the loco went to North Wales - the new name being applied between 1911 and 1913.

The loco was not the same as the 'Alice' type Hunslets at Dinorwic, having a longer wheelbase, stepped frame (dropping the height of the footplate) and a domed boiler, making it similar to the Port Class locomotives at Penrhyn. *Lady Madcap* was apparently fitted with a shorter 'Alice' type boiler (a complex issue to vex historians!) for a time, but the original boiler was reinstated. The loco was withdrawn from service and by the end of April 1952 had been stripped and the boiler removed. By July 1969, the frames were reduced to pieces and had gone completely by January 1970.

It is conventional to identify a locomotive by its frames, and their destruction would normally indicate the loco has been scrapped. However, a number of parts survived, inspiring Andy Blackwell and Dave Ruston to look at recreating *Lady Madcap*. After gathering a collection of original components and 'new' spares, the crucial acquisition was the cylinders, found in store at the Llanberis Lake Railway. With the project now considered viable, the next step will be to have new frames cut.

The components at the time of writing include: cylinders, wheelsets, water tank (made by Dry Dock Co), coupling and connecting rods, crossheads, axleboxes and covers, weighbar shaft, bunkers, two slide bars, handbrake column, reverser quadrant, valve buckles, eccentric straps, links, levers and other miscellany. The dome cover also survives, being amongst components purchased by the owner of *Sybil Mary*, thus it is hoped to borrow it and make a copy.

Although it should be classed as a new-build project, there is an argument that with this number of original components, the resulting loco may be nearly as original as several of the other ex-quarry Hunslets which incorporate numerous parts swapped in their working days, and have received major rebuilds in preservation!

Corris Railway No 7

The original three Corris Railway locomotives were built by Hughes Locomotive and Tramway Engine Works Ltd at the Falcon Engine Works, Loughborough. Two were scrapped in 1920, while No 3 was rebuilt that year. The line needed another locomotive and the GWR (which had taken over the Corris) ordered a Kerr Stuart 'Tattoo' Class 0-4-2ST - KS4047 (delivered 10 June 1921) becoming No 4 on the Corris line, costing £1,825. This loco received a new boiler in 1928. The firebox was condemned in 1948 and the loco withdrawn, the railway closing later that year. No 4 was purchased (with No 3 - for £25 each!) in 1950 by the Talyllyn Railway Preservation Society and while retaining the same number, was named *Edward Thomas*, latterly running as *Peter Sam*.

As restoration of the Corris Railway advanced, Society

This 1 May 1998 picture taken in the works of Winson Engineering in Daventry shows the frames for Corris Railway No 7 in the centre of the workshop floor. Beyond, the Ffestiniog Railway 1918-vintage 2-4-0DM Baldwin *Moelwyn* is being renovated, while to the right, the Welsh Highland Railway (Caernarfon) luxury First Class Dining Saloon is under construction. The skeleton framework to the left is a coach under construction for a railway in Japan.

members looked at securing a steam locomotive for future operations. A survey resulted in 78 offers of financial support, encouraging the Society to proceed. Consideration was given to obtaining a foreign locomotive but nothing suitable was located. Any loco had to have similar dimensions to an original Corris loco to fit the loading gauge and, by summer 1994, the decision was made in favour of the 'Tattoo' type. Key factors included the greater capability and easier maintenance of the Kerr Stuart over the Falcon type, plus the absence of drawings for a Falcon.

The Corris Railway Society launched its Tattoo Locomotive Appeal Fund on 1 February 1995. With the cost estimated at some £70,000 it was recognised that it would probably take around 10 years to bring to fruition. Estimates were received from three companies, and Winson Engineering (then of Penrhyndeudraeth, later Daventry) was selected. An initial problem was the lack of suitable Kerr Stuart drawings. They were understood to exist in Armley Mills Museum, Leeds, but copies could not be obtained. This was overcome in early 1995 when a chance encounter resulted in drawings for the locomotive being secured. After evaluation it was confirmed that building could proceed.

A Quality Plan, including the construction document, copies of the drawings and photographs of the loco in its original form and as modified by the TR was prepared by Colin Blackwell of BB Engineering Services and forwarded to Winson's. They revised their quotation and a formal order for production of a rolling chassis was placed on 10 September 1996 - payment would be made in stages with work progressing as the cash was raised.

Updated General Arrangement drawings were prepared and the manufacture of parts commenced, a visit to Winson's factory in April 1997 allowing viewing of the frame plates, hornblocks

and wheels. More components followed and by February 1998 the frame and wheels were ready for inspection. The Tattoo Locomotive Company was formed in summer 1998 to take the project forwards, and Winson's were asked to design a new welded boiler. With fundraising going well, there was a rolling chassis (with suspension and trailing truck) by April 1999, with fabrication of the inner and outer firebox and boiler barrel also completed. Further work on the boiler and firebox, along with fabrication of the cylinders, proceeded through 1999 and the components were looking like a locomotive by winter that year. With work having started on producing the motion, the project was reckoned to be 50% complete by spring 2000. Work proceeded into 2001, by which time firebox, smokebox and chimney had been completed. Unfortunately, Winson's business problems in April/May 2001 also brought the Tattoo project to a halt. The components have been moved to an undisclosed location where work restarted early in 2002.

The locomotive will be a modern interpretation of Corris Railway No 4 rather than an absolute replica. It will incorporate improvements, including oil-firing (to accommodate Forestry Commission regulations) and air braking, while retaining the overall appearance of Kerr Stuart No 4047. While the TR has owned and operated ex-Corris No 4, a number of changes have been made. These include cab entrances on both sides (the original had access to the cab on one side only), replacement of the original round bar coupling and connecting rods with conventional machined rods and a cab extension. The revived Corris Railway has not used the numbers 1 to 4 for its 'new' locomotive fleet (Nos 3 and 4 still exist at the TR) and has allocated Nos 5 and 6 to internal combustion locomotives at Maespoeth shed, hence its new steam loco has been allocated the No 7.

CHAPTER NINE

New Challenges

Many feel that the Lynton & Barnstaple should never have been closed in the first place, and others have opined that 'if only' it could have hung on for a few more years, it would certainly have been saved. The Welsh Highland probably staggered on for longer than logic says it should have done. Whatever, both have held a very special place in the hearts of narrow gauge enthusiasts and their potential revival has exercised the imagination for many years - tempered with harsh reality in both cases. While the WHR trackbed remained basically intact, the legal complexities in achieving access to it were awesome. In contrast, the L&B trackbed had been sold off into parcels years ago and the reassembly of a line where this has happened is unprecedented in preservation.

There are people, however, who just will not give up - and persistence pays off in the end. Trains have now returned to the WHR trackbed, and in the foreseeable future will run over additional sections, hopefully all the way to Porthmadog. While the return of trains over the full length of the route between Lynton & Barnstaple now seems highly unlikely, at least a section of the line is rapidly heading for a revival - with an excellent chance that this will take place shortly after this book is published.

The saving of the Talyllyn was aided by locomotives and other items from the Corris Railway. In time, some TR volunteers turned their attention to reviving the Corris. A part of the line has already been rebuilt and it should not be too long before passenger services are running, and further sections are also likely to be added. Although still at the earliest stages, the resurrection of at least a part of the Southwold Railway is also now being actively pursued, and who would dare to say this also will not succeed?

The Welsh Highland Railway

The Welsh Highland Railway (WHR) ran from Dinas station, with a cross-platform connection with the LNWR standard gauge line, through Rhyd Ddu to Beddgelert, via the Aberglaslyn Pass to Porthmadog where it connected with the Ffestiniog Railway at Harbour station. Little has ever been straightforward about the WHR. Its construction incorporated predecessor lines, it was always impoverished and closure was

inevitable. And yet, there was something magical about the line which has led many to work long and hard to revive it. Even this has had untold complications and, people who have not followed the twists and turns over the decades remain confused by there being two operational Welsh Highland Railways, each under independent ownership. One does not (quite) run on the original WHR trackbed, although work has started towards this ambition, while the other opened on a trackbed which was previously standard gauge, and only opened over genuine WHR ground in 2000. In passing, it can also be mentioned that the two lines are also built to slightly differing gauges!

History

The gestation of the Welsh Highland Railway is extremely complex and can only be outlined here. Moreover, the present day operation of WHR trains between Caernarfon and Dinas (a section not part of the original WHR) means that one must take an even greater step back in history to set the situation in context.

The Nantlle Tramway - a 3ft 6ins gauge line - connected the slate quarries of the Nantlle Vale (the larger operations including Dorothea and Pen-yr-Orsedd quarries) with Caernarfon where the product could be dispatched by sea. The horse-worked line was incorporated by an Act of Parliament as the Nantlle Railway in 1825 (although Nantlle Tramway is the commonly used description) and opened in 1828. George, and his brother Robert (not to be confused with his better known son Robert), Stephenson were involved as consultants. It ran roughly westwards from the quarries towards Pen-y-Groes, before turning north for Caernarfon, passing Dinas along the way. During the 1860s, construction of a standard gauge line by the Carnarvonshire Railway Co was undertaken, incorporating much of the Nantlle route from a point to the north of Pen-y-Groes, through Dinas towards Caernarfon. In 1870 the Carnarvonshire Railway was absorbed by the London & North Western Railway, which completed the standard gauge line into Caernarfon, in the process making a junction with the Carnarvon & Llanberis Railway. Parts of the old Nantlle route were straightened to accommodate the standard gauge tracks, while what remained in use of the Nantlle Tramway (by then owned by British Railways!) was finally closed in 1963.

Hunslet 2-6-2T *Russell* with a Welsh Highland Railway (Porthmadog) train in 1996.

Following the 1870 absorption of the Carnarvonshire Railway by the LNWR, Charles Eastern Spooner (of Ffestiniog railway renown) developed a collection of proposals for narrow gauge railways which, if all had come to fruition, would have produced a 2ft gauge empire across North Wales taking in Porthmadog, Corwen, Beddgelert, Capel Curig, Betws-y-Coed, Rhyd Ddu and Pwllheli. Of the eight proposed railways submitted to Parliament, three were actually approved in 1872, and of these, nothing further happened to progress the 'General Undertaking' (the line to Betws-y-Coed) which was abandoned by an 1876 Act. Construction did, however, commence on the 'Moel Tryfan Undertaking' with work starting in May 1873. The railway progressed from Dinas on the LNWR Caernarfon to Afon Wen line to Tryfan Junction, where one line swung round southwards and climbed to Rhostryfan and Bryngwyn, the other continued on to Waunfawr and beyond.

The line to Bryngwyn opened for goods and mineral traffic during 1877 and passenger services commenced on 28 January 1878. Beyond Bryngwyn, an incline ran up to Drumhead where a number of lines serving slate quarries converged. On the other route from Tryfan Junction, passenger services commenced from Dinas to the western end of Quellyn Lake on 15 August 1877, were extended to the eastern end of the lake on 1 June 1878 and reached Rhyd Ddu on 14 May 1881 - this station being subsequently renamed (with an eye to marketing but arguable accuracy!) South Snowdon. The financing of the railway

had always been somewhat rocky and, almost as soon as it was built, it was in Receivership. Although it enjoyed some passenger and general traffic, Rhyd Ddu was not the obvious destination for tourists as was Beddgelert, three and a half miles away from the NWNGR terminus. The key to the line's fortunes was slate, a trade which suffered periodic depressions, and the NWNGR never cleared its debts even when traffic was reasonable. WWI was the final straw, passenger services on the Bryngwyn branch ceased on 1 January 1914 and all passenger services stopped from 1 November 1916. The NWNGR was initially equipped with two 0-6-4T single Fairlie locomotives built in 1875 by Vulcan Foundry: *Snowdon Ranger* (withdrawn 1917) and *Moel Tryfan*, which survived to run on the WHR and (in cut down form) on the Ffestiniog Railway, finally being scrapped in 1954 by the fledgling FR preservation effort. In 1878 *Beddgelert*, a Hunslet 0-6-4T (not a Fairlie design) was added, this loco being withdrawn in 1906, and in 1908 *Gowrie*, a Hunslet-built 0-6-4T single Fairlie joined the stock, until being sold around 1915. As will be seen, Hunslet 2-6-2T *Russell* was not owned by the NWNGR, although it worked on the railway.

Despite being in Receivership, the NWNGR obtained the North Wales Narrow Gauge Railways (Beddgelert Light Railway Extension) Order in 1900 under the 1896 Light

Railways Act. This was a defensive measure, for the idea of utilising the Croesor Tramway to link Porthmadog to Rhyd Ddu via Beddgelert was already being mooted. Some work was done, but in 1906 the powers were transferred to the Portmadoc, Beddgelert & South Snowdon Railway. The force behind the PB&SSR was Mr H J Jack, Chairman of North Wales Power & Traction Co. Basically a hydro-electric power generating and supply company, the South Snowdon element refered to the power station in the Gwynant Valley, not the renamed Rhyd Ddu station, and the earthworks for a line connecting the power station with the Croesor Tramway were largely finished although the line was never built. The earlier idea of linking Porthmadog and Caernarfon revived again - now in the form of an electric narrow gauge line - and 10 four-wheel electric locomotives were ordered from Ganz in Hungary (of which at least four seem to have been built) but they were not delivered. Although this scheme never proceeded, the PB&SSR did construct the tunnels in the Aberglaslyn Pass, plainly a crucial element in what would become the WHR route. Other works by this company proved to be abortive following changes in the route to be followed. These included a bridge near the Royal Goat Hotel on the edge of Beddgelert and the abutments of another structure in a nearby field - both of which remain today - along with some further works in the Aberglaslyn Pass which were not utilised. Although the company never completed its railway, it did buy a locomotive, Hunslet 2-6-2T *Russell* being built in 1906. The explanation for this acquisition, by a company promoting an electric railway, appears to be the need to maintain the working of slate traffic on the Bryngwyn branch.

With the NWNGR effectively moribund, the PB&SSR having achieved very little and WWI in progress, the 'grand plan' for a rail link between Porthmadog, Rhyd Ddu and Caernarfon slipped into the background - but not completely away. The proposal was revived in 1921 when an application was made to reactivate the Light Railway Order. The local authorities decided to contribute funding and the Welsh Highland Railway (Light railway) Order was made on 1 March 1922. This transferred the powers of the NWNGR and PB&SSR to the Welsh Highland Railway (Light Railway) Company - although the aim of reaching Betws-y-Coed was finally dropped!

The 2ft gauge Croesor Tramway was a horse-worked line built in 1864 linking the slate quarries in the Croesor valley to the harbour at Porthmadog. Constructed by the use of way leave's rather than Parliamentary powers, the position was regularised by the Croesor & Portmadoc Railway Act of 1865. The section of the tramway between the Harbour, where the line connected with the FR, to a point north of Pont Croesor where the tramway crossed the River Glaslyn, was to be upgraded to form the first section of the WHR. The NWNGR itself was refurbished and work commenced on constructing the 'link' from Rhyd Ddu to Beddgelert, through the Aberglaslyn Pass, Nantmor and to the junction with the Croesor line. The ex-NWNGR section between Dinas and South Snowdon reopened to passenger traffic, as the WHR, on 31 July 1922. This was followed by South Snowdon to Portmadoc New (1 June 1923) and Portmadoc New to Harbour (8 June 1923) making a 22 mile

railway. The Bryngwyn branch was also included in the WHR, although passenger services never returned.

Col Holman F Stephens, famous for the collection of ailing railways with which he became associated, was appointed civil engineer and locomotive superintendent to the WHR and FR on 1 April 1923. Consistent with his reputation for acquiring bargains, 1917-built 4-6-0T Baldwin No 590 was soon bought for the WHR. *Moel Tryfan* and *Russell* were also available (and both were to be cut down in an effort to make them fit the FR loading gauge), and Ffestiniog locomotives were used to supplement the WHR motive power. In addition, various internal combustion locomotives were tried in the search for economies in operation. It was to little avail, for the railway simply did not make money and the WHR went into Receivership in March 1927. Possible salvation came when the FR took a lease for the WHR from 1 July 1934 for a trial period up to October 1934. Despite making a loss, the FR then signed a 42-year lease! The last passenger train ran over the WHR on 26 September 1936 and, at the end of that year, the FR was seeking release from the commitments of the lease but was refused. Occasional goods trains ran until 19 June 1937, and the line was closed on 1 July 1937.

Demolition trains started to take up most of the WHR track for the war effort, lifting commencing in August 1941 and the Baldwin was scrapped. The section between Croesor Junction and Porthmadog was finally lifted during 1948/49 and the link between Madoc Street and the GWR standard gauge had gone by 1950. The standard gauge Caernarfon to Afon Wen line closed in 1964, the station site at Dinas became a Council Highways Department depot, while the old NWNGR yard at the south end of the site was taken over in 1950 by the local water and rivers authority.

The FR negotiated an exit from its lease with the Receiver in August 1943 and, on 26 January 1944, the County Council petitioned the High Court for an Order to Wind Up the WHR. The WHR had a range of debts and few assets. The liquidator appointed on 17 March 1944 made it clear that the share capital was 'irretrievably lost' and there was little prospect of funds being available for unsecured creditors. The subsequent story is taken up in the following sections, suffice to say that the revival of the WHR has been possible because of the unusual situation whereby the trackbed survived as a complete entity in the hands of the Official Receiver.

Welsh Highland Railway (Porthmadog)

The Welsh Highland Railway Society was formed in 1961, reputedly following a conversation on a platform at Crewe station! By 1963 a depot had been established at Kinnerley in Shropshire and the Society became the Welsh Highland Light Railway (1964) Ltd in January 1964. Agreement to purchase the trackbed (for £850!) from the liquidator of the old company was reached, but this deal collapsed when the liquidator died in September 1964 before the exchange of contracts. Responsibility for liquidating the old company then passed to the Official Receiver and negotiations started afresh. In 1973, the '1964' Company purchased the standard gauge Beddgelert

A busy scene at the Porthmadog station of Welsh Highland Railway (P) on 25 October 1997. Bagnall 0-4-2T *Gelert* arrives with a passenger service, while Hunslet 2-6-2T *Russell* waits in the loop with a demonstration goods train.

Siding from BR and two years later, bought Gelert's Farm. The farm was transformed into a railway base and three-quarters of a mile of track was laid to a location named Pen-y-Mount (just short of the route of the original WHR) and opened to the public on 2 August 1980. The company name was subsequently changed to simply the Welsh Highland Railway Ltd with the company having commenced the registration of the Welsh Highland Railway name and crest as a trademark in 1995, the certificates being issued in January 1996.

In the early 1960s, the railway preservation climate was very different from that of today. It was probably even worse in this corner of North Wales, for the local authorities had lost a lot of money in the failures of the old WHR company. Not surprisingly, Caernarfon County Council was totally opposed to the prospect of reopening the railway when first approached. The new WHR company therefore opted to mount a public relations exercise and the local authority (subsequently to become Gwynedd County Council) was steadily won over. In retrospect, it is interesting that some of the '1964' Company pioneers had ideas centred on opening between Caernarfon and Dinas in view of subsequent events, but a railway based at Porthmadog found favour with the Council and by opening and developing a line on the Beddgelert Siding site, the WHR steadily developed a climate which swung opinions behind the long term goal - and demonstrated that the ambition of reviving the WHR could take practical form.

Back as far as 1978 the WHLR (1964) had secured the inclusion of restoring the line to Pont Croesor in the Council's Local Plan. Gwynedd County Council also formed a WHR sub-committee to deal with issues concerning the old route of the line and the proposal emerged that the Council would buy the trackbed from the Official Receiver and lease parts of it to the WHLR company. The railway and Council made a joint application for a Light Railway Order in 1988 to cover the section up to Pont Croesor, but in the following year it was discovered that the Ffestiniog Railway had made a bid to buy the trackbed two years earlier!

A period of conflict between the two organisations followed, which peaked in 1995 when the (then) Secretary of State decided to grant a Light Railway Order to the Ffestiniog, rather than the joint WHR/Gwynedd County Council application. The revival of the WHR now largely, although not totally, passed to the FR and that aspect of the story continues in the section covering Rheilffordd Eryri, more commonly known as the Welsh Highland Railway (Caernarfon).

With the Public Inquiry decision having gone against them and the Transfer Order given to the FR, a number of the Gelert's Farm-based volunteers left. Others adopted a pragmatic approach and by 1998 the two companies had signed a legal agreement which heralded a new era of cooperation. In addition to ensuring that the WHR(Porthmadog) would have access to running trains over the reconstructed route, the agreement allowed for the WHR(Porthmadog) to start work on extending from Pen-y-Mount to Pont Croesor as soon as the FR had opened the line to Waunfawr. As the next section shows, this happened late in 2000 and, following various surveys undertaken in concert with the FR, work started on the trackbed beyond Pen-y-Mount in 2001.

In the meantime, the WHR(Porthmadog) has worked on plans to develop the site and railway into a working museum. Initially, the idea was to restore, or replicate where possible, the infrastructure and equipment used on the WHR during the 1920s period, and present visitors with a flavour of the atmosphere of a narrow gauge railway of that time. The concept was rapidly taken up by many of the volunteers who adopted the clothing style of 1920s working men when on the site. This initial concept has developed further and a comprehensive scheme entitled 'Slate, Sail and Steam' has emerged. Although early days for this major project, it would aim to tell the story of Porthmadog, covering the railway networks which brought the slate from the quarries to the town, from whence it was exported by sea around the world.

Reverting to the existing railway, the station building at Porthmadog houses a shop with a huge range of railway books, along with the renowned Russell Cafe. Part-way along the running line is Gelert's Farm, where trains pause on the outward journey. Just behind the station platform, an area has been developed to house a display of historic wagons from the slate industry, and passengers can visit the carriage shed/restoration shed with covered storage for locomotives which are out of service. Other exhibits include the only known surviving Pwllheli tram car - a horse drawn line which connected Llanbedrog and Pwllheli between 1897 and 1927. Planning permission has already been granted for this building to be virtually doubled in size in order for it to form the centrepiece of the previously mentioned museum.

Old farm buildings on the Gelert's Farm site have become a machine shop and carpenter's shop, while a barn provides covered storage. A signal box has been constructed in the yard, along with a modern building known as the RED shed which houses various small diesel locomotives. The 'eastern bloc'-style red star above the doors is a product of Gelert's Farm humour - the RED actually stands for Railway Extension Department! At Pen-y-Mount, a corrugated iron station building which is a mirror-image of the WHR building which used to be at Nantmor, has been constructed.

Gelert's Farm is also the location of the steam locomotive running shed, which houses the restored Hunslet 2-6-2T *Russell*. The steam fleet also includes Bagnall 0-4-2T *Gelert*, while awaiting heavy overhaul is Peckett 0-4-2T *Karen*, with further locos constituting very long-term restoration projects. These are O&K 0-6-0WT *Pedemoura*, a Bagnall 0-4-2T (a 'sister' of Gelert, but as yet unrestored) and ex-South African Railways 'NG15' No 120. The latter, a 2-8-2 built by the Societe Anglo-Franco-Belge in 1950, arrived at Gelert's Farm in 1994. The

people who imported it subsequently handed ownership to the WHR company and although it has been stripped down, little progress has been made on its rebuild. Other locos on the site include three Polish Lyd2 diesels which are owned by members.

A long-term objective of the railway is to operate a complete train of WHR vehicles. The 'Gladstone Car' (Prime Minister Gladstone rode in the coach in 1892 when he opened Watkins Path up Snowdon) has already been returned to service. The carriage was built in 1891 by The Metropolitan Railway Carriage & Wagon Co Ltd of Birmingham for the North Wales Narrow Gauge Railway on which it was No 8, an all 1st Class bogie tourist observation coach. The ends were open above the waist to afford passengers the best views as they travelled through Snowdonia, with a glazed central section into which they could retreat if the weather deteriorated. It later became WHR coach No 29. The very dilapidated body was recovered from a garden near Harlech in 1987 and the rebuild into original condition at Gelert's Farm included the reconstruction of one balcony end which was completely missing. Physical fruits of the agreement with the FR have resulted in the transfer of several items of rolling stock from the other side of the town, including what remained of Hudson coach No 42 which used to run on the WHR and has been reconstructed into its original form at Gelert's Farm.

Future projects are the construction of a replica centre-door quarrymen's coach of the type which served as a brake van on the Welsh Highland for a short time, and restoration of another NWNGR/WHR vehicle, the so-called 'buffet car'. Built by the Ashbury Railway Carriage & Iron Co Ltd in 1893, this vehicle was NWNGR No 10 until 1922 when it became WHR No 23, then No 36 in 1936. It was then converted into a buffet car by the FR which lowered the body on the bogies and reduced the height of the roof. The vehicle was sold off by George Cohen & Sons in 1942 for £50. The 'buffet car' was taken to a field at Waunfawr where the separated halves of the body lay until 1987 when the remains were moved to Gelert's Farm. Incredibly, the bogies were still with the body and, after recovery, having been sunk into the earth for over 40 years, the journals and brasses have been found to be in near-perfect condition! It has to be admitted that the body has suffered considerably, although the railway is confident it can be restored.

The Welsh Highland Railway Company has had to come to terms with the fact that its objective of restoring the WHR is going to be achieved by means other than those anticipated. But the determination to return trains to this trackbed displayed by this company's pioneers and their successors should be given due credit, for their efforts must be considered crucial in arriving at the situation which exists today whereby trains are indeed, once again, running over the trackbed of the WHR.

Rheilffordd Eryri - Welsh Highland Railway (Caernarfon)

As outlined above, the Ffestiniog Railway first became involved in the revival of the Welsh Highland with its 1987 bid to purchase the trackbed. Those involved at the time appear not to have been trying to secure the WHR trackbed for potential

reopening, but more to avoid competition against the FR. However, the position had changed by the time this secret bid became public in 1989 and changes on the FR Board meant that the people who took the project forward into the 1990s were dealing with a situation which they did not create.

The proposal now was not just the restoration of the WHR between Dinas and Porthmadog, but also the construction of a new 2ft gauge line over the route of the old LNWR standard gauge line between Dinas and Caernarfon, in use as the Lon Eifion cycleway, thus tapping into the tourist attractions of Caernarfon. In 1991, an attempt by the FR to bring the old WHR company out of Receivership failed, so in the following year an application was made for a Light Railway Order which aimed to take over the assets and liabilities of the old company. This was accompanied by an application to cover the Caernarfon to Dinas section. The two Porthmadog-based railways were now in opposition to each other and the WHLR(1964) Company and Gwynedd County Council also made a joint application for an LRO. A Public Inquiry was held to consider the competing applications covering the old WHR route in November 1994 and the Inspecting Officer found in favour of the WHLR(1964)/GCC - but the Secretary of State decided instead to grant a Light Railway Transfer Order to the FR, the Order being made in 1995. This left the joint WHLR(1964)/GCC application, relating to the Dinas - Caernarfon section outstanding. After its initial shock, the

WHLR(1964) Company entered into talks with the FR and by mid-1996 was backing the FR plans, indeed, in July of that year a gang of WHLR(1964) volunteers laid the track at Glan-y-Pwll to accommodate the newly-arrived South African Garratts. The company withdrew its own LRO application for the Dinas - Caernarfon section, along with its objection to the FR's application, and the new unitary Gwynedd Council also withdrew its objections and competing application and backed the FR scheme. The Council granted a 999-year lease on the trackbed to the FR and agreed to sell the old WHR shed and workshop site at Dinas.

The Ffestiniog's vision of a revived WHR was of a very different kind of narrow gauge line from anything previously seen in Britain. A 25-mile route, which included gradients of 1 in 40, called for powerful locomotives which could maintain speeds of 25mph to keep the journey time acceptable to the modern customer. Moreover, trains of 10-12 high-quality carriages were to be operated over track built to the highest standards. The solution was to be found in South Africa, but the total package carried a high price - calculated at £20 million in 1995.

With the arrival of the National Lottery, an application was made to the Millennium Commission which resulted in an

History is made as Garratt 'NGG16' No 143 eases out of Dinas yard at 17.45 on Saturday 5 August 2000 and moves onto the original Welsh Highland formation - the first loco to steam on the route since 1936. *Conway Castle* **is almost hidden behind the four coaches of the train.**

award of £4.5 million towards the construction of the 12 miles between Caernarfon and Rhyd Ddu. This represented 43% of the £9.1 million cost of opening the section by 2000, with further grants secured from the European Regional Development Fund, the Welsh Development Agency and the Wales Tourist Board. The Ffestiniog Railway formed the Welsh Highland Light Railway Co Ltd (WHLR) to undertake the project, supported by the Welsh Highland Railway Society which had been formed in 1993.

The first stage was to build the Caernarfon to Dinas section, along with the reconstruction of the cycleway beside the new railway, and contractors commenced work in January 1997, with the first track - purchased from the Donnybrook Railway in South Africa - being laid in May. Tracklaying was completed in September and the new line was inspected by HMRI on 3 October 1997. The approval certificate was issued on 9 October, followed by the issue of the LRO on the following day, with an unadvertised service commencing over the weekend of 11/12 October.

The construction, in such a rapid timescale, of a wholly new three-mile narrow gauge railway was a major achievement. But at this stage, aside from a few yards of new 2ft gauge metals at

Dinas which lay on land once traversed by Welsh Highland trains, the WHR had not yet been revived and significant hurdles remained. An application was made at the end of March 1997 for the necessary Transport & Works Order, although at this point the purchase of the trackbed from the Official Receiver had still not been concluded. Even so, an opening to Rhyd Ddu by 31 December 1999 was anticipated.

The Gelert's Farm-based WHR Ltd and the FR finally signed an agreement covering their future relationship in January 1998. Key issues included the terminology - henceforth the two lines would be known as the Welsh Highland Railway (Porthmadog) and the Welsh Highland Railway (Caernarfon) - and the WHR(P) would build the line from Pen-y-Mount to Pont Croesor as soon as the WHR(C) had opened to Waunfawr. Other elements covered access to the revived line to operate vintage trains and the development of Gelert's Farm as a heritage centre. Crucially, this agreement also signalled the withdrawal of the WHR(P) objection to the FR's Railway Works Order application, the Public Inquiry into which commenced in December 1997 and continued into January 1998. Unfortunately, Snowdonia National Park Authority and the National Trust were now opposing the WHR reopening. In the case of the latter, this stemmed from a decision made in the autumn of 1997, and created a strange situation in view of its stated policy of wishing to see a reduction in car journeys to its properties, while trying to purchase part of Snowdonia.

The Snowdonia National Park Authority also performed a

U-turn when it published its Eryri Local Plan, for the first draft had supported the reopening of the WHR, but when the new document was published the railway had been deleted from the Plan - apparently following receipt of just three letters of objection, one being from the vice-chairman of the NPA and chairman of its planning committee. By the time the Inquiry started in July 1998, the Authority had received about 30 letters supporting its new position - and over 5,700 letters objecting to the removal of the WHR from its Local Plan! The outcome was finally published early in 1999, the Inspector having concluded that reinstatement of the line was in the public interest and did not conflict with National Park purposes. The Inspector's report was accepted by the National Park Authority, but the RWO decision was still awaited.

The report submitted by the RWO Inquiry Inspector expressed two concerns. In addition to the geological aspects, he believed the FR had not proven its case that the RWO application met a national transport need. The report made it clear that these conclusions were based only on the evidence placed before him. In considering the report, the Deputy Prime Minister, John Prescott MP, was able to take into account the positive outcome of the Inquiry into the Eyri Local Plan and in April 1999 let it be known that he was 'minded to approve' the application for an RWO. This provisional statement was subject to a satisfactory report by a Consulting Engineer into the stability of the rock formation in the vicinity of the tunnels in the Aberglaslyn Pass. The statement not only covered the Dinas to Porthmadog section, but included the 'cross-town link' in Porthmadog which would allow trains to once again pass over Britannia Bridge to run onto the Ffestiniog Railway itself at Harbour station.

The survey, prepared by Ove Arrup, found that there was little danger of rock falls and simply recommended raising the retaining walls between the two tunnels by two metres, with a further metre of stone-catching fence above. John Prescott, MP, as Secretary of State for the Environment, Transport and the Regions, declared himself satisfied with the proposals and not prepared to delay the making of the RWO any longer. The Order was made on 28 June - just before the new Welsh Assembly officially came into being on 1 July - and came into force on 21 July, but actual work on-site could not start until a works programme had been agreed with Council officers and other concerned parties. There was one last potential twist. In early-August, the National Farmers' Union lodged an application with the High Court for a Judicial Review of the decision to grant the Railway Works Order, although no injunction was sought to prevent works proceeding. The challenge was dismissed by the High Court on 24 November, the Court also turning down the NFU's application for leave to appeal.

The way was now clear to move the project forwards and contractors started preparing the trackbed, including fencing and drainage, by the end of 1999. Contracts were also let for lowering the trackbed under six over-bridges to create a larger loading gauge. Work sites were established at Waunfawr and part-way along the line beside the Rhostryfan Road as well as at Dinas. Unfortunately, exceptionally wet weather during the early months of 2000 held up the start of tracklaying. The first rails on the route of the original WHR since 1941 were finally laid over the weekend of 1/2 April 2000, the first loco to run on the trackbed since demolition being *Upnor Castle*, which was based in a temporary shed at the Cae Wernlas Ddu worksite.

The weather continued to hamper progress and several provisional opening dates came and went. The problems were compounded as the trackbed, which had been comprehensively reclaimed by nature in many places, was cleared. A landslip in

Two for the future on the WHR(Caernarfon). A pair of former South African Railways 'NG15' 2-8-2 locomotives, imported for a failed scheme, became available and have been purchased for future use on the fully revived Welsh Highland Railway. This 4 May 1998 picture at Dinas shows No 133 (with very large slab-sided tender) with No 134 just visible behind, the tender for this loco being on another part of the site. Another 'NG15' (acquired previously to this pair) is at the Gelert's Farm base of the WHR(P), although currently dismantled.

The modern new infrastructure developed as part of the revival of the WHR (Caernarfon) is illustrated by the locomotive facility developed at Dinas. Ex-South African Railways 'NGG16' Garratt No 143 is being prepared for service on the new railway, with the bonnet of Hibberd 4wDM *Upnor Castle* just visible on the left of the frame.

Afon Gywrfai Gorge was uncovered, and the original trackbed needed considerable upgrading to meet modern standards and the higher axle loading requirements of the rebuilt line. The HMRI inspection took place on 21 July and was followed by a series of heavy works trains to bed down the formation and act as crew training runs. On the evening of Saturday 5 August, the driver of 'NGG16' Garratt 2-6-2+2-6-2 No 143 was told to keep his loco in steam following the arrival at Dinas of the last service train of the day from Caernarfon. *Conway Castle* was hooked onto the tail of the train, the 'NGG16' eased forwards and crossed the shed access points and at 17.45 ran onto the new track, the first locomotive to steam on the original Welsh Highland formation since 1936. A little after 18.00 the train arrived at Waunfawr to a round of applause from gathered onlookers. The line to Waunfawr opened for passenger services on Monday 7 August, the revised timetable coming into operation when the 10.30 ex Caernarfon terminated at Waunfawr rather than Dinas.

The official opening took place on 15 September, which was also the first day of two-train running on the WHR(C) with *Mountaineer* hauling four FR carriages, brought north in preparation for a 16-17 September gala event entitled WHR Ffestival 2000.

Poor weather and fuel shortages did not deter 1,300 visitors

from travelling to the Ffestival event to see *Russell* - visiting from the WHR(Porthmadog) - running on the Welsh Highland trackbed for the first time since 1937. The loco, the last survivor of the old WHR motive power fleet, ran over the weekend in double-headed company alternating between FR single Fairlie *Taliesin* (also visiting for the event) and *Mountaineer*. *Russell* also achieved a 'first' by appearing in Caernarfon. The two carriage sets in use were the Winson-built WHR(C) set, along with FR carriages 37, 17, 23, 12 and 11. The presence of *Russell*, along with a WHR(Porthmadog) promotional stand in the goods shed at Dinas manned by WHR(P) volunteers in 1920s period dress, emphasised how much the past ill-feeling was being replaced by cooperation. It is also worth mentioning that during the weekend's events, the FR's 0-4-0STT *Palmerston*, accompanied by FR coach No 39 and brake van No 10, were operating on the WHR(Porthmadog).

The station at Caernarfon, not far from the Castle, is not yet fully developed. Trains initially ran straight through to Dinas, pausing only at Hendy Crossing where the line crosses a road on the level but, following requests by local residents, a Halt was built at Bontnewydd and opened early in 1999. At Dinas, trains arrive at the newly-built platform on what used to be the standard gauge side of the interchange shortly after passing the new 12-car carriage shed. The original station building has been renovated, as has the goods shed, now a museum. On leaving the station and passing under the road bridge, the tracks run through the old NWNGR yard where there is a locomotive running shed, complete with pit and wheel drop, and a workshop. The tracks swing into a cutting, which had to be re-excavated and effectively rebuilt, before passing under the main road. Trains run straight through Tryfan Junction where the station building remains in its ruined state, although it may be rebuilt later. At Waunfawr, the semi-ruined station building was dismantled and a new island platform constructed, with the building to be reconstructed in extended form.

As to the remainder of the railway, the next target was Rhyd Ddu to complete the section covered by the Millennium Commission funding - albeit rather behind schedule. Although work started on extending towards Betws Garmon, no rebuilding could take place within the National Park (the boundary lies just south of Betws Garmon, about a third of the way between Waunfawr and Rhyd Ddu) until the remedial works in the Aberglaslyn Pass were completed. This was done in April 2001, but all work on the extension was suspended during the outbreak of Foot and Mouth disease. Work has restarted and Rhyd Ddu will be a temporary terminus while the funding for the final push towards Porthmadog is secured. There is no suitable site for a temporary terminus between Rhyd Ddu and Porthmadog - Beddgelert being ruled out because of potential congestion and steep gradients - so this final section will have to be constructed and opened in one go. Meanwhile, the WHR(P) is working on extending from its Pen-y-Mount terminus to Pont Croesor, ready to meet up with the railhead from the other direction. Once connected, this leaves the Porthmadog cross-town link to the FR at Harbour station, the final part of which will have to be re-routed to avoid the supermarket, built over the original formation. The (revised) aim is to reach Rhyd Ddu in 2002, possibly 2003, with the ambition remaining of trains running between Caernarfon and Porthmadog by 2006.

Two ex-Port Elizabeth Cement Works Funkey Bo-Bo diesels arrived at the FR in 1993. One was radically reconstructed to fit the FR's limited loading gauge and named *Vale of Ffestiniog*. The other, retaining its original form, was named *Castell Caernarfon* and moved to Dinas in 1997. Two Beyer Garratt 'NGG16' 2-6-2+2-6-2 locomotives were obtained from the Alfred County Railway in South Africa. Although supposedly fully overhauled, on arrival at the FR in January 1997 it was clear that substantial work was required before they could enter service. The first to be moved to the new line, having been overhauled and converted to oil-firing, was No 138 (painted in a green livery) and named *Millennium/Milenium*, with No 143 (retaining its historic black livery) following later. A third 'NGG16', No 140 (unrestored and in red livery) was purchased from German enthusiasts for a nominal sum and has remained in store at Glan-y-Pwll since its arrival in April 1997. Meanwhile, work has proceeded on the restoration of Beyer Peacock 0-4-0+0-4-0 No K1 - the first Garratt to be built, in 1909, and repatriated from Tasmania by its builders in 1947. The FR purchased it in 1966, although being far too large for the loading gauge, it was displayed in the National Railway Museum from 1979 until 1995 when the WHR project presented the opportunity of returning it to service.

The Hibberd diesel *Upnor Castle* was sold to the WHLR by the FR for use on construction and works trains, although the first loco to work on the new line was actually the Boston Lodge 39hp Hunslet diesel shunter *Harold*! The FR Alco 2-6-2T *Mountaineer* also provided early steam power on the line, as has Hunslet 2-4-0STT *Blanche* and George Linstal 0-4-0STT *Prince*, these locos being cheaper to operate in the 'shoulder' periods when traffic is lighter. The wagons used by construction trains were from South Africa, while the six-carriage passenger set present from the line's opening was built by Winson Engineering of Daventry, with a further Alan Keef Ltd-built carriage added in 2002 with another to follow. Two further locomotives were purchased in 1998 when a scheme for a new line in Yorkshire was abandoned. These are Franco-Belge 'NG15' 2-8-2s SAR No 133 (FB2683/52) and No 134 (FB2684/52) which were imported, unrestored, from South Africa.

The Lynton & Barnstaple Railway

Calls for a railway to connect the twin villages of Lynton and Lynmouth with the 'outside world' started in the 1850s. The standard gauge first reached Barnstaple in 1854 by way of the North Devon Railway (subsequently part of the London & South Western Railway) from Exeter. In 1873, the GWR-sponsored Devon & Somerset Railway also reached the town, leaving Lynton and Lynmouth surrounded by railways on three sides (with the sea to the north) - but still some 20 miles from the nearest station and served only by horse drawn coaches over poor roads. A series of proposals arose from 1879, that reaching fruition being the 1ft 11½ins gauge Lynton & Barnstaple Railway which ran for 19¼ miles from a station somewhat above Lynton, across Exmoor, to a cross-platform station shared with the LSWR at Barnstaple Town.

Central to this line was the publisher and Liberal MP, Sir George Newnes, who jointly financed the funicular which linked Lynton and Lynmouth in 1890. Influenced by the success of the Ffestiniog Railway, Sir George was involved in meetings during 1894 which resulted in the construction of the L&B and, in the process, saw off a rival scheme for a standard gauge line from Lynton to the GWR at Filleigh Junction. The L&B Bill received Royal Ascent on 27 June 1895 and the 'first sod' was cut on 17 September by Lady Newnes, Sir George being the Chairman of the new L&B company.

The construction contract was awarded to Mr James Nuttall on 5 March 1896, with the aim of completing the line by 1 May 1897. It seems the consulting engineer had misled the company and the contractor concerning the nature of the work and Nuttall found himself involved in heavy earthworks and excavation through rock rather than soil. Costs rose and the contract fell seriously behind schedule, while the company found the purchase of land was costing far more than anticipated. Three locos (from Manning Wardle & Co) and 16 carriages (from Bristol Wagon & Carriage Works Co Ltd) were ordered in November 1896, but during 1896/97 the company had to raise extra capital to complete the railway. *Taw*, hauling a single coach formed the first train over the line in March 1898, followed by an official opening ceremony on 11 May and the commencement of services on 16 May. With costs significantly higher than expected and

Extensive renovations have been undertaken at Woody Bay station in preparation for the time when the grass in the foreground gives way to track – and the revival of part of the Lynton & Barnstaple Railway will have become a reality.

the late opening delaying earnings, legal action between the company and contractor continued through 1898, with the Appeal Court finding in favour of the company in February 1899 - but by then Nuttall was bankrupt.

A pioneering attempt to boost traffic by introducing a motor feeder service was made by Sir George Newnes, in cooperation with the railway company. A coach service between Ilfracombe and Blackmore station was started in April 1903 but foundered when it was caught speeding - at 8mph! The two open Milnes-Daimler coaches were sold to the GWR which founded the GWR Road Transport Department. Traffic did not develop over the line as anticipated and it was 1913 - the year in which the highest recorded traffic was carried over the railway - before a dividend was paid, and this was ½%. A restricted service operated during WWI, followed in the 1920s by increased motor transport competition. Operating costs were also rising and the brief period of relative prosperity ended.

Negotiations for the line to be taken over by the LSWR commenced in 1922. The LSWR was due to become part of the Southern Railway under the Railway Act of 1921, this taking effect on 1 January 1923. Final agreement was reached for the L&B to be taken over by the SR in March 1923, the handover following on 1 July. The end of independence signalled a period of investment in the L&B. The SR provided new sleepers and track fixings, improvements to buildings and the addition of steam heating. In 1925, a new locomotive was provided and, in 1927, four bogie vans and four bogie wagons were added to the stock - plus three breakdown cranes which enjoyed limited employment! The SR augmented the timetable and enhanced the publicity - but to no avail.

By 1931, traffic was falling in the face of increased road competition and economy measures were implemented. The line attracted holiday makers, but the summer season was too

short to compensate for the lack of winter traffic. The end came in 1935 when renewals were needed to the permanent way - and the SR announced that the railway would close at the end of the season. Debate continues over the wisdom of this but, the fact is, the last train ran on 29 September 1935, double headed by *Yeo* and *Lew*. The equipment was sold by auction at Pilton yard on 13 November 1935.

The L&B is fabled for many things, not least its equipment. The original locomotives were 2-6-2Ts built by Manning Wardle & Co, *Yeo* (arriving in 1897 from storage since the line was far from complete) followed by *Taw* (in March 1898) and *Exe*. The trio's appearance progressively changed between 1903-1913 when the cab arrangement was altered. Despite the problems in getting the railway opened, the Board decided that a fourth loco would be needed. Manning Wardle were unable to supply a loco in time and the order went to the Baldwin Locomotive Works in Philadelphia, 2-4-2T *Lyn* being built in May 1898, shipped to Barnstaple in parts, and first steamed in July 1898. The fifth loco, ordered by the Southern Railway in 1925, was *Lew*, another Manning Wardle 2-6-2T. Although basically the same design as the earlier locos, there were some changes - notably the flat cab backsheet and the drip tray under the motion rather than the covers fitted to the original locos. The first four locos were all scrapped at Pilton following the auction, but *Lew* was used to work demolition trains, following which it was exported to Brazil in 1936.

The line was equipped with 16 carriages from the Bristol Wagon & Carriage Co, which set a new standard for quality on the British narrow gauge. They shared the same dimensions and ran on the same underframes, but comprised six different types: saloon, saloon brake, composite, third observation, third and third brake. An additional composite brake was added in 1911, this being slightly longer and probably intended for use in single coach trains. The original goods stock consisted of 14 4-wheel (eight open wagons and six vans) and four bogie (two open wagons and two brake vans) vehicles. Further bogie flat wagons, open's, vans and brake vans were added in subsequent years. Little equipment survived the auction. The most significant item is coach No 2, now preserved in the National Railway Museum, York, in ex-L&B condition. Coach No 15 (SR No 6993) was moved to the Ffestiniog Railway in 1959 and has been rebuilt, now being FR Bar Car No 14 -further details concerning other items follow below.

'To Barnstaple and Lynton Railway, with regret and sorrow from a constant user and admirer. "Perchance it is not dead, but sleepeth".' So read a black-edged card, sent with a wreath, by Paymaster Captain Woolf, RN(Ret'd) of Woody Bay on the day after the L&B closed.

It has been a long sleep, but the time for awakening is approaching. Late in 1961, the possibility of reopening part of the line was floated, resulting in the inaugural meeting of the Lynton & Barnstaple Railway Society in March 1962. By May 1963, it had been determined that cost made reopening the whole line impossible. The Society was offered the chance to buy the trackbed between Lynton and Dean Deep, but the expense of purchasing and rebuilding even that section was deemed too great and more modest targets of preserving relics and setting up a museum were set at the first AGM in January 1963. This early preservation idea ended in 1964 when the Society was disbanded.

A new organisation, The Lynton & Barnstaple Railway Association, was formed in 1979 and has pursued the ambition of reopening at least part of the line. The biggest problem is the fragmented ownership of the trackbed. Following closure, the land and Halts were offered to adjoining landowners, with the remaining property (stations and Pilton yard) put up for auction on 7 October 1938. Land not disposed of at the auction was sold following negotiation: Pilton shortly after the auction, Lynton station in 1939 and Chelfham station in 1940. Subsequent developments have obliterated sections of the old line: a reservoir at Wistlandpound, the Civic Centre across the route preventing entry to Barnstaple, plus road schemes and privately owned buildings at other locations.

In the 1980s, a small section of trackbed was purchased on the edge of Parracombe. A scheme to start from Blackmoor Gate was proposed but never progressed; however, late in the '80s, North Devon District Council offered a lease for land at Hole Ground. This scheme envisaged a new station on the outskirts of Barnstaple and a two mile line to Snapper Halt, but had fallen through by 1994. Meanwhile, at the end of 1993, the Association

had purchased 700 yards of track and eight coaches from Thorpe Park in Surrey. This equipment was collected in early 1994 and taken to the Milky Way near Clovelly where a 900 yard circuit was constructed and opened in May 1994 as the Lynbarn Railway.

While the Milky Way operation was being developed, the opportunity to purchase Woody Bay station and 70 acres of surrounding land, encompassing 300 yards of the trackbed, arose. This purchase was completed in March 1995 and volunteers installed power, dug a bore hole (a dowser found the best water source!) and completely re-roofed the building. Internal renovation followed, while outside, station nameboards were put up and the signal cabin restored.

Planning permission was granted in March 1996 for a line to run from the station, in a south-westerly direction, on the old trackbed as far as Killington Lane, a distance of nearly one mile, although not all of the necessary land had yet been purchased. The permission also included a loco shed at Woody Bay and additional sidings.

A field next to the station land had been purchased and sufficient trackbed secured for 400 yards of line. Opening was expected by late 1999 or early 2000, but various factors delayed progress. A complex land dispute was finally resolved early in 2001. Highway improvements on the A39 to allow public access to Woody Bay also had to be undertaken, along with providing a surfaced car park, before any rails could be laid. Agreement was finally reached with the local authority in December 1999 and the highway work undertaken during 2000, with the car park being finished early in 2001.

The work centred on Woody Bay was guided by the principle of getting something open and then making step-by-step progress, the next objective being to try and buy a comparatively

Following extensive restoration, this December 2000 picture shows the restored deck of Chelfham viaduct, ready to accommodate Lynton & Barnstaple Railway trains, although their arrival at this location is likely to be some time away yet. Note the construction of the viaduct in a series of straight sections, something not at all apparent from ground level.
(Fastline Photographic Ltd.)

A train of ex-Thorpe Park stock - *Sir George*, built by Alan Keef Ltd in 1984, with coaches, inside the Milky Way building of the Lynbarn Railway. To the left is the passenger platform, while on the other side of the tracks are storage sidings. The cab of *Parracombe*, a 1946/47 vintage Baguley, is just visible on the right, then *Titch*, a 1941-built 20hp Simplex. Further down, behind the carriages, is a workshop area.

short section of trackbed to join up with the section purchased all those years ago between Parracombe Lane and Cricket Field Lane. Subject to Planning Permission, this would bring the track length up to 1½ miles.

Meanwhile, Chelfam station, along with half a mile of trackbed and the old stationmaster's house, named *Distant Point*, was put up for sale in November 1998 and the purchase was completed late in April 1999. Some time previously, a group of members had formed the Fairview Partowners Scheme to purchase a house near Parracombe, complete with 300 yards of L&B trackbed, and to be used as a shared holiday home. This house was taken off the market, but the nucleus of prospective part-owners re-formed as the Distant Point Partnership and helped with the Chelfam purchase.

Chelfam Viaduct, immediately adjacent to the station, was the major engineering feature of the L&B line. It carried the tracks 70ft above the Stoke Rivers valley on an eight-arch structure, each 42ft wide. The structure was never disposed of following closure and, during 2000, was the subject of a £450,000 restoration funded by Rail Property Ltd, with contributions from the Railway Heritage Trust and the Lynton & Barnstaple Light Railway Co Ltd. The restoration allows for passenger trains running over the viaduct and the involvement of the Lynton & Barnstaple Light Railway Co ensured that the parapets, removed in 1961, were reinstated and the standard of water-proofing on the deck would deal with the weight of such traffic.

Although the return of trains over the viaduct is now possible, the focus for a revived L&B remains Woody Bay and the aim is to open during 2002. Initially in the form of a fairly basic railway, the long term aim is a faithful recreation of the old L&B. Central to this concept is Project Yeo, which aims to produce a replica 2-6-2T Manning Wardle - see Chapter 8. There are also two items of ex-L&B stock undergoing restoration. In Essex,

coach No 7 is approaching completion. This vehicle is effectively a replica incorporating original material, including the centre section of L&B 3rd Class open-centre 50-seat observation coach No 7, one of four vehicles of the type originally on the railway. Also incorporated are doors collected from other original coaches which became garden sheds, etc. Bogie brake van No 23 has also survived. This 8-ton van, with a fully enclosed guard's compartment, was built at Pilton by the L&B in 1908. The original timber underframe is long-gone and a new underframe has been built, as for the coach, which should ensure the integrity of the restored, largely complete, original timber body. The L&B also purchased an original 1927 8-ton Howard-built bogie van, stored for many years near Great Torrington, towards the end of 2001.

In 2001, the Association purchased a 150hp 0-6-0 Baguley-Drewry diesel named *Leichhardt* from the Illawarra Light Railway Museum in New South Wales, Australia. The loco arrived at Tilbury Docks on 9 November 2001 and was moved to Williton (West Somerset Railway) on 20 November. It is to be renamed *Pilton*, but needs regauging and modifications to the cab before entering service. Meanwhile, Ruston & Hornsby 40DL *Snapper* was moved to Woody Bay at the end of September 2001 and became the first locomotive at the old station since the Lynton & Barnstaple Railway closed. Other locomotives are currently at the Lynbarn Railway, including *Axe* - see next section.

While the Lynton & Barnstaple Railway Association is the 'parent' body for the restoration project, other companies have been formed to meet specific needs. These include the Lynton & Barnstaple Light Railway Co Ltd, The Lynton & Barnstaple Railway Estates Co Ltd (incorporated on 23 June 1997) and The Lynton & Barnstaple Railway Trust which came into existence on 3 April 1998. Also, as seen previously, Manning Wardle & Co Ltd

A train of restored and replica Corris Railway stock behind 4wDM No 5 *Alan Meaden*, pictured part-way between Maespoeth and Corris on the rebuilt section of the Corris Railway.

was formed as a plc in 1997 by two members on behalf of the railway and was intended to provide an engineering support centre for the revived L&B as well as taking on outside work, and traded from an industrial unit between November 1999 and mid-2001.

The Lynbarn Railway

Forming an attraction in an Adventure Park called the Milky Way near Clovelly, this line would not normally fall within the parameters of this volume. However, it has provided income for the L&B Association's efforts to reinstate part of the Lynton & Barnstaple line, given the Association credibility and practical experience in running a railway, and provided a base with some engineering facilities. Having built a railway, the Association has also gained enormous experience operationally, for this little line handles passenger numbers far in excess of many other heritage railways.

Opened in May 1994, for the first season visitors to the Milky Way who wanted a ride paid a fare. The Milky Way later adopted a policy of an all-inclusive charge for a day out and since 1995 visitors have been carried free, the L&B Association receiving an agreed payment from the Centre's operators. The railway, just under a mile in length and employing 20lb 'Jubilee' rail laid on wooden sleepers, was built and is maintained by L&B volunteers, although part-time drivers are employed.

Passengers board the train in a combined train shed/workshop in one of the Milky Way buildings. This provides covered accommodation for the line's operating stock: *Sir George*, (built by Alan Keef Ltd in 1984) which came from Thorpe Park, Surrey along with the coaches, and a 1946/47 vintage Baguley *Parracombe*. Late in 1999 a further locomotive arrived at the site following purchase by an L&B member. A diesel hydraulic locomotive built by Severn Lamb in 1973, it worked trains on the 900 yard Southport Pier Railway until 1997 under the name *English Rose*. Following extensive refurbishment, including fitting

a replacement Perkins engine and the addition of air brakes, it was ready to enter service in mid-2001. Also present are *Titch*, a 1941-built 20hp Simplex and the Ruston & Hornsby 30hp *Caffyns*, both of which can be used on the Lynbarn, but could form the nucleus of 'real' L&B motive power.

Also in the Milky Way workshop is *Axe*, a Kerr Stuart 'Joffre' Class 0-6-0T (No 2451 built 1915) purchased in the early years of the Association. Initially, the lack of a suitable workshop and absence of funds for a new boiler precluded progress, but the advent of the Lynbarn Railway provided both. Work has largely concentrated on the frames, with the intention of providing a pony truck similar to that fitted to *Sgt Murphy*, now working as an 0-6-2T at the Teifi Valley Railway.

The Corris Railway

This charming 2ft 3ins gauge line, which can claim to be the oldest narrow gauge railway in Mid-Wales, closed but was never forgotten and - after years of volunteer work - is about to join the ranks of operational preserved lines, as this is written.

In its earliest form, the Corris Railway was a horse-worked tramway, opened in 1859 to convey slate from the quarries of Corris Uchaf and Aberllefenni to the quays on the Afon Dyfi (River Dovey). In 1863 the standard gauge reached Machynlleth and the new outlet for slate meant the line west of Machynlleth was abandoned and the tramroad became the Corris Railway. Changed ownership in 1878 saw replacement of the original iron rails with steel, and an order for three steam locomotives and ten passenger carriages. Actually, the passenger carriages simply regularised a situation already existing unofficially, since passenger traffic had developed, utilising adapted wagons. One of the quarry owners, fearing his slate trains would be affected, objected to this regularisation - a dispute not resolved until 1883, by which time some of the sharper curves had been realigned, and passenger services were officially approved.

A passenger platform is under construction opposite the shed at Maespoeth in this July 2001 picture of the revived Corris Railway. The line's vintage train stands in the yard behind 4wDM No 5 *Alan Meaden*.

The railway peaked in the 1890s when yearly totals of 80,000 passengers and 18,000 tonnes of slate were carried, but decline set in after 1900. Slate production was already falling by the start of WWI, during which passenger figures also reduced. A brief recovery in the 1920s was only temporary, and in 1930 the line was sold to the Great Western Railway. Passenger services ceased and the railway only ran to serve the Aberllefenni quarry. It kept going through to nationalisation in 1948, but services ceased on 20th August that year following erosion on the approach to the Dyfi river bridge.

Just three years after closure, operation of the Talyllyn Railway in the next valley was taken over by the TRPS. The Corris and Talyllyn were both 2ft 3ins gauge, and it could be argued that the Corris contributed to the success of the Talyllyn in the form of the ex-Corris locomotives Nos 3 and 4 which were sold to the TRPS to become *Sir Haydn* and *Edward Thomas* respectively, along with other items of Corris stock, including a carriage.

In an interesting historical twist the Talyllyn, in effect, created the circumstances which would resurrect the Corris. During the early 1960s, some Talyllyn volunteers started to visit the Corris on their way home after a weekend at Tywyn. The idea of starting a museum took hold and the Corris Society was formed, while a different group of people had formed The Corris Railway Preservation Society. The groups merged, formed The Corris Railway Society, and opened a museum in 1970, having acquired the remaining buildings on the Corris station site.

Although the station itself had been demolished, a few hundred yards of track were laid on the trackbed to the south of the site. Negotiations with British Rail - owners of the trackbed after nationalisation - were slow, but the Society obtained planning permission for the Corris to Maespoeth section and works trains were running over the relaid line by 1985. The Society developed the museum, acquired Maespoeth loco shed, and sought Planning Permission for the line south of Maespoeth to a site at Tan-y-Coed, near the old Llwyngwern quarry, now The Centre For

Alternative Technology, which was granted in 1994. The track between Corris and Maespoeth was upgraded and, in 1996, steam returned to Corris when ex-Corris loco No 4 visited for its 75th anniversary from the TR.

By 2001, the Maespoeth - Corris sections had been completed to passenger carrying standards and a train was ready to be operated, but paperwork issues delayed progress. Two fields south of Maespoeth were purchased to construct a deviation from the original formation (breached by highway works) at Pont-y-Goedwig. The railway could then proceed with its application for a Transport & Works Order to cover the 2.5 miles between Corris and Tan-y-Coed (between Esgairgeiliog and Llwyngwern). The aim is to commence passenger operations between Maespoeth and Corris, hopfully in 2002 with work then starting on building the extension from Maespoeth south to Tan-y-Coed.

The original three locomotives were built by Hughes's Locomotive & Tramway Engine Works Ltd in 1878. Constructed as 0-4-0STs, they were later converted to 0-4-2ST configuration and provided with proper cabs - originally the roof was supported by four pillars. The fourth Corris loco, also an 0-4-2ST, was built in 1921 by Kerr Stuart & Co. Amongst modifications made to this loco under Talyllyn ownership was the fitting of a running plate. The loco has also 'adopted' the guise of *Peter Sam*, complete with red livery, during its time at Tywyn and it was in this form, although with the name covered, that it visited Corris in October 1996. The Corris Society is having a new loco, based on the design of No 4, constructed - see Chapter 8. The Society has three diesel locomotives: No 5 *Alan Meaden* is a Motor Rail (22258/65), No 6 is a Ruston Hornsby (51849/66) 4wDM to which a new cab has been fitted and No 8 is a Hunslet 4wDM.

The original carriages were small, 4-wheel, tram-like vehicles. The first bogie coach arrived in 1888 and had the appearance of the earlier coaches joined together with a central vestibule. The success of this coach resulted in the 4-wheelers being mounted in pairs on new bogie underframes. Two similar bogie coaches were delivered in 1898, making a total of eight. All the coaches had an entrance on one side only, and originally all had normal roofs, although two were later given clerestory roofs. Two of these bodies survived. The remains of one are preserved in the Corris Railway Museum, the other was rebuilt and entered service on the Talyllyn Railway as coach No 17. The Corris Society completed a new passenger coach in 1985. Known as 'Tiger' and based on the design of the original bogie vehicles, it has a shorter body and runs on a 4-wheel ex-NCB manrider chassis.

Maespoeth loco shed, where the Upper Corris Tramway branched from the main line, has been renovated and fitted out with a machine shop, as its main operating base, with the yard area being substantially remodelled in recent years. The original Corris station was most unusual, having an overall roof covering the passenger running line, a carriage shed built onto the back of the station, and a loop behind the building to allow slate trains to run through without passing the passenger platform. A Medical Centre (in a Portacabin) and car park now occupy the site of the original station. Facing this is the old stable block (which houses the museum), and the new station. A single point branches the line into two short stubs, terminating each side of a slightly raised platform. The railway used to pick its way through the village and run to Aberllefeni, the terminus for passenger services, with tramways continuing up the valley to serve the quarries around Ratgoed. There is no prospect of returning trains to this section. To the south, Machynlleth station building still stands and is in non-railway use.

Southwold Railway

When work on this book commenced, the Southwold Railway was set to appear in the chapter covering lines which were sadly departed, but events unfolded during its preparation which led to the feeling that it may become a revival project!

The Southwold Railway provided a rail link between Southwold on the Suffolk coast and the East Suffolk Railway line between Ipswich and Yarmouth. The ESR (later part of the Great Eastern Railway) declined to build a standard gauge branch itself, so an independent company was formed to promote construction. An Act of Parliament was obtained on 24 July 1876 covering the 8¾ miles between Halesworth and Southwold, a branch to the River Blyth at Halesworth and a branch to Blackstone Quay between Southwold and Walberswick. The 3ft gauge Halesworth - Southwold line was opened on 24 September 1879, but shortage of funds meant neither branch was built.

The line which operated as a leisurely country railway certainly contributed to the development of Southwold, generally without financial problems, although the absence of capital reserves caused a somewhat 'hand to mouth' existence. The ever-present danger of flooding also presented problems.

The early 20th century represented the heyday of the line and, by 1907, revised powers were obtained to build the one mile extension to Blackstone Quay, as originally planned. Delays, including proposals to convert the line to standard gauge (to which end some of the bridges and structures were

widened) meant that the extension was not built until 1914. By then, WWI had broken out and the railway came under Government control. This resulted in some heavy usage, but the coastal fishing trade largely disappeared and holiday makers were no longer visiting Southwold. Government control ended in 1921, but so had the hopes of further extensions, gauge conversion and new equipment. The line avoided being grouped under the LNER banner in 1923, but competition from bus services was being felt - hitting hard in 1926 when passenger numbers plummeted. There was some recovery in 1927, but another drop in 1928. The railway approached the LNER and Southwold Corporation for help, but the local authority refused to offer a subsidy and the final passenger train ran on 11 April 1929. This was followed by 'tidying up' operations, and the fire was dropped in a Southwold locomotive for the last time on 20 April 1929.

A couple of schemes were proposed to reinstate services, but nothing came of either, and by 1930 a somewhat bizarre situation had settled over the railway. A Receiver had been appointed, but the Board of the company did not seek an Act of Abandonment, hence the defunct railway was left to rot. A further revival scheme arose, prevented from getting anywhere by WW2 and most of the line and its equipment was demolished during a scrap recovery drive between July 1941 and 1942, the locomotives being cut up where they stood and the swing bridge roughly mid-way between Southwold and Walberswick was disabled by the Army. Although there was precious little left, the early success of the Talyllyn Railway Preservation Society inspired the idea in 1956 of a Society to preserve the Southwold line, but nothing developed. Remarkably, despite the line having ceased operations in 1929, the owning company still existed - albeit with just one surviving director - into the 1960s before the legal position was disentangled and the company finally wound up.

Three 2-4-0T locomotives were built by Sharpe Stewart & Co for the opening of the line: No 1 *Southwold*, No 2 *Halesworth* and No 3 *Blythe*. In 1883, lack of finance meant that No 1 was returned to the manufacturers. It was subsequently regauged to 3ft 6ins and sold in 1888 to the Santa Marta Railway in Columbia. Increasing traffic enabled the railway to order a new No 1 *Southwold* from Sharpe Stewart in 1893, the loco being very similar to the original design, but slightly longer and a 2-4-2T. Anticipating increased traffic from opening the Harbour branch, 0-6-2T No 4 *Wenhaston* was ordered from Manning Wardle and delivered in January 1914. The six coaches, which had end verandas when built but which were closed in during a programme of refurbishment following WWI, and 16 of the wagons, were 6-wheel vehicles employing the Cleminson flexible wheelbase system. There were also 23 4-wheel vehicles consisting of two covered vans, two flat wagons and the remainder being open wagons. The only surviving item of rolling stock is the body of a 4-wheel van, now preserved at the East Anglia Transport Museum at Carlton Colville, along with some small artefacts in the Southwold Museum.

The Southwold Railway Society formed in 1994 and enthusiasm took hold for reviving a section of the line. Proposals were drawn up and put forward for consultation in the Southwold locality in late 2000/early 2001. These received a basically favourable reception from both residents and the local authorities. The Society is aiming at a three-stage project. Initially, the setting up of a depot and museum at Southwold on the site of a decontaminated gas works, with the construction of a replica locomotive and carriage. Stage two would be to lay about 930 yards of track up to the site of the present Bailey pedestrian bridge which replaced the old railway swing bridge. Stage three would be to cross the river, possibly with a new bridge alongside the pedestrian bridge, and continue for another 700 yards to Walberswick. Although the adoption of 2ft gauge was considered, it was determined that if the project was going to be done, it had to be done properly - so any revived line will be of 3ft gauge. The Society also envisages steam power, to be provided by a newly built replica locomotive - probably of the 1893-built 2-4-2T *Southwold*, but oil-fired. The replica carriage would be built in original form with open verandas at the ends. Estimates put the total cost of the project at around £1.5 million.

And more new projects

The addition of narrow gauge lines to the preservation scene shows every sign of being never-ending! The railways covered previously in this chapter are reconstructions of lines which had been thought lost and have to utilise new equipment since little, if any, of the original exists. The following lines are essentially new projects (although there were narrow gauge tracks at Threlkeld) and all are aimed at supplementing other attractions - plus providing more sites to view historic equipment in action.

Derbyshire Dales Narrow Gauge Railway

Development of this new 2ft gauge railway started in late 1998/early 1999, at Rowsley South, the terminus of the standard gauge Peak Rail line. The narrow gauge railway will add to the attractions of the site and provide something additional for Peak

Rail visitors at the station. The stock, including diesel locomotives and coaches, has been acquired from a number of sources over several years by Peak Rail members Henry and Mary Frampton-Jones.

Work commenced on clearing and levelling part of the formation for the line and four locomotives and a passenger vehicle were moved from Radstock, Somerset to Rowsley during February 1999, plus passenger vehicles and wagons, pointwork and rails. Further equipment arrived, with a sizeable shipment in February 2001, when the storage facility at Radstock ceased to be available. This included rails, sleepers, a tipper wagon, the frame of a bogie coach and two 4-wheel coaches. The latter were built on skip chassis and are not for public passenger use - one may be retained in this form for publicity. A further diesel locomotive was added in the following April.

By early 2001, a run-round loop had been laid near the picnic area at Rowsley South, plus sidings adjacent to containers to house the locomotives. Work also started on the passenger carrying 'main line'. By the end of the year, some 200 yards of track had been laid, and it was hoped to add a further 150 yards and a platform in time to run demonstration trains during Peak Rail special events in 2002. Passenger rides (in push-pull form) might commence later in 2002, subject to progress - including fitting air brakes to a second loco - and HMRI inspection.

The 'main line' runs past the containers, along the edge of the site, through the woods behind the large Peak Rail locomotive shed, erection of which commenced in 2001. The total length of the narrow gauge line is planned for 700 yards, although (and no detailed plans have been drawn up) there is the possibility of extending further, somewhat back on itself in a form of U-shape. The main passenger line has been built using 30/35 lb rail spiked onto old standard gauge sleepers cut in half. The sidings are lighter and employ 25lb rail on wooden sleepers.

The initial batch of locomotives were 1960-built Motor Rail No 22070 (ex-London Brick Company) and three Ruston &

This 1999 picture shows some of the track and a selection of the stock of the Derbyshire Dales NGR being developed at the Rowsley South terminus of the standard gauge Peak Rail line – hence the wagon in the background accommodating the engine of a standard gauge diesel, which somewhat dwarfs the 2ft gauge stock!

The original circa 1900 loco shed at the Threlkeld Quarry & Mining Museum near Keswick, Cumbria. This June 1999 picture shows some of the 2ft gauge track which has been laid, and a selection of the diesel locomotives which have been gathered at the site, where a passenger carrying line is being developed.

Hornsby locos: Class 13DL 264252/1952 (ex-Oakeley slate quarry, Blaenau Ffestiniog), Class 48DL 487963/63 (ex-Butlin's Pwllheli holiday camp) and Class LB 393325/56 (British Rail, Chesterton Junction Civil Engineers depot, then Vobster Light Railway). The fifth loco to arrive was a Motor Rail diesel (ex-Arnolds sand quarries, Leighton Buzzard), while the two bogie toastrack passenger vehicles were built by Baguley and were once used at a Butlin's holiday camp. A number of side-tip and flat wagons have also been brought to the site, including several ex-WD wagons.

The line will be worked by diesels for the foreseeable future, although it is hoped that a steam locomotive will visit at some point. A supporting Society may also be formed to help develop the project.

Chasewater Narrow Gauge Railway

Development of the standard gauge Chasewater Railway was held back for many years by 'planning blight' over a new road, land for which was required at its Brownhills station site. When resolved, a new Brownhills West station was built and the railway started to blossom during 2001. As part of this expansion programme, the idea of developing a new narrow gauge line emerged.

The first lengths of 2ft gauge Jubilee track were laid into storage buildings at the end of November 2001 and a 1961-vintage Lister Blackstone locomotive, plus some prefabricated points, arrived with more stock expected to follow. Named The Chasewater Narrow Gauge Railway, the line is being built by Chasewater members under the auspices of the standard gauge line and will initially form a demonstration track within the perimeters of the Brownhills West site as an additional attraction for visitors to the standard gauge railway. Demonstration trains were expected to start running in the summer of 2002.

Longer term plans are being discussed with the local authority, which could result in a quarter mile line linking the car parks in the Country Park with Brownhills West station, although no passenger rides are expected to be operated until 2003. There are no immediate plans for resident steam, although it is intended to bring in occasional visiting locomotives.

Threlkeld Quarry & Mining Museum

A new 2ft gauge railway has been in development at the Threlkeld Quarry & Mining Museum near Keswick, Cumbria, over several years and is expected to commence operation during 2002.

The original rail system around the granite quarry was steam-worked on 2ft 4ins gauge, although later locos seem to have had a slightly wider gauge! There were three steam locos - two Bagnalls and a Barclay. The original circa 1900 loco shed still exists and now accommodates Bagnall 0-4-0ST *Sir Tom* (2135/26) a similar loco to that which worked at the quarry. *Sir Tom* was originally built to 3ft 6½ins gauge and supplied to Callenders Cables Construction Co of Belvedere, Kent, along with sister loco *Woto*, now owned by Patrick Keef. Both ceased work in 1968 and, following a period in the hands of a dealer, were sold into preservation. Like *Woto*, *Sir Tom* has been regauged, and arrived at Threlkeld in 2000 for final re-assembly and return to steam.

The passenger carrying line commences beside the loco shed and runs over the route followed by the original railway up to the lower level of the quarry where a building houses some of the dozen or so 2ft gauge internal combustion locos which have been brought to the site. The aim is to extend the running line to a length of about half a mile, creating a railway with a strong 'working days' atmosphere. Other planned developments include a gravity-worked incline.

The passenger coaches are likely to be basic eight-seater carriages utilising ex-flat wagons to reinforce the 'quarry experience'. Other stock includes some ex-Broughton Moor equipment, and there are items of quarry and mining stock which are part of the Mining Museum. In the longer term, the trackbed still exists for a line of up to two miles in length.

CHAPTER TEN

Museum Collections

Museums need not be collections of static material and modern trends lean towards emphasising the working nature of exhibits. Most of the railways within the pages of this book constitute working museums on their own account and many have separate, but related, museum displays and collections.

This section deals with collections which are specifically museums, but may have a related length of demonstration track. While, ideally, items related to transport are best seen working, there must be exceptions, with compelling arguments in favour of rare, precious and, in some cases delicate, mechanical items being kept secure and in non-working display condition. Thus, original material can be retained and historic construction methods conserved for study. In one form or another, all of these collections combine the opportunity to view equipment in action, with other items placed on static display.

The Narrow Gauge Railway Museum

The Narrow Gauge Railway Museum at the Tywyn Wharf terminus of the Talyllyn Railway grew as a direct result of the preservation of the railway. During the clearing-up work following the 1951 take-over of the line by the Preservation Society, historic items came to light. Not needed for the immediate running of the railway, they were put aside while more pressing priorities were dealt with. Naturally, the suggestion arose that these items should be placed on public display. As potential exhibits from other closed narrow gauge lines started to be offered, housing the growing collection was addressed by taking over the small slate building (originally a gunpowder store) on the southern side of the TR tracks beside the road bridge.

The building was cleaned out and the interior walls colour-washed, while some work was done to the outside. A showcase was placed inside and locomotive nameplates screwed to the walls - with ex-Penrhyn quarry De Winton 0-4-0VTB *George Henry* the star exhibit. This locomotive was joined in 1956 by 0-4-0T Guinness locomotive No 13 from the St. James's Gate Brewery, Dublin. The museum idea was now gathering momentum, and outgrowing the building, for the Guinness loco had to remain outside.

The answer lay in a compound, surrounded by a slate wall, between the station building and the standard gauge tracks beside the wharf edge which had served as a coal yard. The project was adopted by the Midland Area Group of the TRPS, plans produced and work started. The slate walls were raised in height by the use of bricks, a flat roof added and windows installed on the south and west elevations - with double doors in the eastern wall. This building was officially opened on 29 September 1959, but was full before it was finished! In addition to the two locos now inside, there was an original Talyllyn slate wagon, ex-Dundee Gas Works No 2 and 18in gauge 0-4-0WT *Dot. Cambrai* had to remain outside, and plans were drawn up to extend the building.

A generous donation from Mr R C U Corbett of Hampshire assisted towards the cost of a new building with greatly increased space, mezzanine floor, storage and workshop accommodation, and Planning Permission was secured by the end of 1962. A Trust was set up to administer the collection in 1964 which resulted in grants from the Pilgrim Trust and Landmark Trust making it possible for the building to be completed by contractors, the exterior being finished by September 1966.

Early in 2000, plans were prepared for a major redevelopment of the Wharf station site. A new two-storey construction to replace the existing museum and cafe buildings is to be added to the western end of the original Wharf office building, resulting in an upgraded museum, with the first floor incorporating an education room and museum small exhibits gallery. Funding issues were approaching resolution as this book was being written and work should start in 2002.

Today, the locomotive exhibits at Tywyn consist of: De Winton 0-4-0VTB *George Henry* (ex-Penrhyn quarry), 18in gauge Beyer Peacock 0-4-0WT *Dot* (ex-Gorton Works), William Spence 0-4-0T Guinness Brewery No 13 (ex-St. James's Gate, Dublin), Manning Wardle 0-4-0ST *Jubilee 1897* (ex-Cilgwyn quarry, later Penrhyn quarry), Dundee Gas Works No 2 0-4-0WT built by Kerr Stuart and Hunslet 0-4-0ST *Rough Pup* (Dinorwic quarry). Also in the collection at Tywyn, but not yet displayed, is a 1919-vintage Baguley petrol locomotive No 774. The Trust also owns three locomotives which are on loan to other sites: French-built (L Corpet & Cie) metre gauge 0-6-0T

The ground floor of the Narrow Gauge Railway Museum at Tywyn showing Kerr Stuart 0-4-0WT No 2 (721/02) which worked at Dundee Gas Works (centre foreground), 18in gauge Beyer Peacock 0-4-0WT *Dot* (2817/87) which was employed in its builders Gorton works (background) and ex-Penrhyn Manning Wardle 0-4-0ST *Jubilee* 1897 (1382/97) to the left of the frame.

Cambrai now at Irchester Narrow Gauge Railway Museum, 4-wheel vertical-boilered chain driven Sentinel *Nutty* at Railworld in Peterborough and Motor Rail diesel *Penelope* in working order at North Ings Farm Museum, Lincolnshire. The Museum at Tywyn houses several items of stock, including a 4ft gauge Padarn Railway transporter wagon, with three 2ft gauge Dinorwic slate wagons and a brake van. The Museum also contains permanent way materials, name and works plates, tickets, posters, timetables, lamps, station nameboards and other historic material - all encompassing a wide range of narrow gauge lines.

Amberley Museum

Located on the site of a limeworks and surrounded by the faces from whence the chalk for the kilns was quarried, the Museum at Amberley tells the story of working life in the South East of England. A range of working exhibits are located around the site with the total 'experience' enhanced by the use of buses and the train ride to transport people around the old chalk pit complex. The Railway Group operates as part of the wider Museum, not simply restoring narrow gauge equipment but enabling visitors to experience a form of transport from the past.

The working chalk pits at Amberley used railways, albeit standard gauge, now long gone. The entrance path into the Museum is on the route of the line which connected the quarry with the station goods yard, now the car park, while the locomotives were sheded in the building beside the blacksmith's workshop.

Although the tracks have been developed over the years, the narrow gauge railway collection at Amberley dates back to the beginning of the Museum, which opened in 1979. The first locomotives brought to the site were a Hibberd from Chichester Sewage Works and a privately-owned Ruston. In the mid-1980s, Thakeham Tiles at Storington donated the redundant railway equipment from their works and the Brockham collection which had been built up near Dorking was transferred to Amberley in 1982. The now-combined collection has expanded

through donations, purchases and the arrival of privately-owned items and there are more than 30 locomotives, two gauges of operating line and representative equipment covering 13 different gauges.

Most visitors join the 2ft gauge passenger line at Amberley station for the 500 yard trip through the woods to Brockham station. Like all the other transport at Amberley, travel is included in the admission price - although donations are welcomed.

The objective is to portray the use of narrow gauge railways in industry, although obvious compromises are made relating to the standard of track maintenance and the fitting of air brakes in order to carry the public. If a piece of historic equipment is not to be adapted, it is simply limited to demonstration trains. The passenger line may be worked by a battery loco with a Wickham trolley; if the number of visitors climbs, a 60S Motor Rail or a Hudson-Hunslet diesel will haul a couple of coaches, selected from Groudle Glen stock, open ex-Penrhyn quarry coaches, the ex-RAF Fauld coach, or an ex-Lydd Ranges (MoD) vehicle. At busy times, steam is employed.

At Brockham station there is a complex of tracks used for demonstration purposes only, including a rare section of dual-gauge track, the additional rail allowing the use of the 3ft 2¼ins gauge Dorking Greystone Lime Co Ltd stock which forms the Betchworth collection, housed in a building behind Brockham station, which also forms a small exhibits building.

Other covered accommodation for locomotives is inside a tunnel, which dates from 1948 and was dug by the lime makers who worked on the site until the 1960s. In time, the track into this tunnel will also be dual gauge (the current line is 2ft gauge only) although the use of the tunnel is very restricted since it is also the home of a colony of pipistrelle bats, a protected species. Having received Planning Permission early in 2001, work started on a new locomotive shed behind the locomotive running shed. Steam locomotives based at Amberley are Bagnall 2-4-0T *Polar Bear*, Bagnall 0-4-0ST *Peter* and Decauville 0-4-0T *Barbouilleur*. In addition, there are a number

of operational internal combustion locomotives, together with interesting static exhibits including Guinness loco No 23 from the St. James's Gate Brewery, Dublin, together with a transporter wagon which allowed these locos to shunt the 5ft 3ins sidings, and

a hoist which lifted the locos on and off the transporter wagons.

A long-term project to extend the passenger line commenced with work on clearing the trackbed in the winter of 1997. Progress accelerated in late 2000 with the acquisition of suitable 35lb rail and the granting of Planning Permission. The extension, which will double the length of the main running line, commences at Brockham station and runs round the top of the site, behind the workshop building, past the Seeboard Electricity Hall, to a new terminus by the garden area. At the time of writing, there is no projected date for completion, which depends on available resources and volunteer time.

Most of the major locomotive restoration projects have been completed, allowing the Railway Group to concentrate on developing the infrastructure and maintaining what is already running. To this end, there is an ambition to build a 100ft by 50ft exhibition hall devoted to narrow gauge railways.

Bressingham Steam Museum

This collection, now including four railways of differing gauges and a number of standard gauge steam locomotives on static display (plus other steam exhibits) was started by Alan Bloom - as famous as a gardener as he is to steam people.

The collection started with traction engines and road rollers, the first railway locomotive being *Princess* in 1964, a model of

CENTRE: Bressingham Steam Museum took Hunslet 0-4-0ST *George Sholto* (HE994/09) to the Ffestiniog Railway in October 1996. The loco is pictured with Launceston's Hunslet *Lilian* (317/83) at Tan-y-Bwlch on their way back down the FR following an early morning trip to Blaenau.

LOWER: Krupp-built 4-6-2 *Rosenkavalier* on the 15in gauge Waveney Valley Railway at Bressingham Steam Museum in July 1996.

an LMS Pacific. The engine was to work on a new miniature railway in The Dell garden, which was built to the unusual gauge of 9½ins to suit the locomotive. Next, the 2ft gauge Nursery Railway was built. Opened in July 1966, after several extensions, it reached its present length of 2½ miles. This was followed by a second 2ft gauge line, the Woodland Railway, which was less successful than expected and reconstructed to become the 15ins gauge Waveney Valley Railway which opened in 1974. The fourth railway is a length of standard gauge track, a one-time metre gauge line having been removed.

The idea of forming a live steam museum developed late in 1967. Standard gauge locomotives from the National Collection started to arrive on loan, along with a number of privately acquired locomotives including four locos originally purchased by Butlin's for display at their holiday camps, and locos from industry. The nursery business Blooms of Bressingham was sold by the Bloom family in 1996, the sale having no effect on Bressingham Steam Museum, owned and operated by a Charitable Trust since August 1973.

The 9½ ins gauge Dell garden railway was replaced by a new 10¼ins gauge Garden Railway on 6th July 1995. *Princess* was sold and the new line is worked by the 0-4-0 tender engine *Alan Bloom*, built by Bressingham Steam Museum staff - a roughly half scale version of the ex-Penrhyn quarry Hunslet *George Sholto*.

The Nursery Railway now has three ex-Penrhyn quarry locomotives: 0-4-0ST Hunslets *Gwynedd* (HE316/83) and *George Sholto* (HE994/09), now carrying the name *Bill Harvey*, the ex-BR Norwich Shedmaster who helped develop Bressingham, and *Bronllwyd*, which has a Hudswell Clarke 0-6-0 chassis fitted with a Kerr Stuart boiler from *Stanhope* many years ago. *Stanhope*, incidentally, survived and returned to service in 1999 following restoration under the ownership of John Rowlands as part of the Moseley Railway Trust collection.

The 15ins gauge Waveney Valley Railway was constructed following the purchase in 1972 of *Rosenkavalier* and sister engine *Mannertreu* together with suitable rakes of coaches. These Pacifics were built by Krupps of Essen in 1937 for an exhibition park in Dusseldorf. After periods of service in Munich and Cologne, they were stored until sold to Alan Bloom. The Waveney Valley Railway has also been extended and is now about the same 2½ miles track length as the Nursery Railway, although more by coincidence than design!

The Waveney Valley Railway and Nursery Railway routes meet at a scissor crossing. When both lines are working, the 2ft gauge has priority, and the trains parallel each other before diverging on their respective routes. The Waveney line heads towards the far end of the estate in generally wooded surroundings, while the Nursery Railway runs round the more cultivated areas. Both railways are capable of running a two train service at busy times.

Bressingham was formerly famed for footplate rides on the standard gauge locomotives, a practice which ceased in 1991. The standard gauge loco collection is now housed in the purpose-built heated shed, along with a collection of stationary steam engines, and the adjacent locomotive shed. The Exhibition Hall houses the traction engine collection, the Norfolk Fire Service Museum, and a collection of railwayana, together with interpretive displays of railway history.

The Hampshire Narrow Gauge Railway Society - Kew Bridge Steam Museum and Bursledon Brickworks

The Hampshire Narrow Gauge Railway Society (HNGRS) has the unusual distinction of being a Society which owns four locomotives (two steam, two petrol), runs two additional locos they do not own, and operates two railways on different sites. Both railways are owned by museums, neither of which are dedicated to railways, but both tell the story of industries which used narrow gauge lines in their operations.

The HNGRS was formed in 1961 when a small group started out to rescue 0-4-0ST *Wendy*. This 1919-built Bagnall was originally supplied to the Votty & Bowydd slate quarry at Blaenau Ffestiniog but was out of service by 1922. The dismantled loco went to the Dorothea quarry in 1930 and was at work there by the summer of 1935 when she was named after Wendy Wynne-Williams. Having not worked since the 1940s, she was in a sorry state but, having been saved from scrapping, a new home for her was needed. Initially, this was in the corner of a sandpit at Bishopstoke, near Eastleigh. Thoughts then turned to finding a permanent base and several closed ex-BR lines were looked at in Hampshire, especially on the Bishops Waltham to Botley branch. The 1960s were still early times for preservation and the Society pulled out of negotiations as the scale of the commitment became apparent. An offer from a couple of Society members who owned a 2¾ acre garden at Durley resulted in a 770ft long circuit being developed, together with sidings and buildings which accommodated not only *Wendy*, but the ex-Dinorwic quarry Hunslet 0-4-0ST *Cloister* which had been purchased in 1962 by Mr R C U Corbett, and donated to the HNGRS in 1967. Two ex-Ramsgate Tunnel Railway coaches were acquired as passenger stock. *Cloister* ran until withdrawal in 1978 for a major overhaul, but in 1988 the Durley site suffered an arson attack. Although the locomotives were unaffected, much of the stock, including the coaches owned by both the HNGRS and their hosts, was destroyed. The Society left Durley late in 1991 (the railway remains, now upgraded and operated privately by its owners who have restored one steam locomotive and are working on a 'Feldbahn') and the equipment was put into storage.

The Kew Bridge Steam Museum near Brentford, West London is a 'Museum of Water' in the former Grand Junction Water Works Company's Kew Bridge pumping station. The building contains a magnificent collection of working steam power including huge Cornish Beam engines. Around three sides of the perimeter of the site a 2ft gauge railway - intended to show how the narrow gauge served industry - was constructed in stages by the Museum, work beginning in the late 1980s and reaching a length of some 300 yards in 1991. Initially, the Hunslet 0-4-0ST *Lilla* worked on the line. After she departed, Kew looked for a replacement locomotive leading to the arrival of *Wendy* (in working order) and *Cloister* (still only part-overhauled) in 1993 and the HNGRS commenced operating passenger rides,

**An unusual view of Lister 4wDM *Alister* (44052/58), a 'manrider'
and Bagnall 0-4-0ST *Wendy* (2091/19) working the running line
at Kew Bridge Steam Museum early in 1996.**

aided by a Lister Blackstone 12hp diesel (44052/58) named
Alister(!) privately owned but on long-term loan to the Museum.

The method of operating passenger trains at Kew is unusual
due to the short length of line and the absence of turnouts.
Trains are worked by two locomotives, one being used to haul
the passenger vehicle, the other loco following 'light engine',
the roles being reversed for the return trip. Normally, the motive
power would be one of the steam locos and *Alister*, although
both steam locos have been employed. Until 2001, passengers
were carried in a manrider. The fire at Durley effectively
destroyed the two ex-Ramsgate tunnel coaches when their
restoration was virtually complete. The bogies from one were sold,
but parts of the other were retained. Coach No 3 has subsequently
been reconstructed and moved to Kew. With a four compartment
wooden body (originally it had five compartments, it was shortened
in order to fit on the turntable at Durley!) and little more than
the bogies, brake gear and part of the frame surviving from the
original, it now amounts to being a replica. With Westinghouse
brake gear fitted, it 'returned' to service in 2001.

There are plans to extend the Kew running line and, if proposals
prepared by the Steam Museum and nearby Musical Museum
are approved, the track could more than double in length. The
proposal would delete the section of line on the Stand Pipe

Tower side of the Museum, where the 'station' is located.
Instead, the railway would start by the car park (the 'outer terminus') and round past the tea room, but then swing to the right
instead of left. Running roughly parallel to Kew Bridge Road,
it would pass the pumping station next door to the Steam
Museum, and continue to a new terminus behind the Musical
Museum. The track would follow the route once used by a narrow
gauge line which ran beside the filter beds of the pumping station,
so it could be said to constitute a reinstatement! The plan remained
the subject of negotiation as this book was being written.

Kew provided the HNGRS with an operating base for some
of its equipment, but was some way from its spiritual home.
The opportunity to run a railway in Hampshire arose with the
development of the Bursledon Brickworks Conservation
Centre. The buildings date from 1897, the clay being initially
extracted close by, later from pits further away with the clay
brought to the site by an overhead cable system. Construction
of the M27 motorway separated the buildings from the pits,
although a bridge was built under the route of the cable system.
The works finally closed in 1974.

Development of a short 2ft gauge line at the Brickworks
started in spring 1995. Initially, this was laid into a shed to
house the two HNGRS locos, a Simplex 20hp loco
(MR4724/39) built for the American Gulf West Indies
Petroleum Company and presented to the HNGRS in 1961 -
hence her name *AGWI Pet* - and Simplex 40hp (MR5226/35)
properly named *Brambridge Hall*, but more affectionately
Bramble. The railway was rearranged in 1999 when the track
was removed from the main Brickworks building and connected
into shipping containers to house the locomotives, the HNGRS
pair being joined by the Brickworks-owned ex-York Brick Co
diesel *Beccy*. Subsequently, the line has been extended. Early in
2000, the first run-round loop was completed and the line
reached 450 yards in length.

Originally, the Brickworks Trust was not convinced that
passenger rides were desirable, so the line at Bursledon was laid
with light Jubilee track, allowing demonstration industrial
trains to be run. In 1999, an application to the Millennium
Commission to fund an extension of the line up to the main
gates of the Brickworks was unsuccessful, part of the 'millennium
ambition' envisaged by this package being to run steam on the line
for the first time. Although apparently thwarted, the opportunity
arose following a visit by *Cloister* to Amberley in July 2000.
Instead of taking the loco direct from Sussex to Kew, the transporter stopped off at the Brickworks. The chance was too good
to miss; *Cloister* was steamed on 16 July and successfully ran
up the existing line during a Museum Open Day.

There is a plan to build a comprehensive track layout at the
Brickworks linking the various buildings and plant being
restored. This could produce two miles of track, but not in one
run, to perform a practical role in small-scale brick production
combined with the demonstration of past industrial narrow
gauge practice. This potential development includes a plan to
reconstruct the former rope-worked incline to feed a restored
1897-built steam powered Pugmill.

While these developments all relate to the role of the narrow

gauge in industry, the Brickworks Trust has changed its view concerning passenger working. While some 35lb rail has been obtained for potential use at the top end of the line, the current 'main line' climbs very steeply and there are doubts as to whether such a gradient would be acceptable for passenger use. Little can be done about the slope, so an extended passenger line may have to take a different direction. Although at the discussion stage, in theory, a line could be built over the bridge across the M27 motorway under the route of the old overhead cable system. On the far side is the 70 acre Swanwick Nature Reserve - an ideal destination, perhaps, for a 2ft gauge railway!

Running at Kew on two weekends a month provides a regular income, while Bursledon provides a focus for local members. *Cloister*, which returned to steam early in 1998 after a rebuild lasting 20 years, often visits other railways. The Society has acquired three ex-Dinorwic quarry wagons (two slate wagons and a coal truck) which, although needing extensive restoration (and single flange wheels rather than original double flange quarry wheels) will provide a demonstration quarry train to accompany the ex-quarry loco.

The Hollycombe Steam Collection

The Hollycombe Collection dates back to the late 1940s when Cdr John M Baldock realised that traction engines and other steam road vehicles were rapidly disappearing. Having acquired various vehicles, by the early 1960s he concluded that

Hampshire Narrow Gauge Railway Society-owned Simplex *AGWI Pet* (MR4724/39) near the top of the running line at Bursledon Brickworks. The name comes from the loco's first owner, the American Gulf West Indies Petroleum Company.

there were now enough enthusiasts to secure such machines for preservation and transferred his attention to saving fairground rides. As the Collection, now including locomotives and equipment from the Dinorwic slate quarries, expanded the idea arose of opening to the public - and was achieved after many battles with officialdom. Unfortunately, the collection outstripped Cdr Baldock's ability to meet the financial outlays and some rides were sold, although they have subsequently returned. Even with the collection reduced, expenses were still exceeding takings and Cdr Baldock concluded that he could no longer subsidise it at the end of the 1984 season.

Several people suggested opening for the following year on a voluntary basis and a Society was formed. This was successful and the collection expanded. At the beginning of 1999, the majority of the collection was transferred to a new Charitable Trust, made possible by a Heritage Lottery Fund grant which financed the purchase of around 80% of the collection from the Baldock family, the balance remaining on long-term loan.

The collection aims to show the role of steam in Britain's history. Road locomotives were used to build roads which developed the transport network, steam was essential in farming and supplied the power for fairground rides for entertainment,

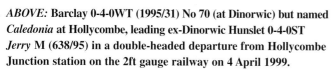

ABOVE: **Barclay 0-4-0WT (1995/31) No 70 (at Dinorwic) but named** *Caledonia* **at Hollycombe, leading ex-Dinorwic Hunslet 0-4-0ST** *Jerry* **M (638/95) in a double-headed departure from Hollycombe Junction station on the 2ft gauge railway on 4 April 1999.**

RIGHT: **Ex-Dinorwic Hunslet 0-4-0ST** *Jerry* **M (638/95) on the 2ft gauge railway at Hollycombe in July 1995.**

and there is an engine from a paddle steamer to represent shipping. Railways are represented by three lines of different gauges. A standard gauge line is worked by 0-4-0ST Hawthorne Leslie (2450/99) now named *Commander B* (after Cdr Baldock) which was purchased in 1985, the passengers being carried on converted ex-BR flat wagons. Previously named *Newcastle*, this is the oldest surviving Hawthorne Leslie loco and used to work at Chatham Dockyard. A 7¼ins gauge railway lies between the fairground and the gardens. In addition to a model of a type '08' diesel shunter, there are two steam locos: *Bob*, a 'Tinkerbell'-type model of a narrow gauge loco built in 1981 and presented to Hollycombe by Mr R C U Corbett, and *Pauline*, built by Bennett Bros of Bristol in 1990 to a 'Romulus' design.

The 2ft gauge line is the most extensive of the railway systems. Hunslet 0-4-0ST *Jerry* M (HE638/95) and a quantity of bullhead rails and chairs, was purchased from Dinorwic in 1967 as the quarries approached closure. Track laying at Hollycombe

started in 1968 and the line reached the old sandstone quarry by 1971, a full loop then being added to bring the track length up to 1½ miles. The second ex-Dinorwic loco, Barclay 0-4-0WT (works number 1995) No 70, was purchased in 1968 and has been named *Caledonia* at Hollycombe, after the Caledonia Works in Kilmarnock where she was built in 1931.

The railway climbs away up the hill, swinging to the right at the top to enter an anti-clockwise circuit, pauses for passengers to enjoy views across the South Downs, passes the quarry and returns alongside fields. On completing the passage of the loop, the train reverses down into the station, adjacent to which is a shed to house both locomotives, and a small signalbox to cover the lever frame. Rides on all three railways are included in the all-in entry price, which covers as many rides as you like, on anything.

An on-going project is the development of a demonstration area in the quarry with skip wagons on tracks up to the 'working face'. These could be worked by a Ruston diesel, with stone moved down the 2ft tracks to a transhipment area behind the station where the standard gauge Grafton self-propelled steam crane will move it to a stone crushing plant, powered by a portable boiler. This will create a road making display from rock face to road roller. In the long term, there could be a Face Shovel working in the quarry - and the possibility has been mooted of looking for a small steam loco to complete the scene. There are several other items of interest around the narrow gauge site, including restored ex-Dinorwic wagons and *Excelsior*, an 1880-vintage 3ft gauge Aveling & Porter loco from the Scout Moor Tramway in the Lancashire Pennines, which, unfortunately, is considered unrestorable and will remain a static exhibit.

Penrhyn Castle Industrial Railway Museum

The formation of a Railway Museum at Penrhyn Castle arose from a coincidence of factors as the final days of the Penrhyn Railway approached. Iorwerth Jones, the regular driver of *Blanche* on the Penrhyn main line was considering how the railway and its locomotives might be saved, while enthusiasts were visiting for a 'final ride' - officially, passenger-carrying had ceased when the workmen's trains stopped in December 1951. The late Bernard Latham had already spoken to Mr W R Parry, Curator for the Castle, on behalf of the Industrial Locomotive Society to see if the Castle might house a preserved standard gauge locomotive. Mr Parry was interested in railway history and, having already accepted a model of the Penrhyn Railway, built by pupils in Penmaenmawr in the 1950s, was receptive to the idea. When the Penrhyn Railway closed in 1962 (the quarry system held on for a further three years) *Linda* and *Blanche* went to the Ffestiniog. Realising that the railway was not going to be saved, Iorwerth Jones also approached Mr Parry and received a positive response. Iorwerth (now back working in the quarry) volunteered to assist in developing the museum.

The model layout was restored and part of the stables area was cleared. When news came that *Charles*, built for the Penrhyn main line in 1882 to replace De Winton locomotives and out of service since at least 1954, was to be scrapped, it was suggested that Mr Parry approach Lady Janet Douglas Pennant, who supported saving the locomotive. Discussions with quarry management resulted in *Charles* being placed on permanent loan to The National Trust and moved to Penrhyn Castle in May 1963. These contacts also resulted in the arrival of the Penrhyn saloon coach, dating from around 1882 and used by Lord Penrhyn and his Agent for trips up to Coed-y-Parc from the Port, along with much else, including trackwork. The earlier ILS approach resulted in the arrival of the standard gauge Neilson & Co 0-4-0WT No 1 which had worked for 92 years at Beckton Gasworks, London. More locomotives followed: Black Hawthorn 0-4-0ST Kettering Furnaces No 3 (3ft gauge), Hudswell Clarke 0-4-0ST *Hawarden*, Hudswell Clarke 0-4-0T *Vesta* and Robert Stephenson & Co 0-6-0T *Haydock* (all standard gauge). Having virtually built the Museum, formally opened on 25 June 1965, as a volunteer (helped by students from Bangor University and others) Iorwerth Jones was offered a full-time job looking after it in 1966 and has remained since. Subsequently, three more locomotives arrived: ex-Penrhyn Hunslet 0-4-0ST *Hugh Napier*, 4ft gauge Padarn Railway Horlock & Co 0-4-0 *Fire Queen* and 3ft gauge De Winton 0-4-0VTB *Watkin* from Penmaenmawr.

Fire Queen is an incredible survivor, being one of two locomotives built in 1848 by A Horlock & Co to work on the 4ft gauge Padarn Railway. The locomotive remains as it was in the late 1880s, albeit cleaned and cosmetically repaired. Both *Fire Queen*, and its companion *Jenny Lind*, seem to have been taken out of service in 1886 when 'modern' Hunslet locos were built to work the Padarn line. By this time, *Jenny Lind* had been modified, including the addition of a cab. Presumably because *Fire Queen* was in original condition, she was selected for preservation and stored in a shed at Gilfach Ddu in 1890 while *Jenny Lind* was broken up. In 1969, when Dinorwic assets were disposed of, *Fire Queen* was privately purchased and placed on loan at Penrhyn Castle, along with the 1896-vintage directors saloon carriage built by the Gloucester Railway Carriage & Wagon Co for the Padarn Railway.

Exhibits are housed in 'The Ride', where horses were exercised under cover, the arches now enclosed by glass. The collection includes coaches, wagons (not just from Penrhyn) and other ex-quarry items, and there are three types of manually propelled machines used on the Padarn Railway: 'Ceir Cicio' *Black Bess* (kicking car - operated by foot pedals), Car Troi *Arthur* (revolving car - worked by hand winding) and an engineer's rail-cycle. There is also a Model Room in the old first floor stable workers' accommodation housing model rolling stock, examples of locomotive model engineering, signs and other ephemera from the locality.

In the courtyard is a display of quarry trackwork in the form of a through line, with a series of turnouts. These range from lever operated stub points, a turnout with cast iron sills (the wagon is directed onto the correct line by pushing to one side or the other), 'spoon points' (where a shaped end piece on a moveable rail is laid over the running line), through to the 'Dump Turnout' where the pieces of cast rail are literally picked up and relocated within castings by hand. The 'through' part of the track forms a short demonstration line on which *Acorn*, the only working locomotive in the collection, can be operated. This 20DL Ruston & Hornsby (No 327904) did not originate from Penrhyn, but represents a type which worked at the quarry in latter days. This example was delivered new to a lime works in Westmoreland, Cumbria, later going to a granite quarry near Shrewsbury. Purchased privately from the quarry then sold to the National Trust, restoration commenced at Penrhyn Castle around 1984 and took some four years. The loco is painted in the maroon livery of most of the Penrhyn diesel fleet and the name *Acorn* reflects the National Trust symbol.

The steam locomotives in the collection will remain static exhibits, except possibly *Hugh Napier*, a Penrhyn Large Quarry Class Hunslet 0-4-0ST built in 1904 which last worked prior to 1964 and passed into the care of the National Trust at Penrhyn Castle two years later. Stripped down for restoration around 1969, work has continued slowly while other projects received attention. At one time, there were thoughts of a demonstration steam line in the Castle grounds, operated by *Hugh Napier*. This idea has been abandoned, but approval to regauge the loco to 1ft 11½ins was given in September 2001. No decision has been made on whether a new steel firebox should be provided, plus a new tubeplate and a set of tubes, but if the money can be found, the loco could steam again - regauging making it possible for *Hugh Napier* to visit other railways. Restoration work is continuing in a small workshop specially constructed in the courtyard.

TOP: **Ex-Pen-yr-Orsedd quarry Hunslet 0-4-0ST *Una* in the yard of The Welsh Slate Museum at Gilfach Ddu**

LOWER: **The author's wife, Carrie, drives 20DL Ruston & Hornsby (No 327904) *Acorn* on the short demonstration line at Penrhyn Castle Industrial Railway Museum.**

The Welsh Slate Museum - Gilfach Ddu

The complex at Gilfach Ddu was built to provide a virtually self-contained engineering and repair facility for the developing Dinorwic quarries opposite Llanberis and is believed to have opened in 1870 in basically complete form, a central courtyard surrounded by workshops on three sides, with an administrative section and Engineer's House on the fourth side. Close by was the interchange where wagons of slate from the 2ft gauge quarry railway system arrived for transfer onto transporter wagons for transit over the 4ft gauge Padarn Railway towards Port Dinorwic. The lakeside part of this trackbed is now used by the 2ft gauge Llanberis Lake Railway.

When the Dinorwic quarries closed in 1969, much of the equipment was put up for auction, but Huw Richard Jones, by then Chief Engineer for Dinorwic, was asked to preserve as much as possible of the building and its contents. The workshops became a Museum, which opened in May 1972 as the North Wales Quarrying Museum, with Huw as its first Keeper. Now The Welsh Slate Museum, it is a major centre for tourists, as well as enthusiasts.

Between 1997 and autumn 2000, a £2.1 million work programme was undertaken following the award of £1.6 million by the Heritage Lottery Fund. Developments included the renovation of the 15.4 metre water wheel built by De Winton's of Caernarfon in 1870 which provided the power for the line shafting in the complex, which in turn drove the machines. The old workshop areas include the iron and brass foundry, blacksmiths' forges and the larger machines along with slate cutting tables and other machines that helped mechanise the production of slate. Four quarrymen's houses from the 1860s have been relocated to the site from Tanygrisau. The piece-by-piece dismantling was undertaken in 1998 with the parts re-erected at the Museum in 1999.

In the courtyard is a large collection of slate quarry rolling stock, and the Museum owns the restored Hunslet 0-4-0ST *Una* which worked in the Pen-yr-Orsedd quarry. She is occasionally steamed and run on the Llanberis Lake Railway.

Between the Museum and the Lake Railway station is Vivian Quarry, which was served by a series of inclines constructed between 1873 and 1877. These were of the 'tanc' type, the slate wagons being loaded onto transporters which run on the inclined rails, rather than the wagons themselves running on tracks. The V2 winding house and incline has been restored with the help of the lottery money. Although operated by an electric motor with the wagons on each transporter being equally loaded, it is possible to demonstrate the only working incline of its kind in Britain.

Moseley Railway Trust

The origins of the Moseley Industrial Narrow Gauge Tramway Museum Society, reconstituted as the Moseley Industrial Narrow Gauge Railway Museum Trust Ltd early in 1999, date back to 1969. Partly as an educational project, a teacher at the Moseley Hall School in Cheadle, near Stockport, Cheshire, laid some 2ft gauge track in the grounds of the school on which a horse-drawn tram was used. The following year, the site of the school, and railway, moved and a 20ins gauge Ruston & Hornsby 20DL arrived from Crowle Brickworks. By 1976 the railway was dual gauge for most of its length, now with a 2ft gauge internal combustion locomotive also at the site and the first advertised opening of the Moseley Industrial Narrow Gauge Tramway Museum followed in 1977, operations being officially inspected and sanctioned by HMRI in 1978.

During 1980, the Moseley school merged with Bulkeley girls school (on the same site), and became the Manor School and the 2ft gauge running line was further extended onto 'Bulkeley Field' to reach a length of some half a mile, although the 20ins gauge had now been removed and the locomotives sold. Operations expanded the following year when visits were made to events with a length of portable track. By 1986, more non-school related people were involved and a formal structure began to be adopted.

The 1990s brought a series of changes. In 1994, the teacher who had started the project left the Society, and two years later the school was closed and became Margaret Danyers College. The College planned to redevelop the site where the railway collection was housed and gave the Society notice to quit. By this time, the running line was 400/500 yards long and a complex of trackwork developed into several buildings, including a loco-motive running shed, a museum and a workshop facility. The locomotive and stock collection had also expanded substantially following much restoration work.

The final operating day at Cheadle was on Easter Sunday in 1998. The entire collection was then placed in storage, the locomotives going into covered accommodation at Whaley Bridge, other equipment being in open storage at a separate site. The Society was converted into the Moseley Industrial Narrow Gauge Railway Museum Trust Ltd, a company limited by guarantee, although it is known as the Moseley Railway Trust. This change was finalised early in 1999. While the search for a site to locate a museum and new running line continued, the collection expanded - six more locos being purchased in the 1998 Gloddfa Ganol sale by Society members - and there were now over 40 locomotives and 80 items of rolling stock in storage. Although the Whaley Bridge site was not open to the public, an open day was held in 1999, followed by another in 2000, when several sections of Jubilee track were laid across the car park, over which some of the locos were operated. To help finance the costs of storage and other overheads, during 2000, the Trust started to publish books of special narrow gauge interest, a fine example being *A Guide to Simplex Narrow Gauge Locomotives* produced in 2001.

Around Easter 2001 it was realised that a number of items had 'disappeared' from the open storage location. A check confirmed that over 30 historic wagons, an engineless diesel loco, spare loco engines, a large quantity of track, a dozen points and a quantity of sleepers had gone, some of the equipment being owned by the Trust, the rest being privately owned by Trust members. It transpired that a new manager of the storage facility had ordered that the items be scrapped without realising they were privately owned! Equipment lost included peat wagons, mine tubs, skips, steel industry bogie flats and bomb wagons along with Jubilee track and heavier rail.

The locomotives at Whaley Bridge were not affected but had to be relocated to a new site, for unrelated reasons, between August and November 2001. The search for a new permanent home continues and, at the time of writing, the Trust has narrowed down the possibilities and has applied for Planning Permission at potential locations. Meanwhile, restoration work has continued.

There are now some 50 locomotives in the collection. Most are diesel, petrol and battery locos, but steam does feature. The star must be ex-Penrhyn Kerr Stuart 0-4-2ST *Stanhope* (2395/17) owned by leading Moseley member, John Rowlands. The loco returned to steam in September 1999, making its first public appearance at the Alan Keef Ltd Open Day on 11 September 1999. It has subsequently been based at the West Lancashire Light Railway pending the Moseley collection finding a new permanent base, but has visited other railways, including the Golden Valley LR and Leighton Buzzard. The collection also includes a large selection of rolling stock. In all, it vies closely with the Leighton Buzzard Railway for the title of being the largest collection of narrow gauge locomotives and stock in the country.

It should be mentioned that the collection owned by the teacher who started the project has been relocated to a farm in

John Rowland's Kerr Stuart 0-4-2ST *Stanhope* **is part of the Moseley Railway Trust collection. The first day of a visit by the locomotive to the Golden Valley Light Railway coincided with the final day of a visit by Patrick Keef's Bagnall 0-4-0ST** *Woto***, presenting the opportunity of the GVLR running double-headed steam trains on 19 August 2001. In this picture,** *Stanhope* **is leading on the climb back from Newlands Inn towards Butterley Park.**

Redruth, Cornwall under the name Moseley NG Industrial Tramway and Museum. Six internal combustion and battery locos, five carriages and around 60 wagons are housed in two large sheds, with about 100 yards of 2ft gauge demonstration track laid, and the potential for adding another half a mile of track. The location is on a working farm, but visits can be made by appointment.

Leeds Industrial Museum

Armley Mills was once the world's largest woollen mill and the first buildings on the site dated back to the 17th century. A fire in November 1805 destroyed the original structures, which were replaced by the buildings standing today. The mills closed commercially in 1969 and were taken over by Leeds City Council. Following conversion, the site reopened as Leeds Industrial Museum in 1982.

The City Museum, first established by the Leeds Philosophical and Literary Society in the 19th century, acquired its first locomotive in 1956, 2ft gauge ex-Harrogate gas works 0-6-2ST *Barber*, built in 1908 by Thomas Green & Co. In 1957,

18ins gauge Hunslet 0-4-0WT *Jack* was acquired with the help of its builders and the Narrow Gauge Railway Society, followed in 1961 by 3ft gauge Hudswell Clarke 0-4-0ST *Lord Granby*. Although part of the Museum's industrial collection, the locomotives remained in storage until 1982, when the locomotive galleries were formed in the old mill dyeshops of Armley Mills. These have been extended by adding the former locomotive shed from Esholt Sewage Works, Bradford.

The collection subsequently expanded and now includes over 20 narrow gauge locomotives, encompassing examples of eight narrow gauges (1ft 6ins, 2ft, 2ft 1ins, 2ft 6ins, 2ft 8ins, 2ft 11ins, 3ft and 3ft 6ins) plus a number of standard gauge locos. The narrow gauge collection includes petrol, diesel and battery electric as well as steam. A number of these, however, are not currently on public display and constitute a reserve collection, including *Lord Granby*.

Jack was fully restored at Bradford Industrial Museum in 1984 and is occasionally steamed on the short 18ins/2ft dual gauge track in the mill yard, the 2ft section being used by a 1928 Hudson-Fordson and 1944 Hudson-Hunslet petrol locomotives. The locomotives on static display include 2ft 6ins gauge Hudswell Clarke 2-6-2DM *Junin*, the world's first commercially built diesel locomotive dating from 1930.

National Railway Museum

The national collection, opened at York in 1975, is predominantly standard gauge, but does include examples of narrow gauge equipment. On display in the main hall are: 0-4-0ST *Pet* (built at Crewe by LNWR in 1865 to work on the 18ins gauge lines within Crewe works), Beyer Peacock 0-4-0ST *Wren* (built in 1887 for the 18ins gauge system in the Lancashire & Yorkshire Railway works at Horwich), 1931 vintage Post Office railway (Mount Pleasant) electric loco No 809, and a metre gauge Hunslet loco and side tip wagon from the Channel Tunnel construction project, plus Lynton & Barnstaple Railway coach No 2, preserved in the condition in which it was acquired (rather than restored) in order to fully conserve the original material and appearance. Various narrow gauge locomotives not owned by the NRM have spent periods on display in the Museum; currently on long term loan is the Ffestiniog Railway's double Fairlie *Livingston Thompson*.

Two further narrow gauge locomotives are owned by the NRM. Ex-Naburn Sewage works 4wDM Ruston & Hornsby (187105/37) was fully restored and placed on loan to the railway at Poppleton Nursery, York. This nursery was started by the LNER in 1942, to provide trees and plants for linesides, station landscaping, etc. A narrow gauge line at the site was started in 1985 and completed to 350 yards by spring 1988. In addition to the NRM-owned loco, a privately-owned 4wDM Motor Rail (7494) from Alne Brickworks ran on the line. By 1999, use of the nursery had declined and the railway ceased to operate. The NRM-owned locomotive and two wagons have been returned to the Museum but, at the time of writing, were not on display.

The only remaining narrow gauge loco on loan away from York, and the only NRM-owned narrow gauge locomotive which can currently be viewed in operation, is WDLR No 3098

(MR1377/18). An example of the 'protected' Simplex type built for service in WWI, this kind of machine worked on the Leighton Buzzard Light Railway which was built in 1919 and employed surplus military equipment. The NRM loco was one of the final batch built but, having missed war service, was one of two long-term survivors at the Yorkshire Water Authority employed at Knostrop Sewage Works in Leeds. Rail operation at this site ceased in 1980 and one of the locomotives was obtained by the NRM, the other going to the Leeds Industrial Museum at Armley Mills. The bodywork of the NRM example was initially restored by 275 Railway Squadron of the Royal Corps of Transport, who applied a No 2275 plate to the locomotive to mark their involvement, although it is not the correct WDLR number. The loco was loaned to the Leighton Buzzard Railway, in non-working condition, in 1990. The Dorman engine was restored by Appleton Engineering of Leiston and returned in 1996. LBR volunteers refitted the engine and completed the restoration to working order, its first appearance under its own power being on 27 June 1999 during the LBR's 80th birthday gala weekend. Finishing touches were complete in time for a 'Diesel Weekend' at the railway on 20 November 1999, and the locomotive has subsequently been used on the line, even running as 'pilot' to the LBR's modern diesel No 80

Hunslet 0-4-0WT *Jack* running on mixed 18in and 2ft gauge track in the early days of Leeds Industrial Museum. This was the occasion of a visit by the Narrow Gauge Railway Society. *(David H Smith)*

ABOVE: Beyer Peacock 0-4-0ST *Wren*, built in 1887 for the 18in gauge system in the Lancashire & Yorkshire Railway works at Horwich, at the National Railway Museum, York. The cab of the metre gauge Hunslet loco from the Channel Tunnel construction project can just be seen to the left.

LEFT: Lynton & Barnstaple Railway coach No 2, kept in 'as acquired' condition, at the National Railway Museum, York.

RIGHT: **Ex-Stewarts & Lloyds 0-6-0ST Peckett No 86 (1871/1934) on the metre gauge running line at Irchester Narrow Gauge Railway Museum. Pictured on 16 December 2001, the loco was in light steam having moved under its own power for the first time in 35 years on the previous day. Behind No 85 is 4wDM Ruston & Hornsby class 49 ED10.**

LOWER: **The cosmetically restored 0-6-0T *Cambrai* (493/88) built by L. Corpet of Paris (on loan from the Narrow Gauge Railway Museum Trust in Tywyn) inside Irchester Narrow Gauge Railway Museum. Beyond *Cambrai* is 6wDM Ruston & Hornsby Blue Circle and 4wDM Ruston & Hornsby *Milford*.**

Beaudesert on two passenger services during positioning moves on 11 November 2001. The NRM has expressed the intention of supplying a new plate bearing the loco's correct 3098 number.

The Irchester Narrow Gauge Railway Museum

This Museum aims to preserve industrial narrow gauge equipment from Northamptonshire. It is also believed to be unique in Britain. having the only metre gauge trackwork, with appropriate locomotives, in the country.

Its origins date back to 1971, for during the 1970s the group which set up the Museum were involved in caring for the standard gauge loco No 70000 *Britannia*. Based in Northamptonshire, they heard that the metre gauge ex-Stewarts & Lloyds Minerals Ltd Peckett No 85 (1870/1934) was on the market in 1977. No 85 was built new for the Wellingborough Iron Company and worked at the Finedon quarries until 1966. It entered preservation at Bressingham Steam Museum and in 1971 was moved to the Yorkshire Dales Railway Museum Trust, marketed as the Embsay & Bolton Abbey Steam Railway since the late 1980s. As a locomotive with local connections, and thinking its restoration would provide a diversion from working on the '7P' 4-6-2 main line machine, it was purchased by the Northamptonshire Locomotive Group.

The loco was moved to the Northamptonshire Ironstone Railway Trust (NIRT) at Hunsbury Hill, but NIRT decided to pursue standard gauge preservation rather than narrow gauge. In 1982, the group moved into the old BR goods shed at Irchester where No 85 was returned to working order two years later, and the collection grew. In 1985 the Irchester Narrow Gauge Railway Trust (a registered charity) was formed and when plans to purchase the goods shed did not work out, they moved to their present location in 1987. The new site is within Irchester Country Park, itself an ironstone quarrying area until 1969, and the Museum running line is on the site of a standard gauge siding adjacent to a 3ft 8½ ins trackbed associated with the industry. The site was cleared and a new building erected - its size being calculated as potentially accommodating every surviving metre gauge locomotive in Britain! A 200 yard metre gauge demonstration track was laid which incorporates a 1 in 36 climb into the compound.

Fellow Stewarts & Lloyds locos Nos 86 and 87 are also located at the Museum. No 87 is a static exhibit, but No 86 is

fully restored, moving under its own steam for the first time in 35 years (and since entering preservation) on 15 December 2001. No 85 last steamed in November 1995 when the boiler certificate expired, but remains complete while the funds for boiler repairs are raised. A fourth metre gauge loco is also in the Museum, the cosmetically restored 0-6-0T *Cambrai* (493/88) built by L Corpet of Paris, presently on loan from the Narrow Gauge Railway Museum Trust in Tywyn. Although this locomotive initially worked in France, it was purchased by the Loddington Ironstone Company in 1936 and worked at Loddington quarries until 1956, when it was transferred to the Waltham Iron Company in Leicestershire. There are also metre gauge diesels: 4wDM Hunslet *The Rock* (2419/1941), 4wDM Ruston (211679/1941) *Milford* and 4wDM Ruston 'ED10' (originally built to 3ft gauge and regauged after moving to Irchester). In addition, there are two 3ft gauge diesels: Ruston 100-DL *Blue Circle* (281290/1949) and a 'Protected' Motor Rail (1363/1918) originally built to 2ft gauge and regauged in 1973 for work at Sundon Cement Works, Bedfordshire. Other exhibits include 3ft gauge wagons, 2ft gauge equipment, and items from the wire-rope worked 1ft 8ins gauge 'portable' railway system from Ravensthorpe reservoir.

CHAPTER ELEVEN

Minimum Gauge

Miniature railways - essentially scaled down standard gauge lines - may have a gauge narrower than standard but are not the same thing as narrow gauge. The divisions, however, become blurred when minimum gauge enters the equation!

Sir Arthur Heywood believed that 15ins gauge represented the minimum gauge for serious use and developed his ideas with a line on his estate at Duffield Bank, near Derby. He designed and built his own locomotives, the first being *Effie* (built 1874) an inside framed 0-4-0T with a launch-type boiler. His subsequent locomotives also had launch-type boilers, but outside frames, and incorporated radial axles allowing them to traverse 25ft radius curves: 0-6-0T *Ella* (1881) and 0-8-0T *Muriel* (1894) the latter being intended to produce the most powerful locomotive possible on 15ins gauge. A railway following his principles was opened in 1895 at Eaton Hall to serve the Duke of Westminster's estate. Heywood-built locomotives for this line were 0-4-0T *Katie* (1896), 0-6-0T *Shelagh* (1904) and 0-6-0T *Ursula* (1916).

Sir Arthur died in 1916. The fate of *Effie* is unknown, not being mentioned after 1894, and is assumed to have been scrapped, but the remaining Duffield Bank locos *Ella* and *Muriel* went to the Ravenglass and Eskdale Railway when it was converted to 15in gauge in 1915. *Katie* also went to the R&ER in 1915, then to Southport in 1919 and to the Fairbourne Railway in 1922. There, she was effectively scrapped in the mid-1920s, her frames being used for a wagon. The frame plates, however, survived and in 1974 were presented to the Narrow Gauge Railway Museum at Tywyn, later being transferred to the museum at Ravenglass. The idea was to construct a static replica based on the frames, but this developed into a full restoration to produce a working locomotive. Of the Eaton Hall locos, *Shelagh* and *Ursula* were scrapped in 1942, the Eaton Hall Railway closing in 1947.

To complete the references to Sir Arthur Heywood, a replica of *Effie* has been constructed for David Humphreys by Great Northern Steam Services of Middlesborough, and James Waterfield has built a replica of *Ursula*, along with a Duffield Bank dining carriage and Eaton Hall brake van.

The Ravenglass & Eskdale started as a 'true' 3ft narrow gauge line, becoming known as 'Rat Trod' (trod equates to path). By the 1890s this had become La'al Ratty, an affectionate term reinforced in 1915 when the gauge was reduced and Heywood minimum gauge equipment arrived, along with miniature locomotives. When the line was sold in 1960, railway preservation was still pretty new ground. The Talyllyn had shown the way, but its pioneering work had then only been followed by the Ffestiniog Railway, Bluebell and Middleton railways - it was certainly the first time that a railway had been acquired for salvation at an auction. With such a history, it must take its place in this volume.

A similar situation applies to the Fairbourne Railway. It started as a 2ft gauge tramway, was regauged and became a miniature line and, following a further gauge conversion, has really become minimum gauge. Moreover, its four steam locomotives are all half size models based on full size narrow gauge prototypes: *Russell* and *Beddgelert* (North Wales Narrow Gauge/Welsh Highland), *Yeo* (Lynton & Barnstaple) and *Sherpa* (Darjeeling & Himalayan).

The Bure Valley Railway also employs smaller reproductions of 'full size' narrow gauge locomotives. The 'ZB' type locos are impressive, 11 ton locos hauling 14 coaches represents 'a pretty handsome piece of kit', as one of the volunteer drivers put it! If these are included, it is hard to see how the Romney, Hythe & Dymchurch Railway can be left out, despite being far more 'miniature' than the others!

Although the Perrygrove Railway is a modern line, it has been included because it has become something of a centre for Heywood equipment. But, as noted, distinctions then become very difficult. For instance, the 12ins gauge Ruislip Lido Railway opened in 1946 as a miniature railway, the gauge being determined by the original steam loco, 4-4-2 *Prince Edward*, dating from 1936. The Ruislip Lido Railway Society was formed in 1980 to take over the railway and has extended from the original ½ mile to 1¼ miles, as well as relaying with heavier rail and erecting several buildings. Motive power now includes *Lady of the Lakes*, a B-B DM built in 1985 by the Ravenglass & Eskdale Railway, and steam returned in 1998 in the form of a half-scale 2-4-0 model of *Blanche*, named *Mad Bess* after a nearby wood.

The Kirklees Light Railway presents a similar quandary, albeit for different reasons. Built on most of the trackbed of a standard gauge Lancashire & Yorkshire Railway branch, the first mile of the 15in gauge Kirklees line was opened between Clayton West and a halt named Cuckoo's Nest in October 1991. The line steadily became four miles long in May 1997 after reaching Shelley station - this extension including the passage of the old Shelley tunnel - the longest 15ins gauge tunnel in Britain! Motive power includes three steam locomotives built by the man who conceived the railway, which is operated professionally with volunteer support. The locos are essentially half-scale narrow gauge machines, 2-6-2T *Fox* being based on a Hunslet which worked in India, 0-4-4-0 *Hawk* is an articulated design based on a Kitson Meyer while 0-6-2T *Badger* is freelance.

Although the 15ins gauge railway at Windmill Farm near Burscough, Lancashire is really more miniature than minimum gauge, the collection of locomotives at the site include examples with Ravenglass and Fairbourne connections. This line opened in 1997 and is some 700 yards in length. There are plans to create a 15in gauge heritage centre to display historic artefacts.

The above examples show how difficult definitions are. One can argue a case either way but, on balance, if these lines were given full coverage, the way would be open for even more debate concerning several other such 'borderline' railways!

The Ravenglass & Eskdale Railway

Although the RH&DR coined the title 'Smallest Public Railway in the World', the Ravenglass & Eskdale Railway probably used the term first in advertising from 1915, when it re-opened as a 15ins gauge line.

The Act of Parliament authorising the construction of the Ravenglass & Eskdale Railway was passed in 1873, making it the oldest narrow gauge railway in England operating a passenger service. The 3ft gauge line was built to transport iron ore mined in the valley needed by the steelworks at Barrow. The locomotives were Manning Wardle 0-6-0Ts named *Devon* and *Nabb Gill*, the former working the first goods train on 24 May 1875. Despite strong criticism of the quality of the line's civil engineering by the Board of Trade Inspector, the first official passenger train ran on 20 November 1876 with two 4-wheel coaches, a 4-wheel brake van and a big 4-wheel saloon.

Within six months the line was bankrupt, although trains continued to run while it was in Receivership. In an attempt to increase traffic, a branch tramway was laid to serve the Gill Force mine at the top end of the railway in 1881, but this failed. The state of the line caused it to become the butt of jokes, but it struggled on serving the local community - and at Bank Holidays so many tourists would turn up that they had to be accommodated in open goods wagons! Passenger traffic ceased on 30 November 1908 following a complaint to the Board of Trade, mainly about the condition of the track. Powers to electrify the route in 1910 came to nothing and the last goods train ran in April 1913.

Two years later, Wenman Bassett-Lowke and Robert Proctor Mitchell were visiting the area. They wanted to run a

River Esk **waits to depart from Muncaster Mill on the Ravenglass & Eskdale Railway.**

'proper' railway using the miniature locomotives which they constructed for pleasure parks. Within seven weeks, a mile of track had been converted to 15in gauge and on 28 August 1915, the railway entered its second incarnation with the start of passenger services between Ravenglass and Muncaster Mill under the control of Narrow Gauge Railways Ltd, a private company formed by Wenman Bassett-Lowke. The 15ins gauge was extended to Irton Road by early 1916, Beckfoot by 20 April 1916 and to Boot by 11 August 1917. When the iron mines at Boot closed, the line was cut back to Beckfoot, but in 1926 the tracks were extended along the old Gill Force branch to a new station at Dalegarth - today's terminus. The railway carried increasing granite traffic as quarries re-opened along the route, between 25,000-50,000 tons per year being transported to a crushing plant at Murthwaite. The stone traffic continued during WW2, although passenger services were suspended until after VE-Day in 1945.

Narrow Gauge Railways Ltd, and the quarries, were sold in 1949 to the Keswick Granite Co. The quarries did not pay and were closed in 1953, with the railway being put up for sale five years later. In need of investment, no buyers came forward and,

***Northern Rock* runs into the Dalegarth terminus of the Ravenglass & Eskdale Railway.**

with just one month's notice, the railway was put up for public auction in 1960 - if there were no acceptable bids, the railway was to be broken up into 60 individual lots. A campaign to save the line started and Muncaster Parish Council became the focus for a preservation society. At the 7 September 1960 auction, the winning bid of £12,000 was made by Douglas Robinson, Clerk of the Parish Council, on behalf of the Preservation Society. Trustees formed a new Ravenglass & Eskdale Railway Company, which is supported by the Ravenglass & Eskdale Railway Preservation Society Co Ltd.

Over subsequent years, the owning and operating company, backed by the Society and its members, have transformed the railway. The line has been relaid, Ravenglass station has been extended with signals and points controlled from the signalbox and new station buildings provided at The Green and Muncaster Mill. The old BR buildings at Ravenglass are now a museum and workshops, while the 125-year old Furness Railway station building is now the Ratty Arms pub. A canopy, recovered from Millom, has been erected, a footbridge from Coniston re-erected and items from other Cumbrian locations have found uses: seats from Seascale, columns from Whitehaven Bransty, signal levers from Brigham station, etc. In 1964, a 700ft cut-off was constructed at Gilbert's Cutting to avoid the previous sharp reverse curves.

The railway has turntables at Ravenglass and Dalegarth, and passing loops at Miteside, Irton Road and Fisherground, with operations controlled by radio between Ravenglass and the locomotives.

After re-opening as a 15ins gauge line, the equipment included locos and coaches from private and public amusement lines and rolling stock originally built for Sir Arthur Heywood's Duffield Bank line. The miniature locomotives were basically one-quarter scale and the first of these to work on the line was

Sans Pareil. These were not up to the task of working the steeply graded line with its sharp curves and, in 1923, Henry Greenly designed a locomotive specifically to deal with R&ER operating conditions. *River Esk* was built by Davey, Paxman Ltd and the 2-8-2 was scaled overall to one-third full size and, having received various modifications over the years, remains in service. In 1928, a 4-6-0+0-6-4 named *River Mite* was produced at Ravenglass, utilising parts of two of the older miniature locos, *Colossus* and *Sir Aubrey Brocklebank*. This loco was scrapped by degrees and is no longer at the railway.

The ex-Heywood locos were 0-6-0T *Ella* (1881), 0-8-0T *Muriel* (1894) and *Katie* (1896). *Muriel*, which arrived at Ravenglass in July 1917, was rebuilt with a larger boiler in 1927, the frames also being extended and a rear truck added. A cab was fitted and the side tanks replaced by the addition of a tender, the rebuilt loco being 0-8-2 *River Irt*. Further modifications include fitting a larger boiler in 1977, which is interchangeable with the other locos. Although now much different from when she was built, *Muriel* lays claim to being the oldest working 15ins gauge loco in the world. *Ella* became a petrol powered loco, ICL No 2, in 1927. The crankwebs from *Ella* were utilised during the 1950s when construction of the diesel *Shelagh of Eskdale* was commenced, this loco therefore being classified as a rebuild rather than a new machine! *Katie* is part of the museum collection and in the process of being rebuilt.

The Preservation Society commissioned the second *River Mite* to run on the R&ER. Built by Clarksons of York utilising the chassis of the former steam powered tender from *River Esk*, it entered service in 1967. The Railway Company subsequently improved its workshop facilities to the point where it could build its own locos. The first to be constructed at Ravenglass was *Northern Rock*, entering service in 1976. This loco was to

Yeo, based on the Lynton & Barnstable 2-6-2T, runs among the sand dunes of the Fairbourne Railway.

a wholly new design, far more akin to a narrow gauge outline than a miniature loco.

Bonnie Dundee was originally built by Kerr Stuart as a 2ft gauge 0-4-0WT and worked at Dundee Gas Works until 1959. Initially privately preserved, it was donated to the R&ER in 1976. The regauged and rebuilt loco entered service as an 0-4-2T in 1982, using the side tanks previously on *Ella*, along with an enclosed cab. A further rebuild in 1996 removed the tanks in favour of a tender and with outside valve gear replacing the previous Stephenson inside gear. Other steam locos include *Synolda*, an identical twin of *Sans Pareil* (scrapped in 1928) normally in the museum but steamed on occasions, and *Flower of the Forest*, an 0-2-2 tram built in 1985 at Ravenglass for the owner of *Bonnie Dundee* and donated to the railway on his death.

The railway has also been home to internal combustion locomotives since 1919 when petrol engined 'scooters' were introduced. Today, the fleet includes *Shelagh of Eskdale*, *Lady Wakefield* and the Railcar *Silver Jubilee*, as well as several smaller locomotives which are either for works train use or museum exhibits.

The railway was equipped with four 4-wheel Bassett-Lowke coaches from Oslo on reopening as a 15ins gauge line. In 1915, the bogie coaches from Sir Arthur Heywood's Duffield Bank line arrived, other vehicles to supplement this stock arriving

later. The old open stock started to be replaced by bogie open carriages around 1928. In 1967, new bogie closed carriages arrived, with new open and semi-open coaches added in 1970. Today's passenger stock are all bogie vehicles with a mix of open, semi-open and closed saloon types, although some of the early carriages remain as museum exhibits.

The Fairbourne Railway

The railway at Fairbourne started as a horse-worked 2ft gauge tramway in 1895 but, in 1916, was converted to a 15ins gauge miniature railway. The late 1920s brought a short-lived and ill-fated experiment with dual gauge when a loco crisis led to the purchase of an 18ins gauge 4-2-2 'Stirling Single', a third rail being added as far as the Golf House, roughly a third of the way along the track. By about 1938, the extra rail had been taken out, the loco having long since departed.

The railway closed in 1940 and suffered greatly during WW2. A combination of zero maintenance, storms and military training led many to suppose it had ceased to exist. The remains of the line were sold in 1946 and the new owners set about a revival. A service was reintroduced to Golf House at Easter 1947 and by 1948 the line was open over its full length to Porth Penrhyn (Penrhyn Point) to connect with the ferry service across Afon Mawddach (Mawddach River) to Barmouth, although on a slightly different alignment from the pre-war railway which had terminated short of the ferry landing.

Things changed again after John Ellerton purchased the railway in 1985. He had run a half-scale narrow gauge railway, worked by *Sherpa* (built by John Milner in 1978) and *Yeo* (built by David Curwen, also in 1978) in Brittany during the 1978/79 season. Immediately after the purchase, the Fairbourne Railway ran as a 15ins gauge line in 1985 - with the 15ins *Sian* converted to an American appearance and running as *Sydney*! The miniature railway stock was then sold and the railway converted to 12¼ins gauge, enabling the use of the locos and rolling stock from the old French line. Subsequently, Beddgelert (David Curwen, 1978) and Russell (originally built by John Milner and Neil Simpkins, 1978) were added to the steam fleet. Russell, incidentally has a 2-6-4 wheel arrangement rather than the 2-6-2 of the 'real' locomotive. Engineering machines were brought in to the works and a replica Sandy River & Rangeley Lakes 2-6-2 (subsequently sold) was built at Fairbourne. A period of decline followed and, by the early 1990s, maintenance and investment had practically dried up.

In April 1995 the line was sold to Dr Roger Melton and Prof Tony Atkinson, who formed North Wales Coast Light Railway Ltd, and work commenced on yet another revival. The tunnel at the far end of the line (basically present for effect, although it helps protect the line from drifting sand) was knocked down and rebuilt and track maintenance tackled. Only steam locos *Beddgelert*, *Yeo* and *Sherpa* had been included when the line changed hands. Subsequently, *Russell* and six coaches (also not in the original sale) were purchased. Staff numbers increased and VHF radios introduced to improve communications along the line.

The track arrangement at Fairbourne, on a confined site between the road, a housing development and the Cambrian Coast standard gauge line, is fascinating. Behind the platform is the facade of what appears to be a station building, but actually is the outer wall of the workshops. Further along is the loco shed, with four parallel roads fronted by a Traverser. At the yard end, beside the standard gauge, three lines meet at a Sector Table, which also can be swung round to access four sidings. The ten carriage shed roads are reached via two normal sidings, one runs onto another Sector Plate leading to a fan of six roads, the other consists of very short lengths of rail with very loosely mounted fishplates. The ensemble slides across metal runners set into the concrete at right angles to provide a flexible connection!

Part-way along the route is a Halt named Gorsafawddachaidraigodan Heddogled Dollonpenrhynareurdraethcereidigion - a contrived but successful attempt at gaining entry into the Guinness Book of Records as the longest station name. It means the Mawddach station with its dragon's teeth on the northerly Penrhyn Drive on the golden beach of Cardigan Bay - otherwise known as Golf Halt! Further along, a small signal cabin marks the entry to the mid-way passing loop where trains

cross during busy periods. At Porth Penrhyn, there is a run-round loop, but the track continues round a balloon loop and rejoins the running line shortly before the tunnel. The choice of using either the balloon or run-round loop at Porth Penrhyn is left to the driver's discretion.

At Fairbourne, an enlarged tea room also forms the entrance to the Indoor Nature Centre, previously a butterfly centre but totally rebuilt as an attraction for children and school visits. The old tea room has been developed into a small museum of the line's history.

Other plans aimed at continuing the stabilisation and improvement of the railway include rationalisation of the carriage stock, with the sale of some excess coaches, although the bogies were retained since most of the purchasers had lines with different gauges. A new coach equipped for wheelchair users has been built, with a second likely to follow. The line is applying new liveries to the coaches, with one rake turned out in chocolate and cream for the 2000 season, with a second rake being finished in blue and cream for the 2002 season. Long-term plans include a new platform in Fairbourne station and thought has also been given to building new locomotives.

Romney, Hythe & Dymchurch Railway

Marketed as 'The World's Smallest Public Railway' when opened in 1927, the locomotives are one-third full size, based on examples of British, North American and German express engines. The 15ins gauge railway is thus really a miniature, or minimum gauge, line rather than a narrow gauge railway. On the other hand, it is hard to exclude a much-loved line which was saved by enthusiastic businessmen and whose full-time staff are backed by volunteers from a supporting association!

The leading figure in the formation of the railway was Captain J E P Howey, one of two wealthy gentlemen who wished to build a miniature line which could also fulfil a public service. The location was apparently suggested by the Southern Railway, which operated the standard gauge branch to Dungeness which had been opened to goods (principally shingle, passenger trains following in 1883) and extended to New Romney in 1894. The principle seems to have been that the new line could serve Dymchurch, remote from their own line, and would help to develop holiday traffic to the then-deserted beaches.

Construction started in 1926 and trains started running from New Romney, through Dymchurch to Hythe, on 16 July 1927 over an almost level route across Romney Marsh - the railway's title does not reflect geographical order but was apparently selected since it sounded better in the order RH&DR! An extension in the other direction from New Romney was opened to *The Pilot* (a public house remains on the site today) on 24 May 1928 and out over the shingle peninsular to Dungeness early in the following August. The entire route of 13½ miles between Hythe and Dungeness was, at that time, double track. Construction of both sections had commenced before the relevant Light Railway Orders had been granted!

The new railway proved very popular with holiday makers and day trippers through the 1930s, but this changed with the

The Bug draws away from New Romney, with *Dr Syn* on the adjacent station road, during a Romney, Hythe & Dymchurch Railway special event on 13 May 2001.

outbreak of WW2. Although holiday traffic disappeared, a normal service continued until May 1940. Local people were evacuated and the railway was requisitioned for military use in June 1940. The railway transported troops between military camps along what amounted to a 'front line' area on the Kent coast, such traffic being run on the Hythe - New Romney section throughout the war. Similar traffic to Dungeness tailed off from about 1942, but this section was heavily used (and consequently damaged) during 1943 in connection with the PLUTO pipeline project in advance of D-Day. The railway was also patrolled by an armoured train, employing *Hercules* and two converted hopper wagons. Plans were made to extend the track from Dungeness to Rye, although never carried out, although a branch for military use was built in the 1920s to serve the acoustic mirrors which the War Department constructed at Hythe. Apparently intended initially to assist with the construction work, the track actually remained in place until about 1950.

When released from military control in July 1945, the railway was very run down, but a major effort by staff, with the assistance of local people and Italian PoWs, enabled the Hythe to New Romney section to re-open for the 1946 season. The New Romney to Dungeness section re-opened a year later - the event being publicised by a visit by the comedy duo Laurel and Hardy in March 1947. Although the line north of New Romney remained double tracked, the section south to Dungeness was now reduced to single track - and remains so.

Boom years followed, but by the 1960s low cost package holidays abroad cut into the traditional holiday traffic and the fortunes of the line declined. Captain Howey died in 1963 and new owners took over in 1964. With the equipment and infra-structure in poor condition, relocating the railway to a new site was considered in 1969, however, The RH&DR Supporters Association had been formed in 1967 to help address the problems. Ideas for shortening the line were considered and complete closure was mooted in 1971, but in February 1972 control passed to a group of enthusiast businessmen led by Sir William McAlpine. A year-round contract to carry school children between Dymchurch and New Romney in 1977 boosted the recovery which followed. Today, the railway is on a sound footing with relaying of the track in progress, a sound locomotive fleet, and is one of the major tourist attractions in Kent.

The stations at New Romney and Hythe still have overall roofs to form train sheds, that at Dymchurch being removed when the station was rebuilt in 1977. There are turntables at New Romney and Hythe so that locomotives can run chimney first, while at Dungeness there is a balloon loop which achieves the same result. The environs of Dungeness have changed radically, the scattered fishermen's cottages and lighthouse being joined by the Dungeness Nuclear Power station. The railway's HQ is at New Romney where the locomotive shed and workshops are located.

Using present day numbers and names for ease of identification (the names of several locomotives have changed over the years) the first five locomotives were basically modelled on LNER 'A1' Pacifics. Built by Davey, Paxman & Co Ltd in 1925, these were No 1 *Green Goddess*, No 2 *Northern Chief* and No 3 *Southern Maid*, followed in 1926 by No 7 *Typhoon* and No 8 *Hurricane*. The same manufacturer supplied a pair of 4-8-2 locos to a freelance design, but resembling the previous Pacifics, in 1926: No 5 *Hercules* and No 6 *Samson*. A pair of Canadian outline 4-6-2s, No 9 *Winston Churchill* and No 10 *Doctor Syn*, were supplied by the Yorkshire Engine Co in 1931. The remaining mainline locomotive is No 11 *Black Prince* which arrived in 1976. This loco was originally built by Krupps of Essen in 1937, along with sisters *Rosenkavalier* and *Mannertreu* (both now at Bressingham) for an exhibition line in Dusseldorf. In addition to the main line fleet is No 4 *The Bug*. This 0-4-0TT was built in 1926 by Krauss to work construction trains. It was sold in 1931 and went to various locations before being 'discovered' in an Irish scrapyard and returned to the RH&DR in the mid-1970s. It was restored to working order by 1977 and now appears during galas and Santa Specials.

Internal combustion motive power arrived as early as 1928 and other machines, basically cars mounted on railway wheels, followed. The last of these was broken up by the early 1960s. The railway now has two mainline Bo-Bo diesels, No 12 *John Southland* and No 14 (unnamed) built in 1983 by TMA Engineering of Birmingham. There are also two 4wPM and one 4wDM machines for works use. The railway has over 60 coaches, including a bar car, and a sizeable fleet of wagons.

The Bure Valley Railway

The 15ins gauge railway between Aylsham and Wroxham was built by a partnership of the Bure Valley Railway Company and Broadland District Council to create local employment and generate tourist income. It was constructed, with a parallel foot-path, on the trackbed of a standard gauge branch built in the late 1870s over which passenger services had ceased in September 1952, but which continued to form a link for freight traffic until January 1982, the track being removed some two years later.

The Council purchased the trackbed and leased it to the BVR company, construction commencing in 1989. The new railway opened on 10 July 1990, but by January 1991 the BVR's parent company was in liquidation and the BVR in Receivership. Broadland Council ran the line during the 1991 season, a new owner took over in 1992 and ran it for a year before selling to yet another new owner just before the start of the 1993 season. This owner operated the railway for two years, before the shares were sold to Westernasset Ltd in 1995.

Although the line lost money in 1994 and 1995, a new era had commenced. When the railway opened, there were 34 full-time staff, but the new management concentrated on building a small, multi-skilled staff (by 1998 there were five full-time employees) and adding people as the railway progressed. Attention was

devoted to every detail. Marketing opportunities were exploited and, probably most important of all, stability was created - this was the first management team to enter a third season!

The railway started achieving a profit, and kept in the black through the winter months, and investment followed to build on increased traffic figures. This has included dealing with a legacy of poor track maintenance and the expansion of the carriage fleet. Progress has been marked by successive record-breaking years, with 1999 being the first year in which the annual passenger total exceeded 100,000, and the trend has continued upwards.

In the early years, steam services were often maintained by hired locos from the Romney, Hythe & Dymchurch Railway. Major change came in 1994 with arrival of the 2-6-2 'ZBs'. Designed and built by Winson Engineering, No 6 *Blickling Hall* and No 7 *Spitfire* are roughly half-scale models of the Indian Railways 2ft 6ins gauge Standard 'ZB' design. Their success resulted in the construction of a privately-owned version at Aylsham from a kit of parts supplied by Winson, which entered service during the 1998 season. This 2-6-2T, No 8 in the BVR fleet, shares a common boiler and mechanical design, including cylinders and wheels, with the coal fired 'ZB' tender locos, but is oil-fired and has the outline of a Vale of Rheidol loco. Also of basically VoR appearance is the steam loco, No 1 *Wroxham Broad*, a 2-6-4T built by Winson's in 1992. The line also has three diesels, the Bo-Bo No 3 *Buxton Mill* built for the opening of the line and subsequently renamed *2nd Air Division USAAF*, No 4 *The Apprentice* used as Aylsham yard pilot and No 5 *Toby* with a wooden tram body for Thomas events.

Broadland Council spent some £3 million on setting up the railway, a large part of which went on the all-new facilities at Aylsham. The complex includes a shop and restaurant, along with the workshop, offices and an open-sided train shed over the platform tracks accommodating all stock under its roof. The locomotives always run chimney first, there being turntables at each terminus of the nine mile railway. There are passing loops at Coltishall, Buxton and Brampton, although the old station buildings are now private homes. The cut-and-cover tunnel shortly after the line leaves Aylsham, built to get the line under the A140 road to Cromer, is the only railway tunnel in Norfolk, and the train may be 'buzzed' at very low level by RAF jets where, just after Hautbois Halt, the line passes the end of the RAF Coltishall runway.

Although the railway is run as a business, it is supported by the Friends of the Bure Valley Railway organisation, formed in October 1990, who actively assist by working as drivers, guards, and on permanent way, etc., in much the same way as members of a preservation society do on other lines.

The Perrygrove Railway

In concept, this 15ins gauge line was to be built as a hobby, it then became a business and is now reverting to being a self-financing hobby expected to keep its owners active into their retirement! Meanwhile, it has also become a centre for keeping alive the Heywood 'minimum gauge' tradition. Michael Crofts and his wife, Frances, looked for a suitable location to build a railway in

RIGHT: Bure Valley Railway 2-6-2 'ZB' No 6 *Blickling Hall* on the return run to Aylsham shortly after leaving Brampton station on 25 October 1998.

LOWER: James Waterfield with his replica Heywood loco *Ursula*, along with the Duffield Bank dining carriage and Eaton Hall brake van at the Perrygrove Railway on 8 September 2001.

1990. Since the plan was for the hobby to become a small business, Planning Permission had to be obtained to allow public opening, and it needed to be in an accessible location. Other factors included an interesting landscape - and an affordable price!

Northumbria and South Wales were investigated until Perrygrove Farm, near Coleford in the Forest of Dean, was found in 1993. The buildings were in disrepair, but the price was right and it fulfilled the other criteria. Planning Permission was obtained for a new railway in 1994, the first sod was cut at Easter 1995 and The Perrygrove Railway opened to the public on 1 August 1996.

The choice of 15ins gauge arose because Trevor and Tony Stirland (Exmoor Steam Railway) had offered to build a steam locomotive to that gauge - the resulting 0-4-2T *Spirit of Adventure* is a great success. The three-quarters of a mile of running line (incorporating rail from four separate sources, including a local mine) commences at Perrygrove station where the sheds are located and initially heads towards Coleford. After traversing a large bend the train, now climbing, heads back in the opposite direction and passes behind the station at a higher level. Still climbing, a further curve is rounded at the Lydney end of the site and the track heads back again (yet higher up the hillside) until swinging round into the terminus at Oakiron, where there is a run-round loop. In time, the line could be extended to a mile in length. Meanwhile, despite the excellent facilities at the Perrygrove terminus, Michael Crofts maintains that he is very conscious that the line is 'unfinished' and

reckons there is 20 years of work to complete the project!

Having adopted 15ins gauge, the idea of creating a Heywood-style line arose. This became reality when James Waterfield decided to base his Heywood replica equipment at the line - *Ursula* hauling the Duffield Bank Dining Carriage and Eaton Hall brake van provides a very attractive vision of the estate railway championed by Sir Arthur Heywood, and ensures that this line has a special place in the British narrow gauge scene, although it is advisable to check in advance whether this train will be in operation before visiting.

Acknowledgements and Author's Notes

With the arrival of the 50th anniversary of the salvation of the Talyllyn Railway - thus the preservation movement itself - a complete overview of the narrow gauge scene in these islands seemed appropriate. Glancing through some of my 30-year old pictures provided confirmation!

I have tried to show the stunning progress made and convey how the narrow gauge has also retained its pioneering spirit. People who care have devoted imagination and hard work - often as volunteers, sometimes it has become their employment - but always done with enjoyment.

I must record the encouragement of the late Michael Harris, who wrote *On The British Narrow Gauge* in 1980. Next, my thanks to David Joy, who edits *Narrow Gauge World*. It has been my pleasure to contribute to every issue of this title since its inception and he was enthusiastically receptive to the concept of a book following this series of features. He refined my ideas into a firm proposition - and, most importantly, offered to publish it! Here, I should add Trevor Ridley, who was equally keen to take the project forwards after acquiring Atlantic Publishing.

Much of the material in these pages has been gathered over years of reporting professionally on preserved lines for various magazines, and only possible with the assistance of the people involved in running these railways - volunteers and professionals - many of whom are counted as friends. They are too numerous to mention individually and much help pre-dated the book, often by a considerable margin. I hope they will not mind if I express my overall gratitude, and not be offended that just a few people who provided assistance very specific to this project are mentioned.

David Smith of the Narrow Gauge Railway Society deserves special thanks, his original offer to help avoid errors slipping through led to rather more work than he may have anticipated - against a rather tight deadline! Other special help in covering British lines was provided by: Dave Allen, John Keylock, Derek Smith, Peter Van Zeller, David Mitchell, Patrick Keef, Jim Smith, Mike Stanyon, Alastair Ireland, Audrey Boston, Neil Dowlan and David Hall. Coverage of the scene in Ireland would have been impossible without the unstinting welcomes and help provided by: Jimmy Deenihan TD, Brid McElligott, Michael Guerin, Maurice Heaphy, Tom Roche, Alan Keef, David Laing, Neil Tee, Ann Temple, Arthur Thompson, Jim McBride, John Griffin, Clifton Flewitt, Richard Condell, James Maher, Christie Spencer, Clare Dowling, Michael Kennedy, Michael Sweeney, Joe Taylor, Maria Kyte and Mark Kennedy.

Finally, my gratitude to Carrie, my wife. She has trudged around railway yards, taken notes, helped reduce drafts to manageable proportions, and photographs to a number which stood a chance of inclusion!

Bibliography

The following bibliography is included to acknowledge specific sources referred to. Much other material has been accumulated while preparing news reports and features for magazine publication. It is thus possible that other sources have been consulted over the years, but could not be specifically recalled while preparing this list.

Quarry Hunslets of North Wales by Cliff Thomas
The Whipsnade and Umfolozi Railway and *The Great Whipsnade Railway* by Cliff Thomas
The Bala Lake Railway by Cliff Thomas (awaiting publication)
The Groudle Glen Railway - Its history and restoration - Tony Beard & Simon Townsend for Groudle Glen Railway Limited
Manx Steam Railway News Issue 110 - The journal of the IOMSRSA
Double Century - Stan Basnett and Keith Pearson
Rails in the Isle of Man - Robert Hendry
Teifi Valley Railway Tourist Guide - Teifi Valley Railway
Corris - A Narrow Gauge Portrait by John Scott Morgan,
Corris Railway Guidebook & Stocklist - Corris Railway Society
A Return To Corris - Corris Railway Society
Bowater's Sittingbourne Railway by Arthur G Wells
S.K.L.R. Stockbook and Guide - Sittingbourne & Kemsley Light Railway Ltd
The Leighton Buzzard Light Railway by Sydney Leleux
Narrow Gauge Tracks in the Sand by Rod Dingwall
Souvenir Guide Book - Padarn Lake Railway
The South Tynedale Railway Visitors Guide - Tom Bell/STR
Portrait of the Welsh Highland Railway - Peter Johnson
The Southwold Railway by Alan R Taylor and Eric S Tonks
Branch Line to Southwold by Vic Mitchell and Keith Smith
Lost Lines - British Narrow Gauge by Nigel Welbourn
Rails round the Rectory by The Rev. E R Boston
Isabel - Stafford's Own - T D Allen Civil
The Isle of Man Steam Railway by Barry Edwards
Snaefell Mountain Railway 1895-1995 by Barry Edwards
Romneyrail by Vic Mitchell and Keith Smith
The Chronicles of Pendre Sidings by John Bate
Rails Through the Sand by W J Milner
The R&ER Stockbook - Ravenglass & Eskdale Railway
The Ravenglass & Eskdale Railway Handbook - Ravenglass & Eskdale Railway
It's been a lot of fun - The Ravenglass & Eskdale Preservation Society
English Narrow Gauge Railways by R W Kidner
Festiniog Railway Locomotives by Taliesin (Rodney Weaver, Paul Ingham, Paul Res and Peter Johnson)
Manx Electric by Mike Goodwin

The Manx Electric Railway, Centenary Year: 1993 Official Guide
Manx Electric Railway, An illustrated guide by Dr R Preston Hendry and R Powell Hendry
The Hunslet Engine Works by Don Townsley
Snowdon Mountain Railway by Norman Jones
Snowdon Mountain Railway official guide
The Lynton and Barnstaple Railway by G A Brown, J D C A Prideaux and H G Radcliffe
Narrow Gauge Railways in Mid-Wales by J.I.C. Boyd
The Vale of Rheidol Railway by C. C. Green
The Welshpool & Llanfair Light Railway by Ralph Cartwright and R T Russell
Welshpool & Llanfair Light Railway - a collection of pictures by Ralph I Cartwright
The Talyllyn Railway (Past and Present Special) by David J Mitchell and Terry Eyres
Portrait of the Festiniog by Peter Johnson
Festiniog Railway in Camera by John Stretton
Festiniog Railway Travellers Guide - Festiniog Railway Co
Return to Blaenau 1970-82 by Vic Mitchell and Alan Garraway
The Padarn & Penrhyn Railways by Susan Turner
The Definitive Guide to Trams by David Voice
Railways Restored - edited by Alan Butcher, Ian Allan Publishing
An Mhuc Dhubh - The Fintown Railway 2000-2001 - journal of Cumann Traenach na Gaeltrachta Lair (CTGL)
Peatland Education Pack - Clonmacnoise and West Offaly Railway
Locomotives & Railcars of Bord na Mona by Stephen Johnson
Irish Narrow Gauge Railways, A view from the past by Michael H C Baker
Irish Railways in Pictures No 4 - The Giant's Causeway Tramway by Michael Pollard
The Irish narrow Gauge - Volume One From Cork to Cavan by Tom Ferris
The Irish narrow Gauge - Volume Two The Ulster Lines by Tom Ferris
The Railway Age in Ireland - Ulster Folk and Transport Museum
The Last Years of 'The Wee Donegal'- The County Donegal Railways in Colour by Robert Robotham
Launceston Steam Railway and Museum Visitors Guide
Volk's Railways Brighton by Alan A Jackson
The Campbeltown & Machrihanish Light Railway by Nigel S C MacMillan
The Campbeltown & Machrihanish Light Railway by A D Farr
The Leek and Manifold Light Railway by S C Jenkins
The Leek and Manifold Valley Light Railway by Keith Turner
The Lincolnshire Coast Light Railway by K E Hartley
The Rye & Camber Tramway - A Centenary History by Laurie A Cooksey
Glyn Valley Tramway by W J Milner
The Jersey Railway by N R P Bonsor
The Ashover Light Railway by K P Plant
The Ashover Light Railway by Robert Gratton & Stuart R Band
Introducing Russell by Peter Deegan
Mineral Railways by R W Kidner
Bagnall: a narrow gauge legacy - Narrow Gauge Railway Society